THE PRESIDENCY OF ANDREW JACKSON

Richard B. Latner

THE PRESIDENCY OF
ANDREW JACKSON
WHITE HOUSE POLITICS
1829–1837

Athens
The University of Georgia Press

Set in 11 on 13 point Caledonia type
Printed in the United States of America

Library of Congress Cataloging in Publication Data

Latner, Richard B.
   The presidency of Andrew Jackson.

   Bibliography.
   Includes index.

   1.   United States—Politics and government—
1829–1837.   2. Jackson, Andrew, Pres. U. S.,
1767–1845.   I. Title.
E381.L37   353.03'13'09034   78–18204
          ISBN 0–8203–0457–3

The publication of this book was supported in part
by a grant from the Andrew W. Mellon Foundation,
administered by the American Council of Learned
Societies. The University of Georgia Press grate-
fully acknowledges this assistance.

FOR ELLEN

Contents

Acknowledgments

During the years this book has been in the making, I have accumulated a large indebtedness to the many people who have provided encouragement and counsel. Most especially, I have benefited from the knowledge, skill, and friendship of Professor Richard H. Sewell, who guided the original version of this work as a dissertation at the University of Wisconsin and who has remained a constant source of cheerful assistance. I am also grateful for the perceptive comments of those who read the manuscript in whole or in part: Ira Berlin, Donald B. Cole, George C. Edwards III, William W. Freehling, Robert Hawkinson, Peter Levine, Kenneth Lockridge, Richard Lowitt, Daniel J. Singal, and Jon L. Wakelyn. Special thanks goes to Professor Robert V. Remini, whose expertise in the Jacksonian period helped focus my thinking. The suggestions and criticisms of these scholars made revising into a creative and challenging endeavor. Whatever defects remain are, of course, my responsibility.

The staffs of the libraries cited in my bibliography, as well as others which I visited, all facilitated my work and made research pleasurable as well as exciting. Barbara A. Volo of the Howard-Tilton Library at Tulane University handled my numerous interlibrary loan requests with efficiency and good humor, while Mrs. Mildred L. Covert expertly typed large portions of the manuscript. At the University of Georgia Press, Malcolm M. MacDonald extended thoughtful and friendly advice. I was also fortunate to receive a grant from the Horace Rackham School of Graduate Studies at the University of Michigan, and two summer grants from the Committee on Research of the Graduate School, Tulane University. This financial aid expedited the conclusion of my project. Portions of this book appeared in different form in articles published by the *Journal of American History*, the *Journal of Southern History*, and the *Tennessee Historical Quarterly* and are reproduced with the kind permission of the editors.

I would also like to express my appreciation for the understanding and encouragement provided by my family, particularly my parents, Samuel and Florence Latner, and my in-laws, Joseph and Sylvia Pechman. Finally, my greatest debt of all is to my wife Ellen. This book is for her—for everything.

Introduction

For those who knew Andrew Jackson, it must have come as no surprise that his presidency turned out to be one of the most turbulent in American history. From the time of his adolescence, Jackson had shown an alarming tendency to make himself the center of controversy. His presidential years similarly provoked conflict and contention as Americans arrayed themselves in rival political camps on a scale that surpassed that of the Federalist-Republican battles a generation before.

The drama of the Jackson years has proved as compelling to historians as to Jackson's contemporaries, and there now exists an extensive literature which explores the meaning of his presidency and the substance of Jacksonian politics.[1] For the most part, scholars have focused on the major issues and the prominent figures of the day, but in recent years there has been a noticeable shift in attention from national politics and political elites towards local issues and the behavior of the electorate. Political historians, following the example of Lee Benson's pathbreaking study of New York politics, have increasingly emphasized the relevance of religion, ethnicity, and culture to nineteenth-century politics. Often aided by quantitative techniques, they have reoriented Jacksonian historiography by detailing the local and particularistic universe of the electorate where political conflicts swirled around ethnic and cultural rather than socioeconomic considerations.[2]

There is no question that these "new" political histories have illuminated the rich and complex world of Jacksonian politics. At the same time, it would be a mistake to overlook the continued need to reevaluate national and elite politics. This study is guided by the assumption that new insights into the nature of Jacksonian politics can be gained by examining the men who were most responsible for determining national policy, the occupants of the executive office—the president, the cabinet, and the president's noncabinet advisers.

During Andrew Jackson's presidency, the White House occupied a central position in the developing party system. From it radiated decisions that largely determined the broad outlines of the Democracy's political program and helped shape its style, structure, and appeal.[3] The White House was also the scene of intraparty disputes which revealed power relationships among the party's ruling elite. A study of White House politics can locate responsibility for political decisions, elucidate the philosophic and practical considerations underlying them, and clarify the manner in which they were determined. Who had influence, how and why that influence was attained, and for what purposes it was used are questions that remain vital to the debate on the meaning of Jacksonianism and invite a reexamination of the Jackson administration.[4]

Jackson's contemporaries recognized the impact of executive decisions on the course of national affairs. Hezekiah Niles, the influential editor, grumbled that under Jackson "the *president* is THE 'GOVERN-MENT,'" and the Whig party made the issue of executive usurpation the common denominator of its opposition.[5] Yet historians have devoted little attention to White House politics during his presidency. There still exists, for example, considerable uncertainty about the membership and functioning of the fabled Kitchen Cabinet, though historians generally acknowledge its importance for decision making.[6]

The failure to probe the workings of the executive office is understandable. Even political scientists encounter serious methodological problems in trying to assess contemporary decision-making processes. The difficulties multiply significantly when one attempts to explore the past, especially when much of the activity of key men took place in private and there can be no recourse to interviews. Nevertheless, there are ways to penetrate the inner councils of decision makers. Political scientists employ two basic devices to assess power relationships, a "reputational" approach, which records observers' and participants' statements about who had influence in a particular decision, and a "case study" approach, which notes the actual activity of participants in each decision. The case study technique provides a check against the reputational method's failure to discriminate between presumed and actual power. Both methods are, of course, part of the historian's stock-in-trade, and I have attempted to apply them rigorously in examining the executive office during Jackson's presidency.[7]

When Jacksonian politics is analyzed from this perspective, Jackson's preeminent position in his own administration becomes manifest. The picture that emerges is not that of a president who simply projected his emotional needs upon the outside world, reacting defensively and personally to the issues that confronted him.[8] Nor is it that of an inexperienced and vacillating leader, prone to manipulation by those who gained his confidence.[9] Rather, one sees that Jackson possessed a relatively coherent set of ideas which generated the controversial measures of his presidency. With the assistance of his advisers, he formulated a program and helped construct a party which sought to reconcile and adjust the heritage of Jeffersonianism to the profound changes occasioned by the rapidly expanding commercial and industrial opportunities of nineteenth-century America.[10] Jacksonian politics was not a carbon copy of Jeffersonianism, but it owed much to the legacy of Thomas Jefferson and the Republican party's principles as formulated during the 1790s. Like Jefferson, Jackson viewed his task as an urgent mission to assure the survival of republicanism and of America as a model to be emulated by the rest of the world.

Of course, Jackson was a man of action and impulse, and no one would claim that he was an original political thinker. Yet these qualities do not necessarily contravene an interest in ideas and programs. Indeed, scholars in a variety of disciplines increasingly recognize man's "symboling" activity, his need to employ ideas to understand and impose order on the world of experience, much as a traveler needs a map to maneuver through unfamiliar terrain.[11] In Jackson's case, activity and emotional energy complemented a deepfelt attachment to Jeffersonian tenets and a determination to pursue the programmatic implications of that philosophy. Jeffersonianism provided in large measure the vocabulary for his understanding of his political responsibilities.

It is equally evident that Jackson was an astute leader who consulted widely on matters of policy and politics. He sought aid from cabinet members, noncabinet officials, members of Congress, and friends and acquaintances outside of government. His advisory system was flexible, pragmatic, and perfectly consonant with his determination to control his administration. Not only was influence contingent upon agreement with his program, but his advisory system, much like Franklin Roosevelt's, depended for effectiveness upon a dominant president to make decisions.

While Jackson had many advisers, he gave special prominence to a group of westerners, particularly Kentucky's Amos Kendall and Francis Preston Blair. These confidants shared with him a basic agreement on political principles and practice. They gave their loyalty first and foremost to Jackson and looked to him for their position and status. All three were slaveholders, but they considered themselves western not southern, and one of their primary objectives was to tie the West permanently to the Democracy in order to ensure the party's dominance.

At the time of Jackson's election, the notion of a uniform and separate West was becoming increasingly unstable, especially in the longer-settled border states of Kentucky and Tennessee, which were rapidly losing their frontier characteristics. Moreover, not only were the inhabitants of most of the older populated areas of the Mississippi Valley the progeny of the Southeast, but the spread of slavery south of the Ohio River emphasized that region's southern roots. More and more, the designation "Southwest" was applied to distinguish this half of the Valley from its northern counterpart. Yet the idea of a distinctive trans-Allegheny West persisted and continued to provide a basis of sectional identification for men like Jackson, Kendall, and Blair.[12] Since, with certain notable exceptions, Jackson's most confidential advisers were from the West, that section made a special contribution to the formation of the Democratic party's program and structure.

Martin Van Buren, on the other hand, had less effect on Jackson's policies than one might expect. Although he was probably the man most responsible for welding the Jackson coalition of 1828, his influence did not predominate in the new administration. Indeed, in a few major policy decisions, Jackson embarked on a program without his full support. Nor did Van Buren control the Kitchen Cabinet. During these years, a clash of interests, ideological and personal, existed between the Blair-Kendall faction and the Van Burenites. While this rift never seriously threatened to split the party, its existence caused misunderstanding, tension, and occasional delays in decision making. That Jackson generally endorsed the positions taken by Blair and Kendall also shows their greater influence relative to Van Buren's.

In emphasizing the West's special contribution to Jacksonian politics, these findings hark back to the writings of Frederick Jackson Turner. Throughout his presidency, Jackson sought counsel from western advisers and displayed a concern for maintaining western strength in the Democratic party. Moreover, to some degree western experiences shaped the program and rhetoric of his administration, particularly its concern for the farming and mechanic population and its endorsement of hard-money, antibanking, and egalitarian principles.

Yet there are significant differences. Turner's idea of the West was enveloped in romantic notions of frontier democracy, and one would be hard pressed, for example, to fit slaveholding, tough-minded politicians like Jackson, Kendall, and Blair into Turner's conception of western democratic idealism. Furthermore, simplistic sectional generalizations must be avoided. Not only were ideas and values that might be identified with the West found nationwide, but the West itself was not a monolithic section. It had many political tendencies, and Jackson and his Kentucky advisers exhibited only one strain—and that not necessarily the most representative one—of western political thinking.[13] Jackson had other western counselors, such as William B. Lewis and Andrew Jackson Donelson, who had no influence on policy formation and, indeed, frequently opposed his decisions.

It is also necessary to avoid underestimating Van Buren's influence in order to establish that of other advisers. Van Buren was certainly the most influential contributor to the Democratic party's position on internal improvements, and his differences with Jackson and with other advisers never jeopardized his standing as the president's probable successor. Nevertheless, for reasons both personal and political and having to do with matters of temperament, style, psychology, and ideology, Jackson gave special attention to western advisers throughout his eight years in office.

Any study is necessarily circumscribed by its methods and purposes, and I have narrowed my discussion to Jackson's domestic policy. Further, I have followed Van Buren's judgment that Indian removal, internal improvements, banking, and tariff reform "were the most prominent of the domestic objects" to which Jackson directed his attention.[14] Decisions involving public land sales, the distribution of the surplus revenue, the use of the mails by abolitionists, and the question of the recognition and annexation of Texas, to name only a few, receive little or no mention. Any assessment of the relative importance of topics must be subjective, and it would be hazardous to discount the significance of other issues. But those which Van Buren listed seem to merit the weight he accorded them, and the pattern of influence they reveal can be tested by the further investigation of White House politics during Jackson's presidency.

A note about terminology. Throughout this book, I have capitalized the word "Bank" when referring specifically to the Bank of the United States and have used the lowercase "bank" when discussing local institutions or general banking attitudes. The two situations are not always easily distinguished; for example, a bias against banks usually, but not always, was reflected in opposition to the Bank as well. Nevertheless, historians acknowledge the distinction as necessary and useful, and I have adhered to it.

1

The Victorious Coalition

The presidential election results of 1828 registered a decisive victory for Andrew Jackson over the incumbent John Quincy Adams. The electoral count stood at 178 for Jackson and 83 for Adams, and both sides agreed that there had been a tremendous outpouring of support for the challenger. The relatively close popular vote, however, indicated that the dimensions of Jackson's appeal were often exaggerated, for Old Hickory had garnered only 647,276 votes to Adams's 508,064. Still, the scale of victory was impressive. Jackson won about 56 percent of the votes cast and carried virtually every electoral vote south of the Potomac River and west of New Jersey. He even managed to poll substantial minorities in parts of New England, Adams's stronghold. The administration had clearly suffered a stinging rebuke, and the capital city accordingly took on a funereal aspect. While the dour president sought solace in Milton's *Paradise Regained*, his administrative officers pleaded illness rather than attend social functions in the waning days of their rule.[1]

Uncertainty about what the new political order would bring added to the pall. Jackson's victory presaged changes in personnel and policy, but their extent and nature remained unknown. His political convictions were Jeffersonian in origin, but they were neither well known nor fully developed, and, in any case, were obscured by the maelstrom of innuendo and slander that constituted the campaign of 1828. The organization supporting him seemed equally problematic, more an uneasy coalition of contentious elements—Calhounites, Crawford "Radicals," Kentucky relief men, and others—than a coherent political party. The Democratic party as an institution with an identifiable ideology, organization, and style did not exist in 1828.

These conditions made political predictions necessarily vague. Daniel Webster, who had cast his lot with Adams, took stock of the situation as he waited apprehensively for Jackson's arrival. "Nobody knows what he will do when he does come," he reflected. "My opinion is that when he comes he will bring a breeze with him. Which way it will blow, I cannot tell."[2] In time, Jackson would make known his intentions. Meanwhile one could profitably cast a look at the nature of his support and the context of his victory for intimations of his future course. As Webster suspected, the substance of Jacksonian politics did not arrive at a stroke but owed a great deal to events of the previous decade.

Politically, the 1820s were a period of transition, transformation, and realignment. The one-party hegemony established by the Republicans with the demise on the national level of the Federalist party created the appearance of national unity and political harmony. Without completely abandoning its Jeffersonian grounding, the Republican party under James Monroe continued its drift, begun at the end of James Madison's presidency, towards the incorporation of Federalist principles, stimulating national economic development by sponsoring banks, protective tariffs, and internal improvements. Monroe, believing that political parties were inimical to republican government, also aspired to their elimination. His desire to create a national rather than a partisan administration, to embrace all elements of American society under its umbrella, bespoke the ideal of an Era of Good Feelings.[3]

Yet Monroe's vision was illusory. Without a potent political opposition to promote cohesiveness, the Republican party organization noticeably deteriorated, opening the way for sectional and factional divisions. Presidential authority was also adversely affected as Monroe was compelled to rally support for his program by first achieving a consensus within his cabinet. The failure of the congressional caucus of 1824 to attract more than one-third of the Republican members of the Congress underscored the collapse of party organization. No longer could a small group of national leaders prevent any Republican with a personal following, even an outsider to national politics, from becoming a serious presidential contender.[4]

At the same time, fundamental changes were occurring in the electoral environment of early nineteenth-century America. Legal barriers to political participation broke down with accelerating speed after the American Revolution, offices increasingly became elective rather than appointive, and a new, closer relationship developed between officials and voters. Ideas of deference yielded to a voter-oriented style of politics in which men lacking the status of previous elites sought the approval of the electorate. More and more, what counted was not a man's wealth or prestige, but his ability to appeal to the voter. Politics began to take on popular, dramatic, even evangelical qualities as politicians exhorted support by means of parades, rallies, conventions, and newspapers.[5]

As styles changed, so too did the politicians' names, and during the 1820s a new generation achieved political maturity. In New York there was Martin Van Buren and Thurlow Weed; in Kentucky, Amos Kendall and Francis Blair; in New Hampshire, Isaac Hill; and in Virginia, Thomas Ritchie. Talented and ambitious, they were in many cases undistinguished by family background, status, and education— qualities that had mattered in previous eras. They looked to politics (and its close associate, journalism) as an outlet for their aspirations, and they proved particularly adept at appealing to, organizing, and manipulating the electorate.[6]

The decline of traditional, gentry politics did not occur uniformly or abruptly throughout the country. The ideal of a disinterested, virtuous elite never disappeared entirely, and those who achieved political power continued to be of a higher socioeconomic status than the general electorate. But more often than in the past, they had risen by their own efforts rather than by inheriting status from their fathers. In short, older political notions and practices were being replaced by ones that tended to be more egalitarian in catering to the demands of an expanded and interested electorate.[7]

These quantitative and qualitative changes in politics were intensified by the panic of 1819 and the ensuing depression. The sharp decline in prices brought distress to all groups, farmers, merchants, manufacturers, and financial interests, and an end to the post-1815 nationalistic exuberance. To combat the depression, some advocated currency inflation and debtor relief legislation. Others advocated a hard-money policy, a return to specie payments, and an end to immoral speculative schemes. Whichever position one preferred, it was hard to remain aloof from the political battle. Thus while voters largely ignored the presidential elections of 1816 and 1820, they flocked to the polls for state elections during this period, with many states experiencing record turnouts of eligible voters.[8]

In some states, the panic weakened the hold of entrenched elites when ambitious politicians like Tennessee's Felix Grundy proposed a popular relief program and forced a realignment of political factions. It also strained the faith of many Americans in their government in Washington. In the South and West, especially, discontent was directed against the Bank of the United States which was blamed for precipitating the panic, the Marshall Court which upheld the Bank, and the general conduct of the national government which seemed remote and unresponsive to the people.[9]

John C. Calhoun sensed the panic's effect when he noted "a general mass of disaffection to the Government not concentrated in any particular direction, but ready to seize upon any event and looking out anywhere for a leader." There existed, he continued, "a vague but widespread discontent, caused by the disordered circumstances of individuals . . . resulting in a general impression that there was something radically wrong in the administration of the Government." To large numbers of Americans, something was wrong with the country's leadership. America had strayed from its Jeffersonian tradition of hostility to special privilege and consolidated government, and the republic was in serious danger of forgetting its special mission of upholding liberty.[10]

In retrospect, it is clear that these complex transformations converged to promote Jackson's presidential candidacy. To some extent, they thrust him forward almost regardless of his will. But Jackson's repeated expressions of disinterest in political office also masked a strong ambition and a political instinct that knew how to take advantage of a favorable situation. As his campaign gathered momentum in the years after 1822, when the Tennessee legislature nominated him for president, Jackson better than anyone else profited from the breakdown of the Republican party organization and from the shifting political practices and concerns of post-1815 America.

Jackson's initial base of support came from his political cronies in Tennessee, the Blount-Overton faction. Since his earliest days in Nashville, Jackson had associated with this group, which included his friends and neighbors, John H. Eaton and William B. Lewis, as well as John Overton and Hugh Lawson White. Although Jackson increasingly distanced himself from their speculative banking and land operations, his personal and political bonds with them remained strong in the 1820s.[11]

As Charles Sellers has demonstrated, most Blount-Overton men first sponsored Jackson's 1824 candidacy as a means of serving local interests. To their surprise, and in some cases chagrin, Jackson's campaign caught fire in large areas of the country, especially the South and West. There is little question that his military fame and reputation for energy and boldness exerted a strong attraction on the minds of his countrymen. An expansive, energetic, and yet anxious society found itself both reflected in and reassured by Jackson's triumph over his lowly origins and the adversities which marked his early career. His orphanhood, reckless adolescence, and near bankruptcy, his brushes with death, and his marriage tainted by the suggestion of bigamy all seemed to reflect on a disproportionate scale the inchoate world of his contemporaries. At the same time, his military triumphs, his rise into the prosperous planting gentry of Tennessee, and his successful forays into politics signified the possibility for a self-reliant man to conquer and control such a fluid and unpredictable environment. Jackson became a charismatic figure for his generation, having the ability to obtain men's loyalty, to lead them, and yet to appear as one of them.[12]

Jackson's personality and background were doubtless important in 1824, but there is also evidence that his independence of established institutions enabled him to take advantage of the social and economic dislocation produced by the panic. Unlike his rivals in 1824, John Quincy Adams, Henry Clay, and William Harris Crawford, Jackson was not directly connected with the Monroe administration or the federal government. Those who were most affected by the panic found in Jackson's candidacy a means of expressing their discontent and disillusionment with Washington politicians. In Ohio and Kentucky, for example, Jackson's greatest strength appeared in areas which had been hardest hit by the panic and where relief sentiment was greatest. Although there are few studies of local politics in the 1820s, it appears that Frederick Jackson Turner was correct in maintaining that the electorate aroused by the panic of 1819 rallied to Jackson. Indeed, his campaign propaganda was designed in part to attract such support. Eaton's "Wyoming Letters," which appeared in newspapers during the canvass, presented Jackson as a Revolution-tested republican who would reverse the trend towards corruption and intrigue which imperiled the republic. In Pennsylvania, and no doubt elsewhere, Eaton's themes found a responsive audience.[13]

The surprising impact of Jackson's effort nevertheless fell short of victory. Although showing great popularity in the Old Northwest, the border area, and the South, he won only a plurality of popular and electoral votes, and the election in the House of Representatives went to Adams. Yet the "corrupt bargain" between the new president and Secretary of State Clay proved a Pyrrhic victory, for over the next three years Jackson's support increased dramatically with the addition of new supporters. Backed by a more efficient campaign organization, the Jackson coalition swept into power.[14]

Numerically, the major difference between defeat in 1824 and triumph in 1828 came from the addition of the followers of John C. Calhoun and Martin Van Buren to the original Jackson men. Both factions also provided the General with political leadership of the first order.

Calhoun moved into the Jackson ranks shortly after Adams chose Clay as his secretary of state. In part, ambition dictated the shift because Calhoun worried that Clay's appointment blocked passage to the White House for sixteen years. But in part, too, Calhoun harbored private resentment against Adams's endorsement of vigorous federal activity, especially tariff protection. Although as vice-president, Calhoun limited himself to public attacks on the "corrupt bargain," he privately informed friends that Adams's policies spelled doom for the South. By 1827, he was encouraging his state's campaign against protective tariffs and was beginning to formulate his theory of nullification.[15]

Calhoun, of course, had not always opposed a generous interpretation of constitutional powers. As a War Hawk and as sponsor of the Second Bank of the United States, the Tariff of 1816, and the Bonus Bill of 1817, he had represented the new generation of Republican nationalists who lacked the constitutional scruples of the Virginia Dynasty. During the mid-1820s, however, he gradually disavowed this nationalistic phase of his career and, as was so often true, his position reflected significant developments in antebellum southern society.[16]

Enthusiasm for measures of economic nationalism had never received the unanimous or wholehearted endorsement of southern politicians. A small band of Old Republicans centered in the upper

South, especially in Virginia, had been decrying the Republican party's gradual drift towards loose construction and Hamiltonian principles since Jefferson's second administration. To traditionalists like Nathaniel Macon, John Randolph of Roanoke, and John Taylor of Caroline, the increasing disposition of Republicans to condone paper-money banking, corporate charters, tariffs, and internal improvements weakened the moral fiber necessary to perpetuate republican government and robbed the honest farmer of his property and liberty.[17]

Throughout the 1820s, Old Republican spokesmen picked up considerable support in the South. Many considerations contributed to the revitalization of their limited government principles: animosity towards the national bank and, by extension, to the Supreme Court whose loose construction doctrines upheld it; federal Indian policy under Monroe and Adams which hindered white expropriation of land and allegedly infringed upon the state's sovereignty over its internal population; and the combination of agricultural depression in the upper South and declining cotton prices which created extensive hostility to protective tariffs and internal improvements expenditures. States' rights principles promised relief from federal taxation and appropriations that seemed inequitable and debilitating to the South.[18]

To some, Jeffersonian tenets also provided protection against potential northern attacks on slavery. Thus Georgia's Governor George M. Troup, provoked by Senator Rufus King's resolution to apply federal land revenue to emancipate slaves, warned that the trend towards increased federal power indicated that at no remote day the government would "openly lend itself to a combination of fanatics for the destruction of everything valuable in the southern country," and John Randolph in denouncing an internal improvements measure in the House asserted that "if Congress possesses the power to do what is proposed by this bill, they may not only enact a sedition law—for there is precedent—but they may emancipate every slave in the United States—and with stronger color of reason than they can exercise the power now contended for." Impelled by the South's hardening commitment to cotton and slavery, a doctrine whose primary focus had been on the preservation of liberty and property from government interference increasingly took on explicit sectional overtones. South-ern support for measures of economic nationalism dissolved, and their proponents' voices were muffled.[19]

In South Carolina this reaction to nationalistic policies was most extreme, and Carolina planters began to criticize the Tariff of 1824 with a vehemence unmatched by planters in other southern states. Calhoun's somersault into nullification reflected this state of affairs. Even his support of Jackson in 1828 was contingent upon the future president's course of action. The election, he confided, was but an "incident" which might "retard or accelerate our fate . . . but which at best affords but the *means* of reform which must take place or we are ruined."[20]

Calhoun's decision to discard his earlier nationalistic program brought him the support of a group of southerners who viewed loose construction principles as a threat to slavery and to the South—men like Littleton W. Tazewell and John Floyd of Virginia, and Robert Hayne and James Hamilton, Jr., of South Carolina. Yet because Cal-houn kept secret his interest in nullification, and because he was reluctant to attack the Bank or all federally sponsored internal im-provements, he was able to maintain the personal allegiance of influential northerners like Samuel Ingham and George M. Dallas of Pennsylvania, Marcus Morton and David Henshaw of Massachusetts, and Levi Woodbury of New Hampshire.[21]

Calhoun did not bring to Jackson's camp a large number of votes. His withdrawal from the campaign of 1824 under the pressure of Jackson's popularity had demonstrated his weakness on the hustings. But his reputation as a statesman and his distinguished career in government brought him the support of large numbers of wealthy, educated, and socially prominent men. If the South Carolinian was vulnerable in the countryside, he was strong in Congress where his politically experienced followers could play havoc with their ene-mies' program.[22]

Shortly after the Calhounites joined forces with Jackson, Martin Van Buren adroitly maneuvered his followers into the growing Jackson coalition. The Van Burenites[23] originated in the aftermath of the Missouri controversy when the willingness of northern Republicans to exclude slavery from Missouri revealed to Van Buren the ominous consequences of the continued erosion of Republican principles and organization. Formerly, party loyalty, tight organization, and dedication to strict construction principles had prevented sectional issues like slavery from endangering the Union. As Van Buren recalled a few years after the crisis, "party attachment in former times furnished a complete antidote for sectional prejudices by producing counteracting feelings. It was not until that defense had been broken down that the clamour agt. Southern Influence and African Slavery could be made effectual in the North."[24]

Sectional conflict was a disturbing possibility, but Van Buren was also dissatisfied with other aspects of postwar Republicanism. The son of a Kinderhook, New York, tavernkeeper, Van Buren followed his father's example by becoming a "zealous partisan" of the Republican party in Federalist-controlled Columbia County. States' rights, economy in government, an agrarian bias, and a basic faith in the "sober second-thought" of the people—if not in their first judgment—as the basis of government were Van Buren's controlling ideas. Increasingly, they clashed with the tendency of Republican presidents like Madison and Monroe to tolerate a national bank, federal aid for internal improvements, and excessive tariff rates. His commitment to Jeffersonianism happily coincided with New York's local interests, such as the protection of its huge investment in the Erie Canal from federally aided competition, and he undoubtedly envisioned a restored Republican organization propelling him into the White House. But Van Buren also sincerely believed in Republican principles, which he identified with the safety of America's republican experiment and the preservation of liberty.[25]

Immediately after the conclusion of the Missouri crisis, Van Buren set out to resuscitate the Republican party on its former basis as an alliance between "the planters of the South and the plain Republicans of the North." By 1823, he had restored the old New York–Virginia alliance, the party's crucial connection in Jeffersonian times, by forming strong ties with the Richmond Junto and its editor-spokesman, Thomas Ritchie. But their presidential hope in 1824, William Harris Crawford, suffered a resounding defeat, which included the loss of New York, and Van Buren was left to ponder the future of his badly bruised faction. After much soul searching and with trepidation, he joined the Jackson coalition.[26]

Clearly, Adams's political philosophy and program had no appeal to the Radicals, as the Crawford men were dubbed. Years later, Van Buren recalled that he "never entertained a moment's doubt" after Adams announced his views on expansive government powers in his inaugural address that there would be a "speedy reunion of the Republican party—excepting the personal adherents of Mr. Clay." But Van Buren nevertheless wanted assurances from the Jackson men that the General would adhere to Jeffersonian principles. By the winter of 1826–27, under the impression he had received them from Calhoun, he set out to convince the rest of the old Crawford faction.[27]

Van Buren's strongest argument was that the addition of Radical influence could prove the decisive element in assuring Jackson's respect for states' rights principles. As he explained to one eminent Crawford leader, "by adding the General's personal popularity to the strength of the Old Republican party which still acted together . . . we might . . . be able to compete successfully with the power and patronage of the [Adams] administration . . . ; that we had abundant evidence that the General was at an earlier period well grounded in the principles of our party, and that we must trust to good fortunes and to the effects of favorable associations for the removal of the rust they had contracted, in his case, by a protracted non-user and the prejudicial effects of his military life." Such arguments helped convince Van Buren's friends, and the spring of 1827 brought public confirmation of the Van Buren–Jackson alliance when Ritchie's Richmond *Enquirer* endorsed Jackson's candidacy.[28]

Few Radicals mustered great enthusiasm for Jackson, and the southern branch accepted him only because they could "get no better." But Van Buren had to make the most of whatever assurances he received because he had no other choice. He could not dismiss the fact that the next election would be a two-man contest, and of the two it was crystal clear that Adams offered nothing but a continuation of Hamiltonianism. Moreover, Jackson looked like a sure winner, and if strict constructionists did not attend the victory dinner, what could they hope for in terms of influence?[29] The Van Buren faction brought Old Hickory a considerable bloc of support, extending into New York, Virginia, Georgia, and North Carolina, and involving a larger popular following than the Calhoun forces. Although it had fewer nationally prominent leaders than the Calhounites, its main spokesman, Van Buren, was a political power unto himself.[30]

There were other adjustments of political lines during Adams's presidency, such as the steady stream of Federalists, especially from the South and Middle Atlantic states, into Jackson's camp.[31] But the most significant movement in its impact on the future Jackson Democratic party was the switch from Clay to Jackson of the relief, or New Court, party in Kentucky. Emerging during the panic of 1819, the relief party had disrupted Kentucky politics by advocating a program of currency inflation, stay and replevin laws, and the replacement of the court of appeals, which had declared much of its program unconstitutional.[32]

Among the leaders of the Kentucky relief party was Amos Kendall. Born in 1789 to a poor Massachusetts farming family, Kendall adopted the moral values of his Puritan ancestors, especially those of hard work, self-improvement, and plain living. A serious and sober young man—his childhood friends called him "the Deacon"—he possessed a small and sickly frame but also keen ambition and expansive intellectual interests. The combination led him to seek a wider field than the confining bounds of rural Massachusetts. "It is inferior minds highly improved which govern the world," he once counseled his son, no doubt with his own career in mind.

Guided by this maxim, Kendall worked his way through Dartmouth College, piously avoiding rowdy student brawls, and graduated at the head of his class. Dreaming of "the active scenes" of politics, he studied law, but opportunities were limited in Massachusetts, and in 1814 he joined the westward movement, hoping to find fame and fortune in Kentucky.[33]

For more than a year Kendall tutored Henry Clay's children and accustomed himself to his new environment which, whatever the pretensions of Lexington's polite society, was more primitive, open, and fluid than that of Massachusetts. He heard his first stump speech and found himself "not so unpleasantly impressed" as he expected. "Time may reconcile me to it," he concluded. He seemed to be a fast learner, for shortly afterwards he noted in his journal that he had "learnt the way to be popular in Kentucky. . . . Drink whiskey and talk loud, with the fullest confidence," although he confessed he had not yet put the lesson to use.[34]

But Kendall's lowly background and insecure status made him uncomfortable in Lexington society and he sought opportunities elsewhere. After a brief attempt at law practice, he found his profession. Under the sponsorship of the Kentucky politico Richard M. Johnson, Kendall turned newspaper editor, and by October 1816 he was half owner and editor of the Frankfort *Argus of Western America*.[35]

The panic of 1819 catapulted Kendall into political prominence as he became a leading propagandist and organizer of the relief forces. Although many men of substance supported the relief party, its strength centered in the least commercial areas south of the Bluegrass, where Kentucky's land-poor debtor and mechanic population was concentrated. Its opposition, on the other hand, was located predominantly in the landed and commercially developed areas of Lexington and the older Bluegrass region. Relief leaders quickly realized the necessity of taking their case to the people, and seizing the standard of democracy, they blasted the established political elite for refusing to help the common man. They also displayed a shrewd awareness of the benefits of political organization, holding rallies, parades, meetings, and political conventions to concentrate the strength of the farming and mechanic population against an entrenched leadership. One branch of the new grass-roots style of politics which marked the Jacksonian period was pioneered during the furious Kentucky relief battles.[36]

Kendall showed a special talent for attacking the Bank of the United States, which many westerners blamed for precipitating the panic and for draining their wealth to profit eastern interests. When the Bank was chartered in 1816, Kendall had welcomed it without enthusiasm. Although he considered it "necessary . . . & useful" to end the financial chaos evident during the War of 1812 and its aftermath, he nevertheless "tremble[d] with apprehension" at the danger posed to liberty by its power and concentrated wealth. He adopted a wait-and-see approach.[37]

The panic brought out in full force Kendall's hostility to the Bank. He published a series of essays denouncing it as a "monied aristocracy" and accusing the national government of reviving the menace of Federalism by again encroaching on the rights of the states and the people. He recommended that the Bank's charter not be renewed and that an amendment to the Constitution be adopted prohibiting the federal government from chartering corporations outside the District of Columbia. In the meantime, he supported the state-chartered Bank of the Commonwealth, becoming one of its directors, and recommended stay and bankruptcy laws to help relieve the severity of the depression.[38]

During this period, Kendall's personal and political association with Francis Preston Blair began. Tall and exceedingly thin—he weighed scarcely more than 100 pounds—Blair was born in Virginia towards the close of the eighteenth century and moved as a child to Kentucky where his father became an active Jeffersonian, serving for over twenty years as the state's attorney general. Raised in a politician's household, Blair adopted the party's tenets, and in 1811 he opposed the rechartering of the national bank and defended the right of a state to tax its branches.[39]

Although he was educated at Transylvania University in Lexington and trained as a lawyer, Blair's poor vocal powers compelled him to find an alternative career. He established himself on a small plot of land near the state's capital, Frankfort, and sought to emulate the Virginia ideal of the gentleman farmer. While he continued to make farming his avocation, Blair increasingly found himself drawn into politics. During the 1820s, he became a major contributor to Kendall's newspaper, served as a director and in 1829 as president of the Bank of the Commonwealth, and was appointed clerk of the new court of appeals.[40]

On the surface it appears incongruous that relief party leaders like Kendall and Blair should later have become key advisers to a president who increasingly emphasized the benefits of hard money and the evils of paper currency inflation. But the discrepancy is more apparent than real, for Kendall and Blair, like most New Court men, favored inflation only as a necessary and temporary expedient to aid hard-pressed farmers and mechanics. Despite their support for Kentucky's Bank of the Commonwealth, they were not connected with commercial banking interests. Rather, they were hard-money men with an agrarian antagonism to all banks. While praising the state's bank for easing the plight of debtors, for example, Kendall criticized its excessive note issues, applauded legislative efforts to place it on a specie-paying basis, and announced that he was "in principle opposed to all paper systems." When the legislature repealed the charters of Kentucky's extensive independent bank system, Kendall placed the news under the heading "RAG SHOPS DISFRANCHISED."[41]

In Kendall's view, a depreciated currency not only hurt creditors but also the "farmer, mechanic and laboring man," who was paid for his labor in depreciated currency while purchasing imported goods at inflated prices. Only speculators, merchants, and debtors profited from paper money. To those who lived by their own industry, it was ruinous. "Let us cling to gold and silver," Kendall implored his readers. But if temporary inflationary expedients were necessary, let the paper be issued by government-operated banks or by private banks subject to governmental regulations, thus ensuring public control over the money supply to serve "the common good."[42]

Moderation also marked Kendall's support for other parts of the relief program. His enthusiasm for stay and replevin laws was circumscribed by a moralistic concern that such expedients merely postponed the day of reckoning and jeopardized public virtue. *The people must pay their own debts at last,* he claimed, explaining that they must ultimately rely on their own resources to better conditions.[43] Kendall's persistent affirmation of the values of economy, industry, and morality during the 1820s cautions against equating his temporary endorsement of banks and paper money with aggressive, entrepreneurial instincts. To categorize Kendall or Blair as ambitious men-on-the-make endeavoring to replace one established economic elite with another ignores their Jeffersonian antipathy towards banking, their partiality for hard money, and their commitment to the concept of republican virtue. Jeffersonian mistrust of banks persisted in the West and, though often dormant, could be kindled into a powerful force.[44]

As in other states which suffered from the effects of the panic, the gradual return of prosperity to Kentucky in 1822 eased the conflict over economic remedies. But party warfare in the state was quickly resumed over a new issue in 1823, when the court of appeals rekindled the reliefers' democratic cause by declaring their program unconstitutional. Most relief men followed Kendall and Blair in sustaining the people's right to pass measures which, however unwise, were constitutional. The emerging New Court party urged the elimination of the court of appeals and the appointment of new judges. To

Kendall and Blair, the battle between the Old and New Court men recalled the earlier Jeffersonian assault on the federal and state courts, and they again defended the right of the people "to rule themselves" against the "'spirit of monarchy.'" They cast themselves as protectors of the Jeffersonian legacy warding off an entrenched group of lawyers and judges who defied the popular will and attempted to curtail the right of self-government.[45]

The New Court party supported Kentucky's favorite son, Henry Clay, in 1824, but by the fall of 1826 a combination of practical and ideological considerations brought them into Jackson's camp. In part, supporting Jackson provided an opportunity for rescuing their political fortunes after the return of prosperity undermined the popularity of their program. Moreover, relief leaders attributed their loss in the state elections of 1825 and 1826 to the aid which Henry Clay provided to the conservative Old Court party. By latching on to Jackson's coattails, therefore, the New Court party could strike back at Clay as well as reverse its ebbing popularity.[46]

But vengeance and political ambition only partly explain their decision to abandon Clay. Depression and battles with conservative financial interests sharpened the relief party's hostility to the connection between government and favored economic and political groups. Jeffersonian antipathy to concentrated power and special privilege gained new vitality as the New Court men attacked the Bank, the Supreme Court, and Kentucky's political establishment. Like Van Buren, Kendall expressed dissatisfaction with Monroe's amalgamation policy, pronouncing the president's principles closer to *"federal republicans,* than *republicans* of the *Jeffersonian school."* [47] When the Adams administration pushed latitudinarianism into new frontiers, relief party leaders turned to Jackson. For them, Jackson represented the means by which farmers and mechanics would overthrow entrenched interests, sever the government's connection with the privileged few, and assure the purity of republican institutions. "I never deserted your banner," Blair explained to Clay, "until the questions on which you and I so frequently differed in private discussion—(State rights, the Bank, the power of the Judiciary, etc.)—became the criterions [*sic*] to distinguish the parties, and had actually renewed, in their practical effects, the great divisions which marked the era of 1798." And Kendall, reminding his readers of the tendency of power to corrupt, denounced the Adams administration for the "grossest encroachments" upon states' rights and claimed that all good Jeffersonians in Kentucky were supporting Jackson.[48]

Although their recent defeats in state elections indicated that they no longer represented majority opinion, the New Court party placed at Jackson's service skilled politicians who had probed the popular mind during the 1820s and had learned the value of appealing to the common man by attacking privilege, monopoly, and abridgments of the popular will. In many respects, they had developed that peculiar combination of demagoguery, idealistic defense of the common man, and organizational ability that would characterize the Democratic party. When Jackson became president and began to develop his political program, he increasingly sought the counsel of the former New Court spokesmen, Kendall and Blair.[49]

While the contribution of the relief men to Jackson's program lay in the future, their shift was immediately perceived as a blow to the Kentuckian. A story went the rounds about the first meeting with Clay after Blair announced for Jackson. Clay had traveled from Lexington to Frankfort in the winter to attend to some legal business. After dismounting from his horse at a tavern door, he encountered Blair, who was just leaving. "How do you do, Mr. Blair?" asked Clay blandly while extending his hand. Blair mechanically took the tendered hand, but was evidently nonplussed and at length said, "Pretty well, I thank you, sir. How did you find the roads from Lexington here?" "The roads are very bad, Mr. Blair," graciously replied Clay, "very bad; and I wish, sir, that you would mend your ways."[50]

As the Jackson coalition was pieced together, it did not project a coherent and uniform platform. The disparate elements of the coalition revealed divergent views on substantive issues that provoked controversy over their narrow material aspects as well as their implications for the kind of society the future would unfold. Tariffs, internal improvements, banking and currency, and similar issues not only involved concrete rewards and sacrifices for different interests, but also inspired broader, value-laden questions about the pace, extent, and texture of economic and social change.[51] Consequently, local Jackson leaders pledged their candidate to contradictory positions, and wisdom counseled Jackson not to risk his popularity by engaging in political debate. He himself possessed a politician's appreciation for necessary ambiguity, and he preferred in the midst of a campaign to "speak . . . with reflection, embracing general remarks. . . ." He and his followers, therefore, were generally content to let Adams's "reserved, cold, austere, and forbidding manners" and his deficiency in the art of getting on with other people take full effect.[52]

Yet even though personalities dominated the election of 1828, there were many indications that a Jackson presidency would be different from Adams's. In part, Jackson's association with the Crawford and Calhoun factions created the impression that he would limit federal power, and his mail bulged with appeals from supporters to restore Jeffersonian principles to government. Van Buren explained to him that "the politics of this state [New York] like those of Pennsylvania & most of the northern states are yet governed by old Party feelings"; a former Crawford supporter urged him to "bring us back to the honesty of the times of Jefferson"; while a leading southern antitariff Calhounite was hopeful that Jackson's southern background, wisdom, and integrity would make him a "PACIFICATOR" on the tariff issue. There was also support for strict construction principles from western Jacksonians. The Kentucky Central Jackson Committee, headed by Blair, wrote that the General's election would "form an era in our Annals, more auspicious to our liberties than that which was signalized by Th. Jefferson, in restoring our Government to its 'Republican tack.'"[53]

Jackson's own political opinions also suggested, though in general terms, his future course. He was not, to be sure, a political theorist with a systematic and interrelated set of beliefs, and historians rightly contrast his emotional and active qualities with Jefferson's greater emphasis on reason and the mind.[54] Nevertheless, Jackson possessed underlying political ideas, values, and prejudices which could be called a persuasion or, without unreasonable flexibility, a philosophy or ideology. These thoughts not only filtered and screened reality but provided the context for his actions. As his career progressed, and especially during his presidency, his thinking became more refined, coherent, and consistent.[55]

Basically Jeffersonian in origin, Jackson's principles reaffirmed the Republican party's concern for preserving liberty and republican government from the perilous influences of power and corruption. This solicitude was itself an outgrowth of the Revolutionary crisis during which Americans crystallized their unique concept of government and society. Renouncing concentrated authority, monarchy, aristocracy, standing armies, and established churches as inimical to freedom, republican proponents based government on the will of the people and relied for its stability on the proper balance of governmental powers and on such essential but intangible qualities as public and private virtue, internal unity, and social solidarity. Republics, however, were fragile and delicate mechanisms that easily fell prey to external attack or to the wicked designs of evil men. They were also vulnerable to internal corruption, particularly from the excesses associated with an evolving market economy—stockjobbing, paper credit, funded debts, powerful monied interests, and an expanding bureaucracy. To the republican mind, liberty was always endangered and one had to guard continually against those who would subvert it.[56]

During the 1790s, Jeffersonians revitalized this Revolutionary heritage to challenge Federalist economic and constitutional doctrines. Confronted by the expansion of executive and federal authority, the establishment of a national bank, a large funded debt, increased taxes, and abridgments of civil liberties, they insisted on strict construction, states' rights, and limited government principles as essential to maintain a free and virtuous republican society. Different views of the Revolution's republican legacy infused the political conflicts of the first party system, but it is generally assumed that the securing of independence with the conclusion of the War of 1812 ushered in a new period of American history, one having its own issues and concerns.[57] The break seems arbitrary, for attention and anxiety continued to focus on the republican ideal after 1815, especially in men like Jackson whose memory of the Revolution remained vivid and whose political ideas were formulated during the heated battles of the republic's early years.[58]

In 1828 Jackson's political philosophy was still evolving and his political record sufficiently ambiguous so that many supporters concluded that he was sympathetic to economic nationalism and expansive governmental powers. He was affiliated with the economically aggressive Blount-Overton faction, which was notoriously involved in banking and land enterprises. Moreover, as a United States senator, he had voted for the patently protective Tariff of 1824 as well as for a number of internal improvements bills. When called upon to explain his position, he explicitly sanctioned "a liberal construction of the

Constitution" and virtually embraced Clay's American System and home market concepts whereby protective tariffs encouraged industry and commerce, eliminated surplus farm labor, and produced a national market for agricultural products. He seemed equally willing to condone the blurring of party lines, having recommended that Monroe appoint a Federalist to the cabinet.[59]

But there were stronger indications of Jackson's essential agreement with traditional Republican states' rights and limited government notions. Throughout his life he identified the achievement of liberty and self-government during the Revolution with the Republican party. Assuming that the foundation of republican government lay in the "virtue, and independant [*sic*] exercise of . . . free suffrage" by the people, he also possessed a deep-rooted and impulsive anxiety that, with the exception of farmers, mankind was prone to treachery and corruption.[60] He viewed the excesses of Federalist rule as evidence of this tendency, and as a member of the House of Representatives had even refused to approve a declaration of sentiments praising Washington's administration. Indeed, if Jackson had any special ties in politics, they were with Old Republican ideologues like Nathaniel Macon and John Randolph who considered themselves the conscience of the party.[61]

Admittedly, Jackson participated in the drift towards economic nationalism during Monroe's presidency, but his Jeffersonian scruples were still evident. When Monroe vetoed a toll bill which entailed federal jurisdiction over the Cumberland Road, Jackson sent his congratulations. When the relief battles broke out in Tennessee and Kentucky, he revealed his hard-money bias and firmly sided with those opposed to paper-money inflation. Declaring that the state banks were unconstitutional and their note issues worthless, he spoke of the "paper banking system" as a corrupting influence on the people's morals.[62] Even his endorsement of the Tariff of 1824 was qualified. To Jackson, the recent war confirmed the need to protect goods essential for national defense, and although this category could be interpreted flexibly, it implied selectivity and restraint in preparing tariff schedules. Moreover, the tariff provided revenue to pay the public debt which, echoing Jefferson, he labeled "a national curse," and he warned of its tendency to create a "monied aristocracy" which bent government to its will and ultimately destroyed liberty. The primary beneficiary of the tariff, in Jackson's thinking, should be the farmer, whom he described as "the main pillar [*sic*] of our national prosperity, and upon which our independence and wealth as a nation rests." [63] His concessions to economic nationalism, then, were framed within a Jeffersonian context.

It is also likely that Jackson became more consistent in his limited government thinking during Adams's presidency. When Adams's first annual message to Congress called for extensive internal improvements expenditures, the establishment of a national university and astronomical observatory, and coastal surveys, Jackson characterized the speech as "well calculated to swell to indignation the dissatisfaction" already created by the president's election and appointment of Clay. He considered the "corrupt bargain" as but one aspect of a dangerous reassertion of executive and federal power, and he accused Adams of repeating his father's errors and reviving "the asperity which marked the struggle of 98 and 1800." [64] The future of republican government was at issue. "Instead of building lighthouses of the skies, national universities and making explorations of the globe, their [the people's] language will be pay the national debt, prepare for national independence & defense—then apportion the surplus revenue among the several states for the education of the poor," Jackson insisted. One astute Adams man accurately perceived the direction of Jackson's ideas. "Your favorite the American system," he informed Clay, "the people of Tennessee is opposed to, and also the Hero if he had no concealment." [65]

Jackson had no intention of embarking on a states' rights crusade and he still retained ideas about national power which did not fully satisfy the Crawfordites or antitariff Calhounites. His approval in principle of tariff protection disappointed and troubled many southerners, and a leading Calhounite informed him that his tariff position was not all that could be desired. [66] Jackson also failed to specify the types of internal improvements that constituted an invasion of states' rights, thus leaving the door open to personal judgment and the continuation of some degree of federal aid. This ambiguity was reinforced by his support for apportioning the government's surplus revenue to the states. A surplus implied a tariff sufficiently high to bring in more money than the government needed for administrative purposes, and Jackson did not rule out its use by the states for internal improvements.[67]

Nevertheless, Jackson's tendency to qualify and limit federal activity distinguished him from Adams. The president was more impressed by the benefits of government activity than by its potential threat to liberty and individual enterprise. Arguing that "liberty is power," he urged his countrymen to enact measures of public improvement. Jackson, however, advanced a moderate states' rights philosophy that deftly appealed to the bulk of his supporters who sought limited aid from the federal government but feared that the abuse or aggrandizement of federal power would corrupt republican institutions. His Jeffersonian vocabulary revealed the conviction that while a republic must be strong enough to maintain unity and independence, its moral fiber must remain unblemished by extravagance, aristocratic pretension, and special interest legislation.[68]

In order to unite their efforts and concentrate their forces against Adams, leaders of the Jackson coalition constructed a more elaborate, extensive, and efficient organization than had ever been employed in national politics before. One must avoid exaggerating its proficiency, for the political machinery created in 1828 was only the organizational skeleton of the Democratic party, the elaboration and fleshing out of which would take years, not being completed until the 1840s. Nevertheless, particularly in the Middle Atlantic states and the West, partisan efforts took on new dimensions, and the Jacksonians demonstrated a particular affinity for stimulating political interest through popular campaign techniques and grass-roots organization. The partisan scruples that had marked the first party system were gradually being replaced by an acceptance of political organization as beneficial to republican government. As early as the 1828 campaign, the Jacksonians showed themselves more willing than their opponents to usher in the new order.[69]

In Washington, the Jackson men united in scuttling Adams's program, harassing the president at every turn and taking the initiative out of his hands. They established their own newspaper, the *United States' Telegraph*, which made its first appearance in February 1826, some time before the Van Burenites endorsed Jackson. It therefore showed the influence of the Calhoun-Jackson alliance; and its editor,

Duff Green, had been an early promoter of Calhoun's presidential ambitions. A former Missouri newspaperman, Green must be acknowledged as one of the pioneers of the national party press. Previously, Washington newspapers had served primarily as internal propaganda devices for the local capital community, but Green took advantage of the expanding national political environment by making the *Telegraph* the central agency of a newspaper network, disseminating pro-Jackson material throughout the countryside and publishing favorable accounts of Jackson's prospects which first appeared in other newspapers.[70]

Green was also the most influential member of the Washington central committee of twenty-four, an organization that distributed to the states election material printed at the center of government. Meanwhile, in the political hinterland, militia meetings, parades, and mass rallies supplemented more formal arrangements for rallying the voters, and by the closing months of 1827, virtually every county, city, and town of importance had a functioning Jackson committee of one type or another.[71]

The numerous state and local Jackson committees were linked together by a central committee in Nashville consisting of Jackson's closest personal friends and advisers, including John Overton, William B. Lewis, John Eaton, and a former Crawford supporter named Alfred Balch. The Nashville committee, which the Adams men labeled the "White-washing Committee," worked closely with political leaders in Washington and in the states, distributed defenses of the candidate, kept tabs on the activity of the multifarious Jackson organizations, and offered advice on conducting the campaign. Because the Nashville committee contained Jackson's closest political friends, and because two of its members, Eaton and Lewis, followed him to Washington as aides, this committee served as a prototype of the Kitchen Cabinet.[72]

Partly out of expediency, the Jacksonian political structures were more efficient and popular than those of the Adams men. As the "outs," Jackson men had to bypass administration politicians and officeholders and rely instead on the masses of citizens who were attracted to Jackson by his personal magnetism or his expected political decisions. But also as a matter of principle, Jackson politicians seemed more in harmony with the early nineteenth century's impulse for greater participation by the citizenry in politics. At the same time, this political machinery provided better opportunities for skilled politicians to direct and channel voter sentiment. The electorate was brought closer to its national leaders, and each was better able to influence the other. As president, Jackson would skillfully exploit this new relationship.[73]

Jackson's own contribution to this developing organization was itself indicative of the changes occurring in American political practice. During the Monroe years he had criticized the continuation of party divisions and had pledged that if he were elected president, it would be by "the people" not by "a party." Always influenced by republican notions of public virtue, Jackson was confident that "the judgment of an enlightened, patriotic, and uncorrupted people" would sustain him.[74] Nevertheless, he also recognized the people's need for organization and information in order to make their influence felt. During the campaign, he collected and prepared material to be sent "eastward & Southward . . . to every printer & Jackson committee in Ohio, Indiana, Illinois, Mississippi, Louisiana and Alabama—and to the north, Pennsylvania, Virginia, Maryland, New Jersey, New York and New Hampshire." He prodded the Nashville committee to action and embarked on a trip to New Orleans in January 1828, ostensibly to celebrate his victory over the British, but actually a thinly disguised effort at vote gathering. He thereby sanctioned the new, more popular campaign style as well as the employment of more systematic techniques to mobilize the electorate.[75]

Just as Jackson's political principles awaited future elaboration, the Jackson coalition lacked the organizational coherence that the Democratic party would attain during his presidency. Although strong enough to defeat Adams, the coalition contained many Jackson men who considered themselves to be as loyal to Van Buren or Calhoun as to Jackson. Their alliance with Old Hickory was largely one of practicality and convenience since they hoped to obtain an influence over the president which would later give them control over the government. Thus in 1826, Van Buren men and Calhounites contested control over the *Telegraph* when Van Buren suggested that Thomas Ritchie either replace Duff Green or establish another Jackson paper in Washington. Similarly, a few of Calhoun's enemies tried to undermine his position by informing Jackson that Calhoun had once desired to punish him for attacking Spanish Florida. Although both Jackson and Calhoun agreed to set aside the matter, it illustrated the precarious unity of the Jackson coalition as men jostled for power and position.[76]

2

Cabinet Formation and Jackson's Advisory System

Andrew Jackson arrived in Washington on 11 February 1829, took up temporary residence at Gadsby's National Hotel, and began to select his official advisers. The city was already buzzing with speculation about the possible makeup of his cabinet, for not only were Jackson's followers divided into rival factions, but there was a widespread belief in his "unfitness" for office. Jackson's appointments would, therefore, reveal something about his political intentions as well as his ability to govern.[1]

Many of Jackson's initial choices turned out to be unfortunate, and he was compelled to reorganize his cabinet halfway through his first term. But the process of cabinet formation indicated a president determined to direct his administration and to make himself the focal point of a large and flexible advisory network. As he gained experience, his future cabinet selections improved considerably, though they were always influenced by a style of leadership that looked beyond formal institutions for advice.

Prior to Jackson's election, cabinet practice had varied considerably, but both Federalist and Republican presidents had generally used the cabinet as a policy forum and as a device for recognizing geographical sections and party factions. With the demise of the first party system and the concomitant weakening of presidential authority, the status and independence of cabinet members had grown until Monroe found that cabinet consensus was the only guarantee of his program's success in Congress. Even the more aggressive John Quincy Adams had struggled to establish control over his cabinet and program.[2]

From Thomas Ritchie, Jackson received the advice that he form an "old fashioned . . . consultative" council, but Jackson came to Washington resolved on circumscribing the cabinet's political and advisory powers and enhancing his own authority. His attitude towards the presidency was not in keeping with traditional Jeffersonian doctrine or experience. In contrast to the Federalists' emphasis on energy in the executive office, Republican theory advocated limited executive discretion, cautioning that a strong president endangered liberty, and Republican presidents had found their powers diminishing as the cabinet grew more assertive. There were, of course, exceptions, especially Jefferson himself, who pioneered in the exercise of presidential leadership; but it is unlikely that even Jefferson achieved full liberation from a suspiciousness of executive authority, and his Republican successors were, in any case, either unable or unwilling to follow his example.[3]

Jackson, however, was prepared to exercise the powers of his office, to require the subordination of his officials, and to reach beyond the cabinet for political and programmatic advice.[4] Experience and temperament helped dictate this course. As a general, he had rarely held councils, preferring instead to consult his aides informally and to make his own judgment. He was also aware of the difficulties Monroe had suffered by failing to control his cabinet, a lesson which doubtless reinforced his intention to concentrate his own authority. Psychologically, too, Jackson displayed a suspicion of human nature that was reflected in his need to be self-reliant. Life had taught him about the ever present danger of deceit and betrayal, and his trust and confidence were gained only by those whose loyalty and worthiness had been tested. "I have been Tossed upon the waves of fortune from youth[h]ood, I have experienced prosperity and adversity," he explained in a revealing autobiographical observation to a friend. "It was this that gave me a knowledge of human nature . . . you will find many, professedly, friends, who by, and from their openness of conduct, and specious professions, the inexperienced youth, at once places the utmost reliance—when in many Instances these professions are made with a view to obtain your confidence that it may be betrayed. To guard against such impositions there is but one safe rule—have apparent confidence in all, but never make a confident [sic] of any untill you have proven him worthy of it . . . never, untill you have well tried him, confide to any a secrete that might be injurious to you if publickly known." As individuals, cabinet members might therefore obtain Jackson's confidence, but as an institution composed of men who were often strangers and who might have independent political bases, the cabinet was not congenial to Jackson's instinct.[5]

In addition to these considerations, Jackson's management of his cabinet was shaped by his view of politics and of the office he had won. According to Van Buren, Jackson presumed that his "strength lay with the masses" and that to labor in their interests "was the special mission assigned to him by his Creator." Confident of his own virtue, he belittled the weight of established and prominent politicians and considered his election a moral triumph by the people over entrenched interests intent on destroying self-government. The executive, therefore, became "the direct representative of the American people," and since no member of his cabinet ever had the popularity or power to controvert his claim, he effectually enhanced the president's power and undermined the independence of the cabinet, making it more an administrative arm of the chief executive.[6]

Hezekiah Niles, the astute and influential editor, protested the change. He criticized Jackson's use of his secretaries "only as . . . *clerks*" and pronounced Jackson's references to "my cabinet" as novel. Niles had a point, for Jackson's conception of presidential leadership was unprecedented. Federalists had shunned the notion of the president as a direct representative of the people, and Republicans had generally looked to the legislature as the voice of the citizenry. Jackson, however, legitimized presidential power by locating its authority in the popular will. While this idea was personally congenial, it was also consonant with what he took to be his mandate, "to increase the value and prolong the duration of American liberty."[7]

In keeping with his limited view of the cabinet's role, Jackson's criteria for selecting its membership were modest. He wanted "plain, business men" rather than eminent politicians who might use their position as a stepping stone to higher office, and he insisted that his nominees "concur" in his moderate states' rights course. Nevertheless, the task of forming a cabinet proved arduous. James Buchanan cogently summed up the major cause of difficulty: "Disguise it as we may, the friends of Van Buren and those of Calhoun are becoming very jealous of each other."[8]

Rivalry between the two factions was intense. Jackson was sixty-two years old, in precarious health, and had indicated during the campaign that he believed in a one-term presidency. The importance of gaining a foothold in the executive office could not, therefore, be denied. It was also widely believed that Jackson lacked political experience and know-how, and that his limited involvement in national politics would, of necessity, force him into the hands of more skilled politicians. And the advantage of being close to Jackson when he reeled under the burdens of office was all the greater because the Democratic party in its infancy offered unique opportunities to establish priorities. Since the party's course had not yet been charted, these early years would set precedents that would be difficult to overturn. For the antitariff radicals in particular, it was now imperative to reverse the trend towards the concentration of power in the federal government and to relieve the South of the hated Tariff of Abominations.[9]

The stakes were large, and members of the Van Buren and Calhoun factions eyed each other jealously and estimated their relative strengths. The Calhounites, according to one Regency man, had "no political character here"; he predicted their political obliteration. Alfred Balch informed Van Buren soon after the election that "Calhoun has already commenced the campaign in Tennessee for the Presidency," but he announced that the Van Burenites were prepared. "The former friends of Crawford here—neither few in number nor weak in talents have an acc[oun]t to settle with Mr. Calhoun which must be settled." Duff Green, on the other hand, privately gloated that Van Buren was "overacting his part." Speculation about the Van Buren–Calhoun rivalry was so pronounced that Green, though a Calhoun partisan, took pains to assure the country that the new administration was not in danger of collapsing.[10]

Settled in Gadsby's, Jackson received scores of visitors, so many that Washingtonians dubbed the hotel "the Wigwam." He listened politely as each presented advice about appointments, but he refused to reveal his intentions. Even Isaac Hill, the political boss of New Hampshire and editor of a newspaper which Jackson read avidly, called upon the president every day but could only "infer" that he would be consulted in the future.[11]

While Van Burenites and Calhoun men jostled for position, Jackson consulted primarily with his longtime Tennessee associates, Senators John H. Eaton and Hugh Lawson White, and his planter neighbor, William B. Lewis. All were members of the Blount-Overton faction and had been Jackson's earliest presidential boosters. They were his personal friends and had served as leading figures in his presidential campaign. It was natural and comfortable to turn first to them for advice.[12]

John Eaton was a man of considerable wealth and leisure. Although a lawyer of some talent, he rarely practiced, being content to live in gentlemanly fashion on his considerable inheritance. His association with Jackson was a long one, dating at least from the time when he served on the general's staff during the War of 1812. He was also, like most Blount-Overton leaders, conservative in his politics, having been a director of the Nashville Bank and an opponent of all efforts to make it resume specie payments during the panic of 1819. Jackson, of course, had favored resumption and had criticized Eaton's stand as well as the inflationary schemes of the relief men.[13]

Despite such policy differences, Eaton had put his ample political talent and energy behind Jackson during the campaigns of 1824 and 1828. He became one of the most influential members of the Nashville Junto, and his loyalty and industry earned him Jackson's trust and affection. The bond between them, however, transcended political attitudes, since Eaton ultimately differed with him on major policy decisions, notably the Bank War and the Maysville Road veto, and he joined the Whig party in 1840. But personal friendship was important to Jackson, and never more so than when he arrived in Washington to take on the responsibilities of the presidency. "I have confidence in other men but I have more in [him]," Jackson declared of Eaton.[14]

William B. Lewis was not only a neighbor and friend of Jackson's but also Eaton's brother-in-law. He too had been among Jackson's earliest presidential backers, and his Federalist background undoubtedly aided in lining up former Federalists and Clintonians behind Jackson. His interest in politics, however, was mostly personal. Less intellectual than Eaton, he cared more about detail than issues or ideology; but his devotion and willingness to perform political chores made Jackson especially desirous of keeping him nearby. Indeed, the president asked him to live in the White House while serving as second auditor of the Treasury Department.[15]

Lewis was also a member of the Blount-Overton faction and a director of the Nashville Bank. But there was always something suspicious about his business transactions, and his financial dealings and land speculations had come under severe criticism in Tennessee. Even Eaton regarded him warily. Lewis, too, eventually differed from Jackson on banking and internal improvements policies, but he remained personally attached to Jackson. "Keep . . . William B. Lewis to ferret out and make known to you all the plots and intrigues Hatching against your administration and you are safe. The major will be faithful," Jackson advised Polk when Young Hickory became president.[16]

Hugh Lawson White was also much in evidence at Gadsby's. Another Tennessean, White too had been a Blount-Overton leader, though his ties with the other members were somewhat strained. His independence had increased in recent years, probably because of his dislike of Eaton and Lewis. Jackson, however, recognized White's considerable reputation as an incorruptible, sensible spokesman of Jeffersonian sentiments. He considered the senator one of his "confidential friends" and requested his opinions about the cabinet.[17]

Finally, James A. Hamilton, the son of Alexander Hamilton, was a conspicuous and frequent visitor to Jackson's room. Hamilton had been an intermediary between the Albany Regency and the Nashville Junto during the recent campaign, and now, in February 1829, he again represented Van Buren's interests. Several of Van Buren's friends had encouraged Hamilton's journey to Washington so that Jackson could have around him "a discreet friend," and Hamilton undertook the responsibility eagerly, doubtless stimulated by his desire for an appointment.[18]

Significantly, the most visible advisers to Jackson, with the exception of White, were partial to Van Buren's political prospects. Hamilton, of course, had come to Washington as a Regency representative, while his mentor remained in Albany presiding over the state legislature. He wanted a cabinet friendly to Van Buren at the outset so that no energy would have to be expended later in order to sway it to Van Buren's side.[19]

The attachment of Lewis and Eaton to Van Buren was largely personal and originated in the factional disputes that marked the Monroe era. Especially important was their dislike of Van Buren's rival, Calhoun. Lewis's hostility began in 1819, when he became convinced that Calhoun, as secretary of war, had disapproved of Jackson's expedition into Spanish Florida and had counseled Monroe to punish the general. Although Calhoun's support for both of Jackson's presidential bids raised his standing, it did not erase Lewis's hesitancies. His doubts may occasionally have been fanned by Alfred Balch, Van Buren's friend on the Nashville central committee. In any event, during the campaign of 1828 Lewis warned a fellow Jacksonian about the "delicate subject" of Calhoun, believing it "a rock upon which we may split." [20]

With Eaton, Lewis, and Hamilton constantly present at Jackson's side during the preinaugural period, many observers concluded that the president's cabinet smacked of a Van Buren intrigue. The reality was quite different. Although associated with the Blount-Overton faction, Jackson had never been its creature, and his habitual independence of mind and faith in his own political intuition served to distance him from his advisers' suggestions. Hamilton, who thought he enjoyed "the General's confidence," merely provided a sympathetic ear and operated as a messenger, inquiring into the availability of possible nominees. And when Eaton, Lewis, and Hamilton urged the appointment of Van Buren's friend Louis McLane to the Treasury Department, Jackson rejected their counsel in favor of the suggestion of the Pennsylvania delegation to Congress. The cabinet, though it reflected the advice of Eaton and Lewis, was not the product of a political intrigue; rather it indicated most of all that Jackson was determined to establish his own leadership of the executive office. [21]

Even before leaving Tennessee for Washington, Jackson was determined to appoint either Eaton or White to a cabinet post. He wanted to "have near him a personal and confidential friend to whom he could embosom himself on all subjects." Soon after arriving at the capital, he selected Eaton as secretary of war, a position especially suited to one who had considerable experience in Indian affairs and who, Jackson believed, had "high standing" in New York, Pennsylvania, and the West. [22]

Jackson had also decided before setting out for Washington to appoint as secretary of state Van Buren, who had made a major contribution towards his election by convincing former Crawford men to rally behind him. Moreover, no president could ignore the benefits of tying New York to his side. Although a few Virginia antitariff radicals were disappointed in the choice, probably because they bitterly resented

Van Buren's vote supporting the Tariff of 1828, no one was surprised by it. Even the Calhoun faction generally acknowledged its appropriateness, though with what enthusiasm it is difficult to say.[23]

With these two appointments out of the way, Jackson concerned himself with the others. Because of its relationship to the divisive tariff issue, the Treasury Department proved the most troublesome. In line with his endorsement of moderate tariff reform, Jackson had decided "not to put into this office either an ultra tariff or an ultra antitariff man." Furthermore, he wanted to give this seat, the second most prestigious in the cabinet, to Pennsylvania, a state which had boomed his candidacy in 1824 and had given him overwhelming support in both campaigns.[24]

Jackson's own preference was for Henry Baldwin, a Pittsburgh iron manufacturer, politician, and tariff spokesman who had been one of his earliest supporters. But Baldwin's political base in Pennsylvania was a liability. His faction was identified with Federalism and, in a state where Van Buren had few sympathizers, with loyalty to Clay rather than Calhoun. The state's dominant "Family party" insisted on one of its own, and under the urging of Pennsylvania's congressional delegation, Jackson waived his choice of Baldwin in favor of Samuel Ingham.[25]

As a member of the entrepreneurial-minded Family faction, Ingham had first supported Calhoun in 1824, but when the South Carolinian withdrew from the contest, he became one of the most prominent Jackson men in Pennsylvania. A successful paper mill operator and proficient county boss, Ingham was an intelligent but unimaginative, rigid, and self-important man. During the 1820s he had been chairman of the Post Office Committee in Congress, where he learned the importance of patronage for party purposes. He was hoping to put his skills to work as Jackson's postmaster general when the new president offered him the Treasury Department. His appointment has generally been attributed to Calhoun's influence, but this seems unlikely. Ingham's considerable efforts for Jackson merited a high position, and once Jackson had decided to give the Treasury Department to a Pennsylvanian and a moderate on the tariff issue, Ingham was the logical choice. He had been one of the "seven traitors," the seven Pennsylvania congressmen who had voted against the increased protection of the Woolens Bill of 1827, and he had failed to record a vote on the Tariff of Abominations.[26]

Jackson's collaboration with his Tennessee friends was most evident in the appointments of attorney general and secretary of the navy. He had no apparent preference for either seat, though, since the other positions were given to the North and West, equity dictated that the nominees should come from the South. Predominantly upon the recommendations of White, Eaton, and probably Lewis, Jackson nominated John Branch of North Carolina for the Navy Department and John McPherson Berrien as attorney general.[27]

Branch was a planter of considerable wealth and prominence, who had abandoned Crawford during the 1824 campaign in order to capitalize on Jackson's popularity in North Carolina. His aristocratic manners led some observers to speculate that Jackson had appointed him to enhance the social prestige of the administration, but he had other noteworthy qualities as well. He had a long acquaintance with Eaton, both men having been born and reared in the same county of North Carolina and having attended the University of North Carolina. Moreover, he had visited Jackson a number of times during trips to Tennessee, where he owned land, and he never lost an opportunity to ingratiate himself with the General. It is also possible that Jackson wished to acknowledge the constant support that North Carolina had given Republican candidates without ever having received a cabinet appointment. Branch, who was extremely popular in his home state, would thus have come readily to mind.[28]

An avid proponent of states' rights principles, Branch had also been an outspoken critic of banks and internal improvements legislation. But neither Lewis nor Jackson seemed to know that he was deeply committed to immediate and drastic tariff reduction, and Lewis mistakenly thought him a Van Buren partisan, possibly because of his early connection with Crawford.[29]

John McPherson Berrien was a cautious and conservative man whose sternness and aloofness were noted even by his friends. Like Branch he was a wealthy plantation owner, but he had achieved recognition and prominence primarily for his legal abilities. With his extensive reputation as a lawyer, he was clearly qualified to be a distinguished attorney general. Berrien's political career remains enigmatic. A former Federalist, he retained some elements of that party's nationalistic thinking; at the same time, however, he was an ardent defender of the South and slavery. Aligned with, but not intimately attached to, the Troup-Crawford faction in Georgia, Berrien had supported Crawford in 1824, but had not then transferred his political affiliation to Van Buren. His relations with the New Yorker were "never confidential nor particularly cordial," and he had engaged in numerous political disputes with other members of the Crawford set.[30]

The reasons for Jackson and his Tennessee counselors' choice of Berrien, apart from the Georgian's stature as a lawyer, are largely unclear. However, a serious controversy between Georgia and the federal government had flared up when the Adams administration failed to remove the state's Indian population, and though Jackson's desire to remove the southern Indians to land west of the Mississippi River promised to resolve the issue, retaining a Georgian as attorney general could prove useful to him. It is certain that Berrien's only significant contribution in his brief cabinet career was as a mediator between Jackson and Georgia on Indian policy.[31]

Jackson's final selection was John McLean of Ohio as postmaster general. McLean had served in this position during Adams's presidency, but he had used his patronage and influence to promote Jackson's election. A close friend of Calhoun, he also had his own presidential ambitions, with a base of support in his native Northwest and among Methodists throughout the country. His political strength made him a valuable ally for the administration, and probably as a means of satisfying McLean's ego and acknowledging his political standing, Jackson decided to give the office cabinet status. McLean, however, quickly found that despite its enhanced prestige the job no longer suited his needs, and he soon exchanged it for another appointment.[32]

Jackson completed his cabinet by 19 February, but postponed the official announcement until the 26th. The delay was due to the outcries of discontent that greeted rumored reports of the choices and cast a gloomy shadow over the new administration even before it evicted the Adams men.[33]

The Calhounites were particularly unhappy at Jackson's list. "I am perfectly cool—damn cool—never half so cool in my Life," the South

Carolina radical James Hamilton, Jr., grumbled. In Hamilton's view, Jackson's actions were confirmation that the president would surround himself with men who could provide no moral leadership and that he would cater, instead, to "Whiskey House popularity."[34]

Jackson's selections doubtless ruffled Hamilton's aristocratic feathers, but the nullifier was primarily disturbed at what the selections revealed about Jackson's moderation on the tariff issue. Hamilton had been observing the secret sessions at Gadsby's, and the more he learned about them, the more his irritation increased. Using Calhoun as an intermediary, he sought an interview with Jackson. Hamilton made known to the president his particular solicitude about the Treasury Department, which, he felt, must go to a man in favor of immediate tariff reduction, a man "highly acceptable to the South."[35]

Jackson, however, refused to budge on his appointment of Ingham, emphasizing his decision not to appoint either a radical tariff or antitariff man to the post. As if to confirm his intentions further, the president soon thereafter told Hamilton that he might have had a seat in the cabinet but for his "ultra tariff violence" in recent months, and it was generally known that Jackson had rejected for similar reasons the suggestion that Littleton Tazewell be given the Treasury post.[36]

Meanwhile, a chorus of protests began to concentrate on Jackson's appointment of Eaton. Among those expressing disappointment was Duff Green. While the proud and egotistical editor may have been disgruntled by the apparent influence that Eaton and Lewis seemed to have on the president, he was most directly concerned that Eaton was undermining his position as the new administration's official spokesman.

Before Jackson's arrival in Washington, and probably without his authorization, Eaton asked Amos Kendall whether he would be willing to enter into partnership with Green or, failing that, to set up an independent newspaper. Kendall, who had carried Kentucky's electoral vote to the capital, also brought with him an outstanding reputation for political acumen and editorial cunning. In fact, Green himself so greatly appreciated Kendall's talents that in 1828 he offered him an assistant editorship of the *Telegraph*. Kendall, however, demanded a full partnership and Green then withdrew his offer.[37] Now, in the preinaugural days, Kendall agreed to Eaton's proposition, but with the condition that Green approve the arrangement. The Kentucky relief leader greatly respected Green for the support which the *Telegraph* had given Jackson during the campaign, and he had no desire to precipitate a feud. When the editor refused to divide his power, the matter was dropped; but Eaton's actions had wounded Green's pride and made him suspect a plot to undermine him and his friend Calhoun.

A number of Tennessee politicians, especially Blount-Overton enemies, also expressed anger at Eaton's appointment and were outraged that Jackson was relying extensively upon his and Lewis's advice for cabinet selections. A large portion of the Tennessee delegation to Congress approached Jackson and requested a reconsideration of Eaton's appointment. The dissatisfaction even spread to the president's own household. Jackson's nephew Andrew Jackson Donelson had accompanied his uncle to Washington to serve as his private secretary and to shield him from unnecessary annoyances. His wife, Emily, was to serve as White House hostess, Jackson's wife having recently died. An opponent of the Eaton-Lewis clique in Tennessee, Donelson regretted their apparent influence with Jackson, and his wife ridiculed Lewis's position as the president's companion. "Here is that sycophant Lewis that pretended to come along out of friendship to the Genl has got himself into a fat office and to save himself all expense has taken his quarters here for the next 4 years," she complained. But Jackson would not yield on either Eaton's or Lewis's appointments. "I was born for a storm and a calm does not suit me," he said of this situation.[38]

Most of the opposition to Eaton was politically motivated, but his opponents also made use of personal or "family matters" to undermine his position. Eaton's recent marriage to Margaret O'Neale Timberlake had outraged Washington society. The daughter of a Washington tavernkeeper and admittedly "frivolous, wayward, [and] passionate," Peggy had gained an unsavory reputation for being too forward with her father's boarders. Whatever her actual transgressions may have been, Peggy's affairs became an affair of state when she married Eaton on New Year's Day, 1829. Eaton had been a frequent boarder at the O'Neale tavern and the gossipers had a field day. One prominent Washington socialite thought Eaton's talents and virtues could not overcome "his late unfortunate connection," and that his marriage would be "an obstacle to his receiving a place of honor, which it is apprehended even Gen. Jackson's firmness cannot resist."[39]

The various complaints about Eaton's appointment made his seat the focus of a complicated series of maneuvers among Jackson's nominees in the week between their appointment and the official announcement. John McLean's embarrassment in the Post Office Department began the activity. Jackson had informed McLean of his desire to remove those officeholders whose appointments "controverted the will of their constituents" or who had used their offices for political war against him. McLean at first agreed to these principles but upon reconsideration realized his predicament. If forced to remove some of his previous appointees, he would undercut his own popularity as well as risk the anger of those not appointed to the vacancies. It was a situation no presidential hopeful could relish. McLean requested another position and, probably desiring to weaken the Van Buren faction, suggested that Eaton and he exchange posts. Jackson agreed to the change but made it clear that the Post Office would retain its cabinet rank.[40]

Meanwhile, John Branch, under the false impression that Jackson now thought Eaton a liability, believed he could "save the feelings of the President and Eaton himself" by urging the latter to give McLean the War Department and allowing the president to decide whether he or Eaton should have the navy portfolio. Eaton gave his assent to Branch's proposal, doubtless knowing that Jackson would give him the more prestigious Navy Department.[41]

The situation was becoming increasingly complex. James A. Hamilton suspected a Calhounite plot to ease Eaton out of the cabinet, and Jackson, tired of the maneuvering, felt he was being pressured by an effort to separate Eaton from himself. He therefore declared that the cabinet would stand as it was, and on 26 February the *Telegraph* published the list. McLean, however, still chafed in his position, and some Jackson men, fearing he would not adhere to the president's course of removing officeholders, put a few cases before him. McLean hesitated to commit himself and, realizing his precarious position, requested and received a seat on the Supreme Court.

McLean's replacement was William T. Barry, a Kentucky relief man who had been closely associated with Kendall and Blair during the

1820s. Like Blair, Barry was a Virginian by birth, having moved to Kentucky as a child. A lawyer by profession, he was especially renowned for his oratory and had been Transylvania University's first law professor and lecturer. Andrew Jackson Donelson had studied with him, though Jackson was not without qualms about some of the constitutional principles Donelson absorbed from his teacher, particularly those relating to the right of a state to issue paper money.[42]

Barry was small and slim and physically unimpressive, but he had expended all his energies and scarce resources in 1828 in supporting the Jackson cause in Kentucky. Now that he was out of office and considerably in debt, his Kentucky friends urged his appointment as a Supreme Court justice. Possibly Jackson also took into account his connection by his first marriage with John Overton, patriarch of the Blount-Overton clan. In any event, the president tapped Barry for the Court, and when McLean decided to leave the Post Office, he simply moved Barry from Court to cabinet.[43]

Barry's political views were more resilient, especially concerning the Bank of the United States, than Blair's or Kendall's, and he would make no positive political or administrative contribution to Jackson's administration. He was not an avid spoilsman either, and some removals went against his personal feelings. But he accepted their necessity and was willing to carry them out: "Policy called for them; indeed justice to the administration required it," he explained to his daughter. "Mr. Clay is at work; his partisans who have abused their stations and who are still devoted to his interests cannot or ought not to remain in office."[44]

Jackson felt pleased with his appointments, thinking the cabinet "one of the strongest . . . that ever have been in the United States." But a great many politicians and political observers disagreed. Webster called it "a very *weak* Cabinet," and Louis McLane thought it could "make no appeal to the moral intelligence of the country. . . ." "The selection of the Cabinet is in my mind conclusive evidence of the old General's incompetence," grumbled one disappointed Jacksonian.[45]

Such criticism in fact, only underscored Jackson's purposes. Most men still thought of the cabinet as a policy-making institution, embodying the wisdom of eminent statesmen and factional leaders. But Jackson primarily sought out "plain, business men" who would administer his program. With the exception of Van Buren, none of his nominees was considered a major national political figure, and most occupied precarious positions in their local settings. Berrien, Ingham, Eaton, and Barry all had substantial opposition at home. Even Van Buren still lacked political stature; he had emerged from his gubernatorial election in New York with only a plurality of votes, and his reputation as a political manipulator made him suspect to men who had grown to political maturity under the Virginia dynasty. Many of Van Buren's closest friends thought he still needed seasoning before seeking the presidency. One influential Regency man acknowledged the justification for Jackson's choices: if the president had selected men with independent political bases, C. C. Cambreleng explained to Van Buren, "you would have had all leaders and no wheel-horses and the first hill you reached would have up-set you all." Jackson's appointments signaled his determination to lead his administration. Surrounding himself with lesser politicians, he hoped they would be dependent on him for their status.[46]

Jackson's cabinet also showed his ability to maintain his independence against the Van Buren and Calhoun forces. To be sure, Ingham was a Calhoun partisan, but his appointment had come from the recommendation of Pennsylvania Democrats and had not been warmly received by Calhoun's South Carolina friends. John McLean, though considered a member of the Calhoun faction, had presidential ambitions of his own, while Barry, McLean's replacement, was indifferent to the pretensions of either Calhoun or Van Buren. He considered himself a Jackson man. Branch and Berrien were not considered Calhoun supporters at this time, and their attitude towards Van Buren was a matter of speculation. Branch had once been a Crawford supporter and Lewis thought him "decidedly friendly" to Van Buren, but he was never identified with Van Buren and the New Yorker never expressed a desire to have him in the cabinet. As for Berrien, his lack of cordiality with Van Buren makes it difficult to believe that Lewis, Eaton, or Jackson thought him a Van Buren follower.[47]

Indeed, the disappointment expressed by leaders of both factions only bears out Jackson's autonomy. Hamilton and Robert Hayne both protested the selections to Jackson during the week before the official announcement. Calhoun, though publicly silent, indicated his distress that Jackson's choices signified a lack of commitment to immediate tariff reform. But Van Buren was no more pleased with the cabinet. He had wanted Jackson to appoint "practical, intelligent and efficient men . . . in whom the people have confidence," and he was unpleasantly surprised at the final list. "I had not heard or thought of Messrs. Branch and Eaton as members of the Cabinet, and but slightly of Mr. Berrien," he noted glumly. Van Buren confessed to James Hamilton, Jr., his inability to influence Jackson's selections, and he later recalled that "there was probably not one of those malcontents more disappointed than myself by the composition of the administration." Even James A. Hamilton, who had labored to ensure a cabinet favorable to Van Buren, acknowledged his failure and thought Van Buren would have to rely on his own talents to sway it in his direction.[48]

If the cabinet revealed no special partiality for Van Buren or Calhoun, it made clear Jackson's intent to draw the line against Clay and Adams. Appointing only his own supporters to office, Jackson patently disregarded former party allegiances. Branch, Ingham, Berrien, and possibly Barry had once acted with the Federalist party, as had Louis McLane, who became minister to Great Britain. Cabinet selection, therefore, gave a boost to the second American party system just as it helped to conclude the first. "We shall now have, what was at one time feared we should not have, a party administration," Cambreleng assured Van Buren.[49]

It is evident that Jackson's popularity and independence increased his flexibility in forming a cabinet. Feeling no need to rely upon other men's power and influence, he could more safely discount their "local weight, and the influence of their States." Of course, he did not completely flout traditional considerations. Throughout his presidency, for example, his executive appointments continued to draw upon the same high social strata of the population as did John Adams's or Thomas Jefferson's, and his future cabinet selections, with the exception of Amos Kendall's appointment as postmaster general in 1835, never incurred the odium attached to the first ones.[50]

Moreover, contrary to historical tradition, Jackson also consulted regularly with his cabinet on matters of policy and patronage. To be sure, during his first two years in office, his prejudice against councils, combined with the divisive effects of the Eaton affair, made cabinet meetings infrequent. He preferred to meet with each person separately in order to avoid collisions, and when the cabinet convened, as it did to discuss his annual messages to Congress, one close observer seemed greatly relieved that a session could be held without acrimony. "The Cabinet Council of yesterday went off well," James A. Hamilton reported in November 1830. "There was very little daubing, and consequently but little reparation to be made."[51]

After the spring of 1831, however, the cabinet gathered once a week, first on Saturdays, later on Tuesdays. During crises, such as the winter following the removal of the government's deposits from the national bank, the cabinet met every day. Nevertheless, Jackson never lost his distaste for cabinet sessions, and at least one secretary complained in 1834 that the president "shuns consulting all, as he is so military & dislikes councils of . . . cabinet." According to Levi Woodbury, only public pressure and the urging of his secretaries compelled the reluctant Jackson to call on his cabinet for advice.[52]

Jackson's lack of enthusiasm for this institution also influenced its deliberations. The cabinet certainly did discuss and advise on major diplomatic and domestic matters—the commercial treaty and claims dispute with France, the North East boundary controversy with Canada, the removal of the deposits, the Specie Circular, and the distribution of surplus revenue to the states, among others. It also dealt with practical issues of patronage and personal claims against the government. Secretary of State Louis McLane requested a cabinet meeting before Jackson announced his selection of district attorney in Philadelphia, so that the president might "be unanimously sustained" in such an important matter. Even the post office in Portland, Maine, was a subject of cabinet deliberation.[53]

But consultation rather than policy formulation appears to have been the most conspicuous activity of Jackson's cabinet. The more important the issue to the president, the more he used the cabinet only as a means of gaining political support for a predetermined policy. According to Francis Blair, editor of the administration newspaper and a confidant of Jackson's, the president would "sacrifice his own predilections, and indeed his determinations, in regard to appointments, to the preferences of his secretaries," but when "important principles are concerned . . . he is inexorable." Blair later summarized Jackson's procedure for the benefit of Abraham Lincoln: "Leading measures resolved on, the cabinet should be accommodated to them

& those who hoped for any thing as party men would follow in the wake." Although the evidence is inconclusive, it appears that Jackson never polled his cabinet. Questions were discussed and opinions solicited, but Jackson remained the center of decision making. Both Blair and Amos Kendall agreed that he never asked his cabinet to make a decision, reserving that instead for "his own judgment."[54]

Paradoxically, Jackson's acceptance of his decision-making responsibility made him tolerant of opposing opinions among his cabinet members. He regarded open, candid, and well-intentioned differences of opinion as "evidence of firmness as well as honesty of purpose," and he seemed to discount the damage such dissent could cause when it went beyond the confines of the White House. Perhaps he thought it better to have the dissidents within the administration where they could be watched, but in retrospect it appears that Roger Taney's assessment was correct and that Jackson's determination to "act upon his own opinions" made him too easygoing about the public expression of opposition by secretaries. As a result, Jackson's presidency was marred by unfortunate appointments and frequent cabinet changes, which embarrassed his administration and endangered its success.[55]

The problem was most acute in his first cabinet selections, when he was politically inexperienced and failed to investigate carefully the men whom he appointed—later he recalled the "maneuvering of men . . . from which I learned a lesson of caution." He accepted the recommendation by some Pennsylvania congressmen of Ingham over his own choice of Baldwin, and he acquiesced in the suggestion of Eaton, Lewis, and White that he appoint both Branch and Berrien. Had he scrutinized the credentials of his nominees, he would have discovered that his cabinet contained men with serious disagreements about the party's direction and future leadership.[56]

Even as Jackson's primary concern was directed towards his cabinet, he was signaling his intention to reach beyond it for advice. In particular, the new president was showing marked attention to Amos Kendall, who had arrived in Washington bearing his state's electoral vote and his own expectation of a rewarding government appointment. Both Jackson and Kendall realized that the Kentuckian was "too new a man" to be acceptable for a cabinet position, but the president assured him at one of their early interviews that he was "fit for the head of a department" and would be placed "as near the head as possible." Kendall accepted an auditorship which paid the then handsome salary of $3,000 a year, a sum which parsimonious living in Georgetown, away from the capital's social life, made sufficient for him to support a growing family and make payments on his personal debts.[57]

There were many reasons for Jackson's partiality. As editor of the *Argus of Western America*, Kendall had developed a vivid and comprehensible style which reflected the grass-roots political appeal of the New Court party, and he had displayed considerable mental agility in explaining a variety of public issues. He therefore could assure Jackson of having a skilled and resourceful editor at hand in case Duff Green was unable or unwilling to support his policies against the opposition. Further, it was Jackson's political instinct to pitch his appeal to the people. Although not averse to working through established political channels, he looked to the electorate as his main support. However much some politicians might grumble that it was "evil to see the President & the People divorced from the politicians," Jackson was always ready to take his case to the country. He recognized the need for his presidential messages to be understood, and labored to make them intelligible and persuasive. Kendall's propagandistic talents perfectly matched Jackson's requirements.[58]

Kendall's knowledge of Kentucky politics heightened his attractiveness. With Henry Clay the most likely contender in 1832, Kendall would be a valuable political asset. Whether Jackson considered this when appointing him is uncertain, but once in office Kendall expended considerable energy organizing the Democratic party of Kentucky in an attempt to prevent Clay from being elected senator. "Be up and doing in Kentucky," he charged his second in command, Francis Blair. "Organize, organize. Take hold of the Argus—You shall not want for information from Head Quarters. . . . A fig for the faint hearted men who are ready to surrender because I leave the state."[59]

Kendall's political skills were so well known in Washington that Van Buren, Calhoun, and John McLean all offered him prominent positions before Jackson arrived. But Kendall recognized that an acceptance would entail an implied commitment to one of these presidential hopefuls. Considering himself exclusively a Jackson man, he resolved to wait for the President's expected offer so that he would "depend on Old Hickory only" and could take his choice "between the future candidates . . . without 'entangling alliances' with any of them." He combined this independence of major competing factions with a bent for ideological warfare. "The ground for us to rally upon," he counseled Blair shortly after arriving in Washington, "is the support of Jackson's administration, opposition to Clay, state rights, and amendments of the constitution. Fixed in our principles, we must ultimately take *him* for our candidate who can best unite the party." Kendall's direct loyalty to Jackson and fervent commitment to principle greatly impressed the president. "I can assure you of one thing," Jackson once declared of him, "that the least coolness shown by the President to Mr. Kendall and neither his poverty, or love for the salary could retain him in office five minutes." [60]

Most important for the future, it was evident from their first discussions that the two men basically agreed on essential political matters. Whatever the ambiguities of his campaign, Jackson took his election as mandate to restore Jeffersonian principles and practices to the government. In private discussions with Kendall shortly after his inauguration, he disclosed the general direction he intended his administration to pursue. He stressed government retrenchment by curtailing excessive expenditures, eliminating unnecessary offices, and providing honest and efficient administration. He planned to pay the national debt, to quiet the tariff issue by adopting "a middle and just course," and to place limits on federal internal improvements projects by avoiding "every thing which can touch the jurisdiction of the states," such as tollgate profits. At the same time, he allowed the possibility of some federal assistance by means of distributing surplus revenue, "if any there should be," to the states, but he expressed himself only as "rather favorably inclined" to the idea. He may also have made known his grave doubts about continuing the Bank of the United States under its present charter. [61]

Kendall listened appreciatively, finding that the president's moderate states' rights opinions coincided with his own. Although allegiance to Henry Clay and the nationalistic mood of the post-1815 period had once led him to commend tariff protection, a home market for American products, and federal aid to the West for internal improvements, Kendall's enthusiasm for these measures had ebbed considerably throughout the 1820s. [62] The reasons for this shift are uncertain, but his endorsement of economic nationalism had always been qualified, and the panic of 1819, the inexorable expansion of the Marshall Court's authority, and his abandonment of Clay for Jackson occasioned in Kendall a resurgence of Jeffersonian scruples about the inequities and abuses of federal legislation. He began to criticize "modern federalists" who believed in the right of the federal government to make and control roads, and he censured tariff extremists who transformed what should properly have been "a temporary tax" into a "monopolizing measure" for privileged groups and special interests. Kendall still affirmed some degree of federal economic intervention, and during the election of 1828, he assured westerners and Kentuckians in particular that Old Hickory was in favor of protection and internal improvements. But he spoke as much about the limitations of federal aid as he did about its benefits.[63]

Like Jackson, Kendall was convinced that there were "horrible abuses" in government and that "radical reform" was necessary to "preserve the purity and efficiency" of its elements. Shortly after receiving his auditorship from Jackson, he enthusiastically undertook to lop off excess expenditures, uncover acts of official corruption, and rotate opposition officeholders out of their positions. He boasted of saving the government thousands of dollars and proudly revealed that his predecessor, Tobias Watkins, a furious Adams partisan, had misappropriated government money for his own benefit. Adams was shocked on learning of the defalcation, but for Jackson and Kendall it merely confirmed the corruption that had set in.[64]

Kendall wished to adjust the increasing demands upon government according to the dictates of Jeffersonian principles, and he regarded Jackson's election as replicating Jefferson's achievement in returning government "to its republican tack." At the time of Jackson's inauguration, he did not consider himself one of the president's confidants; like everyone else in Washington, he recognized the special proximity of Jackson's old Tennessee friends.[65] But Jackson suspected that his measures might stir up violent opposition, and he knew that Kendall, unlike his Tennessee advisers, possessed both the ability and principles to further his program. As the administration progressed, Kendall moved gradually but surely into Jackson's inner circle to replace those early aides.

Jackson's indications of favor to Kendall, as well as his reliance upon the advice of his Tennessee cronies, signaled the first appearance of his "Kitchen Cabinet." Historians have traditionally claimed that the term originated during Jackson's presidency as a label derisively applied by the opposition to a group of aides, mostly outside the cabinet, who specialized in political manipulation, wire-pulling, and patronage. It is generally implied that these men shared similar goals and worked closely together in achieving them. There exists, how- ever, a suspicion that the Kitchen Cabinet was largely a figment of the opposition's imagination. The difficulties in identifying its member- ship or meetings imply a lack of the regularity and formality that one demands of an institution like the regular cabinet. Nevertheless, the concept of a Kitchen Cabinet persists, and recently it has been argued that it performed important noncabinet functions and served as an early version of what later became the party's national committee.[66]

In reality, the label "Kitchen Cabinet," though used on rare occa- sions in private correspondence as early as the winter of 1831, was not publicized until March 1832, towards the end of Jackson's first term, when Calhoun followers, such as Senator George Poindexter of Mis- sissippi and Duff Green, angry at what they considered a Van Burenite plot to alienate Jackson and Calhoun, applied it as an alternative to such previous expressions as the "malign influence" or "Van Buren, Kendall, & Co." Blair alleged that Poindexter first used the term in an essay denouncing the administration that he wrote for the *Telegraph*, and the charge was never denied. References to Jackson's Kitchen Cabinet became increasingly prominent as the election of 1832 ap- proached.[67]

While the Kitchen Cabinet certainly lacked the institutional self- identification, established rules of procedure, and regularized pat- terns of interaction associated with the cabinet, it was also something more than an organization with the limited political purpose and power of a national party committee. Rather, it most resembles the modern White House staff, a group of aides personally attached to the president and having his special trust.[68]

The organization of the White House staff depends on the president. Dwight David Eisenhower, for example, adopted a pyramidal, hierar- chical, and formalistic system which emphasized order, efficiency, and specialization of tasks. Franklin Roosevelt, on the other hand, instituted a highly competitive system of delegated responsibility and overlapping authority, resembling a circle with the president at the hub surrounded by generalists selected for individual assignments. Other presidents have created an organization falling somewhere between the poles of these two models. Whatever the case, White House staffers are chosen only for their ability to serve the president's needs and understand his thinking. They share his perspective in overseeing the general direction of the administration rather than the more limited view of department heads or bureaucrats.[69]

White House staffs generally have inner and outer positions, the inner circle being composed of assistants who are engaged in assignments of great importance to the president and whose opinions he seeks on a variety of issues. The modern president has allocated so much authority to these inner staff assistants that they not only participate in policy making but sometimes issue instructions to cabinet officers and their subordinates. The boundary between cabinet and White House staff is often erased, with propinquity to the president largely determining influence.[70]

The analogy with the modern White House staff is admittedly imperfect; recent presidents can draw upon the services of more than five hundred aides, a number that even Jackson's most imaginative enemy would not have associated with the Kitchen Cabinet. More significantly, Jackson's inclusion of certain cabinet members, especially Van Buren, cautions against too neat a comparison. Nevertheless, the resemblance between the two organizations is real, for the Kitchen Cabinet was a political and personal arm of the president and represented part of the enlargement of presidential power that occurred under Jackson.[71] Not only did it perform most of the functions of the modern staff in serving the president's personal, party, public relations, and programmatic needs, but its incursions into the traditional role of the secretaries stirred up similar resentment from the opposition. The *National Intelligencer*, for example, alleged that Jackson removed the deposits from the Bank "upon the wisdom of the Kitchen Cabinet, his Cabinet proper protesting against it in vain," and the paper chided him for having "other financial *counsellors*" than the secretary of the treasury.[72]

Despite its prominence, the membership and the manner of functioning of the Kitchen Cabinet remain obscure. Duff Green maintained that its membership was subject to change and that the names of all except the most conspicuous participants were "known only to a few." He never published a promised list of its personnel. A number of suggestions can be hazarded, however, about its composition, structure, and functions.[73]

In the matter of general influence, Jackson's longtime Tennessee associates, particularly Eaton and Lewis, were gradually displaced during his first term by Kendall, Blair, and Van Buren. Unlike the Tennesseans, the new inner circle was fully compatible with Jackson's evolving program. Of the three, Kendall and Blair shared the greatest influence. This was partly because of their intimate association with the paramount issue of Jackson's presidency, the Bank War, and partly because their position as administration propagandists brought them into the president's confidence frequently and on a variety of issues. But their access to Jackson also depended on personal considerations. Like him, they were westerners and outsiders to the Washington community, somewhat ill at ease with the capital's social set. Furthermore, Kendall and Blair both lacked substantial independent political backing, and like most close presidential aides their status and fortunes were tied exclusively to the president himself. Indeed, they seem to have regarded Jackson with an almost filial devotion, for as Blair put it, Jackson's advisers looked up to him "rather with a reverence and respect which recognizes in him almost a parental authority." It was a situation that appealed to Jackson's disposition to control and dominate events.[74]

Van Buren, on the other hand, was urbane and adept at navigating the troubled waters of Washington's social and political world. He also had his own political base and presidential aspirations. Temperamentally cautious, he contrasted with the doctrinaire and zealous Kentuckians. Thus, although he exerted considerable influence and gained Jackson's personal trust and affection, Van Buren generally remained somewhat in the shadows of the president's western advisers.[75]

Jackson's advisory system was flexible, however, and like Roosevelt, he often brought others into his confidence when circumstances warranted. Roger Taney, though scarcely known to Jackson at the time he was appointed attorney general, rapidly emerged as a staunch supporter and personal friend during the later stages of the Bank War. Jackson continued to consult with Taney even after the Senate rejected his nomination as Treasury secretary, and the president underlined Taney's special position by inviting him to stay at the White House while they conferred.[76]

Taney was only the most prominent of a number of men whose aid and advice Jackson solicited on important programmatic matters. Attorney General Benjamin F. Butler, for example, assisted Kendall and Taney in preparing the administration's defense of its decision to remove the deposits, and Senator Thomas Hart Benton advised Jackson in his drawing up of the Specie Circular.[77] Indeed, it would be an exaggeration even to assume that Blair, Kendall, and Van Buren, the core of the inner circle, were apprised of every presidential decision. Kendall, for example, apparently had little prior warning of Van Buren's intention to resign from the cabinet in the spring of 1831, though Blair was consulted. Moreover, Kendall and Blair sometimes had their own disagreements, and on at least one occasion the former's high standing offered no protection against Jackson's anger. However influential these members of the inner circle might be, the president never permitted them to monopolize access to him.[78]

The Kitchen Cabinet also had an outer circle of less influential advisers. Men like Andrew Jackson Donelson, the president's nephew, William B. Lewis, and earlier John H. Eaton contributed little to programmatic decisions, but performed personal and political services for the president. Donelson, who could be relied upon to keep a confidence, served as private secretary, drafting letters, notes, and presidential messages. Eaton's presence at the beginning of his presidency brought Jackson the necessary security of personal friendship and provided him with a trusted aide whose "intimate knowledge of public men and of parties was to guide him safely through all collision." Lewis, who in Van Buren's words was "an intimate personal friend" of the president, attended to party and patronage matters, but acted only at Jackson's direction.[79]

Among their services, members of the outer circle gathered information on the political climate; occasionally intervened in local party matters to help a loyal Jacksonian, as when Donelson furnished James K. Polk with damaging information about a political opponent; helped establish local Jackson newspapers; and advised the president on appointments and removals. Their functions were not specialized, however, and members of the inner circle like Kendall and Blair also performed such political tasks.[80]

No complete enumeration of Kitchen Cabinet members can be offered with great confidence. On some matters of politics and patronage, Jackson consulted such men as William T. Barry, Isaac Hill, James A. Hamilton, Reuben M. Whitney, and, at least at the beginning of his administration, Duff Green, with a regularity that would qualify them as occasional and peripheral members of the Kitchen Cabinet. Hill, for example, was a channel of communication between the White House and New England Jacksonians, but on a major issue like the removal of the deposits, he was kept in the dark until after Jackson had made his decision. There is no evidence that any of these men performed services for Jackson with the frequency of Donelson, who lived at the White House throughout his uncle's presidency, or Lewis, who lived there for most of the first term.[81]

The difficulty in identifying the Kitchen Cabinet's membership attests to the flexibility of Jackson's advisory system. Viewed schematically, it resembled a series of interlocking circles surrounding the president at the hub. Cabinet members, government officials, members of Congress, friends, and, on rare occasions, acquaintances moved in complex patterns around the president. Members of the cabinet like Van Buren and Taney could find themselves alongside minor officials and nonofficeholders like Kendall and Blair within Jackson's closest groups of advisers. On the other hand, disagreement with the president's program could lead to exclusion from the inner circle, as happened with Lewis, whose resistance to the Bank War and friendship with the conservative Louis McLane led one cabinet member to remark in January 1834 that he was "not now called of the Kitchen Cabinet." Jackson could also consult friends like John Coffee, with whom he frequently corresponded, and acquaintances like Reuben M. Whitney and Thomas Ellicott, whose familiarity with banking procedures brought them to his attention. Thus, even though the Kitchen Cabinet was a central feature of Jackson's advisory system, the president also sought counsel elsewhere, both within and without the government. The observation of a perceptive student of recent White House politics seems equally applicable to Jackson's day: "the orbits of advisers . . . that revolve around the President do not, like the heavenly bodies, follow a fixed and settled course."[82]

There were, of course, liabilities in Jackson's system; for example, disagreements between members of the inner circle, especially be-

tween Van Buren and Kendall and Blair. And although the administration paper denied it, there was also friction at times between
cabinet members and aides. "No well digested system of operation
here by Pre[si]d[en]t, Cabinet, or his friends in Cong and no watchful,
prompt & plentiful writer or Editor for the Globe to aid Blair & sustain
Adm[inis]t[ratio]n at every point," complained Navy secretary Levi
Woodbury during the removal crisis.[83]

However much such friction must have irritated and frustrated
Jackson, it is apparent that he preferred to rely on his advisory system
rather than on the formal cabinet or a more hierarchical arrangement
of official and unofficial aides. Although the divisiveness of his first
cabinet itself encouraged this practice, it was also perfectly consonant
with his style and with his determination to control his presidency.
Indeed, a large and flexible system of advising necessitated a dominant president if decisions were to be made at all.[84]

Those closest to Jackson acknowledged his central position.
"Whenever anything involves what he conceives the *permanent*
interest of the country," Blair observed, "his patriotism becomes an
all-absorbing feeling, and neither *kitchen* nor *parlor* cabinets can
move him." Kendall's conclusion was the same. "They talk of a
Kitchen Cabinet, etc.," he explained to James Gordon Bennett.
"There are a few of us who have always agreed with the President in
relation to the Bank and other essential points of policy, and therefore
they charge us with having an influence over him! Fools!! They can
not beat the President out of his long-cherished opinions, and his
firmness they charge to our influence." To be manipulated by others
was out of character for a man who had always reserved for himself the
final determination and responsibility for a decision. "I should loath
myself did any act of mine afford the slightest colour for the insinuation that I follow blindly the judgment of any friend in the discharge of
my proper duties," Jackson assured a friend.[85]

3

A More Cohesive Party

Now to my tent, O God, repair,
And make thy servant wise;
I'll suffer nothing near me there
That shall offend thine eyes.

The man that doth by his neighbor wrong,
By falsehood or by force,
The scornful eye, the slanderous tongue,
I'll banish from my doors.

I'll seek the faithful and the just
And will their help enjoy;
These are the friends that I shall trust,
The servants I'll employ.

—Andrew Jackson[1]

Jackson's expectation of changing the principles of government suffered an initial setback when turmoil in his cabinet and conflict with his vice-president, John C. Calhoun, diverted energy from more substantive matters. For two years, the executive office was the scene of often bitter personal and political contention. Yet what resembled mere factional intrigue over such minor matters as the Eaton affair and the Seminole controversy also involved broader issues of policy and resulted in the establishment of a more coherent party structure and philosophy. As Amos Kendall observed in the midst of these disturbances, "a new division of parties" was materializing. On the one side stood "the democracy of the northern, middle, western, and part of the southern states," supporting a simple, virtuous, and efficient government, a gradual reduction of duties, and "the abandonment of all pretensions to powers which necessarily create collisions with the states." On the other side were the joint forces of "the furious anti-tariff men of the South and the furious tariff men of the north with the corrupt portion of the late coalition party." At the same time, the upheaval redrew and clarified lines of influence in the White House, establishing a basic pattern of authority that persisted throughout Jackson's presidency.[2]

Discord appeared first within the cabinet and ostensibly involved the unwillingness of certain secretaries and their families to socialize with John and Peggy Eaton. The Eaton affair has often been characterized as a petty social feud primarily involving the personal considerations of a bereaved president defending a close friend's wife.[3] Some historians have recognized its political implications by describing it as the decisive battle in the war between Calhoun and Van Buren for the succession.[4] In truth, the Eaton affair had both personal and political dimensions and was the first of a series of interrelated events that ultimately brought Jackson and Calhoun to a parting of ways. But the incident also had a broader significance, for it became a vehicle for contesting the programmatic direction of Jackson's presidency, especially his tariff policy.

At the time of Jackson's inauguration, Washington was still a self-contained community whose social stability had been assured by the continuity of officeholding under the Monroe and Adams presidencies. Jackson's victory and the demands of his backers for removals and "rotation in office" posed a threat to this order. "Never before did the city seem to me so gloomy," one socialite noted shortly after Jackson's arrival. "So many families broken up, and those of the first distinction and who gave a tone to society." Even when wholesale proscription failed to materialize, every appointed official felt the insecurity of knowing his tenure depended on the will of the administration. Consequently, the distinction between Washington's permanent residents and its less permanent officeholding population began to develop.[5]

Many Washingtonians also viewed the Jackson administration as an egalitarian challenge to their way of life, particularly when the president appointed westerners and "editors of the foulest presses" to office. Since Jackson generally selected men of the same socio-economic position as did former presidents, it would appear that the capital city's anxiety was exaggerated. But as Sidney Aronson has shown, Jackson's officials tended more often than those of past administrations to be self-made men or the offspring of families whose high status was restricted to the local level.[6] Some Washington social leaders, therefore, snobbishly claimed that the Democrats had fewer "respectable and fashionable people" than the opposition, and on occasion facetious comments were directed at their lack of social standing. Thus in 1836, a distinguished Virginia senator good-naturedly assured his wife that they would live "in the *fashionable* quarter of the town; for since Editor Blair has established himself on the President's square . . . the gentility, among the members of Congress at least, seem instinctively to have fled from it, & collected at the opposite end of the City."[7]

In turn, some key Jacksonians considered themselves outsiders who were fortunate to escape the corruptions of court society. Postmaster General Barry from Kentucky condemned the capital's "aristocracy . . . claiming preference for birth or wealth," which allowed "none but sycophants who cringe to them to have standing or character." Kendall, who preferred Georgetown where rent was cheaper and social demands fewer, thought Washington "the center of extravagance"; and when Blair was preparing to come to the city to replace Duff Green, Kendall advised that Mrs. Blair could have her choice of society but, he added, "I think she will not have much taste for that which is called the *very first*." Blair clearly agreed with his friend's assessment, for sometime after his arrival he referred to the "vulgar great of the City." Jackson's own opinion was similarly unflattering. "Our society wants purging here," he exclaimed to one correspondent.[8]

Political hostility doubtless helped widen the social split. Many Washington socialites opposed Jackson and, therefore, ostracized the Democrats. During the heated congressional session following his removal of the government's deposits from the national bank, society divided along political lines and, according to one fashionable observer, "in society, as well as in politics the opposition carries the day."[9]

The impact of Jackson's administration on Washington society should not, however, be overstated. With the exception of the first two years, when the uproar over the Eatons disrupted the city, the Jackson period brought few marked changes to Washington's social life. Relatively few officeholders were removed and the distinction between resident and nonresident, which later characterized the city, was merely adumbrated. Presidential levees and gala dinners continued, and Jacksonians generally mingled with the opposition at social functions. But the advent of Jackson evidently did bring some fresh air into the staid Washington community, and there is little doubt that the community distrusted him, especially when he first took office. Thus when Eaton was appointed to the cabinet, Washington's social leaders rallied against his wife.[10]

In Washington, politics and society are closely knit, and cabinet officials constitute a significant element in society. When the families of Calhoun, Ingham, Branch, Berrien, and Donelson snubbed Peggy, "polite" society applauded them for their "*noble* stand," but their actions inevitably had political repercussions.[11]

Foremost among the Eatons' prominent defenders was the president himself. Jackson possessed a romantic and exalted appreciation of the family as an enclave of morality and virtue in a world of uncertainty and strife. Having approved the Eatons' marriage, and doubtless recalling the slanderous attacks directed by the Adams press against his own wife, he readily connected Washington's social intrigue with the political corruption he attributed to the previous administration. He was convinced that the attack against the Eatons emanated from Clay and was designed to undermine his presidency by compelling him to dismiss a confidential friend. It was "neither astonishing or unexpected," he claimed, that "the hired slanderers of Mr. Clay" would resort to defamation and intrigue. He confessed himself "astonished and mortified," however, that some of his own supporters lent aid to "such unhallowed work."[12]

Lewis also sided with his brother-in-law and toiled relentlessly to gather evidence attesting to Peggy's virtue. He was assisted by Barry, who was then living with the Eatons, having come to Washington without his family. To the postmaster general, Peggy was a "sincere and friendly" woman. "She may have been imprudent," he admitted, but "most of the women here are." Barry attributed the attack on her to Washington's "aristocracy," which was outraged that a tavernkeeper's daughter should have the good fortune to marry into the fashionable world.[13]

Van Buren also associated with the Eatons, having determined after a careful assessment of the situation to deal with Peggy as he would with the wife of any cabinet officer. His decision had little to do with loyalty to John Eaton, for Van Buren thought Eaton's personal integrity questionable and his political notions "lax." From their service together in the Senate, he must have known that Eaton approved the Bank and favored federal aid for internal improvements. But Van Buren recognized the necessity of standing by Eaton, who was his political ally. More important, Eaton was Jackson's personal friend, and Van Buren had no intention of antagonizing the person who bore his hopes for restoring the Republican party as well as for advancing his own political career.[14]

Kendall also rallied behind the Eatons. Like Van Buren, he apparently never had confidence in the secretary of war's abilities, and would undoubtedly have agreed with Blair's conclusion that Eaton "although reputed to be so near to Genl Jackson was . . . 'of no consequence at all.' " But he thought a conspiracy existed against the president's friend, and loyalty to Jackson dictated his response.[15]

From the day of his inauguration, Jackson found his officers arrayed in opposing camps over the Eaton question. Throughout the summer and fall of 1829, he struggled mightily, but unsuccessfully, to convince Washington society of Peggy's virtue and his cabinet of the need for harmony. Sometime in autumn, however, the context of the issue changed radically. Jackson became convinced that the continued persecution of the Eatons was directed not by Clay, but by Calhoun. In November, he contended that the Eaton affair was "founded in political views, looking to the future," and that because Eaton would not be one of Calhoun's puppets, "it was necessary to put him out of the Cabinet and destroy him regardless what injury it might do me or my administration."[16]

Why Jackson now fixed upon Calhoun has never been determined. The Calhouns had returned home to South Carolina immediately after the adjournment of Congress, and they were not in Washington while the controversy continued and when Jackson determined their guilt. Possibly Jackson noticed that the Inghams, Calhoun's warmest friends in the cabinet, were especially prominent among Peggy's detractors. But circumstantial evidence points to the significant role of Jackson's closest advisers at this time. Eaton and Lewis, as well as James A. Hamilton, still a frequent visitor to the White House, disliked the vice-president, and if they did not plant the idea of Calhoun's culpability, they certainly did nothing to discourage Jackson when he identified the South Carolinian as the source of the Eatons' embarrassment.[17]

In any event, Jackson's conclusion helped polarize the White House into supporters and opponents of Calhoun. To identify with Eaton was taken as a sign of hostility towards Calhoun; to oppose Eaton was ipso facto evidence of pro-Calhoun sentiment. By February 1830, Barry no longer viewed the Eaton affair as Peggy's challenge to Washington's aristocratic values, but as involving the "extreme jealousy of some of Mr. Calhoun's friends" who believed Eaton was "more friendly to Mr. Van Buren than to Mr. Calhoun." He was somewhat perplexed to find that his support of the Eatons made him the object of hostility by some of Calhoun's friends and thought their behavior "utterly without cause, for I like Mr. C. as I do Mr. Van B., but I like General Jackson better than either."[18] At the same time, Kendall also reported the widespread belief that Calhoun's friends were the principal instigators of the Eaton affair. He noted that Calhoun had treated him "rather coolly" in recent months and he could see no cause for it "unless it be that I openly denounce the conspiracies against Eaton." He judged Calhoun "a madman if he promotes it, and he is not a wise man if he does not put an end to it."[19]

Jackson may have been correct in thinking that Calhoun had the power and influence to put a stop to the Eaton affair, especially by compelling his close friends the Inghams to associate with the Eatons. But his assumption that Calhoun provoked the controversy to further his political ambitions was an oversimplification too often repeated in historical accounts.[20] Although Ingham's attachment to Calhoun was "extreme,"[21] there is evidence that hostility to Van Buren and, relatedly, to high tariffs weighed more in the calculations of Branch, Berrien, and perhaps Donelson than did partiality for Calhoun. They hoped to prevent Van Buren from gaining influence in the administration, especially because they viewed him as a proponent of protective tariffs. If their antagonism to him or to high tariffs ultimately worked to the benefit of Calhoun, they would not object; but they did not consider themselves as Calhounites.

Both Eaton and Van Buren were popularly associated with the Tariff of 1828, the ill-conceived offspring of a marriage between the demands of northern and western farmers and manufacturers for increased protection and the dictates of presidential politics. In the South, the tariff was regarded as an abomination, and the activity of Eaton and Van Buren in sponsoring, promoting, and voting for the bill was duly noted. The South Carolina radical Robert Hayne attributed the measure to "*Eaton* & others" who "with their eyes open" had "wholly disregarded the South," while Duff Green not only held Van Buren responsible for the bill but believed the New Yorker intended to rally the protectionists behind the Democratic party. Green even worried that Van Buren's ambition would lead him to join forces with Clay and thereby "continue a system of measures onerous upon the South, and provoking discontent bordering upon, if not terminating in, disunion." [22] Van Buren's own Regency newspaper, the Albany *Argus,* did nothing to discredit such thinking when, even before Jackson's inauguration, it denied that Van Buren voted for the tariff only because he was under instruction. Van Buren, the *Argus* assured its readers, genuinely favored the measure. [23]

Eaton's special relationship with Jackson and his encouragement of Van Buren's political interests were therefore of considerable moment to those who were deeply distressed about the South's plight. Eaton's presumed influence implied that Jackson would do nothing to bring about immediate tariff reform, and his attachment to Van Buren augured ill for future relief. Although the evidence is not conclusive, it appears that both Branch and Berrien were largely swayed by such considerations.

Neither man considered himself a Calhounite or nullifier. Branch later denounced attempts to connect him with nullification, and Lewis had judged him "decidedly friendly" to Van Buren when the cabinet was formed. As late as October 1830, Kendall retained a high regard for Branch, whose honesty and integrity he praised. But Branch was a planter aristocrat, devoted to old-style gentry politics and to expanding the South's influence in the federal government, particularly through tariff reform. He regarded himself as "a republican of [the] school of '98, but never an advocate of 'demagogical . . . *democratic* republican[ism].'" And immediately after his expulsion from the cabinet in the spring of 1831, he returned to North Carolina and attacked the tariff and Van Buren, whom he held responsible for the Tariff of Abominations. "We must resist him on *principle* and every other *tariff* candidate," Branch urged. [24]

Berrien's case is similar. He, too, continually protested attempts to identify him with Calhoun or nullification. "Our private relations," he later recalled of Calhoun, "were kind, but never intimate, and politically, we were almost always opposed." But his resentment of party politics and his commitment to radical tariff reform reinforced the personal coolness to Van Buren that had originated in a political disagreement during Adams's presidency. Like Branch, Berrien denounced the "new system" of politics for which Van Buren was noted, whereby "men are moved in *masses* by *party machinery*." He opposed Jackson's rotation policy and looked upon the electorate with the hauteur of an old school politician accustomed to power in the hands of a natural elite.[25]

Before entering the cabinet, Berrien had declared the Tariff of 1828 and all protective tariffs unconstitutional, and had predicted opposition to it by the slave states. Later, after his dismissal from the cabinet in 1831, he rushed to Philadelphia to attend a free trade convention where he again argued against tariff protection. Berrien always denied he was a nullifier, but his refusal to cooperate with the South Carolina radicals was due primarily to his belief that their program was impractical and unrealistic. His own outrage at the unjust and inequitable sacrifices imposed on the South by protective tariffs closely approached theirs, and like them he denied the right of the federal government to coerce any state which sought to "interpose its sovereignty to arrest the evil." He never made clear his alternative to nullification, but he leaned towards a southern convention for rallying a united South against the protective principle. Berrien's attacks on Van Buren, however, won praise from the nullifier James Hamilton, Jr., who promised that South Carolina would sustain him "to the death."[26]

While Donelson does not appear to have been an antitariff extremist, he shared with Branch and Berrien a distrust of Van Buren. Recalling the "Magician's" support of Crawford and the vicious Crawfordite attacks on his uncle during the 1824 campaign, Donelson came to Washington "full of misconceptions" about Van Buren. Already predisposed against Eaton and Lewis from years of fighting their clique in Tennessee politics, he became distressed when he found they were "sowing the seed of glory for Mr. Van Buren," and he naturally gravitated to the side of the anti-Eaton forces. He did not, however, labor on Calhoun's behalf, and certainly opposed nullification, but he thought that Eaton, Lewis, and Van Buren were conspiring to bring about Calhoun's demise, something Donelson regarded as sure to "disorganize the party" and lessen his uncle's prestige in order to suit Van Buren's "ambition."[27]

Donelson's position undermined the president's confidence in his judgment. When Blair arrived in Washington in late 1830, Jackson warned him about his nephew. "I raised him. Let him do what he will, I love him. Treat him kindly but if he wants to write for your paper you must look out for him." Shortly thereafter, Donelson left Washington to spend six months in exile with his wife, returning only after Jackson revamped his cabinet in April 1831. Even then he remained cool towards Van Buren's bid for the vice-presidency.[28]

The Eaton affair was, therefore, more complicated than Jackson thought. Although attributable in part to the jealousies of the rival Calhoun and Van Buren factions, it was also an expression of hostility to Van Buren and to protective tariffs which was unconnected with Calhoun's personal fortunes. To some extent, then, the controversy involved questions of access to the president and of the direction of the administration's program. But in the tense political atmosphere of Jackson's first year, such subtle distinctions were clouded, and it was not surprising that Jackson, fully appreciating the coalitional nature of his early backing, identified Calhoun as the sole cause of his difficulties.

At about the time he concluded that the vice-president was behind the Eaton matter, Jackson received convincing evidence that Calhoun had advised Monroe to punish him for invading Florida in 1818. The controversy surrounding Jackson's Seminole campaign has been related so often that it is necessary to summarize it only briefly. The General had chased the Seminole Indians into Spanish Florida under the impression that he had the endorsement of Monroe and his secretary of war, Calhoun. His actions triggered a congressional investigation, which he thought the work of Clay and Crawford, and he was certain that Calhoun supported him. Although some of his friends, including Lewis, knew that Calhoun had suggested to Monroe that he be punished, Jackson never found their protests sufficiently convincing to question the overtures of friendship that Calhoun proffered during the years after the Florida invasion.[29]

During the campaign of 1828, however, James A. Hamilton and Lewis, ostensibly attempting to reconcile Jackson and the Crawfordites and to gather information to rebut allegations of Jackson's wrongdoing, procured a letter from Georgia's Governor John Forsyth quoting Crawford to the effect that he, not Calhoun, had defended Jackson's Seminole actions. Given Lewis's and Hamilton's attachment to Van Buren, it is likely that they solicited this information to puff their favorite at Calhoun's expense. The Forsyth letter was not revealed to Jackson but in the course of the campaign he opened a correspondence with Calhoun and Monroe about the Seminole incident. Apparently satisfied with their explanations, he quickly dropped the issue in the interest of unity against Adams. Here matters remained until late autumn 1829, when Lewis announced to Jackson that one of Monroe's confidants had just revealed that Calhoun had been "the first man" to move in the cabinet for Jackson's punishment. Lewis also mentioned the Forsyth letter confirming the charges against Calhoun, and Jackson immediately requested that he secure it.[30]

For various reasons, Jackson did not have Crawford's statement in hand until May 1830, and he then sent it to Calhoun, expressing his "great surprise" at the allegations of Calhoun's duplicity and asking for explanations. By that time, however, the two men were entirely estranged and the ensuing correspondence was written with eventual publication in mind. Jackson, of course, emphasized Calhoun's personal treachery, while Calhoun, knowing he could not deny his opposition to the Florida invasion, underlined the role of the Crawfordites in reviving old issues. His real target was Van Buren, the present leader of the Crawford men.[31]

Calhoun was undoubtedly correct in thinking that his enemies had raised the Seminole issue to weaken his standing with Jackson. Lewis and Hamilton were especially prominent in bringing this stale issue to the president's attention. But it is more significant that in the fall of 1829 Jackson was willing, as he had not been before, to pursue the matter. The continuing Eaton imbroglio had certainly reduced Jackson's confidence in Calhoun and conditioned him to think of his vice-president as being motivated by "ambitious views" and "base hypocracy [sic]."[32]

However much the Eaton affair and the Seminole controversy

served to alienate Jackson and Calhoun, ultimately it was policy disagreements that drove them apart. By December 1829, Jackson believed that Calhoun was implicated in South Carolina's nullification movement and, consequently, could not support his program of moderate tariff reform, distribution of surplus revenue, and immediate payment of the national debt.[33]

The tariff was a major obstacle to Democratic party unity, for Jackson's followers disagreed over every aspect of the question, including its constitutionality. As Daniel Webster put it, the Jackson men were "irreconcilable; they cannot stir against the tariff."[34] Jackson's position of "a middle and just course" was therefore politically expedient, but it also expressed his own conviction that a degree of protection was essential to maintain national security, to establish economic parity with Europe, and to pay the national debt. Once the debt was erased, for example, the tariff could be lowered further. Thus in his annual report of 1829, Jackson declared that the Tariff of 1828 had "not proved so injurious . . . or so beneficial . . . as was anticipated," and he called for lower rates on products which did not compete with American labor.[35]

The same message also explained the likelihood that "until a remote period" any tariff satisfactory to the nation's needs would produce a revenue in excess of government expenditures, and Jackson recommended that Congress consider distributing this surplus revenue to the states according to their federal apportionment. His language, however, suggested doubts about the measure's constitutionality, and he urged the adoption of a constitutional amendment authorizing distribution to give assurance of the government's right. His constitutional scruples were genuine and were related to "deeply rooted convictions" that limited government should not be undermined by "overstrained constructions." Privately, Jackson also revealed that he favored distribution less for the policy itself than for its effect on other objectives. He expected that the lure of gaining future revenue would encourage Congress to hold back expenditures until the national debt was liquidated. "The moment the people see that the surplus revenue is to be divided among the States, (when there shall be a surplus) . . . they will instruct their members to husband the revenue for the payment of the national debt," he explained to a close friend.[36]

Jackson's position on the tariff and distribution was in keeping with his republican ideals. The tariff would adjust competing local and national interests within a limited government framework, while distribution, by returning excess revenue to the states, promised to avoid jurisdictional conflicts with the federal government. Distribution also possessed a proper Jeffersonian lineage, having originated with Jefferson himself. Jackson's moderate course, therefore, received a warm endorsement from Van Buren and Kendall. Van Buren had long concluded that the protective principle "could only be loosened by degrees and by means which would not rouse the prejudices of its supporters." And Kendall, while denouncing the inequities produced by overzealous protectionists, thought the "interest of the country" required that protection not be wholly abandoned. He also warned that precipitous action would hazard the party's political strength in the middle states, especially Pennsylvania.[37]

Jackson's position placed Calhoun in an embarrassing situation. The vice-president was privately committed to his state's radical antitariff crusade, and during the summer of 1828, he had written an *Exposition* developing the idea that a state could render a federal law null and void within its boundaries while still remaining in the Union. He also found Jackson's interest in distribution worrisome, for he considered the plan "the most odious and unconstitutional of all measures," presumably because it implied the indefinite continuation of protective rates, and portended the prostration of state governments by making them dependent on the federal government for revenue.[38]

Yet Calhoun's ingrained conservatism and political ambition prescribed the cautious stance of avoiding a challenge to Jackson and restraining more radical nullifiers. As William W. Freehling has documented, though Calhoun intended nullification as a conservative and peaceful device to protect the South within the Union, he recognized that the theory was controversial and could easily be construed as treasonous, and that before it could be applied time was essential in order to explain its mysteries to the nation. Similarly, Calhoun's desire to be president and his naive confidence that he would eventually win Jackson's favor also counseled moderation, for the president had already made clear in his cabinet appointments that he would not reward extremism. Calhoun, therefore, expressed his hope of giving Jackson "an honest and decided support," whenever it could be done "without abandoning principles." He was willing to defer tariff relief to pay the national debt, and though he considered Jackson's cabinet choices "in several respects unfortunate" and could not "concur in some of his measures," he did not anticipate these differences would drive the two men apart. His frustration, however, was perceptively noted by a southern senator who described Calhoun in January 1830 as "much disposed, though afraid, to declare himself against the leading measures of the present Administration."[39]

Calhoun's stand was unacceptable to Jackson. His refusal to endorse publicly the president's policies led to suspicion; his inability to moderate southern radicals led to estrangement. Jackson, after announcing his misgivings about the Bank, censured Calhoun for remaining "silent on the Bank question." His anger again flared up when the modest tariff proposal in his annual message of 1829 was attacked by leading Calhounites and when he received reports that Virginia Calhounites had attempted to withdraw the public printing from Ritchie because of his "warm *general* approbation" of the message.[40] Calhoun himself acknowledged the harm his associates were doing to his position, but he could only acquiesce in their actions. He had wanted to hold Jackson responsible for those official expressions on the tariff and distribution "most favorable to the South, and to wait for the great and successful effort for relief [in] the period of the payment of the public debt." But, he noted with regret, "a different course was taken."[41]

The difficulties that some of Jackson's appointments encountered in the Senate further confirmed the president's grave doubts about his vice-president. The most prominent example was Isaac Hill, who lost his auditorship partly because Levi Woodbury, Hill's New Hampshire rival and Calhoun's personal friend, refused to defend his character. Compounding this irritation was Calhoun's action, as president of the Senate, in preventing a reconsideration of the rejection vote and then requesting Jackson to appoint his political friend Virgil Maxcy in Hill's place. Whether Calhoun's action was a display of political ineptitude or of frustration, it called into question his loyalty to the administration. "A little *new* leaven trying to mix itself with the *old* lump," Jackson commented sourly about the willingness of Calhoun's partisans to ally themselves with the Clay forces.[42]

The well-known Jefferson Day Dinner in April 1830 provided a public forum for displaying the increasing gulf between Jackson and

Calhoun. While the dinner had been organized to celebrate an alliance between Democrats of the West and South, some Calhounites used the occasion to legitimize nullification by clothing it in the mantle of Jeffersonianism. Perhaps knowing beforehand the nature of some of the Calhounite toasts, Jackson reportedly glared at Calhoun and declared: "The Federal Union. It must be preserved." He intended his toast as a rebuke to what he considered the seditious statements made by some of Calhoun's friends. Afterwards, he explained to Kendall that he was a disciple of Jefferson and "many of the sentiments uttered at the dinner, were such as Jefferson abhorred."[43]

Well before February 1831, when the Seminole correspondence was published, Calhoun had lost all influence with Jackson. By the fall of 1830, Kendall reported a "total alienation" between them, and at the same time, Duff Green informed Calhoun that Jackson was bitterly hostile to South Carolina's nullifiers. The vice-president's standing suffered a similar decline with Kendall, who had come to Washington favorably disposed to Calhoun's prospects. As evidence mounted that Calhoun was unable to stand behind the president, Kendall remarked that he was "a noble fellow; but . . . too impatient." By the spring of 1830, Kendall envisioned the probability of "open war" between the administration and "the Anti-Tariff Hotspurs" led by Calhoun. "You will foresee his fate if he suffers his restless ambition to hurry him into such conflict," Kendall warned.[44]

Calhoun himself realized he could no longer be loyal both to nullification and to Jackson. In October 1830, he confided to his friend Ingham his support of nullification and expressed his willingness to stand on its principles: "If entertaining these opinions is to proscribe me from the honors of the country be it so." With his influence plummeting, Calhoun became increasingly certain that Jackson would never provide security for the South. Whereas in early 1830, he thought the administration controlled by men who were "either ignorant, or indifferent" to the South's interests, by early 1831, he was convinced that Jackson and his advisers were as "hostile" to him and to the South as Clay. As for Jackson's moderate tariff policy, Calhoun denounced it as an insidious attempt to reconcile both tariff and antitariff sentiment. He thought it now necessary to oppose the president so that the South could be united against the protective system, a system which Jackson "more than half supports."[45]

As Calhoun and other antitariff radicals lost Jackson's confidence, their rival, Van Buren, rose in Jackson's esteem. By January 1830, Jackson had concluded that his secretary of state should be his successor, and despite some political differences in the coming years, he never changed his mind.[46] Yet at the outset of Jackson's administration, Van Buren's prospects had not appeared encouraging. He had accepted Jackson's offer of a cabinet position with some misgivings, disliking Jackson's other selections and being unsure of the president's programmatic intentions. He was even uneasy about his own reception as leader of a faction that had bitterly attacked Jackson four years earlier and that had been the last to join Old Hickory's campaign against Adams. Indeed, in some respects Van Buren possessed handicaps that Calhoun did not, for while Jackson took office believing that Calhoun was a staunch and loyal friend, his previous association with Van Buren had been brief and impersonal.[47]

Personalities have an intangible but undeniably important effect in determining a president's assessment of his advisers, and without question, Van Buren's steady, trusting, and supportive demeanor favorably impressed Jackson and earned his affection. When shortly after the new administration commenced, Jackson imperiled Van Buren's position as Regency leader by selecting for positions in New York two men who were repugnant to Van Buren's party, a stunned Van Buren tactfully solicited Jackson's permission to assure his friends that the president had acted with honest purposes and not out of hostility to him. Van Buren's willingness to put the best face possible on an awkward situation and not to think ill of Jackson's motives was eventually reciprocated by the president's confidence.[48]

Other actions by Van Buren followed the same pattern. His decision to call upon the Eatons and his solicitude about the president's emotional and physical condition established bonds of friendship in the early days of Jackson's presidency. Soon the two men were going riding together, and Jackson was complimenting Van Buren as "true, harmonious, and faithful," doing everything to "render my situation, *personally*, as pleasant and comfortable as the nature of my public duties will admit."[49]

However helpful these personal qualities were, it was Van Buren's political skill and support for Jackson's programs that cemented their ties. Although historians have focused on Jackson's domestic program, the president avidly desired a successful foreign policy as well. As secretary of state, Van Buren managed to restore the West Indies trade and to bring France to an agreement on spoliation claims dating from the Napoleonic period. His performance added luster to the administration's public image and enhanced Van Buren's standing with the president.[50]

In domestic matters, Van Buren's formidable political skills and his understanding of the ins and outs of Washington politics nicely complemented Jackson's more personal approach to governing, especially in the early days of the administration. Moreover, Jackson was able to say of Van Buren that which he found impossible to say of Calhoun—"he is . . . Republican in his principles." Both sought to reverse the trend towards expanding federal authority, to limit internal improvements expenditures, and to reduce the tariff. They also agreed in their opposition to nullification and the Bank. As Van Buren worked diligently on the tariff section in the president's first annual message and on the Maysville Road veto, the contrast to Calhoun was evident. Van Buren has "identified him[self] with the success of the administration," Jackson noted approvingly. Kendall described Van Buren's growing influence in different terms: "Van Buren glides along as smoothly as oil and as silently as a cat," he reported in March 1830. "If he is managing at all, it is so adroitly that nobody perceives it. He is evidently gaining from the indiscretions of Calhoun's friends. He has the entire confidence of the President and all his personal friends, while Calhoun is fast losing it."[51]

Although Van Buren gradually drew close to the president, his influence with Jackson was not unrivaled. Saddled with a contentious cabinet and an unreliable vice-president, Jackson increasingly confided in Kendall, who busily prepared for publication defenses of the Eatons, continued to battle against defaulters and excess expenditures, and worked on presidential messages.[52] Of the utmost consequence was Kendall's undertaking the responsibility for bringing his friend Blair to Washington as administration spokesman. Contrary to Calhounite accusations, they did not establish the Washington *Globe* to advance Van Buren's interests, but to better promote Jackson's measures and to protect the administration if Duff Green should follow Calhoun into opposition.

From the start, Green's position as the administration's editor was precarious. Van Buren's friends suspected his allegiance to Calhoun and voted him the public printing only because his competitors were outright Clay and Adams men. "There is much of the old Crawford leaven operating against him in the bosoms of some of the Jackson members," Kendall observed in January 1829. If Green thought it compatible to support both Jackson and Calhoun, some of the president's closest friends thought otherwise. Early in 1829, both Eaton and Lewis tried unsuccessfully to undermine Green's autonomy, first by forcing him into a partnership with Kendall, and then by making Lewis the channel of communication between the *Telegraph* office and the White House.[53]

But ultimately it was Green's inability to reflect Jackson's views and to provide a rallying point for the president's policies that brought him down. His intense pride and inflated sense of self-importance led him into a succession of petty feuds with cabinet members, including Calhoun's friend Ingham. He even flaunted his independence of the president. When Jackson nominated the protectionist and anti-Calhounite Henry Baldwin for a position on the Supreme Court, Green attempted to undermine the confirmation proceedings by publicly representing the nomination as "unfortunate for General Jackson—for the party who elected him to office—and for the country."[54]

Green's attachment to Calhoun also weakened his standing. In the spring of 1830, the editor tried to blame Van Buren's followers for the Senate's rejection of Isaac Hill's nomination. Hill labeled Green's action "very imprudent." Meanwhile, Gideon Welles, a prominent Connecticut editor and Jacksonian, garbled an account of an interview with Green in which he received the impression that Calhoun would challenge Jackson for the presidency in 1832. Although Green had actually stated that Calhoun would seek the office only if Jackson refused renomination, Welles's report angered Jackson's advisers. "What sort of an administration editor is Gen. Green?" Kendall fumed upon hearing Welles's allegation. Green attempted to balance his support for both Jackson and Calhoun. "Is friendship for one incompatible with friendship for the other?" he asked. But the response of the president's followers was increasingly that of Kendall: "General Green is considered more devoted to Mr. Calhoun than to General Jackson."[55]

On substantive issues, Green also found his situation delicate and, ultimately, untenable. Although he pleaded with South Carolina militants to "moderate your public men," he remained an ardent critic of protective tariffs. His particular remedy for the South's ills was an alliance with the West to effect a lower tariff and to clear a path to the White House for Calhoun. Therefore, when Jackson refused to endorse a significant and immediate tariff reform, Green objected. In the spring of 1830, he purposefully distorted the president's moderate tariff sentiments at the conclusion of the Maysville Road message, making it appear as if Jackson were promising an eventual end to the protective system. He also published an explanation of Jackson's Jefferson Day toast, denying that it showed hostility to the southern antitariff movement. The president saw through the ruse, however, and bitterly complained that Green had perverted his ideas. To Jackson, the editor was overly disposed to identify the administration with nullification.[56]

It was, finally, Green's wavering course on the Bank that caused Jackson to seek another newspaper. Although Green was no friend of the Bank, he opened the columns of the *Telegraph* to his South Carolina allies, who were assailing Jackson's policy. In July 1830, he printed George McDuffie's favorable report on the Bank and promised to review the document. But the analysis never appeared, thus leaving the administration's supporters with only the Bank's side of the controversy. This was the final straw for Jackson. On his way to Tennessee, he fired off a letter to Lewis, denouncing "the conduct of Genl. D. Green" who "has professed to me to be heart and soul, against the Bank, but his idol controles [*sic*] him as the shewman does his puppits, and we must get another organ to announce the policy, and defend the administration."[57]

Jackson had mentioned the possibility of another newspaper before, but his letter to Lewis gave the matter new urgency. While the president remained in Tennessee, Lewis consulted with E. W. Gooch of Virginia about coming to Washington to replace Green. In choosing Gooch, Lewis probably had Van Buren's interests in mind, since the Virginian had previously worked for the Richmond *Enquirer* as Ritchie's partner. But Gooch demanded assurances and pledges of support which were impossible to satisfy. Moreover, Lewis failed to press the issue because Green, under pressure, professed a change of tack, to provide "entire and *exclusive* devotion to the reelection of Jackson."[58]

While Lewis was negotiating with Gooch, however, the two former Kentucky relief leaders, Kendall and Barry, had conferred about the need for a new paper, and Barry had suggested Francis Blair as a replacement for Green. Kendall jumped at the suggestion, for he and Blair were steadfast political allies and their thinking on political issues almost always coincided.[59] Kendall did not trust Green's summer professions of support for Jackson, and despite the diminished interest in a new paper displayed by others, he continued to press Blair to come to Washington. He was certain that Jackson, upon returning from Tennessee, would accept Blair. "Your sentiments in relation to the Bank will make him zealous for you," he assured Blair. Kendall was right, for when Jackson returned in September, he announced his determination to have a new paper exclusively devoted to his policies, one which was not connected in any way with Calhoun and the nullification movement.[60]

With Jackson's promise of support, Kendall made final arrangements with Blair. They planned to make the newspaper exclusively a Jackson organ; it might also aid Van Buren, but only because the New Yorker identified himself with Jackson's success, not because he controlled the presses. When a friend of Van Buren approached Kendall, requesting assurance that Blair would use the paper to support Van Buren, Kendall explained that neither he nor Blair could give any pledges, but that "such would probably be the natural result" of Blair's position and principles. Van Buren nevertheless approved the new paper, especially because of Blair's spirited blasts against nullification, and Kendall informed Blair that he would probably have the New Yorker's support as well as that of Jackson. "But," he counseled, "I do not wish you to be considered under any pledge to him, express or implied. I wish you to stand just as I *do*—the friend of General Jackson and his administration, having no future political views other than the support of his principles."[61]

By the first week in October, Jackson had given his final approval, and Blair prepared to leave Kentucky. His purpose was not to replace Green, but to establish his press as a *"coadjutor"* which would loyally support Jackson regardless of Green's future course. Hoping not to provoke a fight with Green, Kendall assured him that Blair was coming to Washington "wholly unpledged to *man* or *men*." Green was not placated and thought Van Buren responsible for the situation. But he was wrong. Blair's was to be a *"Jackson paper,"* Kendall noted, adding that Van Buren had little to do with its establishment. "He was not even consulted so far as I know." [62]

Van Buren himself acknowledged that Blair's paper was not his organ. Until the publication of the Jackson-Calhoun correspondence in February 1831, Van Buren considered Blair as "personally favorable to Mr. Calhoun," which was not fully accurate since Blair had come to Washington uncommitted to either Van Buren or Calhoun. But Blair certainly showed no hostility to Calhoun until shortly before the vice-president took his dispute with Jackson to the public. And Van Buren also informed his political friends that he had no control over the policy of the paper. Indeed, even after Calhoun's departure, Blair's interest in supporting Jackson sometimes led him to disagree with Van Buren about political matters. Blair, like Kendall, had his own base in Jackson's Kitchen Cabinet, and when Van Buren was elected president, Blair offered his resignation so that Van Buren could have "the selection of the Journalist who must to some extent have confidential relations with the Administration." Van Buren asked Blair to remain, and the two men grew increasingly intimate.[63]

Blair was not a physically imposing sight when he arrived in Washington. Slightly disheveled and bandaged from a mishap to his coach, he first encountered Major Lewis in the president's office. "Mr. Blair, we want stout hearts and sound heads here," said the disappointed Lewis.[64] The Kentuckian, however, possessed the requisite qualities. His anti-Bank and hard-money notions promised Jackson a staunch ally on those issues. In editorials for the *Argus of Western America*, he had also warmly commended Jackson's tariff and distribution statements. While expressing affection and pledging relief to the South, he had condemned nullification as disruptive of sectional harmony. As he explained to Duff Green, "I have somewhat of Southern feeling, & am desirous to modify the policy . . . and accommodate it in a spirit of compromise . . . [but] I cannot adopt the doctrine of Nullification." [65]

Equally relevant was the fact that Blair proved an unusually capable and effective administration and party editor. The Washington *Globe*, which probably adopted its name from *Le Globe*, the Parisian newspaper associated with the recent July Revolution in France,[66] not only broadcast defenses and explanations of Jackson's program but perfected the techniques employed by Duff Green's *Telegraph* during the election of 1828 in functioning as the party's central press. Through subscriptions, exchanges with other Democratic newspapers (Blair estimated exchanges with over 400 papers by the summer of 1833), and the encouragement and aid it provided for the establishment of other party journals, the *Globe* served as a clearing house for political information and propaganda, enabling Jackson to tap public opinion more effectively.[67]

Since Jackson was often more popular among a politician's constituents than the official himself, the *Globe* was especially successful in commanding attention in the hinterland. "You know the influence of a favourable notice in a Washington paper of a member [of Congress] upon the people," one representative reminded Blair, and another thanked him for publishing the proceedings of a political celebration in his district. Jackson carefully exploited the *Globe*'s grass-roots influence, sending articles to Blair for publication and franking newspapers for circulation around the country. On occasion, he requested public exposés of those who opposed his policy, explaining that the notices "would have a good effect upon the public & enlighten the minds of the people in their choice of Representatives." In general, according to Blair, the president's "mode was to have a pretty thorough going organ that would do . . . [his] bidding and whip *in* or *out* restless men, and that was the only way of making a united party."[68]

Upon Blair's arrival in Washington, he and Jackson soon became fast friends. The president explained the state of affairs—the impending nullification fight, the Bank's transgressions, the combination against Eaton—and taking Blair under his wing at a state dinner, he showed him marked attention. Blair reciprocated this confidence with fervent devotion. In some respects he soon became closer to Jackson than did Van Buren, for Blair had more of the president's impulsive energy. A few months after coming to Washington, the editor reported that "if Van Buren says, 'You are rash in this business, Mr. Blair,' the old hero says, 'you are right Mr. Blair. I'll stand by you.'" Jackson was also particularly fond of Blair's family and found hours of comfort and solace at the Blair home, establishing a lifelong personal bond that even Kendall did not share with the president.[69]

At the same time that Blair, Kendall, and Van Buren were gaining increased access to Jackson, the president was securing his own control over the emerging Democratic party. As evidence of Calhoun's treachery mounted, Jackson and his aides undertook a campaign calling for his renomination. By more closely identifying Jackson's fortunes with those of the party, they made manifest their opinion that resistance to his will would be subversive of party unity.

Jackson was silent about his future plans when he entered the White House, though Duff Green was probably right in thinking that the president's "jealous eye to his future fame" would make him desirous of another term. The major contenders for the succession clearly expected him to seek office again. Calhoun considered it futile to challenge Jackson if he wanted a second term, and Green speculated that Jackson would pave the way for Calhoun's advancement in 1836 by resolving the tariff issue. Van Buren warmly endorsed a second term, in part because it provided time to erase his reputation for political manipulation, a task that would be made easier if by continued association some of Jackson's popularity were to rub off on him. He probably also shied away from battling Calhoun when the vice-president seemed strong.[70]

Those independent of Calhoun or Van Buren supported Jackson's renomination for other reasons. Barry, deprecating the rivalry between Van Buren and Calhoun, looked to Jackson's reelection as a means of preventing "division in our ranks." Kendall agreed, and in the spring of 1830 he implored Blair to have the *Argus of Western America* urge a second term. "Our friends forget, that they ought to think only of supporting Jackson and Reform and are looking out for new leaders," he asserted.[71]

During the winter and early spring of 1830, reports circulated in Washington that Calhoun would attempt to force Jackson into retirement at the end of his first term, or that he might even challenge Jackson if the president decided on a second term. Kendall fretted that the South Carolinian's impatience was responsible for "a secret coalition" with John McLean. "They desire to take the field forthwith," he reported. And Lewis also thought Calhoun would hold Jackson to his election promise of a one-term presidency.[72]

There is very little direct evidence that Calhoun wanted to contest Jackson's reelection, but the Kitchen Cabinet considered Green's handling of the *Telegraph* as especially ominous. In March 1830, the editor blasted as "ill timed, unadvised, and unauthorized," an article in another paper declaring Jackson to be the only candidate of the party. Privately, Green explained to Ritchie that Jackson should not "*now*" be declared a candidate since his program had not been set decisively upon a states' rights course. Only when this was done would it be proper to discuss the president's reelection. Kendall was furious at Green's behavior and accused him of catering to Calhoun's ambitions. "Our party and principles must not be sacrificed for any *man*," Kendall exclaimed.[73]

Genuine or not, the possibility of a challenge to Jackson's leadership led Lewis, who was particularly skilled in this type of political intrigue, to recommend to a Pennsylvania anti-Calhoun editor that the Democratic members of the Pennsylvania legislature adopt a resolution endorsing Jackson's renomination as the only means of preserving party harmony and defeating Clay. To make sure the resolution was appropriate to the occasion, Lewis enclosed one of his own for the members to sign. Shortly afterward, a Pennsylvania legislative caucus adopted a resolution similar to the one Lewis suggested.[74]

Under the direction of the Kitchen Cabinet, and with the kind of political coordination that had marked the previous presidential campaign, the renomination movement soon spread to other states. New York Democrats quickly followed Pennsylvania's example, and New Hampshire, Ohio, and other party organizations soon lined up behind the president. Jackson himself approved, if indeed he did not suggest, these proceedings. He closely watched their progress and thought they would prove to be a damper on Calhoun's ambition. The Calhounites, he asserted, would have "to yield to the determination and will of the people."[75]

The movement to secure Jackson's leadership was eminently successful in giving greater coherence to the Democrats. John Quincy Adams correctly noted that Calhoun was now reduced to the alternative "of joining in the shout of hurrah for Jackson's reelection or of being counted in the opposition." By April 1830, Van Buren happily observed that the people were getting right and rallying behind Jackson's renomination. And the Massachusetts Democrat, Marcus Morton, at that time a Calhoun partisan, reported that "within the last month the opinion of the Democratic Party in Massachusetts and I believe throughout New England seems to have taken a new and decided direction. . . . It is now generally understood and believed that General Jackson will be a candidate for reelection."[76]

The benefits of this campaign became fully evident the following year when Calhoun published the Seminole Correspondence. No matter how carefully he tried to direct his charges against Van Buren and Crawford, it nevertheless appeared that Calhoun was dividing the party and challenging the president. "The supporters of Jackson are the Republican party," Blair claimed. "We recognize no subdivision. 'He who is not for us is against us.'"[77]

Undoubtedly, Calhoun's identification with nullification weakened his case with many of his early supporters, especially in western Georgia and Pennsylvania. But it is also true that many abandoned him simply because they now recognized Jackson as head of the party and chief spokesman for Republican principles. Marcus Morton stated the new relationship most succinctly in explaining to Calhoun that although he had indeed been the victim of a Van Burenite intrigue, the people would blame him for injuring the party. "The Administration having been brought into existence by the voice of Democracy; having been founded and in most respects conducted on Democratic principles, there is a strong desire on the part of Democrats, notwithstanding its mistakes and errors, to sustain it," Morton contended. "The President cannot be separated from the Administration. The Administration cannot be separated from the Democratic party. And the friends of the latter feel constrained to support the two former."[78]

In similar fashion, when Van Buren's and Eaton's resignations in April 1831 cleared the way for Jackson to discharge Branch, Berrien, and Ingham, the three officers tried to blame the cabinet shakeup on Van Buren. But Blair countered by depicting their attack as an insinuation that Jackson was not the leader of his administration and by charging them with dividing the party, supporting Calhoun, and undermining Jackson's policies. His strategy was so effective that even Ingham's friends in Pennsylvania refused to come to the former secretary's aid. "I would be censured for bringing the state administration in to broil and collision with the . . . Genl Government," a Pennsylvania leader explained to Ingham. And Kendall exulted at the way men flocked to Jackson's support. "Old Hickory shines brighter the more they rub him," he declared.[79]

Most historians have viewed the turmoil in Jackson's first cabinet and his dispute with Calhoun as petty anomalies in a presidency marked by so many momentous issues. There is no contesting the fact that Jackson expended an enormous amount of time and energy concerning himself with inconsequential, and sometimes shabby, details of the Eaton and Seminole controversies. Nevertheless, the upheavals of the first two years had significant implications both for the Jackson Democratic party and for the executive office.

The Eaton and Calhoun incidents first demonstrated the keen disappointment of antitariff radicals, even those unattached to Calhoun, with Jackson's moderation in returning the republic to a policy of more limited government. They believed that the influence of Eaton coupled with Van Buren's appointment signaled Jackson's intention to perpetuate the injustices of the protective system.

It is difficult to say how extensively this hostility penetrated in the South. Calhoun asserted that Jackson was "not only weak but in fact odious" in that section, and in the aftermath of the rupture caused by Calhoun's departure and the cabinet reorganization of 1831, a number of prominent politicians, primarily from the slaveholding states of South Carolina, Georgia, Alabama, and Mississippi, deserted the party. Moreover, some southerners who formally remained Democrats sympathized with the zealots but stood by Jackson because his popularity made opposition impracticable.[80]

Most southern Jacksonians, however, stayed with the president and doubtless agreed with Ritchie that despite some drawbacks, Jackson's program was better than any other politician's and might be improved in the future. They found Jackson sufficiently sympathetic to the South to secure their allegiance, though their support exposed them to charges by Duff Green of repudiating their section and "joining in the crusade against the South." Although strained at times, the continued loyalty of moderate southerners more than compensated for the defection of the radical antitariff elements, and it resulted in a party more cohesively united around Jackson's states' rights program.[81]

The alienation of the dissenters also left Jackson as the indisputable leader not only of his administration, but, through his renomination, of the Democratic party. Consequently, the ambitions of presidential aspirants were necessarily deferred for six years, and time was gained for Jackson to execute his program. At the same time, the ties between the Van Buren faction and Jackson grew more secure as Van Buren's charm, tact, and support for Jackson's program won him the president's confidence and affection. John Branch exaggerated when he claimed at the time of the cabinet shakeup that Van Buren "had become latterly the almost sole confidant and adviser of the President," but he was generally correct in recognizing that Van Buren was among Jackson's most trusted advisers.[82]

Van Buren's increasing influence was evident in the new cabinet selections. Jackson had constructed his first cabinet without consulting him. In the spring of 1831, however, the two men worked together to form another cabinet, and Van Buren was directly responsible for the appointments of Louis McLane as secretary of the treasury and Edward Livingston as secretary of state. Both Livingston and McLane disagreed with Jackson's banking and internal improvements views, but the president reluctantly yielded to Van Buren's "earnest solicitations," rationalizing his indulgence by stating that he could never have a cabinet which would agree with him on all policies.[83] While Levi Woodbury as secretary of the navy, Roger Taney as attorney general, Lewis Cass as secretary of war, and William Barry, who remained as postmaster general, were not Van Buren's personal friends, neither were they hostile to him. The new cabinet, therefore, reflected the changed political situation of 1831. No member was hostile to Van Buren, no member was a radical antitariff man. As a southern radical bitterly remarked, the cabinet contained "no friend of the great Southern interests & there seemed to be a careful exclusion of Mr. Calhoun's friends."[84]

To some, the appointments apparently confirmed Van Buren's power over Jackson. Calhoun thought the cabinet would serve Van Buren's interests, and it is probable that Hugh Lawson White rejected an offer to become secretary of war because he thought an acceptance would commit him to Van Buren. But both Calhoun and White exaggerated the situation by overlooking its basic feature—loyalty to Jackson. Barry, Taney, and Cass were not known as Van Buren partisans, and though Woodbury had been identified with Calhoun, he was selected under the assumption that he was now exclusively a Jackson man. It would thus be more accurate to consider the cabinet as primarily bound to Jackson rather than as pro–Van Buren.[85]

The balance of power within the executive office altered in other ways during this formative period. The quick replacement of the *Telegraph* by Francis Blair's Washington *Globe* proved to be of enormous significance. While an embittered Duff Green publicly blamed "Van Buren and his agents" for his banishment and privately spread rumors that the administration was capable of such gross folly as the holding of "a large Negroe ball in the president's House," Blair provided Jackson with a party press such as no previous president had possessed—a paper designed to stimulate and direct public opinion as a counterweight to the resistance of opposition politicians. Blair himself became one of Jackson's most valued advisers and soon was boasting that in many important matters Jackson preferred his opinion over that of Van Buren. His close associate Amos Kendall also rose in Jackson's confidence, and in the early summer of 1831, he gave evidence of his new status by compromising with his abhorrence of Washington life to move from Georgetown to near the State Department and thus closer to the president.[86]

The dramatic rise of Blair and Kendall shifted power away from Jackson's other western advisers. In 1829 the president conferred with Eaton and Lewis, but by the spring of 1831 he was looking for counsel to the two Kentuckians; they agreed wholeheartedly with his program whereas Eaton and Lewis found it difficult to do so. Lewis remained in Washington as Jackson's personal friend, carrying out certain political tasks, but the president's diminishing reliance on his advice was evident when he moved out of the White House in early 1832. Eaton, having resigned from the cabinet in April 1831, left Washington a few months later, and never regained his early importance.[87]

Kendall and Blair, on the other hand, continued to earn Jackson's trust. While they agreed with Van Buren about many policies, they did so from an independent vantage point, for neither was a protégé of the "Magician" or committed to a particular candidate for the succession. Both considered themselves loyal only to Jackson. They gave the Jackson administration a dose of relief politics while attaining an influence that frequently exceeded that of Van Buren.[88]

The departure of Calhoun and the alienation of antitariff radicals did not, then, leave the administration in the hands of Van Buren or the protective tariff advocates, as Duff Green had feared. Instead, by reorganizing his cabinet and promoting his own renomination, Jackson established himself as the head of his administration and party. Van Buren remained a powerful figure around the president, but his subordinate status was illustrated when he reluctantly acceded to Jackson's wish that he become minister to Britain. At the same time, the emergence of Blair and Kendall indicated that even among Jackson's counselors Van Buren's influence was not unrivaled. The agitation of the early days of Jackson's presidency had, in the end, clarified the contours of the developing Democratic party.[89]

4
Elaborating a Program

In the midst of the storms that wracked the White House, Jackson set about formulating a program in keeping with his resolve to restore Jeffersonian principles to government. Affirming the values of limited government, individual initiative, and moral constraint as essential elements of republican society, he displayed a keen sensitivity to the corrosive effects of special privilege, monopoly, and excessive government power. By harking back to the ideals of an earlier period, Jackson's program evoked nostalgia for a pristine agrarian world, which doubtless contributed to its appeal. At the same time, however, it proved a resilient and effective instrument for adjusting the divergent and competing interests of an expansive and pluralistic nation.[1]

As Jackson charted his course, he established the pattern of decision making that would mark his presidency. While seeking counsel from a number of men, he relied especially on Van Buren, Kendall, and Blair. But the president himself remained the hub of activity and generally initiated policy. Although he often personalized the opposition and claimed to be the innocent victim of its attacks, it would be simplistic to say that he merely reacted vindictively and in self-defense to the actions of others. Rather, his instinct was to reach out for issues, to formulate the context of debate, and to oversee the controversy to its conclusion.[2] As a result, there commenced, in Amos Kendall's somewhat exaggerated words, a "general shaking . . . which was destined, after a long agony to separate parties on original principles, much better defined and understood than they were even in the days of Jefferson."[3]

When the twenty-first Congress assembled in December 1829, John Quincy Adams, observing the indeterminate nature of politics, predicted that before long "a new organization of parties" would take place. "There are combustibles enough: they only want kindling; and the torches are at hand," he noted. Among the explosive possibilities, Adams listed "the Indians." Indeed, the notion that Jackson's Indian policy would spark controversy was widely accepted, and the official Jackson organ, Duff Green's *Telegraph*, forecast that Indian removal would "no doubt, be one of the subjects agitated" by Congress.[4]

The relations of the southern Indian tribes with federal and state governments had been one of the few issues distinguishing Adams from Jackson in the campaign of 1828. During his presidency, Adams had become embroiled in a controversy with Georgia over the removal of the Creek Indians. Claiming that a removal treaty negotiated by federal commissioners and certain Creek chiefs was illegal, Adams refused to countenance it and renegotiated a second treaty, one somewhat less favorable to the state. When Georgia officials, led by Governor George M. Troup, complained loudly and refused to recognize the new pact, Adams announced to Congress that Georgia's actions were "in direct violation of the supreme law of this land." Despite the militancy of his message, however, Adams rejected his cabinet's suggestion that he send troops to uphold federal laws and treaties. He did not doubt the right, only the expediency, he said. Instead, he concluded another treaty in early 1828 which ceded the disputed land to the state.[5]

At the time of Jackson's inauguration, attention continued to be focused on the southern Indian tribes, especially the Cherokees who in 1827 had adopted a constitution proclaiming them an independent nation with complete sovereignty over tribal land in Georgia, North Carolina, Tennessee, and Alabama. Having adopted an agricultural way of life as well as other trappings of white civilization, the Cherokees were determined to preserve their tribal integrity and land. But Georgia was equally adamant. As a leading politician noted, the Cherokees occupied "some five or six millions of acres of the best lands within the limits of the State," rendering it obvious that "the resources of Georgia could never be extensively developed" until settled by "an industrious, enlightened, free-hold population." Arguing that the Indians could not create an independent nation within the state's borders, and reminding the federal government that it had agreed in 1802 to extinguish the Indian title as soon as possible, Georgia officials resolved to undermine tribal unity and to encourage removal by extending the laws of the state over the tribe. Georgia acted shortly after Jackson's election, and Alabama and Mississippi passed similar legislation before the new president was inaugurated.[6]

Jackson wasted little time in indicating his support for the position of these southern states. He told a member of the Georgia delegation to inform the Cherokees that the state possessed a right to extend its jurisdiction over them, and that "it was for them to make their election, to go west of the Mississippi, and possess land which they and their children should not only possess forever, but have the friendly and protecting arm of the United States government thrown around them, or abide the consequences of such rules of action as Georgia might prescribe for their government." Secretary of War John Eaton conveyed the same message directly to the Cherokees. "The arms of this country can never be employed, to stay any state . . . from the exercise of those legitimate powers which . . . belong to their sovereign character," he announced.[7]

It was not until his December 1829 message, however, that Jackson elaborated on his policy. Drafted with the aid of Kendall and Donelson, the message recorded the dismal results of previous Indian policy in attempting both to civilize and to remove eastern tribes. It skillfully argued against Cherokee independence, and employing the rhetoric of states' rights principles, claimed for the southern states the same right to rule over their Indian population as that held by the states of Maine or New York. Should the federal government countenance the Cherokee position, Jackson alleged, it would follow "that the objects of this Government are reversed, and that it has become a part of its duty to aid in destroying the States which it was established to protect." In order to avert calamity, Jackson recommended the setting apart of an area west of the Mississippi to be guaranteed to removing tribes in exchange for their lands in the East. Those remaining in the states would be subject to their laws and "ere long become merged in the mass of our population."[8]

Jackson's recommendation was hardly novel. American Indian policy since the Federalist period had variously emphasized removal as well as civilization and assimilation. Adams himself, no doubt in frustration, had urged its consideration in his last presidential message. Jackson's proposal, therefore, was not so much a radical change in purpose as a shift in emphasis. Efforts at civilization would now be conducted in the West, where the Indians would be removed from the baleful influence of white frontiersmen, and the federal government would now more vigorously stimulate removal by refusing to recognize tribal integrity east of the Mississippi.[9]

Jackson's conclusion that removal made sense for white men, Indians, and the nation derived from years of involvement in Indian affairs. Recent scholarship has made clear that he was not simply the Indian-hater depicted in standard texts. Although ethnocentrism and his early frontier and military experiences made him no admirer of Indian life, his view of these peoples was also shaped by Jeffersonian humanitarian and states' rights traditions, concern for national security, and a vision of an industrious agrarian republic.[10]

In the decade following the War of 1812, Jackson had personally presided at more than half the major treaty negotiations and had exerted considerable influence over federal Indian policy. As early as 1817, he had questioned the legitimacy of Indian treaties and, in denying tribal sovereignty, had established a justification for the assertion of federal and state legislative authority over the tribes. He called treaty making "an absurdity" since Indians were "the subjects of the United States," and he explained the practice as an expedient which had been adopted when the federal government was weak and which could now be abandoned in favor of legislative policy. As president, Jackson simply extended this argument, claiming that the failure of the *states* previously to extend their jurisdiction over the Indians had also been a matter of weakness and had not involved the renunciation of sovereignty over their internal population.[11]

Jackson had also urged upon President Monroe the necessity for removing Indians westward and concentrating the remaining population in small areas in the East. Such a policy, he asserted, would aid national defense by placing white men on American borders in the South and Southwest. Equally important, it would replace a primitive, savage, and hunting population with a progressive white society. "What is the vallue [sic] of the soil, compared to the vallue of the population that section of the country will maintain," Jackson wrote in encouragement to his friend John Coffee, who was negotiating a cession treaty with the southern tribes. "Labour is the wealth of all nations." [12]

But Jackson also believed that removal was equally advantageous to the American Indian. Reflecting a Jeffersonian desire both to treat them liberally and to introduce elements of white culture, Jackson considered removal "just and humane." In the West, "free from the mercenary influence of white men, and undisturbed by the local authority of the states," the tribes could either reaffirm their customs or, preferably, adopt civilized ways. The government would do its share, exercising "parental control" over their interests and helping to perpetuate their race. Failing to perceive the growing complexity and market orientation of Cherokee society, Jackson contended that only a few Indians had managed to adopt the white man's customs, and he distinguished them from the mass of "real" Indians who still "retained their savage habits" and who would benefit from removal. To Jackson, the minority "whitemen and half breeds" exploited "the annuities, the labours, and folly of the native Indian," and represented the same kind of "corrupt and secrete combination" of privileged interests that he encountered in contending against the Bank and internal improvements logrolling.[13]

Whatever the Indians' fate in the West, however, Jackson was adamant that the states had full sovereignty over their land and population, and that the central government must protect this right even if it meant reducing its power in areas where some claimed it could legitimately act. "An absolute independence of the Indian tribes from state authority can never bear an intelligent investigation," he argued, reminding his secretary of war that actual Indian title to the land would nullify the states' grants of their western domain to the federal government. "Such a doctrine would not be well relished in the West," he warned.[14]

Jackson's solicitude for the Indians' welfare, therefore, was heavily laced with elements of paternalistic coercion, and, with no evident recognition of the iniquities involved, he manipulated the granting of annuities, withdrew federal protection against intruders, refused to enforce the Intercourse Act of 1802, and threatened to make the Indians pay the costs of removal themselves if they did not sign cession agreements quickly. And always in the background was his refusal to interpose the federal government between the states and the Indians. The rhetoric of Jackson's program emphasized its philanthropic ideals, but the substance revealed a great deal of manipulation and effectual coercion.[15]

Jackson's determination to make Indian removal his first major policy was probably dictated as much by his familiarity with the problem as by the critical situation existing between the southern states and their tribes. Van Buren recalled that Jackson took up the Indian problem "at the earliest practicable moment," and that removal "was emphatically the fruit of his own exertions. . . . There was no measure, in the whole course of his administration of which he was more exclusively the author than this." Jackson himself acknowledged that removal "was a measure I had much at heart and sought to effect because I was satisfied that the Indians could not possibly live under the laws of the state." He also supervised the removal process "with great vigilance," a chore he found "the most arduous part of my duty." [16]

What assistance Jackson required came at first primarily from his western aides. Eaton, whom Jackson had placed in the cabinet largely for personal reasons, was appropriately situated in the War Department, where his close relationship with Jackson and his experience in Indian affairs made him an effective spokesman for the president. It was generally assumed in the early days of Jackson's administration that on this issue Eaton was "better informed of the views and policy of the executive than any other individual. . . ." He helped draft Jackson's initial announcement of removal to the Cherokee Nation in the spring of 1829, as well as Jackson's special message of February 1831 explaining his refusal to enforce the Intercourse Act of 1802.[17] Eaton's Tennessee colleagues, Lewis and Donelson, were also in evidence when Indian affairs were discussed, and Donelson's hand is visible in a number of presidential messages dealing with removal. Kendall, who had once favored a policy of assimilation, "civilizing and christianizing our savages" by settling white families among them, also contributed substantially to Jackson's presidential messages.[18]

As far as can be determined, Van Buren took a decidedly subordinate role in Indian policy. He advised Jackson on constitutional questions relating to removal and endorsed emigration as "the wisest and in the end most humane policy." But he acknowledged Jackson's primacy in this matter, recalling that the president consulted him "chiefly to the manner of doing what he thought ought to be done," and he could hardly have been enthusiastic about identifying himself too closely with a measure that stirred considerable humanitarian opposition in New York and Pennsylvania. He, as well as his followers in the Albany Regency, would consistently emphasize the voluntary and philanthropic aspects of removal and work arduously to bring a peaceful resolution of Georgia's conflict with the Cherokees.[19]

Jackson's announcement of a new Indian policy generally elicited warm applause from key groups of supporters. Duff Green spoke of its enlightened philanthropy, emphasized its benefits to the South and West, and categorized its opponents as "traders, runaway negroes . . . refugee whitemen, and half breeds." The influential Richmond *Enquirer* indicated southern support for Jackson's "respect . . . to the unalienated rights of the States," while Van Buren's organ, the Albany *Argus*, complimented the president for finding a plan that satisfied both the "interested states" and "the philanthropist."[20]

But removal also sparked the first major political battle of Jackson's presidency, helping to distinguish Jacksonians from their opposition. Tennessee's John Bell, a friend and neighbor of John Eaton and a supporter though not an intimate of the president, sponsored a removal bill in the House, while another Tennessean, Hugh Lawson White, proposed a similar bill in the Senate.[21] Debate began in the spring of 1830, when opponents of the measure charged that Jackson had withdrawn protection from the Indians and made federal treaties subordinate to state laws. They emphasized the coercive implications of the plan, denounced the "mercenary motives" of the South and Southwest, and defended the Indians' right to the soil and to independence from state authority. Even at this early stage in Jackson's presidency, the nascent opposition explored the theme of executive tyranny, criticizing the president for his "exclusive interpretation of treaties" and his "abusive exercise of . . . power" in failing to provide against possible bribery and fraud in the removal process.[22]

Jackson supporters, led by the Georgia delegation, retorted that treaties had never made the Indians sovereign, that Georgia retained control over its lands and peoples, and that removal was a humane policy for "a race not admitted to be equal to the rest of the community." Opposition to removal, they alleged, was largely motivated by partisan feelings.[23] Administration forces were well prepared for the contest. Jackson had personally supervised the composition of the House Committee on Indian Affairs, and the two relevant committee chairmanships were safely in the hands of the loyal Tennesseans White and Bell. Moreover, Speaker of the House Andrew Stevenson was always ready to break a tie vote, as he did on three important occasions, to save the removal bill.[24]

The fate of the Indian bill remained in question throughout the spring of 1830. Daniel Webster noted the "great state of *uncertainty*" in Washington during this first legislative session following Jackson's victory. Not only were former Adams men active, but there were ominous signs that some Jacksonians, bitter about Indian removal as well as the unfavorable response by Jackson leaders in Congress to internal improvements projects, were deserting to the enemy. These two issues were closely joined because advocates of the latter insisted that the considerable expense of removing Indians gave an additional cause of complaint to those who considered internal improvements measures burdensome and unconstitutional. Congressman William Stanbery of Ohio, elected as a Jackson man, explained his opposition to the Indian Removal bill on the grounds "that its passage would strike a death-blow to the whole system of internal improvement," and he claimed that the measure "received the support of all the enemies of internal improvement."[25]

Indeed, most of the heated debate over Indian removal occurred in the interval between the passage of the Maysville Road bill and Jackson's announcement of his veto. Some opposition members cleverly tried to delay a vote on removal long enough for Jackson to be compelled either to sign the Maysville bill and save his Indian plan or to send in his veto and risk the loss of votes by outraged internal improvements advocates. Webster, for example, maintained that the action of administration friends in killing another internal improvements measure, combined with the "expected" Maysville veto, would hurt the president. In fact, he asserted, "I should not be at all surprised, if the conduct of the President & his friends, on these two measures should be the means, with Heaven's blessing, of preventing the passage of the Indian Bill." And it was Hezekiah Niles's conviction that if the Maysville Road veto had "appeared half an hour previous to the final vote on the Indian bill, *it would have been rejected by a much larger majority than that by which it was carried.*"[26]

Encouraged by the knowledge that the Indian bill was a "leading measure of the executive," Jackson supporters overcame strong resistance and narrowly passed the measure on 26 May 1830, one day before Jackson issued his Maysville Road veto. It passed the Senate by a vote of 28 to 19, and the House by 102 to 97. An analysis of the vote indicates that the strongest support for removal came from the Southeast, Southwest, and the border-West region, which divided 63 to 16 in favor. The Old Northwest, the Middle Atlantic states, and New England were opposed. But regional alignments were not perfect, and party considerations weighed heavily in some cases. New Hampshire, for example, voted unanimously in favor of removal. Maryland and Indiana also backed Jackson, and New York gave him a substantial minority. This combination of sectional and partisan affiliation yielded Jackson his small majority on the bill. It was his only major legislative triumph of his first term, and the *Telegraph* celebrated its passage by asserting that "next to the reform of abuses, and the payment of the public debt, it will stand forth as one of the great measures of national policy, which will distinguish the administration of President Jackson." [27]

Nevertheless, there had been defections, especially among northern Jackson men. Since party lines were still in an embryonic stage, it is difficult to determine the extent to which Jackson's Indian policy bred rebellion, a matter further complicated by the connection between Indian removal and internal improvements. It seems likely, however, that Indian removal contributed to the alienation of Stanbery, David Crockett of Tennessee, and some members of the Kentucky, Pennsylvania, and New York delegations. Moreover, many who cast their votes with the president had little enthusiasm for his policy, and some congressmen thought that they had been betrayed in their expectation that support for Indian removal would be reciprocated by Jackson's approval of the Maysville Road bill. When the House received the veto message, there immediately arose the question of whether the Indian bill had not actually passed into the president's possession so that a reconsideration might take place. Webster reported "unusual excitement" in the House. "There is more ill blood raised, I should think, than would easily be quieted again." [28]

Jackson later blamed Calhoun's friend, Treasury secretary Samuel Ingham, for the "divisions of Pennsylvania on the Indian question," and it is true that Ingham considered the president's plan inimical to Pennsylvania's pride in "the fair and humane manner in which she had acquired her territory from the aborigines—not by cutting their throats and murdering them, as most of the other states had done." But

Jackson clearly underestimated the moral scruples that many northerners felt towards the implicitly coercive nature of Indian removal. Loyal Jacksonians like Henry Muhlenberg and James Buchanan of Pennsylvania either voted against or abstained from voting on the bill. And according to Van Buren, the policy cost the Democrats "eight or ten thousand voters" in western New York in 1832.[29]

Just as Adams had foreseen, Indian removal became one of the issues that drew party lines during Jackson's presidency. As early as the spring of 1830, shortly after passage of the Indian Removal bill, Adams viewed the measure as part of a concerted effort to diminish the power of the federal government to do good. "The Indians are already sacrificed . . .; domestic industry and internal improvement will be strangled; and when the public debt will be paid off and the bank charter expired, there will be no great interest left upon which the action of the General Government will operate," he lamented. Adams's concerns were shared by Jackson's opponents, and the National Republican platform, which accused the president of failing to uphold treaty rights and of leaving the Indians "entirely at the mercy of their enemies," made Indian removal an issue in the 1832 election.[30]

But Jackson, convinced that removal was the only way to arrest the deterioration of the Indian tribes, pursued his policy with vigor.[31] With the arrival of Francis Blair to edit the Washington *Globe*, he had an enthusiastic spokesman who shared his convictions. Blair had been in Kentucky when Jackson initiated his policy, and though he had reservations about Georgia's militancy, he endorsed Jackson's proposal and attacked Clay and the opposition for manipulating the issue to foment sectional hostility between North and South. By advocating colonization for blacks while opposing it for Indians, Blair charged, Clay was "willing to catch at the prejudice of the non-slaveholding States and pay any price for their support. He would divide our country upon the Slave question, the Indian question, or any other question, so that he might lead the majority to subserve the views of his private ambition."[32]

Immediately upon arriving in Washington, Blair continued his sallies. Indeed, his association with Jackson seemed to harden Blair's views, and during the winter of 1831, he published a three-month series of essays defending Jackson, Georgia, and the other southern

states in their contest with the Indians. He justified Georgia's assertion of authority over the Indians as consistent with states' rights,
accused the Supreme Court of adopting "the nullifying doctrine in a
new shape" by trying to annul the criminal jurisdiction of a state, and
argued that Georgia and other southern states had only followed the
example of northern states like Massachusetts and New York. He
conceded that earlier treaties had misled the Indians into thinking
they were independent nations, but, he continued, those agreements
had violated the legitimate rights of Georgia and were therefore "unconstitutional . . . as to her, entirely null and void." The president's
removal plan was the proper "reparation for the bad faith of this
government," and failure to adopt it would only lead to further de-
moralization and even the extermination of the Indians.[33]

Blair also touched upon themes of special appeal to the West,
glorifying removal in the name of the irresistible westward movement
of "progress." "Who can arrest the march of our population to the
West?" the *Globe* asked in one editorial. "HE only, who can thrust out
his arm and arrest the sun in its course. It will roll on, until stopped by
the western ocean." To resist this current would make "our teeming
fields . . . become a howling wilderness, our comfortable habitations
give place to rough regions, and our twelve millions of civilized,
christian and happy people be swept from the face of the earth that a
few savage pagans and the beasts on which they live, may resume
their ancient dominions."[34]

At the same time, Blair persisted in characterizing opposition to
removal as the work of "hypocritical politicians" and misguided
philanthropists. As was so often the case, the *Globe* emphasized the
narrow political motivations of Jackson's foes, accusing them in particular of trying to embarrass the administration by promoting division
between the North and South. Indian removal, it claimed, had been
"converted by Mr. Clay and his partisans into a political question for
the purpose of increasing the dissentions between the different portions of the Union." To counteract such efforts, Blair exploited northern racial phobias, asking whether northerners would permit "*free
Blacks*" to colonize and establish independent governments within
their state limits, and warning of the possibilities of race war if the
federal government should intervene in the affairs of states to protect
distinct groups. "If the general government has a right to make treaties

with the Indians living within the States, because they are red, it has an equal right to make treaties with the negroes because they are black," he argued. While it would be an exaggeration to assert that Blair treated Indian removal as having the same importance as the Bank War, he did nevertheless contrive a potent defense, skillfully blending the themes of states' rights, unionism, economic progress, racism, and philanthropy against what he considered the efforts of ambitious and hypocritical politicans to halt progress, endanger the Indians, and promote sectional division.[35]

Over the course of Jackson's eight years in office, the United States ratified some seventy treaties and acquired about 100 million acres of Indian land at a cost of approximately 68 million dollars and 32 million acres of land in the West. The Creeks, Choctaws, Chickasaws, and Cherokees were among the tribes that agreed to removal, but Jackson did not focus exclusively on the South. Especially after the Black Hawk War of 1832, he also urged settlements with the weaker tribes of the Old Northwest. One after another, northern as well as southern tribes joined the migration westward. It was with evident satisfaction that Jackson announced at the end of his presidency that he had managed both to save "this unhappy race" and to remove a long-standing obstacle to state improvement.[36]

Indian removal was among the earliest policies to give greater ideological and structural coherence to the Democratic party. It was particularly popular in the South and Southwest, where it promised assistance in ridding the region of a population which was considered inferior and an obstacle to economic growth. Furthermore, Jackson's insistence on disclaiming federal powers which infringed on state authority reassured southerners who worried that the consolidation of power in Washington could unsettle domestic relations. "The jurisdiction claimed over one portion of our population may very soon be asserted over *another*," Georgia's George M. Troup declared of those who defended the Indians, adding that "in both cases they will be sustained by the fanatics of the north." And Thomas Ritchie cautioned that northern efforts on behalf of the Cherokees threatened "another Missouri Question."[37]

Yet even Ritchie recognized that the Indian question was more than a sectional one. It was also "a *party question*," and support for Indian removal became a distinguishing feature of the emerging Democratic party. Although the *Globe* acknowledged that some genuine Jackson men did not support the removal bill, it generally tied opposition to removal with "factious motives." Many northern Democrats, therefore, endorsed the policy despite their own moral scruples and the fear of antagonizing humanitarian sentiment. Consequently the Indian Removal bill helped differentiate the emerging parties, a circumstance borne out by the strong relationship between areas that voted against the bill and those that supported Adams in 1828 and would later support the Bank.[38]

To some extent, however, Indian removal stands apart from most of Jackson's other programs. As an issue of his earliest days in office involving problems familiar to westerners, it was the only program of his presidency in which he relied upon his longtime Tennessee advisers, especially Eaton. Moreover, Jackson seems to have treated Indian removal as distinct from the general impulse of his presidency to restore Jeffersonian principles to government. At the time of his inauguration, he did not mention it among the policies and principles he intended to implement. Nor was it cited among his accomplishments in the document that served as the Democratic party's campaign platform in 1832.[39] To be sure, Jackson's reliance on state authority in preference to centralized control, as well as his desire to protect the "real" Indians from what he considered to be exploitation by a specially privileged Indian elite and their self-interested and politically motivated white allies, link Indian removal with other presidential concerns. But it is questionable whether Jackson ever accorded Indian affairs the centrality that he gave his monetary and banking policies.[40]

As stated earlier, the issue of internal improvements was intimately related to Indian removal, and shortly after arriving in Washington, Jackson explicitly announced to Kendall his opposition to federal internal improvements expenditures that encroached on the rights of the states. His concern derived from a number of considerations, constitutional, philosophical, and practical, and though he acknowledged that the nation would benefit from improved navigation and overland transportation, he thought that past practice had raised serious objections and had been undertaken "at the expense of harmony in the legislative councils."[41]

To Jackson, the Founding Fathers had bequeathed a government of limited, not general, powers. The fate of liberty and republicanism depended upon the preservation of this system, and as early as 1822, in applauding Monroe's objections to the construction of federal tollbooths on the Cumberland Road, he had expressed concern about excessive federal authority. Equally worrisome were the implications of federal investments in local corporations, which he considered "injurious and destructive to the morales [sic] and liberty of the people," and the increase in public burdens, which delayed payment of the national debt. In Jeffersonian thought, heavy public taxation was a sign of oppressive government, and Jackson had indicated during the course of his public career that he considered national debts dangerous to liberty.[42]

Finally, Jackson believed that the previous mode of internal improvements expenditures entailed a chain of inequities and indefensible practices. Among the most glaring was "flagicious logg-rolling," which he decried as destructive of legislative harmony. It reinforced the tendency for some sections and states to benefit more than others from federal expenditures and promoted irritation and jealousy among the states. Jackson was profoundly impressed by the pluralistic quality of the United States, the "diversities in interests of the different States," and he regarded past governmental practice as tending to reward those states demanding improvements while requiring undue sacrifices from those without need. Limited government, then, would "neutralize" the impact of federal power by equalizing appropriations.[43]

Jackson's doubts about federal involvement in internal improvements reflected the concern of many Americans, especially in the South, where such expenditures were considered in much the same light as protective tariffs. But even in the North and West, where enthusiasm for federal aid generally ran high, one also found pockets of opposition. Here, however, there tended to be less interest in constitutional quibbling and more concern for the expense and inequities that resulted from logrolling. In his first annual message, Jackson briefly drew the attention of Congress to these various sources of dissatisfaction.[44]

When Van Buren entered the cabinet, Jackson found a ready ally for reversing the internal improvements tide. As a New Yorker, Van Buren had a vivid illustration in the Erie Canal of how a state could finance internal improvements on its own, and he certainly had no desire to jeopardize his state's commercial supremacy by endorsing federal aid for roads or canals in competing states like Pennsylvania. Also, as the leader of the old Crawford faction, Van Buren realized his southern allies were upset about federal expenditures and the latitudinarian philosophy which justified them. He himself shared their concern, and his self-interested objections to continued federal involvement were infused with Jeffersonian convictions of the need to establish limitations on appropriations for such projects.[45]

In Van Buren's view, Jackson's election provided an auspicious occasion to identify the emerging party with a new policy. Realizing that popular sentiment generally favored federal aid and that more than good arguments would be needed to reverse that opinion, Van Buren sought a counterpoise in the president's "extraordinary popularity." With Jackson squarely behind the policy, the public would be compelled to follow or abandon their venerated General. This strategy would be employed throughout his presidency to gain public support for a dramatic change in policy, leading one dissenter to complain about the "*strong measures* adopted solely on the ground of Gen. Jackson's personal popularity."[46]

When Van Buren raised the matter of internal improvements with Jackson, the president responded enthusiastically and gave him freedom to choose the battleground. Van Buren unquestionably received a free hand largely because he was one of the few men in the executive office who agreed with Jackson in this matter. The president's old friends, Eaton and Lewis, saw nothing amiss in federal appropriations, a position shared by fellow westerner Barry.[47] On the other hand, Kendall seemed a likely ally. He had criticized the "all absorbing system" of Adams and Clay for neglecting to consult with the states and for drawing to the administration "a new set of dependants of the richest and ablest men" who provided loans for the projects. He thought it safer, more economical, and more efficient for the states to act vigorously on their own resources and abandon visions of plundering the national treasury. But Kendall's enthusiasm for western settlement had once made him more favorably inclined to federal aid, and he was still disposed to support a general system of internal improvements if the dangers posed by federal authority to the states could be avoided. He, like Blair, could therefore be expected to follow the leadership of others on an issue which, after all, never engaged his attention the way the Bank did.[48] As for Branch and Berrien, both of whom had been outspoken critics of federal aid for internal improvements, they had sacrificed Jackson's confidence because of their zealous opposition to the Eatons.[49]

Jackson therefore turned to Van Buren to initiate a program more in keeping with his notions of republican government. "The people expected reform, retrenchment and economy in the administration of Government," he reminded Van Buren. "This was the cry from Maine to Louisiana, and instead of these the object of Congress, *it would seem*, is to make mine one of the most extravagant administrations since the commencement of the Government. This must not be; the Federal Constitution must be obeyed, State-rights preserved, our national debt *must be paid, direct taxes and loans avoided* and the Federal Union preserved. These are the objects I have in view, and regardless of all consequences, will carry into effect." [50]

As Van Buren looked over congressional legislation during the 1829–30 session, he selected the Maysville, Washington, Paris, and Lexington Turnpike Road bill as appropriate for Jackson's stand. It called upon the federal government to buy stock in a corporation to construct a road in Kentucky from Maysville to Lexington. Although not actually a part of the Cumberland Road system, its advocates claimed otherwise, and because the federal government had continually appropriated money for the national road, the measure's sponsor, Congressman Robert Letcher of Kentucky, introduced it in April 1830 as one which "would occupy but little time." [51]

Debate over the Maysville Road bill revealed a split within the Democratic party. Most of its opponents came from the South or border region. A North Carolina congressman declared that the federal government had no power whatsoever over internal improvements, while a Georgian thought the bill too local in character to merit federal support. On the other hand, western Democrats generally lined up behind the proposal. Dedicated Jacksonians like Edward Livingston, Richard M. Johnson, and Thomas Hart Benton voted for it.[52]

The most prominent exception among westerners was James K. Polk of Tennessee. Polk, though initially sympathetic to Calhoun, was not identified with either the Calhoun or Van Buren factions. He was, instead, a personal friend of Jackson whose agrarian bias for limited, plain, and economical government mirrored his patron's and gained him increasing prominence in the House and eventually, in 1835, the speakership. When the Maysville Road bill came before Congress, Polk announced his objections. Paying scant attention to constitutional issues, he damned the internal improvements system as a "lavish mode of expending the public money," which drained the treasury and prevented payment of the national debt. His views were obviously congenial to Jackson, who soon chose him to aid Van Buren in drafting a veto message. But however much he spoke Jackson's sentiments, Polk failed to sway a majority of western Jacksonians, and with their support and the backing of many Democrats in Pennsylvania and the Northwest, the measure passed both houses of Congress by early May 1830.[53]

Van Buren, however, thought the bill well suited to Jackson's purposes. Its local character, involving the connecting of two cities in a single state, made it a clear example of federal extravagance. That the road lay in Clay's home state and the senator was avidly pressing it only enhanced its attraction for a president who always preferred taking the battle to his enemy.[54]

Having made his selection, Van Buren consulted privately with Jackson on the veto message. It appears that only Polk aided in drafting the document, and few men knew the president's intentions. According to Van Buren, this secrecy was designed to prevent Congress from amending the bill to make it less local and, therefore, more ambiguous constitutionally. This was perhaps true, but their furtiveness was also politically motivated to permit Jackson's congressional supporters to pass the controversial Indian Removal act.[55]

Van Buren's was the major responsibility for articulating Jackson's reasoning, though the existence of notes in Jackson's handwriting shows that the product was more a collaborative effort than the performance of one man. Despite Ritchie's plea that the president "seize the whole ground with a decided grasp," the veto stopped somewhat short of a conclusive denial of federal power. While the message praised in the abstract what Jackson took to be the Madisonian principle that no federal money could be appropriated for projects not specifically enumerated in the Constitution, it affirmed as policy the more practicable compromise established by Monroe that Congress could appropriate money for "purposes of common defense, and of general, not local, national, not State, benefit." This was not, Jackson admitted, the "construction of the Constitution set up in 1798," but as on other occasions, he admitted the necessity of making some concessions to the conditions of the times. If "sleepless vigilance" were the price of constitutional purity, as he contended, it was the lesser evil to have your constitutional pocket picked when your eyes were open.[56]

The Maysville Road veto offered more than constitutional objections to the bill. It also recalled the United States' responsibility to perpetuate "the republican principle" by lightening public burdens and ending wasteful expenditures that perpetuated the national debt. It further warned of the deleterious consequences of an intimate connection between private enterprise and the public treasury. Permitting government to minister to personal ambition and private profit, the president cautioned, would "sap the foundations of public virtue and taint the administration of the Government with a demoralizing influence." Jackson, then, offered a compelling argument to advocates of internal improvements, especially in the West, warning that extravagant appropriations and large-scale government participation in the economy endangered pure, frugal, and equitable government. Declaring that advocates of internal improvements should look elsewhere for assistance, he stressed other public values in hopes of shifting priorities in a Jeffersonian direction.[57]

The Maysville Road veto did not completely satisfy nervous southerners. Virginia's Philip P. Barbour thought the president did not go far enough, and Thomas Ritchie agreed that the message did "not exactly come up to our Virginia Doctrines." But both men recognized that it reversed the nationalistic policies of the Adams administration and was therefore a significant step in returning the government to states' rights principles. "Our friends are . . . in high spirits for Gen. Jackson's Message," Ritchie boasted. "It does a great deal, by arresting corrupting local appropriations for the benefit of this and that sectional improvement. . . . The obligations we owe 'Old Hickory' for stepping in at this crisis & saving the Constitution almost at its last gasp are great indeed." As with Indian removal, the warm reception given the message in the South helped assure the administration continued support from there at a time when Jackson's dispute with Calhoun was reaching a crisis.[58]

However gratifying it may have been, the South's response was expected. It remained to be seen how the West and North would react. Van Buren himself had been apprehensive, and recognizing that even Jackson's popularity could not withstand a total repudiation of federal aid for internal improvements, he framed the message with a view to making it as palatable as possible. For this reason, Jackson reluctantly upheld the constitutionality of appropriations for national projects.[59]

The congressional reception indicated that a number of Democrats were willing to support the president once he announced his policy. Henry Daniel of Kentucky, an original proponent of the Maysville bill, explained to the House that he would support the veto to give the people an opportunity to consider Jackson's arguments. The president, he told the House, "was elected on the principle of economy and reform; and if the representatives of the people refuse him a proper support . . . it is impossible that the object for which he was elected can be obtained." On reconsideration, two other congressmen joined Daniel in switching their votes, while nine representatives who had voted with the majority abstained after Jackson indicated his policy. Having initially passed the House with 102 yeas and 86 nays, the tally after the veto stood at 96 to 90. In the Senate, the story was much the same, showing a distinct tightening of party lines.[60]

More important to Jackson was the veto's impact on the countryside. His political style was always to rely on the people to sway their representatives, and he had worked over the message with Van Buren to ensure its clarity and precision "so that the people may fully understand it." He had consciously and conspicuously reached out and seized the internal improvements question and, as the *Telegraph* announced, "placed his reputation" squarely behind his veto.[61]

Any assessment of the public's response, however, is hazardous. The Jacksonians lost some state elections in the North and West held in the aftermath of the veto, but this could well be attributed to the normal off-year decline in support for the party in power. It is also possible that the greatest dissatisfaction occurred in those areas of commercial dominance that were already unfriendly to Jackson.[62] On balance, the evidence indicates that the veto alienated some who in 1828 believed Jackson favorably inclined to internal improvements, and a number of prominent Democrats at the time thought it safest to ignore or oppose his decision. Secretary of the Treasury Ingham reflected the prevailing sentiment of his state and never supported it. Duff Green, perhaps fearing the loss of western support for the party and Calhoun, gave the veto only a lukewarm reception; and for some early Jackson men, like Ohio's William Stanbery, the veto was an influential consideration in their renouncing of support for the president.[63]

But the veto also seems to have attached more firmly to the party those who gave it support. New England's Isaac Hill thought the message had strengthened Jackson by consolidating party lines. "Old Hickory is completely identified with that Democracy in New England," he informed a political associate. "It is a division now as perfect as it was in Jefferson's time, between the Democracy and Federalism of the country." Van Buren agreed that the veto had given the Democrats a rallying point, and he reported to Jackson that New York felt "universal satisfaction" with the decision. "The same may be said of Pennsylvania and New Jersey. . . . The South looks better than it has done for years."[64]

In the West, especially in areas outside major transportation routes or in regions that had already received internal improvements aid, many Jacksonians responded favorably to the president's goal of ending logrolling and preserving a simple, republican government.[65] When Kendall, Barry, and Blair organized a Democratic nominating convention in Kentucky, they decided to take the offensive and provide a full endorsement of Jackson's principles. One participant reported that when resolutions were offered approving the veto, "the old grey heads, & furrowed faces seemed young again . . . the doctrines announced 'fell upon their ears like music of other days' . . . I could almost imagine that I was carried back by time to the days of Jefferson." In Tennessee, Felix Grundy, who had counseled Jackson to sign the Maysville bill, played down reports of Democratic defections and asserted that the veto's most important benefit was its clarification of party lines. "Altho your friends may not be numerically increased," he bravely conceded, "their attachment is now of a stronger texture. Formerly, it consisted in a degree of affection for the man and an admiration of his character & public services and confidence in his virtues. Now is added, an adherence to political republican principles."[66]

Jackson took heart at such expressions of support. Indeed he welcomed and encouraged the partisan division that resulted from his veto. "The line, it is said, has been fairly drew [*sic*]," he announced after issuing the message. "My veto upon the Maysville bill [is] the theme of the opposition and . . . where it has lost me one, it has gained me five friends." When Blair began the Washington *Globe*, he helped keep the line distinct by informing the party's followers of the need to preserve republican simplicity. The *Globe* applauded the principles of the veto as a means of eliminating petty projects that corrupted republican government and obstructed natural channels of trade, leaving Duff Green to protest attempts to make support of Jackson's action an "*exclusive* test of party loyalty." [67]

The Maysville Road veto thus identified the Democratic party with the limiting of federal power over internal improvements. In the coming years Jackson and Van Buren intensified their assault on the internal improvements system, further refining the permissible bounds of federal activity and cautioning against measures that entailed "unnecessary expense" or investments in private corporations. Jackson even attempted to establish limits on federal appropriations for lighthouses and harbor improvements, an area in which even the most doctrinaire states' rights advocate admitted federal responsibility. At the same time, he gradually abandoned his early guarded recommendation to distribute surplus revenue to the states, a proposal which had promised indirect but considerable federal assistance. [68]

Although Jackson frequently sweetened the pill for his western supporters by approving such expenditures as he deemed in the national interest, and thereby incurred the displeasure of his southern following, his general line of policy contrasted markedly with that of Adams. Nowhere in his messages can be found a plea to Congress to undertake new responsibilities. Instead, he consistently stressed the constitutional and pragmatic limitations to federal spending, ever striving to convince his western supporters that the improvements they desired would entail unwanted and excessive taxation. [69]

Jackson's performance forged a bond between Van Buren's followers, particularly in the South, and the Democratic party. But equally noteworthy was his accomplishment in eliciting support from westerners like Blair and Kendall. Kendall drafted a party platform for the coming election of 1832, which extolled "simple and cheap" government and called for lowered taxes to support government only "in the performance of its legitimate functions." As a frequent contributor to the *Globe*, he also helped counter the desire for federally aided developmental projects by associating the values of individual industry, morality, and equity with limited government principles. Positive and active government, he warned, ceased to be merely a protector of man's rights and became an instrument to aid some men over others. Government's object, he declared, "is not to make a few men *great*, but all *happy*." If the federal government were left to the simple task of carrying out only its enumerated powers, "industry would be carried, by the labor and skill of individuals, to the highest degree of perfection. . . . For his standing and wealth, each man would rely on his own integrity and industry." [70]

The conduct of Jackson's western advisers demonstrated that a program based on circumscribing government activity, while not necessarily the dominant political tendency of their section, could draw upon persistent Jeffersonian values. Coming at a time when the states were increasingly undertaking responsibility for internal improvements, Jackson's arguments found a more receptive audience than the view of the West as unvarying in its devotion to extensive federal assistance would have led one to expect. [71]

While Jackson leaned most heavily on Van Buren in formulating an approach to internal improvements, the energy behind his bank policy came from his western advisers, especially Blair and Kendall. And since it was Jackson's banking and currency battles that most vividly imprinted on the Democratic party its distinctive values and beliefs, the West must therefore be credited with having made a special contribution to Jacksonianism. The rise of these Kentucky advisers did not mean that Van Buren lost any of the confidence he had gained during the first two years of Jackson's presidency. Letters exchanged between the two men indicate that both retained their mutual affection. Nevertheless when Van Buren returned from England in July 1832, he had to share with Kendall and Blair the power and distinction of being Jackson's closest adviser. [72]

Jackson's own hostility to the Bank of the United States derived from his suspicion of all banks. He knew from personal experience the potential risks of deviating from hard-money orthodoxy, having once been brought to the brink of insolvency by speculative adventures. Possibly his aversion to paper-money banking can be attributed to the psychology of self-reproach, but one must also acknowledge the effect of a persistent western agrarian suspicion of banks.[73] In any case, by the 1820s, he opposed economic activity associated with speculation or get-rich-quick schemes, and considered the paper inflation of state banks during the 1820s unconstitutional, dishonest, and demoralizing. He predicted it would take Kentucky twenty years to recover from the "new fangled projects of wild speculators and unsound politicians." Years later, when he was president and his opponents tried to prove he had once supported the Bank, Jackson hotly denied the charge. "I have been opposed always to the Bank of the U.S. as well as all state Banks of paper issues, upon constitutional ground," he insisted.[74]

Jackson's thinking about banks, and the Bank of the United States in particular, placed him in opposition to many of his close political associates. Eaton and Lewis, as members of the Blount-Overton faction, were economic conservatives who had been involved in Tennessee's state banking system and were now increasingly interested in the Nashville branch of the Bank of the United States. Disagreeing sharply with Jackson on financial matters, they tried to prevent him from attacking the Bank. It was probably they who convinced him to omit a reference to the Bank from his inaugural address.[75]

Indeed, Jackson's first cabinet contained no one who thought it wise to criticize the Bank in 1829. Ingham and Berrien were both strong friends of the Bank, and even those who were hostile to recharter thought the Bank question should be ignored in the president's first annual message.[76]

That Van Buren was among those who advised against an early assault on the Bank controverts the influential notion that he was the agent of its demise. He was indeed the Bank's foe, just as he was the enemy of irresponsible state institutions, but his animus was neutralized by weighty considerations. As recent scholarship has shown, the Bank under Biddle's direction had increasingly become the recipient of public favor not only in the West and South, where it often provided a large portion of the circulating medium, but even in Van Buren's own state, where there was little enthusiasm for unsettling

well-established and profitable relationships with state institutions.
The Bank's strong position cautioned the ambitious Van Buren against
provoking a conflict, as did the widely held, though erroneous, opinion that New York bankers were determined to wrest control of the
nation's finances from Philadelphia. To attack the Bank would leave
Van Buren open to charges of serving petty local interests.[77]

Even Van Buren's southern friends, to whose wishes he was always
sensitive, had ambivalent attitudes about the Bank. Ritchie had edito-
rially denounced it and John Marshall's decision upholding its constitutionality, and his fellow Virginian Andrew Stevenson echoed
Jefferson's prediction that a national bank would "in time overthrow
the liberties of the Country." Yet the intensity of their opposition was
offset somewhat by their fear that precipitate action would disrupt
orderly government and ruin Virginia's stable banking system. Years
later, Van Buren reminisced about how his anxious southern followers
"were kept in constant apprehension" that Jackson would "through
passion or ill advisement, commit some rash act." He also recalled that
at the time of the Bank veto, Ritchie "scarcely ever went to bed . . .
without apprehension that he would wake up to hear of some *coup
d'etat* by the General, which he would be called on to explain or
defend." [78]

Van Buren's delicate situation made him an unlikely orchestrator of
a challenge to the Bank, and Biddle was by no means certain of his
enmity. From some informants Biddle heard that Van Buren and the
New York Democrats were determined to destroy his institution; but
he also learned, sometimes from these same sources, that Van Buren
had nothing to do with Jackson's public criticism of the Bank and that
blame should be placed on "a mania in the West against the present
Bank. . . ." Only after the Bank War waxed hot did Biddle erroneously
conclude that Van Buren was the sole cause of his troubles.[79]

Rather than on Van Buren, Biddle should have focused attention on
Jackson and his Kentucky aides, Kendall and Blair. The personal inclination of the president to seize the initiative was whetted by rumors
of Bank influence during the presidential campaign. He therefore resolved to stimulate public debate before the Bank could secure an
overwhelming majority in Congress favoring recharter. Despite
promptings by Lewis, Van Buren, and James A. Hamilton to exclude

references to the Bank in his first annual message, Jackson persisted. "Oh! My friend, I am pledged against the bank," he explained to Hamilton.[80]

Jackson does not seem to have confided in Kendall his opposition to the Bank until the fall of 1829, but when he did, Kendall enthusiastically enlisted for the duration of the Bank War. Although the Bank's reputation had improved considerably in Kentucky and the West, Kendall's opinion had not changed. His motto remained "*'Delenda est Carthago.'*"[81] Kendall apparently helped write an early version of the Bank section for Jackson's presidential message of December 1829. When James A. Hamilton arrived in Washington in November, he found a rough draft that attacked the Bank "in a loose, newspaper, slashing style," and Kendall was the only person with journalistic experience involved in constructing Jackson's message. The auditor was certainly responsible for informing the New York *Courier & Enquirer* of the impending attack, and the paper's editor placed Kendall's note on the editorial page. By the spring of 1830, Jackson was calling upon him to write essays for the *Telegraph* criticizing McDuffie's favorable report on the Bank, and Kendall was claiming that there would be no compromise on this question. "Whoever is in favor of the Bank will be against Old Hickory," he predicted to Blair.[82]

When Blair arrived in Washington in December 1830, Kendall and Jackson had another efficient friend in their camp. Indeed, Blair's long-standing opposition to the Bank was a major consideration in Jackson's decision to ask him to replace Duff Green, and the new editor quickly familiarized the party with his anti-Bank ideas. His denunciations of Biddle's "banking monopoly" heartened those Jacksonians who had despaired when Green failed to attack the Bank. Isaac Hill applauded the *Globe*'s position, and Kendall reported in the summer of 1831 that the paper "gives the U.S. Bank no rest. I am more sanguine than ever, that we shall prostrate that strong hold of aristocratic power." Blair's provocative course did not please everyone in the White House. Lewis, for example, pleaded with him to cease "initiating subjects which divide *our friends*." But Blair had Jackson's complete endorsement for his attacks and never let up. Along with Kendall, Blair provided the president with the energy and zeal of the relief cause and, as Blair later recalled, helped identify "the policy of that Administration somewhat with that which characterized the canvass in [Kentucky]."[83]

When Jackson questioned "both the constitutionality and the expediency" of the Bank in his first annual message, he stunned Biddle, who had miscalculated both the direction and force of the president's views. Having relied upon Lewis's assurances that the president supported the Bank, Biddle had attempted to win favor with the new administration by appointing Jackson men to various branch offices. But while changes of personnel may have placated those like Lewis who sought to forge closer ties with the Bank, they did nothing to change the opinions of confirmed anti-Bank men. Biddle's concessions, therefore, did not stay Jackson's attack, and throughout 1830, while Biddle worked with Congress to publicize the Bank's sound condition, the president continued to denounce the "few Monied Capitalists" who profited from its transactions. He thought any new national bank must be so organized that its profits inured to the whole country and its procedures protected the rights of the states.[84]

Shortly after his arrival in Washington, Blair helped formulate more precisely Jackson's thinking. Expressing a deep appreciation of the advantages of decentralized authority in a pluralistic society, Blair drafted an outline of a banking system that would "partake of the nature of our Institutions . . . that the checks & balances thus produced, may protect against the tyranny which there is reason to apprehend from an Establishment, holding an absolute control over the currency." Without conceding the necessity for a national banking system, Blair thought the safest arrangement would consist of a national bank in the District of Columbia working with state banks chartered for this purpose. In order to prevent a flood of paper from the state banks, he insisted on guarantees that the government revenue would be safe and that the currency would be "every where redeemable in specie."[85]

Blair's ideas closely paralleled those in Jackson's annual message of December 1830. The president reiterated his apprehensions about the "dangers" of the Bank "as at present organized," and proposed as an alternative a national bank which would be an adjunct of the Treasury Department and which would work in conjunction with state banks to ensure a currency equivalent to specie. Before submitting his Bank statement to Congress, Jackson had forwarded it for Van Buren's appraisal, but the manuscript sources indicate that the New Yorker had nothing more to do with Jackson's early banking policy. Jackson's decision to press his campaign against the Bank was his own, and only his Kentucky advisers, Blair and Kendall, aided him to any appreciable extent.[86] Their efforts derived from a hard-money, states' rights outlook, though their implicit pledge to utilize state banks attracted portions of the banking and commercial community to their cause.

Jackson's message of 1830 greatly disturbed Biddle. The Bank's chief had rationalized the president's first statement as a personal rather than administration or party expression. But he correctly interpreted this second attack as evidence that Jackson would make the Bank's destruction an article of party faith. He fully concurred with his informants that the Bank would "now be made an administration question" and that "the president's name and authority will be wielded against" the Bank by all "its enemies."[87]

The gloom that settled over Bank partisans in December, however, seemed to lift when the cabinet reorganization of April 1831 brought into office some prominent Bank sympathizers. The new secretary of the treasury, Louis McLane, a former Federalist who had not completely disavowed the party's latitudinarian ideas or its admiration of good breeding, character, and manners, responded to Jackson's anti-Bank remarks with noticeable coolness. He belittled the president's constitutional scruples and thought the charter could be amended so as to increase the government's power over its operations. McLane's inflated ambition for high office, including the presidency, also made him wary of engaging in a cause which would disorganize the party and stir opposition to the administration. Biddle, upon hearing of McLane's appointment, referred to him as "a known friend" of the Bank.[88]

The Bank also gained by Edward Livingston's replacement of Van Buren in the State Department. Van Buren had been hesitant to identify himself with anti-Bank activity, but once Jackson made clear his determination to prevent recharter, Van Buren's political philosophy and his need to retain Jackson's affection brought him to the president's side. Livingston, however, was a Bank partisan whose efforts to secure recharter were so conspicuous that he embarrassed both himself and Van Buren, who was primarily responsible for his appointment.[89]

Although McLane and Livingston were the most zealous Bank proponents, they received some support from other members of the executive office. Lewis Cass, the new secretary of war, was disposed to continue the Bank, while both Levi Woodbury, Branch's replacement in the Navy Department, and Andrew Jackson Donelson were wary of arousing the ire of the Bank and its formidable knot of supporters.[90]

In the new cabinet, only Barry and Roger Taney supported the president, and Barry, having once had an extensive legal association with the institution, lacked the firmness of his fellow relief friends, Kendall and Blair. Some political observers thought Barry could be rallied to the Bank's cause, but most simply discounted his influence on Jackson. The president himself seemed to rely on him only for the kind of personal fellowship that Eaton had formerly provided.[91]

However, Taney, who had noticeable states' rights leanings, was strongly against the Bank. The new attorney general never seems to have forgiven it for its unsound inflationary activity during its early years or the corruption of some of its officers in the Baltimore branch. His own ties with state banks in Maryland probably buttressed these objections, but in any case, he considered the Bank's influence and power inimical to republican government. His firmness surprised some Jacksonians. Cambreleng, noting the preponderance of pro-Bank men in the cabinet, informed Van Buren that "strange as it may seem," Taney was the best democrat among them. Yet he was little known to Jackson at this time, attended cabinet meetings only occasionally, and was rarely consulted on banking matters during Jackson's first term. Only with the removal controversy would Taney's influence soar.[92]

Since Jackson knew from experience the vexation that disgruntled officers could cause, one must assume that he probably did not realize how divisive the Bank issue would become when he formed the cabinet. As long as his confrontation with Biddle lay dormant, as it did during the congressional recess of the summer and fall of 1831, Jackson retained a "high opinion . . . of the talents and worth" of his cabinet. But soon after the commencement of the 1831–32 congressional session, he became annoyed at its pro-Bank members. He complained about "the little Federal leaven" in McLane and criticized the personal judgment of Livingston and Cass.[93]

Jackson's grumbling must have been related to the difficulties he was now having with his Bank policy. McLane and Livingston, after secretly conferring with Biddle, were suggesting that the president now leave the subject of the Bank in the hands of Congress. And McLane had informed the president that he would use his Treasury report to speak "in a most favorable manner" about the need to recharter the present Bank, "with such modifications as without injuring the institution might be useful to the country and acceptable to the Executive." [94]

Jackson's anti-Bank advisers, however, were equally adamant that the President continue to apply pressure. Kendall drafted a statement for the annual message of 1831 assailing the institution, while Blair's assaults in the *Globe* elicited McLane's complaint that the paper was "an unfit organ for the adm[inistration]." They were joined by Taney, who warned Jackson that the course advised by McLane and Livingston would indicate to the country that he had changed his mind about the Bank.[95]

For reasons which have never been convincingly identified, Jackson showed a remarkable leniency towards McLane and Livingston. He initially raised no objection to McLane's intentions and agreed, "tho' reluctantly," to the two men's request that he refrain from attacking the Bank in his message. In response to Taney's complaint, Jackson agreed to revise the Bank section, removing any implication that he disclaimed his previous position. But the statement still lacked vigor. While affirming his misgivings about the Bank "as at present organized," he refused to ask Congress to begin making arrangements for the government's financial operations after the Bank's demise. Instead, he ambiguously left the whole subject "to the investigation of an enlightened people and their representatives." Taney was still not pleased.[96]

Jackson's moderation may have resulted from the recognition that his own bank proposal had received little support and that the Bank issue would best be left until after the coming presidential election. Whatever his reasons, it is evident that he had no intention of compromising his opposition to the present Bank. He assured one anti-

Bank Virginian that he still considered the Bank unconstitutional and inexpedient, and he explained away McLane's report as merely expressing a belief that a charter "might" be so constituted as to avoid his objections. Lewis, whose pro-Bank thinking made him a close friend of McLane, knew that Jackson had not changed his views. "Let the question rest until after the next presidential election," he begged one newspaper editor. "I advise this course . . . as a friend to the Bank itself." [97]

Nevertheless, Jackson's indulgence of McLane rankled the president's inner circle. To be sure, the Treasury secretary took pains to disassociate the president from his praise of the Bank, and he qualified his approval of recharter by endorsing it only "at the proper time" and with modifications. But it looked as though the administration had given way to the Bank's influence. Van Buren hoped that the Treasury report would "produce no permanent injury," but he was plainly embarrassed at McLane's regrettable behavior. Blair reacted more sharply. Seeking to undercut the impact of McLane's report, he explained that the secretary spoke only for himself, and that his views differed from "those heretofore expressed by the President and which it is clear are still entertained by him." Blair also expressed his own "dissent from the doctrines of the Report," and promised to continue his discussions of the Bank.[98]

Stung by Blair's barbs, McLane attempted to organize a coup to depose the editor. He found support for his intrigue among some prominent Van Burenites, who regarded Blair as too independent of their leader. In particular, they believed that Blair was not joining wholeheartedly in the movement to elevate Van Buren to the vice-presidency after the Senate rejected his appointment to Britain. McLane himself intimated to Van Buren that Blair's attacks on his report were designed to discredit Van Buren's friends in the cabinet; and the New York politicos Cambreleng, Jesse Hoyt, and James Watson Webb, sharing the secretary's distrust of Blair, gathered in Washington early in February 1832 for a caucus with cabinet members to discuss the possibility of replacing Blair with Kendall. It was thought that Kendall would edit "a more efficient" Van Buren press.[99]

McLane's basic concern, however, was not Van Buren's political future, but Blair's anti-Bank policy. The latter's son, Montgomery, who learned of the incident soon after its conclusion, later recorded that the "intrigue" was inspired by McLane with the connivance of other "Bank men" like Cass to replace Blair with "an Editor . . . who would be less obnoxious to the Bank party." McLane's idea of replacing Blair with Kendall was probably a pretext for the elimination of Blair, after which a pro-Bank editor such as New York's Mordecai Noah would take over the *Globe*.[100]

McLane's intrigue, which coincided with a period of financial difficulties for the *Globe*, led Blair to contemplate resigning his position in exchange for another office from Jackson. While the old assumptions of political status had eroded, they still exerted some force, and Blair was uncomfortable about antagonizing established political leaders of higher official position. Perhaps fearful that Jackson would abandon him rather than challenge his official council, Blair delivered a message to the cabinet proposing his resignation. Suddenly, however, the plot collapsed. Although Montgomery Blair's narrative with its garbled chronology does not indicate exactly how the intrigue was exposed, when Jackson learned of Blair's action, he resolutely stood behind the editor and requested that he remain at his post. "I had no temporizing policy in me and urged you on in your course," Jackson recalled to Blair years after the incident.[101]

McLane's maneuver is less significant for its consequences than for the insights it yields into the power relationships of Jackson's White House. Blair continued as editor, and McLane was soon promoted to the more prestigious cabinet post of secretary of state. Jackson may never have learned the full story of McLane's activity; he may have decided to overlook it rather than expend more energy in reorganizing an institution that he scarcely relied on for policy. But the episode reveals how the pro-Bank elements in the party feared Blair's influence with Jackson and his vigorous prosecution of the Bank War. It indicates, too, the distance that separated Blair from Van Buren, for this was only the first of a series of incidents in which Van Buren partisans rubbed against Blair and sought to undermine his key position in the Kitchen Cabinet.

Above all, the proceedings demonstrated Blair's special position in the administration. Jackson's use of confidential advisers like Blair inevitably generated tensions with more conservative cabinet members. Yet Jackson stood by his editor, at one point even reminding resistant secretaries like Livingston of the need to provide the *Globe* with public printing.[102] In the case of the McLane intrigue, Jackson's refusal to muzzle Blair was especially noteworthy. Coming at a time when many anti-Bank Democrats feared Jackson was losing his zeal for the campaign, Blair's continuing editorial thrusts indicated to perceptive observers that the president was by no means determined to recharter the Bank. Biddle, for example, cast a worried look over the *Globe*, and the editorials shook his confidence that Jackson would approve recharter under conditions that would allow the Bank to function as usual.[103]

The Bank's formal application for a new charter in January 1832 suddenly changed the context of debate. Its immediate consequence for the White House was to strengthen the hand of Blair, Kendall, and Taney against the pro-Bank cabinet members and their satellites like Lewis, who were forced to concede that Biddle had made the Bank a political issue. Only Livingston continued to plead the Bank's case, as he struggled without success to effect a compromise between Jackson and Biddle.[104]

Yet the apparent unity in the executive office masked a deep schism, the point in dispute being how strong to make the veto. The Bank's supporters wanted Jackson to hand down what Taney called "a milk & water & half way veto," which would not preclude the administration's approving a recharter bill at another time. Their commitment to a national bank was so strong that they refused to assist Jackson in preparing a veto message if he should make his opposition to the Bank conclusive.[105] This vehemence disquieted but did not dissuade Jackson, who in mid-June impatiently awaited Van Buren's return from England. He wanted the New Yorker's moral support, and in early July after Congress passed the Bank bill, Van Buren rushed to Washington to offer reassurances about the need for a veto. But Van Buren did not compose the message. That document was largely Kendall's doing.[106]

Although Taney, Woodbury, and Donelson refined and polished its contents, it was Kendall who was responsible for the substance and style of the Bank veto. Taney later recalled that Jackson had "regretted the necessity of calling for the aid of any person out of his cabinet on such an occasion," but with Taney temporarily out of town and most of the cabinet refusing to assist, Jackson "placed his decision and his reasons for it in the hands of Mr. Kendall whose opinions coincided with his own." The veto itself rang with the rhetoric of the Kentucky relief wars, and echoing arguments that Kendall had leveled against the Bank a decade before, it pronounced the institution a private, privileged corporation which exercised inordinate power over the foreign and domestic exchange, drained the West of specie, and was impervious to state taxation. The Bank's special privileges were neither necessary nor proper for the government, and therefore constituted an unconstitutional extension of federal authority and an invasion of "rights scrupulously reserved to the States." [107]

The message urged Americans to rely on themselves rather than to seek favors from the government. The "true strength" of government, it argued, "consists in leaving individuals and States as much as possible to themselves—in making itself felt, not in its power, but in its beneficence; not in its control, but in its protection; not in binding the States more closely to the center, but leaving each to move unobstructed in its proper orbit." Government, then, should confine itself "to equal protection, and, as Heaven does its rains, shower its favors alike on the high and the low, the rich and the poor." But the Bank bill violated these precepts by having government add "artificial distinctions" to natural and just differences among men, thereby making "the rich richer and the potent more powerful." [108]

Jackson and Kendall pitched their appeal to those they called "the humble members of society—the farmers, mechanics, and laborers" who suffered when "the rich and powerful" employed their position as a lever to gain further advantages. Although couched in language implying class conflict between the rich and the poor, their concern was not inequality but special privilege, monopoly, and the abuse of government powers. The rivalry of sections, interests, and people for special consideration constituted a deviation from the intentions of the Revolutionary heroes and Founding Fathers and jeopardized republican government and the Union. [109]

The Bank veto cleverly skirted the issue of replacing the present Bank. Jackson's followers exhibited a great diversity of opinions on banking and currency, ranging from inflationists who hoped the Bank's demise would release the economic energy of state institutions, to hard-money and antibank elements who suspected all banks and wanted only gold and silver as a circulating medium. The veto did not specifically declare in whose name the Bank was to be sacrificed.

Instead it spoke to the fears of those Americans who perceived the national bank's powers as a threat to their liberties, and it spoke to their hopes that the destruction of the Bank would enable each person to "enjoy an opportunity to profit from our bounty."[110]

At various points, however, the message touched upon the general suspicion of note-issuing banks which inspired Jackson and Kendall. Unlike the original charter, the new one permitted state banks to return the Bank's notes at any branch office. Jackson declared this an injustice to private citizens who did not have the same privilege, and playing upon latent misgivings about banks which had been re-kindled during the depression of the 1820s, he warned that it would create "a bond of union among the banking establishments of the nation, erecting them into an interest separate from that of the people." The message also made reference to Jackson's belief that "the only currency known to the Constitution" consisted of the specie coined by mints and the foreign coins whose value Congress regulated. But these paragraphs appeared as diversions from the major thrust of the argument—the dangers presented by Biddle's institution. Since Jackson and his advisers had not yet developed an alternative to the Bank, they focused on its transgressions.[111]

Like the Maysville Road veto, the Bank statement tapped an emotional attachment to fundamental values associated with America's republican mission. It offered a choice between Biddle and Clay, the status quo, special privilege, and monopoly on the one hand, and Jackson, equal opportunity, self-reliance, and limited government on the other. Some politicians thought the veto was in bad taste. Alexander Everett of Massachusetts asserted that "for the first time, perhaps, in the history of civilized communities, the Chief Magistrate of a great nation . . . is found appealing to the worst passions of the uninformed part of the people, and endeavoring to stir up the poor against the rich." And Clay's organ, the National Intelligencer, pointed to Kendall as the responsible party and damned his presentation as "the very slang of the leveller and demagogue." But Jackson was confident that the veto would build pressure from below to force hesitant politicians into line. Blair encouraged this development by identifying it with allegiance to Jackson and the party. The message, he declared, was "but a transcript of the President's own mind," and Jackson took full responsibility for it. He denounced as traitors those who refused to support its principles, while welcoming into the fold those who deserted Clay and the Bank.[112]

It is difficult to measure the effect of the Bank veto on the Democratic party's constituency. A variety of complex influences determine voter behavior, and without the aid of public opinion polls historians must be satisfied with incomplete data. The standard electoral returns for the presidential election of 1832 show that Jackson's majority increased slightly over that of four years earlier, from 56.0 percent of the popular vote in 1828 to 56.5 percent in 1832. But this data is unreliable and according to Robert V. Remini's recalculation, Jackson's majority dipped slightly in 1832, making him the only president in American history to register such a decline. It is also probable that a large majority of states recorded decreased levels of participation by eligible adult white males compared to the election of 1828, indicating that the veto was not sufficiently controversial to attract larger percentages of the available electorate to the polls.[113]

Yet there are also indications that the veto strengthened the Jacksonians in many areas of the country. Jackson's portion of the total vote either increased or remained the same in eighteen of the twenty-one states for which there is relevant data, indicating that outside of Pennsylvania, where the veto hurt Jackson severely, the defection of pro-Bank men was generally balanced by new voters or apathy on the part of the opposition.[114] What little damage the veto may have done was not, therefore, general. According to William Barry, if the veto hurt Jackson in areas where the Bank was popular, it strengthened him in those areas where his following was enthusiastic about attacking a monopolistic institution. As Duff Green ruefully acknowledged, while some thought the veto would injure Jackson, "the kitchen cabinet *knew* better." [115]

Many Jacksonians, of course, gave the veto only grudging support. Pennsylvania's Senator George M. Dallas expressed "fears and doubts" about the veto's principles, and Louis McLane never fully endorsed Jackson's decision. But it was unmistakably clear even to them that Jackson considered the veto a fundamental part of the party's program and ideology, and that he expected his followers to rally behind it. The veto did not always elicit enthusiasm from Jacksonians, but many must have found themselves in Dallas's position, reluctantly supporting it out of loyalty to Jackson and the party. "As to the Bank, let that go," Dallas decided. "We ought to have it but we can do without it." [116]

Largely as a result of the work of Jackson, Van Buren, Kendall, and Blair, the Democratic party had by the election of 1832 considerably refined its program, ideology, and constituency from what they had been in 1828. Jackson's second term would bring further clarification, but the administration had already demonstrated its commitment to revitalizing Jeffersonian principles. To be sure, Democrats within the states sometimes went their own way, but even they generally had to make concessions to decisions emanating from Washington.

This Democratic philosophy was best summarized in Kendall's "Address from the Central Hickory Club (of Washington) to the Republican Citizens of the United States," a document intended as the party's platform for the 1832 election. The address broadcast the party's adherence to the still venerated republican and Jeffersonian concept that liberty was best maintained by circumscribing governmental power. Viewing government as a necessary but regrettable institution, the address claimed that no government could make man "*more free*"; instead, its only legitimate object was "to *protect him in the enjoyment of his freedom.*" Government, it continued, "is to *keep off evil*. We do not want its assistance in seeking after good." Even if rulers acted with the best of intentions and undertook to promote human happiness, they would infringe on personal freedom and risk tyranny and oppression. "He is as much a slave who is forced to his own good, as he who is unwillingly plunged into evil," Kendall asserted. The address reaffirmed traditional Jeffersonian notions about safeguarding the rights of the states, but its emphasis was on the dangers of excessive government to individual liberty and initiative.[117]

The address was not simply a stale and reflexive rendering of outmoded principles; rather, it had a vitality that attested to its grounding in contemporary needs. Jacksonian America was a society increasingly involved in the marketplace, and accelerated economic growth was evident in indices of manufacturing, banking, urbanization, agricultural production, transportation improvements, and other aspects of modernization.[118] Yet these developments did not occur uniformly, and a careful observer readily appreciated the country's diversified, fragmented, and pluralistic qualities. The United States was a patchwork of sections, interests, and people pursuing divergent objectives, at different paces, in different ways. How could one govern such a nation? How could a republican government based upon the people's virtue be preserved when so many things were undergoing change? The Democratic party's answer was to let the country govern itself as much as possible, taking care only that one man's liberty not infringe on another man's rights. "Our confederacy is *unity in plurality*," delcared the *Globe*. While National Republicans and Whigs sought to impose uniformity by endorsing a coherent national program of tariffs, banking, and internal improvements, and by emphasizing values of social and class homogeneity, the Democrats asked, "How long would our Union last, if the people of Massachusetts had a right to legislate for the slaves of Virginia, or if the planters of Virginia had a right to legislate over the small farmers of Massachusetts?" To Democratic policy makers, power was safer if dispersed throughout the political system.[119]

In affirming decentralization and diversity, Jackson and his advisers advanced a philosophy that proved compelling to disparate groups and interests. Southern planters who believed that broadened federal authority picked their pockets to benefit the North and might, if extended far enough, ultimately threaten slavery, rallied to Jackson as a means of restoring respect for states' rights. So too did many northerners and westerners who never benefited from internal improvements projects and who regarded extensive federal spending as a financial burden at best and a conspiracy to aid privileged interests at worst. That the construction of some road or canal might compete with their own trade routes, or transfer authority from local agencies, which were closer to the people, to the more remote federal government, constituted additional reasons for responding to Jackson's appeal.

In some places, the party's emphasis on greater self-reliance and hostility to monopoly and special privilege proved particularly attractive to the less affluent or to certain ethnocultural groups, like the Irish Catholics, who found its doctrines congenial to their own customs and beliefs.[120] But the same ideas also gained adherents among energetic men-on-the-make who sought to break down established interests and open new avenues to wealth. The Boston merchant and Democratic politico, David Henshaw, for example, avidly supported a war against Biddle, but wanted to replace the Bank with another and larger one.[121]

While Democratic ideals spoke to wide elements of American society, they were primarily intended as a moral appeal to planters,
farmers, and mechanics who constituted the bulk of the population
and upon whose virtue republican government depended. These
were the "honest and upright" men, in Kendall's words, who asked
"for no advantage over others," while insisting "that others shall have
no advantage" over them.[122] Like republican ideologues of the Revolutionary period, Jackson assumed that the foundation of republican
government lay in the virtue of the people, and his determination to
restore to government the principles of '98 was predicated on the
assumption that "whatever demoralizes the people, must tend to
destroy Institutions founded solely upon their virtue." Whereas
Whigs were inclined to admire communal authority and social
homogeneity, Democrats relied on individual morality and virtue as
the adhesive to bind society together, and they claimed that the bond
was strongest when government was limited. Many historians have
stressed the high moral tone of the Whig party, but few have recognized the essential moral underpinning of the Jacksonian appeal.[123]

5
Van Buren for Vice-President

The Democratic party's first national convention, which met in Baltimore in the spring of 1832, has received little attention from students of Jacksonian politics. For those who interpret the conflict in the early days of Jackson's presidency simply as being a contest between Van Buren and Calhoun, or who perceive the Kitchen Cabinet as Van Buren's personal instrument, the nomination of Van Buren as Jackson's running mate seems a foregone conclusion and the convention merits consideration primarily for what it reveals about the party's institutional development. Indeed, the organizational implications of the Baltimore convention were significant; however, it is also evident that from the perspective of the White House, where a division into Van Buren and western factions was already evident over policy matters, the New Yorker's selection in Baltimore was not so inevitable.

The call for a Democratic national convention was largely inspired by practical problems concerning the vice-presidency. Jackson's split with Calhoun apparently left the office vacant for the president's second term, but party leaders recognized that the Constitution still permitted Calhoun, or one of his associates, to steal into it. To be sure, the vice-presidency might not be pleasant under these circumstances, but as head of the Senate and vice-president of the United States upon his own standing, a Calhounite could prove vexatious to Jackson's program. The sanction of party loyalty could clearly help prevent this development. Democrats throughout the country must know and unite behind the man Jackson and the party wanted for vice-president.

In the spring of 1831, Calhoun's intentions remained a mystery, but it was widely believed that he would either challenge Jackson for the presidency or, more likely, seek reelection as vice-president. In April, Duff Green asked Virginia's Governor John Floyd to begin a movement to retain Calhoun as Jackson's running mate, and in the following month, Lewis and Kendall learned that Green had urged party leaders in Massachusetts and Connecticut to do the same.[1]

In addition to the possibility that Calhoun would foist himself on the party, there was also the problem of choosing a substitute. Jackson preferred Van Buren, and in the summer of 1831, he even hinted to the New Yorker that if they were elected, he would step down from the presidency once the national debt was eliminated and leave Van Buren as his successor. However, Jackson soon abandoned this fanciful scheme and suggested instead that Van Buren return from England after two years to become secretary of state again.[2]

Jackson's change of heart was dictated by Van Buren's reluctance to accept the vice-presidency. The New Yorker's aversion had little to do with modesty, for he was politically ambitious and had accepted a foreign mission with great reluctance, fearing that his leaving the country for even a few years would jeopardize his future. But Van Buren was also a realist, and he recognized that a vice-presidential movement in his behalf would enhance his reputation as a political Machiavellian, perhaps ruining his presidential prospects forever. He had resigned from the cabinet, alleging as his motive the need to preserve the party and the administration from factional warfare. If he then became Jackson's running mate, he would be open to the charge of having resigned only to advance himself. Thomas Ritchie in fact had already warned him that in such a case Virginia Democrats would never support him. However alluring the prospect of associating with Jackson, then, Van Buren acknowledged the dangers by informing his friends that he was not available.[3]

In the spring of 1831, most Democrats assumed that Van Buren was out of the running and a large number of party leaders expressed interest in the vice-presidency, including Virginia's William C. Rives and Philip P. Barbour, Georgia's John Forsyth, Delaware's Louis McLane, New Jersey's Mahlon Dickerson, Kentucky's Richard M. Johnson, and Pennsylvania's William Wilkins. The possibility of factional discord was manifest, and in May, when Kendall on a visit to New England learned that Duff Green had been working with some success to promote Calhoun's reelection as vice-president, he advised William B. Lewis that the situation had reached a critical point and "ought to have our immediate attention." Having already discussed the issue with Isaac Hill, whose opinions on New England politics both he and the president valued highly, Kendall tentatively suggested Barbour as the candidate most likely to secure the support of northern and southern Democrats. He asked Lewis whether the New Hampshire Democratic party should nominate or recommend Barbour at the next legislative session.[4]

After receiving Kendall's letter, Lewis conferred with his friends, undoubtedly including Jackson and Blair, and suggested that Kendall and Hill have the New Hampshire Democrats call for a national convention. The selection of a vice-presidential candidate satisfactory to all sections would be very difficult, Lewis admitted, and Barbour's antitariff views while acceptable to the South would not win votes in New York or Pennsylvania. Lewis, therefore, recommended that "the Republican members of the respective Legislatures . . . propose to the people to elect delegates to a national convention," where the party could concentrate its strength on one candidate and prevent Calhoun from maneuvering into another term. "If the friends of the administration, when brought together from every part of the Union, in convention, cannot harmonize, I know of no other plan by which it can be done," he declared. Recognizing that Calhoun was stronger among political leaders than among the electorate, Lewis suggested that the influence of the former should be minimized by meeting after Congress adjourned. Kendall and Hill undertook the necessary negotiations, and in June the Democratic members of the New Hampshire legislature passed a resolution calling for a national convention to choose a vice-presidential candidate. Blair promptly gave it notice in the *Globe*.[5]

In urging a delegate convention to resolve its difficulties, party leaders were resorting to an institution long familiar to American politics. Political conventions appeared in America as early as the eighteenth century and had gradually become the prevailing method of nominating local and state candidates in most parts of the country by the time Lewis suggested the device for selecting a vice-president. The national convention, therefore, was a logical and natural extension of state and local practice, and developed partly out of necessity with the demise of the congressional caucus.[6]

Yet more than expediency dictated the call for the first national convention. The idea also attested to the efforts by Jackson and his advisers to construct a political organization which would uphold and perpetuate their principles. Van Buren, of course, had submitted the case for the revitalization of the Jeffersonian party in the aftermath of the Missouri crisis, and as early as 1827, he had propounded the benefits of a national convention to improve the condition of the Republicans "by substituting *party principle for personal preference*." [7] Kendall and Blair also had political objectives that transcended the immediate issue of Jackson's reelection, having agreed even before Old Hickory's inauguration that the Jackson party must establish its principles before worrying about future candidates. From their experience in Kentucky, they fully appreciated the advantages of conventions in promoting party unity, and they now applied their lessons to national politics. Under their guidance, the *Globe* recommended a national convention as "the best plan which can be adopted to produce entire unanimity in the Republican party, and secure its lasting ascendancy." [8]

Jackson also encouraged, if he did not lead, the movement for a national convention. During his presidency, he continued to evolve a more favorable opinion of the benefits of party organization until, by the close of his second term, he had almost completely discarded the suspicions he harbored during the Era of Good Feelings. Parties, he now avowed, not only provided the public support without which "no one can carry on this Govt.," but, when they adhered to proper principles, safeguarded the republic. "I have long believed," he professed in 1835, "that it was only by preserving the identity of the Republican party as embodied and characterized by the principles introduced by Mr. Jefferson that the original rights of the states and the people could be maintained," and he asserted that he had "labored to reconstruct this great Party" and to secure "its permanent ascendancy." [9]

Jackson's efforts on behalf of the Democracy did not reflect, however, an unequivocal endorsement of a party *system*, for he revealed at times the continuing influence of a more traditional view of political parties. As Richard Hofstadter has shown, the Founding Fathers considered parties as inimical to the public good, and they relied on the structure of government and the character of the people, not on the interplay of competitive parties, to assure liberty. Even the architects of the Jeffersonian Republican party could not bring themselves to accept the legitimacy of permanent political competition, and they hoped eventually to absorb the Federalist opposition, leaving only an impotent remnant of intractables to protest Republican rule. Republican leaders regarded their party as the organized expression of public virtue, preserving the republic from the conspiratorial actions and perverse principles of Federalism. It was a party to end parties, and there was nothing inconsistent in a Republican like James Monroe being a party man with ardent antiparty convictions.[10]

Gradually the idea of equally legitimate groups permanently competing for and alternating in power took hold in the early nineteenth century, and, indeed, found one of its most persuasive advocates in the person of Van Buren. But older notions persisted, and the Republican quest for unanimity remained a conspicuous feature of Jackson's political thought. Identifying his party with "the great mass of the people" and with "the cause of the Country," he resolved to establish its permanent ascendancy. To Jackson, the opposition was not representative of the people's virtue, but a party based upon corruption and fraud. He maintained this view even after his presidency; for example, the sudden death of President William Henry Harrison following the Whig victory of 1840 he considered as an "act of an overruling providence . . . to preserve and perpetuate our happy system of republicanism and stay the corruptions of this combined cliqe [sic]."[11]

Yet Jackson's reflections on political parties were neither frequent nor entirely consistent, and he acknowledged the possibility that the opposition would periodically return to power. Thus after Polk's presidential victory over Whiggery, Jackson expressed his belief that the Democratic triumph would "put down . . . whigism . . . forever, at least for a quarter of a century." He also practiced politics as though partisan contention were natural, inevitable, and unceasing, and unlike his predecessors, he did not condemn parties as evil or make serious efforts to do away with the opposition.[12] Nevertheless, Jackson tended to identify the Democratic party exclusively with the public good, and in the extraordinary circumstance of the nullification crisis, he briefly contemplated extinguishing former party distinctions and converting large numbers of the opposition to his side.[13]

Whatever his ambivalence about a competitive party system, Jackson affirmed the usefulness of party discipline and the benefits of such organizational devices as the convention. Convinced that the opposition would endeavor to divide the Democratic party, thereby permitting a minority to rule over the majority, he explained that conventions would enable the people to "retain in their own hands, the election of President and Vice President." They were, he reasoned, essential to the unity of "the friends of the same principles." [14]

The call for the first Democratic national convention, therefore, reflected and reinforced the evolution of the Jacksonians from the coalition of 1828 to the political party of eight years later, and it might well have been held even if no controversy had emerged over the vice-presidency. In any event, the national convention harmonized with the propensity of leading Democrats to appeal for support to the electorate. Blair perceptively noted this innovative, citizen-oriented aspect of conventions in responding to criticism that the Baltimore selections would be mere party nominations. "Very true," he conceded. "It is such a 'regular nomination, according to the party-style,' as concentrated the efforts of the republicans of 1800 in favor of . . . Jefferson . . . with the additional advantage of being of a more popular character than any of its precursors." [15]

The national convention was not universally acclaimed, even by Democrats. Like many institutional changes, acceptance varied according to local traditions and conditions. Resistance appeared among leading Democrats like Thomas Hart Benton, who refused to attend the Baltimore meeting, and Thomas Ritchie, who preferred a constitutional amendment providing that a contested election be returned to the people, thus eliminating the need for conventions to narrow the voters' choice of candidates. Conventions were often charged with being partisan, irresponsible, and unauthorized assemblies composed largely of officeholders which imposed their will on the people, and the second Democratic convention, meeting in 1835, must have thought the institution still required justification because it appointed a committee to defend it from such criticism.[16] But the advantages of a national convention to provide coherence for a national party were apparent to increasing numbers of Americans and among its leading advocates were Jackson and his Kitchen Cabinet.

With the *Globe*'s commendation, the New Hampshire resolution gained support among Democrats throughout the nation, and in the year between the proposal and the assembling of delegates at Baltimore in May 1832, state organizations chose their representatives. Some used a legislative caucus, others left the choice to local meetings of city and county party members, while a few held state conventions for the purpose. About half the states adhered to New Hampshire's recommendation that each delegation should be equal in size to its quota in the electoral college; the remaining states sent either more or fewer delegates than this standard determined.[17]

As plans for the convention materialized, the opposition grew increasingly insistent that the meeting had been called by "Lewis, Kendall, & Co." to further Van Buren's career, and Duff Green accused Van Buren's "regency in this city" of introducing in national politics "the same system by which he controls the State of New York." But such charges misrepresented Van Buren's position among Jackson's advisers and overlooked the initial purpose of the convention in providing a forum for achieving party unity on a vice-presidential selection. Blair refused to commit the party's newspaper to any particular candidate and advised the states to do likewise. He suggested they "recommend" but not nominate a candidate to the convention, and he hoped that when states "express their preference . . . they will not fail to resolve that they will acquiesce in and support the nomination" of the Baltimore convention. However, as 1831 drew to a close, party sentiment seemed to focus, not on Van Buren, but on Kentucky's Richard M. Johnson.[18]

Johnson was a longtime friend of Blair and Kendall, and it had been under his auspices that Kendall first ventured into Kentucky politics. Johnson's political views were flexible. He favored federal internal improvements expenditures, though he reluctantly conceded that Jackson's Maysville Road veto was justified. As a Kentucky relief man in the 1820s, he had criticized the Bank and Hamiltonian constitutional doctrine, but he was not a committed foe of national or state banks and when Congress voted on the Bank's recharter in 1832, he was conspicuously absent. Johnson clearly lacked the ideological fervor of Blair and Kendall on most matters relating to political economics. Yet he could be relied upon to follow the general direction of Jackson's program, and he possessed a considerable political reputation of his own. In addition to his military fame, which derived from his alleged slaying of Tecumseh during the War of 1812, his proposals for lower land prices, and his strong stands against imprisonment for debt and for the delivery of the Sunday mails won him popularity in the West and made him a hero to eastern workingmen.[19]

Johnson's foremost sponsor for the vice-presidency was Blair. In the fall of 1831, he urged Johnson to come to Washington as a senator and prepare himself to be Jackson's running mate. They also discussed political strategy, with Johnson recommending that Blair pressure local party leaders to hold large rallies in his favor. Kendall, who had earlier leaned toward Isaac Hill's favorite, Virginia's Philip P. Barbour, also turned to Johnson. A Van Buren partisan who visited Washington in December 1831 found both Blair and Kendall in favor of a westerner for the vice-presidency, while at the same time, Duff Green informed a friend that "Johnson is the chosen man of the palace."[20]

It was Blair's opinion that Johnson would have been chosen at Baltimore had not the Senate rejected Van Buren's nomination as minister to Great Britain. Improbable as it may seem with their party aspiring to national dominion, Jackson and the Kitchen Cabinet had decided on two westerners as their candidates for 1832. Perhaps they thought Johnson's border state background would make him a suitable compromise between northern and southern Democrats. But it is also likely that they were focusing attention on the party's fortunes in the West, believing the South would never desert Jackson for Clay. A Johnson nomination would counteract Clay's popularity and enhance the Democratic party's appeal in the West. Certainly, Blair and Kendall considered themselves westerners and labored arduously to assure the Democracy's ascendancy in that section.[21]

Whether Johnson would have succeeded at Baltimore became a moot point when, on 25 January 1832, the Senate rejected Van Buren's nomination by the casting vote of Calhoun. The action provided Van Buren's friends with an eagerly sought after opportunity to advance his claim. Many Regency men had never approved his decision to eschew the vice-presidency, and as late as December 1831, Cambreleng, the New York editors Webb and Noah, and James A. Hamilton had all hoped that circumstances would somehow permit Van Buren to seize the Baltimore nomination. Indeed, in early January 1832, Cambreleng informed Van Buren that many of his closest friends wished a Senate rejection as "the only thing that can remedy your error in going abroad." Thomas Hart Benton even refused to participate in the Senate debate on Van Buren's appointment, hoping the opposition would be successful in rejecting it. "Rejection was a bitter medicine," he recalled, "but there was health at the bottom of the draught."[22]

Although Van Buren's partisans were compelled by party considerations to vote for his confirmation, they were ecstatic when the opposition defeated it. "I most sincerely congratulate you on your rejection by the Senate," Cambreleng wrote. "I consider this as a providential interposition in your favor. . . . Indeed, altho' I had ardently desired it, I could not persuade myself to believe that their passions would drive them into a measure the inevitable result of which might have been seen by a schoolboy. . . . The thing is admirable. You will be our V.P. in spite of yourself." [23]

Jackson immediately recognized the opportunity presented by the Senate's action. Refusing to submit Van Buren's name for reconsideration, he denounced the "disgrace done to our country and national character" by the coalition of nullifiers and Clay men, and began to exert pressure on Democrats in Congress and in the states to redress both Van Buren's "injured feelings, and the insult offered to our government." Van Buren, Jackson announced, should be elevated to the vice-presidency "by acclamation." Lewis, whose responsibilities were limited to organizational matters, responded by urging Regency leaders not to hazard Van Buren's future by electing him governor upon his return from England. "If the party do not seize the present occasion for bringing him prominently before the *Nation*," Lewis warned, "he will . . . inevitably go down as a politician. If the Republican party cannot, under existing circumstances, make him Vice-President, they need never look to the Presidency for him." [24]

Blair and Kendall also moved into line. With the president directing the movement for Van Buren, and with party sentiment obviously swinging in his direction, the Kentuckians needed little prodding. But it is also likely that they, too, felt indignant at the opposition's slap in the face of the administration. Kendall declared that the party must do Van Buren "justice," while Blair assured Van Buren that he would receive the party's nomination at Baltimore. On 30 January, the *Globe* affirmed that the Senate's action had changed the complexion of the vice-presidential race. Denying there had previously been a secret movement to promote Van Buren's nomination, it promised that the party's delegates would record the people's judgment of the Senate's "wanton and unjust rejection." [25]

Van Buren, of course, greatly welcomed this show of support. "The spirit excited in the U. States by my rejection has exceeded the most sanguine expectations of my warmest friends," he exulted. Only two weeks before the Senate vote, he had once again informed Jackson that he could not risk a vice-presidential bid, but shortly after learning of his defeat he indicated to the president that he would accept a nomination at Baltimore. On 14 March, he penned a letter to Senator William Marcy publicly acknowledging his willingness to be on the Jackson ticket.[26]

Despite the apparent unanimity with which the executive office rallied behind Van Buren, the *Globe* refused to endorse him. Blair instead maintained the same public neutrality he had previously adopted towards the numerous other vice-presidential candidates. Even after Van Buren had signaled his designs on the vice-presidency, he refused to make it a closed convention by laying down the party line in his favor.

Blair's course may have been nothing more than good politics. Having advocated a national convention to choose a nominee, it would be unseemly to announce the party's choice beforehand. Probably, too, he was reluctant to cast abruptly aside his close friend and fellow westerner, Johnson. Yet it is also possible to speculate that Blair was protecting the party in the eventuality that Van Buren failed to receive the Baltimore nomination. Van Buren had many enemies and some believed he would prove so unpopular as to be forced to withdraw his name. Indeed, some opposition leaders, convinced of Van Buren's weakness, hoped the Democrats would place him on the ticket where he would pull Jackson down to defeat.[27]

In the early months of 1832, pockets of resistance to Van Buren were increasingly evident. Some western Democrats blamed Van Buren for the administration's internal improvements policy and refused to support him. In Pennsylvania, where Democrats agreed on little else, they united in opposing Van Buren. Pennsylvanians regarded Van Buren as hostile to internal improvements and the Bank, and in March 1832, they gave vent to their disaffection at a state convention which nominated William Wilkins for vice-president. Pennsylvania Democrats also refused to appoint delegates to the national convention, and the state was represented at Baltimore by a dozen self-appointed delegates, few of whom were major political figures.[28]

The strongest opposition to Van Buren, however, came from the South, an area where he should have been strong because of his leadership of the former Crawford faction. Many southerners were unenthusiastic about a northern candidate, especially one so closely identified with the Tariff of Abominations and with a style of politics that often grated on southern sensibilities. William Drayton, an antinullification leader in South Carolina, thought his state's Baltimore delegation would "feel themselves restrained from voting for Van Buren in consequence of the part he acted in the passage of the Tariff Act of 1828." And James Iredell of North Carolina expressed the view of many when he asserted that "a large number of Genl J's original friends" would not vote for Van Buren. "We want if possible an antitariff or at least a *moderately Tariff* man & we want a man who will not introduce into the General Government the principle that the whole contest for power is for the *emoluments of office.*" Under these circumstances, even confirmed southern Van Buren men worried about defending him during an election campaign.[29]

Southern anti–Van Buren sentiment took substance in the movement to nominate Philip Barbour at the party's convention. A Virginian and a federal judge, Barbour had been considered a leading possibility for the vice-presidency until the Kitchen Cabinet decided that his strenuous antitariff convictions would antagonize the North. But his opinions were hailed in the South, where Barbour attracted support even after the Senate made Van Buren's selection seem inevitable.[30] Some Barbour men were either Calhounites or antitariff radicals who looked to the judge as a vehicle to undermine Van Buren and weaken Jackson in the South. But others were loyal Jacksonians who thought Barbour safer on the tariff issue than Van Buren, and even Van Buren's Albany *Argus* had to admit that the Virginian was causing defections among friends of the administration. Barbour's candidacy clearly presented a serious challenge to Jackson's plan to place Van Buren on his ticket. After failing twice to have a caucus of Virginia Democrats nominate Van Buren, Ritchie asked the president to renominate Van Buren as minister to Britain rather than bring him before the Baltimore convention.[31]

Van Buren's friends acknowledged these difficulties but were all the more determined to capture the nomination. Close association with Jackson might cause some of Old Hickory's glow to radiate on Van Buren's modest eminence, and a party nomination would strengthen him in the West and South. But for Blair, whose loyalty was primarily to Jackson, a preconvention endorsement of the "Magician" was hazardous. If Van Buren were forced out of consideration, the party would be in better shape if the *Globe* had never been pledged to him. Admittedly such a contingency was unlikely, but in April 1832, Duff Green was reporting rumors that "the Kitchen Cabinet . . . [was] despairing of Van B. and inclined to take R. M. Johnson at Baltimore."[32]

Blair's independence of Van Buren intensified the latent rivalry between Van Burenites and Jackson's western advisers. Regency men naturally mistrusted those around the president who were not personally attached to their own leader and who could use their access to Jackson to urge measures that might embarrass Van Buren. With the Bank War gaining momentum, Regency congressmen particularly stressed the value of having the politically experienced Van Buren close to Jackson, since the president was surrounded by men "whose democracy is so different from our notions of it." Some Van Burenites now betrayed their anxiety by participating in McLane's intrigue to oust Blair from the *Globe*. While these New Yorkers were probably unaware that McLane's underlying purpose was to replace Blair with a less zealous anti-Bank editor, they were enthusiastic about the prospect of having "a more efficient" Van Buren press in Washington.[33]

The McLane intrigue failed when Jackson stood resolutely behind Blair, and tension between the Van Burenites and Blair gradually subsided as the *Globe* grew friendlier towards Van Buren with the approach of the Baltimore meeting. But the editor's changing posture had more to do with the increasing expectation of Van Buren's nomination than to any pressure exerted on him by Regency forces. As one Van Burenite noted after conversing with both Blair and Kendall, Van Buren "had nothing to hope from their *friendship*, but everything from their *interest*." The Kentuckians were Van Buren's "*friends* but no further so, than . . . [Van Buren's] popularity with the people and . . . [his] political power will render *prudent*."[34]

The Democratic convention which met in Baltimore from 21 to 23 May was not the first national political convention. The Antimasonic and National Republican parties had already completed their deliberations by the time the Democrats met. But it was the most national of the three, having more delegates from more states than the others.[35] Three hundred and thirty-four delegates assembled from every state but Missouri to hear the first major speaker assert that the convention's purpose was "not to impose on the people, as candidates for either of the two first offices in this government, any local favorite; but to concentrate the opinions of all the states." He urged the delegates to continue "this mode of nomination" in future years.[36]

The convention's primary business took place on the second day when balloting began for the vice-presidency. Only one ballot was needed as Van Buren tallied 208 votes, considerably more than the necessary two-thirds. Johnson received twenty-six votes from Illinois, Indiana, and Kentucky, while Barbour polled forty-nine votes from Virginia, South Carolina, North Carolina, Maryland, and Alabama. Immediately upon the announcement of Van Buren's total, all the Johnson and Barbour delegates voted to make the nomination unanimous.[37]

As it turned out, the first Democratic meeting had become a ratification session for delegates to confirm the party's ticket. Nevertheless, the convention also performed a significant function in establishing greater party coherence. Democrats throughout the country knew that a vote for candidates other than the official selections would be considered political apostasy. The duly elected representatives of the party had spoken, and it was incumbent upon all party members to support the general will.[38]

The point was broadcast to all Democrats by Blair after the convention adjourned. "The line is now fairly drawn between the parties by the ticket now presented to the public," the *Globe* announced. "The true friends of the President and of the democracy will not refuse to support it from any personal objections to Mr. Van Buren, or from personal preferences indulged for another. No party or principle can be sustained, if individual views are permitted to thwart the counsels of the mass of the community." Blair commended the action of those delegates who had first voted for Johnson or Barbour but had subsequently endorsed the convention's choice, and he called upon Wilkins and Barbour to follow Johnson's example by publicly waiving all claims to the vice-presidency. The effectiveness of his strategy was not lost on Duff Green, who complained that "Van Buren is now put up as the *party* candidate, and Mr. Calhoun and his friends are denounced because they will not support him on *party* grounds."[39]

A national convention, therefore, had advantages beyond its function of nominating candidates, which a caucus could also have accomplished. With its delegates, who presumably represented party members throughout the country, a convention gave the nominee the legitimacy of selection by "the mass of the community." Of course, then as now, many criticized the convention system as a democratic façade for the activity of political bosses. "It is strange that the talents for packing Herrings in a Barrel with just salt enough to keep them from stinking should be of so high account," commented one disgruntled Democrat about his party's enthusiasm for conventions. And there is some validity to the charge. Many delegates were self-appointed or had been selected by state legislatures rather than the party members in the electorate. Moreover, by the time the convention assembled, most Democrats realized that Jackson was exerting pressure to assure Van Buren's nomination.[40]

But it is also true that the convention opened the process of candidate selection to more people than the congressional caucus. And in all likelihood the convention accurately registered party sentiment. If Jackson ardently desired Van Buren's nomination, a majority of Democrats probably shared his feelings. In any case, the convention revealed that combination of political organization and popular participation which was becoming increasingly evident in nineteenth-century America, a style of politics in which Jackson men like Kendall, Blair, and Van Buren excelled.[41]

Guided by Blair's deft handling of the *Globe*, the administration promptly used the Baltimore convention to undermine the Barbour movement. Many of Barbour's supporters had followed Blair's counsel and rallied to the Baltimore nominations rather than "run the risk of dividing the party." But others continued to plead the Virginian's cause over Van Buren who was, according to the resolutions adopted at one Barbour meeting, "decidedly in favor of continuing the odious system of taxation under which we are suffering." Blair, however, derided leading Barbour partisans as Calhounites and warned the dissidents that by dividing the Jackson party they were aiding the opposition.[42]

Meanwhile, the editor and Lewis circulated reports of Barbour's weak standing among party members to show that his chances were hopeless, and Jackson made clear that Barbour men would receive no federal patronage. It soon became evident to even the most resolute Barbour supporter that Van Buren would triumph in the election. As one North Carolina Barbour man noted, "Genl. Jackson's name & the machinery set on foot as I have no doubt by the cabal at Washington" was being worked in Van Buren's favor. "We have presses that would oppose him but they *dare* not." [43]

In October 1832, under this pressure, Barbour withdrew from the contest. Declaring his action necessary for party unity, he asked his friends to support the regular ticket. A few dissenters still cast votes for Jackson-Barbour electors in Virginia and North Carolina, but the regular ticket won handily in both states. [44]

During the campaign itself, Blair and Kendall used all their organizational and editorial skills to aid the Democratic ticket. The *Globe* made sharp thrusts at the National Republicans, their candidate Clay, and, especially, the Bank. Like the *Telegraph* in 1828, the *Globe* became the focal point of a national network of Democratic newspapers, feeding information to other papers and collecting news of local events for distribution throughout the country. Blair and Kendall also issued a special campaign *Extra Globe*, designed to "be circulated and read in *every neighborhood*." In order to assure this extensive circulation, Kendall requested local Jackson politicians to give him the name "of a good, honest, 'whole hog' Jackson man" at each post office. "Every neighborhood must be reached to meet the slanders and falsehoods of our adversaries," he declared. "We are to have 'war to the knife and the knife to the hilt.' Give me *fighting men* who will take some pains for the party, if need be." [45]

Kendall also encouraged the formation of a chain of Hickory Clubs, which supplemented the activity of other state and local Jackson committees. He himself organized the Central Hickory Club in Washington, which was designed "to give tone and character to all other clubs throughout the country." Through its committees of correspondence, the Central Hickory Club became a channel of communication between local and national politicians and was an especially useful tool for circulating campaign material. [46]

Kendall also provided a party campaign platform. In the absence of an official statement by the Baltimore convention, his "Address from the Central Hickory Club (of Washington) to the Republican Citizens of the United States," already described, became the party's statement of principles. Frequently paraphrasing presidential messages and vetoes, the address was a ringing affirmation of Jackson's policies, upholding the principles of states' rights and limited government while denouncing nullification and special privilege legislation. It attempted to explicate the party's articles of faith so that Democrats would follow them even "after President Jackson shall no longer move among our Statesmen."[47]

So conspicuous was Kendall's hand in forging links between the local, state, and national party organizations that Duff Green attributed to him virtual "control of the electoral franchise of this country. . . . The party leaders take their cue from the party press . . . and he who controls the leading papers controls the party. What press is the organ of the Jackson party? *The Globe!* Who is the master spirit of the Central Hickory Club? Amos Kendall!! Who controls the Globe? *Amos Kendall!!*" Of course, other members of the executive office shared the responsibility for oiling the party machinery. Van Buren and his New York friends raised money to help establish newspapers. Lewis surveyed the political terrain in various states and advised the president on allocating patronage. Jackson himself carefully oversaw these efforts, giving the final word on patronage disputes, charging Kendall to circulate material, and requesting Blair to print editorials attacking the opposition. Nevertheless, the contribution of Kendall and Blair in organizing the electorate and broadcasting party ideology was unsurpassed.[48]

With the endorsement of the Democratic convention and the aid of the party's extensive organization, Van Buren easily triumphed on the Jackson ticket. Only Pennsylvania held back and gave its electoral votes to a Jackson-Wilkins ticket. The New Yorker would once again be among the president's advisers in Washington, this time with the added prestige of being the front-runner for the Democratic presidential nomination in 1836. Yet it remained to be seen whether his influence on Jackson's policies would match his new status.

6

Nullification

The nullification crisis stands out among the controversies of the Jackson presidency because it was not strictly a partisan question. Unionism versus secession, sectional harmony versus civil war, the republic versus republican subversives, these were the issues posed by South Carolina radicals. Yet no controversy is without its political implications, and nullification demonstrated the predominance of the Jackson-Kendall-Blair axis of the Democratic party as well as the vital contribution of republican ideology to Jackson's political vocabulary.[1]

By the spring and summer of 1831, the southern antitariff crusade entered a more militant phase. For two years, Jackson had recommended only minor changes in the tariff, declaring it more important to discharge the national debt. He had also acknowledged the possibility that rates would never be reduced to the level of ordinary government expenditures and urged consideration of a plan to distribute surplus revenue to the states. Nullifiers, however, regarded tariff reform as the most pressing issue before the country and opposed distribution for its tendency to maintain high tariff levels. When Jackson's annual report of 1829 asserted that the Tariff of 1828 had "not proved so injurious . . . or as beneficial . . . as was anticipated," George McDuffie countered with a series of speeches denouncing the protective tariff system, demanding the repeal of many of the 1824 and 1828 rates, and proposing his forty-bale theory which asserted that protection punished the southern cotton producer rather than the American consumer. A year later when Jackson called for only the mildest reform, a South Carolina congressman threatened action. "Gen. Jackson's message contains some principles that no name or party can make me swallow," he asserted. "I will not, and you shall see it." Their protests having no discernible effect, nullifier leaders decided in the spring of 1831 to take the offensive against the administration.[2]

For Calhoun, the radicals' decision brought "matters to a crisis" and compelled him to affirm his belief in nullification. In July 1831, therefore, he issued his Fort Hill Address, which argued that a state could render a federal law inoperative within its jurisdiction while remaining a part of the Union. Although Calhoun viewed nullification as peaceful and conservative, he now maintained that tariff reform would not be achieved until a state actually applied his remedy. Protests would no longer suffice. If South Carolina interposed, he declared, other southern states would follow.[3]

In Washington, Jackson viewed the situation in South Carolina with repugnance. His profound contempt for nullification is well known. Discounting Calhoun's contention that nullification would preserve the Union, he treated it as tantamount to secession. "This abominable doctrine ... strikes at the root of our Government and the social compact, and reduces every thing to anarchy," he announced. He described himself as a Jeffersonian and distinguished between its states' rights formulas and nullification. "One will preserve the union of the states," he explained. "The other will dissolve the Union by destroying the Constitution by acts unauthorized by it." He often likened the Union construed by the nullifiers to a bag of sand with both ends open, observing that "the least pressure and it runs out at both ends."[4]

While Calhoun's association with nullification doubtless increased Jackson's antipathy, his opposition by no means depended on personal considerations. He had denounced South Carolina's "ultra tariff violence" even before concluding that Calhoun was its leader.[5] More influential was a fervent nationalism and devotion to the Union, which had been stimulated by his military career and, perhaps, by his association with the West. Jackson identified the fate of the American republic with the Union, and pictured the tragic consequences of a separation in words that recalled the arguments of the *Federalist Papers*. "Without Union," he reminded his countrymen in the aftermath of nullification, "our independence and liberty would never have been achieved; and without union they never can be maintained. ... The loss of liberty, of all good government, of peace, plenty, and happiness, must inevitably follow a dissolution of the Union."[6]

Jackson's thoughts were seconded by Kendall and Blair. Kendall condemned nullification as equivalent to having no government whatsoever, while Blair denounced Calhoun for concocting "a scheme to shatter our republic." Under their direction, the *Globe* countered the antitariff radicalism of Duff Green's *Telegraph* and broadcast the administration's charge that Calhoun was driving "the people of South Carolina and of the whole South, into a league of revolt." Like Jackson, they genuinely viewed nullification as a threat to the republic and had criticized it before concluding that Calhoun was its leader.[7]

In condemning nullification, however, Jackson and his advisers portrayed it in a distinctive manner. It was, in their account, a conspiracy against the republic by reckless and "unprincipled men who .would rather rule in hell, than be subordinate in heaven." According to Jackson, the nullifiers' objective was "to destroy the union, and form a southern confederacy bounded, north, by the Patomac [sic] river." The "wickedness, madness and folly of its leaders," he claimed, was unparalleled in the history of the world.[8]

In Jackson's eyes, Calhoun was the conspiracy's leader, an "ambitious Demagogue" who, having failed to achieve power by legitimate means, would now "move heaven and earth . . . to gratify his unholy ambition." He characterized Calhoun as "devoid of principle" and willing to sacrifice "friend . . . country . . . and . . . god, for selfish ambition." He accused the South Carolinian of leading astray such "high minded honorable" patriots as James Hamilton, Jr., and Robert Hayne.[9]

The *Globe* spread the idea that the source of nullification was disappointed ambition, not protective tariffs. "It is . . . [Calhoun's] interest to keep up the excitement—to make a SOUTHERN LEAGUE— and to acquire importance as its LEADER," Blair alleged. Driving home the point, his editorials drew parallels between ancient republican subversives described in Plutarch, their American counterparts like Aaron Burr and the Blue Light Federalists of the Hartford Convention, and the nullifiers. "These ambitious malcontents," Blair concluded, "are too far removed from the center of gravity in our present government. They wish to become the center of another system."[10]

Nullifiers categorically denied the administration's narrow view of their purposes. Duff Green called one such *Globe* essay "a cock and bull story" and claimed that the nullifiers preferred to rectify injuries to their section rather than scramble for political rewards. Repeatedly the *Telegraph* complained of Blair's "constant endeavor" to represent nullification "as the factious proceedings of a few noisy politicians, in which the mass of the people took little or no interest." But Jackson and the *Globe* remained impervious to attempts by nullifiers to explain and justify their doctrine.[11]

Jackson's appraisal of nullification clearly owed something to his quarrel with Calhoun. Calhoun's implication in the Eaton affair, his duplicity in the Seminole matter, and his public recantation of his earlier loose-construction nationalism provided the detail for the unflattering portrait of an inconsistent, opportunistic, and devious politician who would stop at nothing "to exalt himself to office." But Jackson's view can also be attributed to the persistent influence of republican ideology, which warned that republics were fragile mechanisms which easily fell prey to external attack or to schemes of ambitious and disgruntled citizens. Liberty was always endangered by corruption and power, and one had to guard continually against both foreign threats and internal subversion. The Burr conspiracy, the Hartford Convention, and the War of 1812 constituted potent reminders to Americans of Jackson's generation of their responsibility to preserve liberty from the perils posed by domestic and foreign adversaries.[12]

Jackson was profoundly concerned about the corruption that eroded virtue and undermined republican institutions. Among the sources of internal decay that he identified were privileged monopolies, paper-money banking, speculation, and excessive government expenditures. But nullification was equally ruinous, and he warned that "from disappointed ambition and inordinate thirst for power . . . factions will be formed and liberty endangered."[13] Nullification, then, was as much a test of the country's republican experiment as the Bank.

Jackson's political assumptions made him take nullification as a serious challenge, but they also contributed to distortion and misrepresentation. By focusing on political ambition as the sole impulse behind nullification, he exaggerated Calhoun's position in the movement and failed to acknowledge the depth of South Carolina's anger, frustration, and worry when contemplating the course of national politics.[14]

The "foundation" of nullification, as the Charleston *Mercury* declared, was hostility to tariffs, for nullifiers viewed protection as "a system of sectional and tyrannical legislation" which drained the

South of wealth for the benefit of the North and West. But nullification was also something more than an antitariff movement. As its able chroniclers suggest, leading radicals viewed the tariff as representative of the evils of consolidation, and they brooded that the South's minority position in the Union invited continued sacrifice to the interests of the majority North. Calhoun himself acknowledged that the tariff was but "the occasion, rather than the real cause" of southern unrest, and that since the South's slaveholding economy placed it "in opposite relations" to the majority of the Union, it must seek protection in the reserved rights of the states.[15]

Perhaps, too, South Carolina's extremism was fueled, as William W. Freehling compellingly argues, by an acute sensitivity to actual and potential challenges to slavery. Although the relationship between slavery and nullification rests more on indirect than direct evidence, it is likely that at least some nullifiers were motivated by concern about abolitionist activity in the North.[16] But however South Carolina's position is explained, it remains clear that Jackson and his aides discounted any but the most narrow political impulse. As the *Globe* put it, "there is a motive in all this hallucination," but it "will be found a *politician's*, not a *planter's*."[17]

In the summer and fall of 1831, the situation in South Carolina did not warrant decisive action by the president. The nullifiers, though resolute, had not yet gained sufficient support to defy the central government. Nevertheless, Jackson initiated steps to defuse the controversy by recommending tariff reform. He hoped to "annihilate the Nullifiers" by proposing substantially lowered schedules.[18]

Pressure from antitariff radicals obviously influenced Jackson's decision. Yet his determination to identify the Democratic party with a low tariff policy was also consistent with the limited government, antimonopoly thrust of his presidency. He had always acknowledged that the tariff of 1828, even as modified in 1830, was imperfect, but he had postponed reform in order to collect revenue to liquidate the national debt. By the fall of 1831, the anticipated end of the debt freed him to recommend lower rates.[19]

He announced the change in his December 1831 annual message to Congress. Dropping all reference to distributing surplus revenue, he declared that the retirement of the public debt required an adjustment in the tariff. He recommended duties which would reduce "revenue to the wants of the Government" while still providing limited protection for articles necessary for national defense and for counteracting foreign trade barriers. It was an astute compromise between those who advocated protection and those who insisted on a revenue tariff only; yet the downward direction was manifest.[20]

Jackson himself appears to have initiated the new policy, but he was fully supported by his key advisers. Kendall worked with him on the message and Blair vigorously defended the need for lower rates. Significantly, their position had as much to do with the needs of the West as of the South. An excessive tariff, they claimed, benefited the manufacturer at the expense of ordinary farmers and mechanics, and was therefore a form of special privilege. As Blair explained in the *Globe*, Democratic ideology could not condone a "system which proposes to sustain monopolies in the hands of a few, by levying . . . a tax on the many," and which channels surplus revenue into "the coffers of joint stock companies." This emphasis on the egalitarian and democratic virtues of low tariffs either influenced or reflected Jackson's own views, for the president echoed the *Globe*'s sentiments a short time later in December 1832 in his fourth annual message. The policy of protection, he now asserted, provoked "discontent and jealousy," not only in the South where it was considered "unconstitutional and unjust," but in other sections where it was viewed "as tending to concentrate wealth into a few hands, and as creating those germs of dependence and vice" characteristic of monopolies and destructive of "liberty and the general good." [21]

For the details of a revised tariff, Jackson turned to Treasury Secretary Louis McLane, whose support of the Bank's recharter had recently embarrassed the administration. But McLane's tariff views more closely coincided with Jackson's than did his opinions on banking, and the talented and ambitious secretary eagerly seized the opportunity to recoup some of his lost standing with the president and to enhance his future political prospects. By the spring of 1832, McLane had completed his work, presenting a proposal with substantial reductions on existing rates.[22]

Congress, however, greeted the measure with little enthusiasm. Southern Democrats, finding many provisions objectionable, only reluctantly agreed to support it. More damaging was the bill's failure to win the approval of nullifiers or of most protective tariff advocates, including a number of New York Democrats. Tariff reformers therefore rallied behind a bill sponsored by John Quincy Adams, which contained slightly higher duties than McLane's proposal. It was not what Jackson wanted, but it still provided significant reform and was, in Blair's words, *"an experiment"* that could be further modified as circumstances dictated.[23]

Jackson made Adams's bill an administration measure. In addition to the *Globe*'s approving notices, he designated Lewis to impress upon party members in Congress the need for concessions. To be sure, southern Democrats again complained that the rates were too high and that the principle of protection remained intact, but Blair urged them to consider the new measure as an indication of the administration's sincere desire for reform. The future, he promised, would bring further revision. In the end, Democratic votes assured passage of the Tariff of 1832.[24]

Jackson and his advisers were pleased with the new tariff. The Tariff of Abominations was gone, and a troublesome and potentially embarrassing issue to the Jackson–Van Buren ticket seemed to be compromised. Van Buren, returned from England, expressed satisfaction with the display of party loyalty and mutual concession which marked the bill's passage. And Jackson thought the new tariff had "killed the ultras, both tariffites and nullifiers." He was confident that the overwhelming majority of southerners would be satisfied with the specific reductions in duties on cotton bagging, blankets, and coarse woolens, and would appreciate the party's general commitment, as expressed in Kendall's Hickory Club Address the following October, that taxes "should be sufficient in amount only to support" the government in "the performance of its legitimate functions."[25]

The Tariff of 1832, however, did not halt the nullifiers. To antitariff radicals, the provisions of the new law were deficient and its failure to repudiate the protective principle intolerable. Calhoun dismissed the tariff as completely unsatisfactory. "I no longer consider the question one of free trade, but of consolidation," he confided to an ally. "If, after ten years of remonstrance and denunciation of the system, as unconstitutional, the Southern States should now yield their ground, where can a stand be hereafter made? When will such another opportunity, as that of the discharge of the public debt, be ever again presented? Let the occasion pass, and it is easy to see what must follow—corruption, oppression, and monarchy." [26]

Other nullifiers agreed with Calhoun's assessment. The radicals' leading newspaper, the Charleston *Mercury*, totally rejected the tariff, claiming that "whilst the protective principle is retained in all its odious force, the system itself has been rendered more unequal and oppressive." The nullifiers increased their efforts to control South Carolina, and in October, they won more than two-thirds of the seats in the legislature, enough to call a state convention to put Calhoun's theory into practice. On 19 November, the nullifiers convened in Charleston and demanded a tariff at the uniform rate of 12 percent. They also adopted an ordinance declaring the tariffs of 1828 and 1832 null and void in South Carolina, and proclaimed that after 1 February 1833 it would be illegal to enforce the payment of import duties within the limits of the state. The convention warned the federal government that any congressional action authorizing military force against the state would be viewed as "inconsistent with the longer continuance of South Carolina in the Union." [27]

South Carolina's response to the Tariff of 1832 confirmed Jackson's suspicions that the nullifiers were intractable. As early as the fall of 1831, he had entertained the notion that southern radicals would reject his tariff suggestions and had "only indulged in their vituperations against the Tariff for the purpose of covertly accomplishing their ends." When he later proclaimed that the Tariff of 1832 had "killed" the nullifiers, his rejoicing had less to do with the prospect of having mollified these bitter opponents of protection than with his conviction that by removing valid grievances he would leave further complaints exposed as the work of "disappointed ambition." Tariff reform increasingly became a means of isolating South Carolina from the rest of the South. As the *Globe* noted, new concessions would "disarm the Nullifiers by taking the Tariff weapon out of their hands, and deprive them of the means of practicing further on the credulity of the people of the South." [28]

At the same time that he was losing faith in tariff reform as a means of placating the radicals, Jackson was increasingly directing his attention to military measures. His limited conception of nullification had initially led him to underestimate the nullifiers' popularity. Until the fall of 1832, he had expected public opinion in South Carolina to compel them to desist and he had dismissed as "groundless" reports of their increasing strength. But as autumn brought further information from his South Carolina correspondent, Joel Poinsett, of nullifier victories, Jackson confessed his "astonishment" at the people's delusion and concluded that the nullifiers were "in a state of insanity." He commanded Secretary of War Cass to have the army ready to defend the forts and garrisons surrounding Charleston and dispatched George Breathitt, brother of the governor of Kentucky, to South Carolina to assess the overall military situation. "Wisdom says, *be* always guarded against the . . . combination of the wicked," he explained to Van Buren.[29]

By early December 1832, Jackson had evolved a strategy to deal with the growing crisis. Carefully avoiding actions that might provoke a clash of arms, he planned to isolate South Carolina from the rest of the South by intimidating her with the specter of tens of thousands of armed troops poised within and without her borders. He therefore sent arms and equipment to the loyal Union party in South Carolina, readied the army and navy, and called for expressions of patriotism throughout the country, seeking to array, in Kendall's words, "so strong a moral force . . . on the side of the administration that the incipient treason shall be awed into obedience." He directed South Carolina Unionists to act as a posse comitatus in case the nullifiers resisted federal laws, and promised prompt federal military intervention if this first line of defense proved insufficient. States' rights, he contended, did not permit a state to secede at will, and if South Carolina attempted secession, "the people comp[o]sing this union have a perfect right to coerce them to obedience."[30]

Kendall and Blair fully sustained the president's policy. Privately, Kendall declared that "temporizing with the mischief may extend it and lead to consequences all must deplore," and he collaborated with Blair on essays for the *Globe*, accusing the nullifiers of seeking disunion and justifying federal force if South Carolina acted. "The crisis is at hand," the paper announced. "It is impossible longer to shut our eyes to the design of the leading Nullifiers of South Carolina: It is to dissolve the Union, 'peaceably if they can, forcibly if they must.'" So long as nullification wore "the panoply of war," the *Globe* argued, it would be "criminal in the General Government not to take precautions against it," and nullifiers were warned that the president intended to "PRESERVE THE UNION AT EVERY HAZARD."[31]

When Congress assembled in December, Jackson displayed a deft combination of compromise and coercion designed to isolate South Carolina further. His annual message stressed his commitment to tariff reform, and McLane proffered another tariff proposal as evidence of the president's good faith. But this conciliatory carrot was primarily dangled in front of moderate southerners. It is apparent that Jackson did not believe that new concessions would appease the nullifiers who, he thought, had *run mad.* A leading Democrat reported after talking to Jackson that the president did not expect a new tariff would "prevent an open rupture . . . but he hopes it may keep the other states south steady while he disciplines Messrs. Calhoun, Hamilton and Hayne."[32]

In this context, Jackson's nullification proclamation of 10 December possessed more vigor and spirit than is often attributed to it. The origins of the proclamation are obscure, but Jackson seems to have turned for help in composing it to those aides who most firmly supported a strong assertion of federal authority, Kendall, Blair, and, especially, Edward Livingston. Kendall's draft bears little resemblance to the final proclamation, being legalistic and spare in its phrasing.[33] Jackson, however, desired a brief that would be "argumentative" to counter nullification's heresies, and also eloquent to "strike to the heart and speak to the feelings" of the "deluded" Carolinians. He therefore went over another draft with Blair before sending it to Secretary of State Livingston, urging him to let the document "receive your best flight of eloquence."[34]

The proclamation acknowledged the actions of the South Carolina convention and announced Jackson's response that "the power to annul a law of the United States, assumed by one State, [is] *incompatible with the existence of the Union, contradicted expressly by the letter of the Constitution, unauthorized by its spirit, inconsistent with every principle on which it was founded, and destructive of the great object for which it was formed.*" Jackson directly rebutted the nullifiers' claim of state sovereignty and of the right to resist federal law or even secede from the Union. The Constitution, he asserted, formed "a *government,* not a league," and each state, having expressly given up a part of its sovereignty to join the others in "a single nation," could not possess the right to secede. Only the natural right of rebellion legitimized secession.[35]

Assuring South Carolinians that the tide of public opinion now favored tariff reform, Jackson promised that duties would be reduced "to a just and equitable scale." But he warned that they could not continue their resistance peacefully. Placing the blame squarely on their leaders, he warned that the nullifiers' object was disunion, and that "disunion by armed force is *treason*." He pledged himself "to execute the laws," but promised that no blood would be shed because of "any offensive act on the part of the United States."[36]

While the proclamation's solicitous tone indicated a flickering hope that the voice of reason might yet prevail in South Carolina, the document was not designed to convince South Carolina's leaders of their error. Rather, it was directed at the followers of nullification, at South Carolina Unionists, and at nationalists everywhere whose unionism Jackson sought to intensify. Its pledge to execute the laws revealed Jackson's concern that the movement's leadership was immune to reason. On 9 December, just one day before signing the proclamation, Jackson informed Poinsett that if South Carolina raised troops he would consider it "positive treason," and he would meet it "at the threshold," arrest and arraign the leaders, and put down the rebellion.[37]

As the nullifiers continued to make their own military arrangements, Jackson fixed his attention on the impending conflict. In mid-January, he fully expected to hear that civil war had broken out in South Carolina, and he mentioned the possibility of arresting the governor of Virginia should the passage of federal troops through the Dominion be obstructed.[38] His Force Bill message of 16 January 1833 reflected this concern. Drafted with the aid of Treasury Secretary McLane, the message informed Congress that South Carolina's legislature had enacted nullification, and requested authorization for measures to continue collecting the revenue.[39]

As a recent discussion of nullification has noted, most of Jackson's specific suggestions were designed to avoid rather than precipitate conflict, or at least to compel the nullifiers to strike the first blow. He requested permission to move customs houses away from the shoreline, to receive duties in cash rather than bonds, and to establish jails if state authorities refused to house lawbreakers.[40] But the message also contained recommendations of a more provocative nature. Jackson not only requested explicit congressional confirmation of his power to employ state militias and federal forces against the dissidents, but also sought power to call out the military without issuing a prior proclamation, a proposition Congress refused in the end to sanction. "The conflict, we fear, must come," the *Globe* warned. "Nothing can be done by Congress which will divert the nullifying leaders from their attempt to dissolve the Union."[41]

Jackson's commitment to the Union won support from most Americans. In his own state, for example, the proclamation elicited public and private declarations of loyalty to the nation, and temporarily refurbished the president's popularity among his increasingly numerous and vocal opposition. In contrast to Tennessee's reaction, however, was the dissatisfaction expressed by some of Jackson's own followers with aspects of his policy. In particular, southern Democrats and Van Burenites disputed the president's constitutional arguments, implied that he was insufficiently attuned to southern anxieties, and pleaded for a greater emphasis on conciliatory reform and less on military might.[42]

Southern Democrats were more prone than Jackson to attribute nullification to northern dictation and tariff legislation rather than to the machinations of ambitious demagogues. Ritchie pronounced nullification unconstitutional and rash, but asserted that the "whole South is indignant at the oppression and obduracy of the tariffites." He especially abhorred Jackson's saber rattling and discounted the possibility that southern soldiers would aid the federal government in suppressing the nullifiers. Virginia would be "loth indeed to send a man or musket" to subject South Carolina, he pledged.[43]

Southern dissent first focused on Jackson's proclamation. Nathaniel Macon, a longtime spokesman of Republican principles, criticized Jackson's contention that a state could not secede at will, while John Randolph thought the document's arguments against nullification and secession had bound Jackson hand and foot to "the ultra federalists–ultra tariffites–ultra internal improvement and Hartford convention men." Ritchie, too, complained of the proclamation's erroneous principles in denying a state the right to secede peaceably from the Union. He declared that Jackson had not attended "sufficiently to . . . [its] details."[44]

Ritchie also led the chorus of protests against the Force Bill. He applauded those features designed to avoid confrontation, but considered the measure inflammatory and excessive. "Who . . . can expect to keep together an Union like this, by stern and unqualified force?" he asked. He contended that Jackson should do nothing until after South Carolina acted, and even at this "very last moment," the president should only convene Congress and submit the issue "to the collective wisdom of the co-states." He urged southern congressmen to postpone action on the bill and give priority to tariff reform.[45]

Such grumblings were by no means limited to Ritchie and the southern Old Republican element of the Democratic party. Roger Taney, absent in Maryland during most of the crisis, thought the proclamation had gone overboard in upholding national power and had obscured the difference between Democratic philosophy and Federalism. Both he and Levi Woodbury also disagreed with Jackson's determination to arrest the nullifiers as soon as South Carolina raised troops. They thought it best to await an overt act.[46] Additional dissent appeared among some of Van Buren's closest Regency associates. Cambreleng severely criticized the proclamation for its "broad errors in doctrine on some of the fundamental principles of the constitution." He and Silas Wright also disapproved of Jackson's reliance on Livingston and McLane, men whose Republican grounding was suspect, and who in McLane's case possessed presidential ambitions that competed with Van Buren's.[47]

As for Van Buren himself, South Carolina's resistance placed him in a precarious situation. He opposed nullification and probably agreed with Jackson's disparaging assessment of its motives. His Regency newspaper echoed the *Globe*'s charge that the nullifiers were "ambitious aspirants," who used the tariff as a "pretext" for agitation to destroy Jackson and to shatter the Union. Moreover, with considerable enthusiasm for protective tariffs evident in his own state, especially among wool growers, Van Buren was not sympathetic to radical and immediate tariff reform. He preferred instead to lower rates "only . . . by degrees."[48]

Yet his own interpretation of Republican doctrine and leadership of the New York–Virginia alliance made Van Buren more sensitive than Jackson to nullification's ability to infect moderate southerners. He was particularly apprehensive that Jackson's temper would provoke a large-scale conflict and elicit sympathy for the South Carolina radicals. He also appreciated the damage done to his own image in the South by his well-publicized vote for the Tariff of Abominations and the evidence of continued tariff sentiment in New York. Van Buren knew that if he expected to harvest southern votes in the future, he would have to demonstrate his trustworthiness.[49]

As a result of these conflicting demands, Van Buren approached the developing crisis with trepidation, and as with so many other conflicts that generated intraparty division—the Bank veto, the enactment of the Tariff of 1832, and the removal of the deposits from the Bank—he was not in Washington while nullification raged. He remained in New York, no doubt happily removed from a direct confrontation with his own southern supporters and with the president himself. Although promising Jackson "the best aid in our power," he explained that "the safe conduct of our affairs here, requires, from the diversity of opinion which exists in regard to the Tariff, & the violence of feeling which has grown out of the late election, great discretion & good temper."[50]

From this discreet distance, Van Buren tried to moderate what he considered Jackson's overly forceful stance. He confessed to Jackson his own disappointment with the proclamation's interpretation of states' rights principles, and privately blamed its "objectionable passages" on Livingston's Federalist bias.[51] He also urged Jackson to avoid warlike measures, and in December 1832, upon learning that the president regarded a legislative act raising military units as sufficient grounds to arrest the nullifiers for treason, he strongly suggested that federal troops be employed only after South Carolina had actually resisted federal laws. "You will say I am on my old track—caution—caution," he conceded. "But my Dr Sir, I have always thought, that considering our respective temperaments, there was no way perhaps in which I could better render you that service which I owe you as well from a sense of deep gratitude as public duty."[52]

The following month, amid rumors of an impending presidential communication dealing with nullification, Van Buren gently warned against discharging a firebrand, remarking that his correspondents were "very anxious" at the prospect of violence. When Jackson issued his Force Bill message, Van Buren again murmured disapproval, informing the president that both he and Benton thought the military provisions of the bill were "unnecessary to the administration." He suggested that Jackson withdraw the bill's military features to appease the South, and advised that efforts concentrate on lowering the tariff. Van Buren himself directed New York Democrats in Washington to work avidly to pass a new and lower tariff proposal, and they responded by promoting the ill-fated Verplanck bill. Meanwhile Regency leaders in the New York State legislature tried to pigeonhole resolutions fully endorsing Jackson's policy.[53]

Van Buren later claimed that his suggestions caused Jackson to scrutinize more carefully his actions and rhetoric. To an extent he was correct, for shortly after receiving one of Van Buren's appeals, Jackson modified his strategy. He now determined to wait until South Carolina actually defied the law before calling out federal forces to arrest its leaders.[54]

But this was Jackson's only concession. Refusing to admit any divergence from Jeffersonian tenets, he denied that a state could peaceably secede from the Union. Publicly and privately he declared that the proclamation reflected his own "settled opinions." The *Globe* backed him up, taking Ritchie to task for the *Enquirer's* constitutional qualms, and boldly announcing that Jackson's whole policy was simply "a re-assertion of the Virginia Doctrine, as brought to bear in legal enactments by Mr. Jefferson in the case of the embargo." Moreover, while Jackson applauded efforts at tariff reform as a means of assuring southern support for the federal government, his enthusiasm was muted by doubts of its ability to halt the nullifiers. Viewing the crisis as a test of republicanism, he assured Van Buren that he would act with "forbearance," but vowed not to sit with folded arms. "The crisis must be now met with firmness," he announced, "our citizens protected, and the modern doctrine of nullification and secession put down forever."[55]

It is difficult to determine whether the criticism leveled at Jackson by Van Buren and his Virginia friends was justified and that the president had deviated from Republican orthodoxy in combating the nullifiers. States' rights theorists had never made clear the conditions under which a state could secede from the Union, or the responsibility of the remaining states to preserve it. Moreover, although Jackson's proclamation at times appeared to veer from sound Jeffersonian doctrine in referring to a constitutionally created nation of *"one people,"* a close reading shows its adherence to the theory of dual sovereignty,

whereby the states had voluntarily relinquished to the federal government certain powers which must be strictly construed. Indeed, the
longer the *Globe* debated these points with Ritchie's *Enquirer*, the
narrower became the area of disagreement between them, and by
September 1833, after emotions had cooled, Ritchie professed himself
satisfied with the *Globe*'s commitment to a confederated, rather than a
consolidated government.[56]

Jackson's differences with Van Buren's New York–Virginia axis,
then, were never so great as to rupture their partnership. Both worked
within a similar, though not identical, states' rights tradition, and the
distance that separated them was considerably less than that between
either one and the southern radicals. Nevertheless, their disagreement involved something more than casuistic speculation over the
nature of the Constitution or the right of peaceable secession. It
showed a concern that Jackson was not sufficiently heedful of southern sensibilities, and the recognition, even among southern moder-
ates, that the president was his own man.

In addition to his other difficulties at this time, Van Buren also
received disturbing indications that Kendall and Blair were using the
nullification crisis for partisan purposes. In November 1832, Kendall
apprised Van Buren of his views about the future course of the administration. The recent presidential election, Kendall explained, had
sealed the fate of both the Bank and the National Republican party,
and men would be casting about for new political moorings. Kendall
therefore suggested that while staying clear of opposition leaders, the
Jackson party strengthen itself, especially in the Senate, by unfurling
the banner of unionism. "All men of all parties in the northern, middle
and western states may be united upon the question of *the Union
against Nullification*, and an immense majority of the South may be
rallied in the same cause," he asserted, adding that "no men who
would rally around the union would be excluded from the pale of the
friends to the administration."[57]

Van Buren's response is not preserved, but he must have detected in
Kendall's words a hint of the old quest for Republican unanimity
which, in Van Buren's opinion, had threatened ruin to the Republican
party's principles and organization during the 1820s. Kendall's
suggestions, therefore, jeopardized Van Buren's vision of a revitalized
Jeffersonian party as well as his own political ambitions. At the same

time, Kendall's emphasis on the North and West implied the possibility that southern states' rights sensibilities might be disregarded in the coming struggle with the nullifiers. Undoubtedly, Van Buren warned Kendall against a policy that would blur party lines and bring prominent nationalists like Daniel Webster into the Democratic fold.[58]

In spite of Van Buren's cautions, Kendall's reply was hardly reassuring. Although agreeing that opposition leaders "must be held at arms length," Kendall reiterated his position that their followers could be "severed from their leaders and, I may say, from their principles," and he announced that he and Blair were preparing essays which would appeal to "all true republicans to rally around the man of the people in aid of his determined efforts to preserve the government and tranquilize the country." Even more ominously, Kendall concluded with a blunt demonstration of his independence by asserting that while he now looked upon Van Buren as Jackson's successor, "the events of a few years may make it necessary to its preponderance that its favor and support shall be bestowed upon another."[59]

The Globe's policy in the following days showed the influence of Kendall's thinking. While editorials compared nullification's threat to the Union with that of the Hartford Convention, thus stigmatizing both Calhoun and Webster, the paper also called for the formation of a "UNION PARTY." It declared that nullification was not a partisan issue and urged that the nation be placed above men and party. Nullification "is no party question," one editorial asserted, "it is a question on which all parties and all persons who love their country, under whatever banner they may have fought in the recent elections, may meet and harmonize. It does not involve the question whether this man or that shall be President, but whether the United States shall ever have another President. . . . Here then is the basis of a great patriotic party, an UNION PARTY."[60]

As the crisis deepened, evidence began to mount of cooperation between Jackson and Webster himself. The Massachusetts senator warmly praised Jackson's stand against the nullifiers and assumed responsibility for managing the Force Bill through the Senate. Jackson in return applauded Webster's speech rebuking Calhoun, and the Globe ceased referring to the "Triumvirs"—Clay, Calhoun, and Webster—and commended instead "the pledges given by those hostile to the President personally and politically, in support of the cause of the Union." When Clay announced his compromise tariff measure, Blair proclaimed the formation of a "New Partnership," a "triple alliance . . . composed of Clay, Calhoun, and the Bank"; Webster was conspicuously absent from the list. The point could not have been lost on Van Buren when John Eaton urged him to go to Washington. "A crisis is at hand in reference to men & things," Eaton explained. "The snail modestly may go into his shell and interrupt no one; but then, as none will see him, all will pass him by. I tell you my good Sir, at such a time as this, when new shoals are being made, & new currents forming, the old pilots should be out upon the coast, or they will make bad navigators. You should be here." [61]

Just how serious the Jackson-Webster movement was remains a matter of conjecture. Webster, reduced to secondary status behind Clay in a party which had recently suffered a clear-cut popular rebuff, was certainly interested in exploring a coalition with Jackson, and he received encouragement from conservative Democrats like Cass and Livingston, men whose political principles and style approximated his own. At the same time, Webster was careful not to break completely with his former allies, and he had no intention of abandoning support for tariff protection and a national bank.[62]

Jackson's approach was equally tentative. Not only did he differ widely from Webster on issues of banking and tariffs, but every sign of a possible alliance brought shrill protests from Van Burenite presses. Van Buren himself warned Jackson of the implications for party unity of a formal association with a man whose principles were "antagonistic" to the president's.[63]

One can only surmise that the national crisis posed by nullification temporarily intensified traditional antiparty prejudices and induced Jackson, Kendall, and Blair cautiously to probe the possibility that Webster, with the Bank dead and his party in shambles, would bring his followers into the president's camp. The union, however, would be made on Jackson's terms, and would involve no sacrifice of his program. Kendall, when broaching to Van Buren the idea of wooing National Republicans, asserted unequivocally that he "would never consent to compromise" on the bank question, and the *Globe*, even as it applauded Webster's support for "the principles of the Union," pointedly remarked that his standing would be greater had he "at an earlier day given his aid to the Administration in reducing the tariff and defeating the machinations of the present coalition." Jackson's friend William B. Lewis probably best expressed the administration's intentions. "I do not think we should court Mr. Webster or any other person, but at the same time I think we should not treat him or his friends harshly," Lewis argued. "I would not *invite*, nor would I repel any man or set of men. If they think proper to adopt our principles and fall in with us, I say let them do so."[64]

The insolubility of a mixture of Jackson and Webster elements became apparent early in the session of Congress following the removal of the deposits. By the end of January 1834, Webster fully appreciated Jackson's intention not to recharter Biddle's bank or *any* bank, and the senator returned to the opposition fold. Notions of restructuring party lines evaporated as antiparty suspicions gave way to partisan strife. But during the period between Jackson's reelection and the opening of Congress, Webster remained immune to attacks from the *Globe*, and he received a warm reception from Jacksonians when he toured the West in the aftermath of nullification. The discrepancy between such treatment and the rough handling he received from pro–Van Buren papers was not lost on the opposition, and Duff Green contended that "very different feelings are entertained towards Mr. Webster by the democracy of the west and those of the north and east. . . . The west are quite enthusiastic."[65]

The strained atmosphere produced by a possible coalition with Webster, when combined with Blair's passionate defense of Jackson's nullification policy, his chiding of Van Buren's southern allies, especially Ritchie, and his early advocacy of withdrawing the government's deposits from the Bank, apparently incited during this crucial period another unsuccessful attempt to push Noah, the New York editor, into a partnership with him. Although Blair publicly denied there were any problems with the *Globe*, his brother-in-law, with whom he corresponded on personal and political matters, was "pleased to hear you will have nothing to do with Noah. . . . If your party wants him let the money be forthcoming and sell out your establishment for a price. . . . [obliterated but apparently "Va"]n B—— will pay liberally and so will the rest of the party. [If?] they think he will answer their purpose, do not hesitate if they make advantageous offers. There is no friendship among political asparants [*sic*], as you well know. . . . Old Hickory appears to be deserted by his old friends."[66]

Prospects for a peaceable resolution of the nullification controversy brightened considerably when, on 21 January 1833, a public meeting in Charleston, South Carolina, resolved to postpone nullification until Congress completed deliberations on tariff reform. A few weeks later, in mid-February, Clay and Calhoun made public their agreement to underwrite a compromise tariff which would provide a face-saving retreat for the nullifiers. Jackson, however, refused to shift his priorities and make Clay's bill an administration measure, and thus left Democrats to vote as they wished. He knew that Clay's proposal was assured of congressional approval and would relax tensions, but he found it distasteful. A month before Clay introduced it, Jackson had observed that an effort was underway to "save Calhoun" which "would disgrace . . . [the] country and the Executive." Nevertheless, he acquiesced in the compromise.[67]

At the same time, he insisted on passage of the Force Bill. He considered it necessary not only as security against the possibility that the nullifiers might disavow the compromise and secede, but also as a symbol of the permanence and vitality of the Union. The Force Bill would "show to the world" that the United States was prepared "to crush in an instant" rebellion and treason. It was over this measure that his friendship with Van Buren was most severely strained. Jackson expected the New York legislature to support the bill, and when no such resolution was forthcoming, he was furious. "Why is your Legislature silent at this eventful crisis," he demanded of Van Buren. "Friendship, with candor, compels me to say to you, that your friends are astonished at the silence of your Legislature, and gives rise to dark innuendoes of your enemies, that you command them."[68]

With the *Globe* broadcasting Jackson's resoluteness and chastising those who wavered, the Force Bill easily passed both houses of Congress. But southern dissatisfaction was evident in the number of abstentions in the Senate. Only nine of the twenty-four senators from slaveholding states voted in favor of passage; with the exception of John Tyler's adverse vote, the rest went unrecorded. In the House, the story was somewhat different. There were fewer absentions, but virtually all of the forty-eight nays came from representatives of the slaveholding states, and well over half of the membership from the

South cast their votes in opposition.[69] The Force Bill arrived on Jackson's desk the same day as the new tariff, and he signed it first, declaring that it gave "the death blow" to nullification. The end of the crisis thus found him vigorously affirming the federal government's authority and power in opposition to what he deemed a conspiracy against the republic.[70]

With the conclusion of the nullification crisis, most Americans breathed a sigh of relief that civil war had been averted. Perhaps because the conflict with South Carolina resembled a military campaign, they had witnessed a display of presidential leadership unrivaled by any other decision of Jackson's presidency. One prominent Democrat was astonished by Jackson's firmness and self-confidence during the crisis. "He is a much abler man than I thought him," George M. Dallas reported. "One of those naturally great minds which seem ordinary except when the fitting emergency arises."[71]

Jackson had drawn upon the talents of a number of advisers in responding to South Carolina's challenge. Livingston and McLane made their only positive and significant contributions to his administration during nullification, helping to draft the proclamation, the Force Bill message, and the administration's initial tariff proposal. Kendall and Blair also provided assistance, especially in rallying public support behind the president. Van Buren, however, had little effect on Jackson's policy. He remained safely away from Washington until late February 1833, explaining that his presence at the capital would only further inflame irritated feelings. His disagreement with what he considered Jackson's errant Jeffersonian notions and precipitous military preparations taxed the president's patience and good will. Yet Van Buren was able to rebound quickly, and the two men soon returned to their normal amicable relations. Doubtless Jackson appreciated the awkward situation in which Van Buren was placed by his special association with former southern Crawford men, and he recognized that Van Buren would be at his side if the need arose. In the end, both New York senators voted with the majority to pass the Force Bill.[72]

It would be hazardous to claim that Jackson's nullification policy had any permanent effect on the Democratic party. In the North, party lines were temporarily blurred as Jackson won the plaudits of many whose political beliefs normally placed them in the opposition. There

were widespread rumors during the controversy of a permanent alliance with Daniel Webster and the formation of a new Union party.[73]
However, party lines quickly regained clarity when Jackson renewed
his assault on the Bank by removing the government's deposits.

In the South, Jackson's vigorous stand provided the occasion for a
number of states' rights extremists to bolt the Democratic party and
form one element of the emerging Whig organization. But the great
majority of southern Democrats remained loyal. To be sure, many
regretted that the president was not sufficiently orthodox in his political beliefs. But it was also evident that his views more closely harmonized with theirs than did those of Clay, Webster, or the other
possible alternatives, and that if Jackson and his key advisers were
sensitive to southern demands to a lesser degree than Van Buren,
Ritchie, and their associates, he still agreed that the tariff should be
reformed, sectionally divisive legislation eschewed, and the Constitution strictly construed. The South, although not dictating policy,
found sufficient grounds for continuing its firm attachment to the
Democracy.[74]

This southern connection was facilitated by nullification's effect in
identifying the Democratic party with a low tariff platform. Although
Jackson would eventually have called for a reduction in rates regardless of nullification, southern protests certainly sharpened his desire
to pursue reform. From 1830 to 1833, his annual messages to Congress
revealed a growing insistence on the need to adjust tariff levels equi-
tably for all interests.

The rhetoric in which Jackson announced his demands for limited
protection, however, indicated that he viewed tariff reform as part of
the party's broader antimonopoly and antiprivilege ideology. Excessive tariff schedules not only encroached on states' rights, but by
aiding special interests they threatened fair and honest government.
Expressing ideas that coincided with those of Kendall and Blair,
Jackson objected to Clay's compromise tariff because he thought its
surplus revenue would be employed to secure a new Bank charter and
to construct extravagant internal improvements. Lower duties, therefore, were essential to assure republican government and were as
beneficial to the North and West as to the South.[75]

The passage of the compromise tariff and Force Bill freed Jackson to
turn to other issues, notably the Bank. However, even though he

asserted that nullification was "dead," the president worried that southern radicals would continue to stir trouble. Since he attributed nullification to political ambition rather than to discontent with the tariff, he remained skeptical that Clay's compromise would bring permanent peace. Indeed, the bill's provisions confirmed his doubts. Asserting that the new rates both retained the principle of protection and levied higher duties than the Tariff of 1832 on such necessities as coarse woolens, he claimed that the new tariff "was only a pretext and disunion & a southern confederacy the real object."[76]

In the aftermath of the crisis, the *Globe* similarly contended that economic discontent was not the nullifiers' primary concern. South Carolina's great staple, the paper noted, was rice, a crop which continuously brought "immense wealth" to South Carolina in the period preceding nullification. Since the tariff scarcely affected this crop, why did planters hurl defiance at it? The *Globe*'s response was that the tariff was merely a screen for the pursuit of power. "Political objects, and not pecuniary distresses," it concluded, "have been the real cause of these lamentations, which have been so well feigned by the S. Carolina orators."[77]

In the spring of 1833, some nullifiers denounced the compromise tariff and called for continued and unceasing efforts to protect southern institutions from prejudicial legislation. They also defended slavery more directly from what they considered the threatening activity of northern abolitionists who, Duff Green alleged, had received "a new impulse" from the doctrines of Jackson's administration.[78] Jackson sensed trouble ahead for the Union. He predicted that the nullifiers, having failed on the tariff issue, would grasp "the negro, or slavery question" as their "next pretext." Blair also warned that the radicals were determined to use slavery "as the next cause of excitement . . . for the purpose of embodying the Southern States against those North of the Potomac." According to the *Globe*, the "malcontents," no longer able to exploit the tariff issue, would seek "to produce a dissolution of the Union . . . through agitation of the Slave Question."[79]

Whether southern radicals responded realistically or evidenced a paranoid reaction to early abolitionist efforts is debatable.[80] What is certain, however, is that Jackson's political assumptions filtered reality in such a way as to prevent him from fully appreciating southern anxieties or conceding that the nullifiers had sincere and principled motives. Instead, he perceived radical dissent as the product of political ambition and conspiratorial drives. Declaring that the radicals' dire accounts of northern hostility to slavery were a "false tale," he contended that they would work with intriguers like Clay to "blow up a storm on the subject of the slave question," disrupt the republic, and elevate themselves to power. Slavery was simply a pretext, and those who agitated the subject were, in the *Globe*'s words, exciting "alarms which have not the slightest hold, even on the imaginations of those who originate them." [81]

7
Destroying the Bank

Nullification was not an issue of Jackson's own choosing. Southern radicals had forced this crisis in federal-state relations and diverted his attention from other concerns, especially the Bank. Shortly after its resolution, Jackson resumed his campaign against the "mamoth [*sic*] of corruption," resolving to destroy Biddle's institution by removing the government's deposits.[1] Historians have generally focused on the consequences of Jackson's decision for the nation's economy and for the development of presidential powers.[2] Yet removal also had significant political and ideological implications that made it the most momentous decision of his second term. For the Bank forces, it effectually ended hopes of obtaining a new charter. For Democrats, it reaffirmed their party's institutional cohesiveness and commitment to the principles of limited government, antimonopoly, and individual initiative. Jackson's second assault against the Bank also marked the high point of Kendall's and Blair's influence. It was they who, along with Jackson, were most responsible for the conclusion that severing the Bank's ties as the government's fiscal agent was vital to the perpetuation of the republic and the Democratic party itself.

The idea of withdrawing the government's deposits from the Bank had been discussed in White House circles ever since the inception of Jackson's anti-Bank campaign in 1829. In November of that year, when Kendall informed the New York *Courier & Enquirer* of the president's impending attack on the Bank, he indicated that the deposits might, at a future date, be placed in state banks. However, although Jackson, Kendall, and Van Buren continued to discuss the possibility of employing state banks as an alternative to Biddle's institution, they primarily focused on a decentralized national bank plan. This scheme, which vaguely resembled Van Buren's later independent treasury proposal, was suggested in Jackson's first and second annual messages. Congress, however, refused to consider it, and Jackson, concluding that any national bank would probably fall into the same hands as the old one, abandoned the idea. By the time of the Bank veto, then, the president had not resolved on a substitute agency.[3]

The veto itself did not compel an immediate change in the government's relationship to the Bank. The charter did not expire until 1836 and then it permitted the Bank two years more to wind up its affairs. Thus the government could continue dealing with the Bank throughout Jackson's second term and avoid the problem of finding an acceptable alternative.

The Bank's conduct in the period after the veto, however, decided Jackson on taking further measures against the institution and establishing a new financial system. He charged that Biddle had used Bank funds to aid Clay's presidential campaign, and he denounced the Bank's exclusion of the government's directors from major responsibilities as evidence of its irresponsible, secretive, and dictatorial management. When he then learned that Biddle had violated the Bank's charter by contracting with an English banking firm to delay payment of American 3 percent loan certificates, he became suspicious that the Bank was insolvent and, therefore, unsafe for federal funds. That its action had also postponed the accomplishment of his cherished goal of liquidating the public debt provided additional evidence of the Bank's untrustworthiness. In Jackson's eyes, Biddle would neither work harmoniously with the government nor acknowledge his defeat. His behavior confirmed Jackson's understanding that a privileged, centralized, and powerful monied institution like the Bank posed a threat to republican government. "The hydra of corruption is only *scotched, not dead*," the president asserted.[4]

Taking his reelection as a popular mandate for his anti-Bank position, Jackson considered the means of bringing the institution to heel, either by removing the government's deposits or by issuing a writ of scire facias, a legal action that would bring the Bank before a federal court to determine whether by its conduct it had forfeited its charter. In November 1832, he raised this subject for his cabinet's reflection and promised that he would return to it at a future time.[5] In his annual message to Congress the following month, he placed the Bank on notice by criticizing its handling of the 3 percents and recommending an investigation into its affairs. The inquiry, he declared, was warranted by the numerous charges against the Bank, which "if true may justly excite the apprehension that it is no longer a safe repository of the money of the people." [6]

Jackson was urged on in his course by Blair and Kendall. As early as September 1832, the *Globe* warned the Bank that its electioneering activity would lead to retaliation by the government, specifically the withdrawal of "the national deposits from the control of the Bank." That winter, while the nullification controversy raged, Blair found room in the paper to denounce the Bank's transgressions, to raise doubts about its solvency, and to threaten action. "If the public deposits cannot be had for the public service from the Bank . . . it is time to try other banks. The government cannot be worse off, and may be better," he asserted.[7] At the same time, Kendall adamantly contended that further action was imperative to weaken the Bank and prevent it from throwing its weight behind an opposition candidate in 1836. He informed Van Buren that he would resign if he had to give up the battle against the Bank. "I can live under a corrupt despotism, as well as any other man, by keeping out of its way," he declared.[8]

Taney, too, argued vigorously for withdrawing the government's money. At a cabinet meeting in November, he maintained that the Bank's handling of the 3 percents indicated it was "no longer trustworthy as the agent of the government and ought not to be continued as such." He also warned that the longer the Bank stayed alive, the better its chances of securing recharter after Jackson left office.[9]

But Jackson's early suggestion of intensifying the Bank War encountered opposition. McLane opposed removal, claiming the government had no evidence that the Bank was financially unsound. His suggestion that the president consider a writ of scire facias rather than removal was interpreted by Taney as a subterfuge to save an institution that McLane considered essential to a stable and prosperous economy. The legal case would be heard in a Pennsylvania court where the Bank could expect a favorable reception.[10]

Van Buren was also flustered by further anti-Bank activity. He informed Blair that removal would be "both injudicious and impolitic," and he held an interview with Kendall to criticize continued agitation in the face of a recently adopted House resolution declaring the government's deposits safe. Van Buren's political instincts told him that his presidential ambitions would best be served by keeping the party on an even keel for the remainder of Jackson's presidency, and he considered speculation about the Bank's insolvency too flimsy a defense to withstand the expected political outcry against contravening the House resolution.[11] McLane's resistance was indicative of the potential danger. He had little influence with Jackson, but was respected by conservative Democrats, especially those with Federalist antecedents, who deplored attacks against the Bank. Van Buren's partiality to McLane, shown by continuing recommendations for prominent political appointments, attested to his desire to keep such men within the party's ranks. Removal, however, would jeopardize their allegiance.[12]

Even more worrisome was the reaction of Van Buren's own southern allies, particularly in Virginia. Southern Democrats rallied enthusiastically to Jackson's Bank veto, but the prospect of removing the government's deposits was not received with equal ardor. A recent study of attitudes towards the Bank at the time of removal, for example, aptly labels Virginia bankers as only "cautiously hostile" to the institution. The state's banking community was conservative and stable, and, though opposed to Biddle's bank, it was not overjoyed at the possibility of disrupting established business relationships and stimulating new competition.[13]

Politically, too, removal risked another controversy over presidential authority and governmental powers. Many southern planters still adhered to traditional notions of political leadership, and therefore feared the rise of demagogues who not only appealed to the mob but also utilized political machinery and patronage to control the government. An executive order affecting the government's revenue evoked especially alarming images of financial disorder and the dreaded union of the sword and the purse. Jackson's firm course on nullification had already provoked criticism from the influential Richmond *Enquirer*, and many southerners had refused to support the Force Bill. Removal might stir an even stronger reaction and lead to massive defections from the party. As early as November 1832, Ritchie warned House Speaker Andrew Stevenson of "the mischievous consequences of removing the Deposits." According to Ritchie, southerners resented Jackson's aggrandizement of executive power, and he predicted that an order withdrawing the deposits would bring a whirlwind of trouble in the South.[14]

Finally, it is clear from Van Buren's later actions that he feared another move against the Bank would leave the administration vulnerable to charges of working in the interest of New York bankers. Since the port of New York collected the bulk of the nation's import duties, Empire State banks stood to gain enormous profits upon receiving the government's revenue. And as Van Buren's close friend Silas Wright observed, there were a number of New York Democrats who fairly itched to get their hands on these funds. The justice of the president's policy might therefore be confused by the activity of speculative bankers, and Van Buren would be indicted for deranging the currency in order to satisfy the demands of "a monied junto in N. York. . . ."[15]

In the winter of 1832–33, such considerations made the vice-president oppose talk of removal. However, the vehemence with which Kendall defended the policy to him warned Van Buren that resistance might jeopardize Jackson's backing for the succession. Thus a short time after Van Buren's discussion with Kendall, Lewis found him reluctantly defending removal. When asked about his change of attitude, Van Buren explained that the president had made up his mind to act and the question was therefore settled.[16]

Van Buren's assessment of Jackson's position was accurate, for even as nullification absorbed his energies, the president was engaged in selecting a new Treasury secretary who would expedite removal. The Treasury post was of special importance since the Bank's charter invested it with the power to remove the deposits. Secretary of State Livingston, uncomfortable with Jackson's Bank policy and having found the burden of his cabinet responsibilities too great for his nearly seventy years of age, was scheduled to become minister to France. By November 1832, Jackson had decided that McLane should replace him and someone more in favor of removal should go to the Treasury Department.[17]

Jackson looked to Pennsylvania for his appointment. Opposition to his Bank and internal improvements policies had weakened the Democratic party in that state, and the appointment of a native son might, therefore, revitalize party loyalty as well as identify the state with future actions against the Bank. But finding a suitable man was not easy. The state organization was divided into contentious factions, each of which would resist the nomination of a rival. Furthermore, most of Pennsylvania's leading politicians had refused to support Van Buren in 1832, thus eliminating themselves from consideration by a president determined to appoint no one hostile to his vice-president. However, the name of William Duane "flashed into" Jackson's mind, for Duane appeared to have impeccable credentials. The son of the famous Jeffersonian newspaper editor, he was an opponent of the Bank. He had also remained independent of Pennsylvania's factional bickering while supporting Van Buren in 1832.[18]

Duane was offered the post in December 1832 but did not take office until the following June, after the nullification crisis had abated and Congress had adjourned. His appointment turned out to be singularly unfortunate. Although firmly opposed to the Bank, he was unwilling to take further action against it, least of all by placing the government's money in state banks.

Ironically, Duane shared many of the president's own hard-money beliefs. He held that the Constitution forbade local banks to issue paper money and that such paper caused "fluctuations, revulsions and panics," while generating "inequality in condition, luxury and vice." He predicted that the state banks would misuse the government's deposits and flood the country with the despised paper currency. However, he had no alternative plan of his own and when Jackson later asked for suggestions, the secretary could reply only vaguely that the government might somehow separate itself from all banks.[19]

Duane's monetary notions were not insurmountable obstacles to the successful performance of his duties—had he been willing to make concessions. But the Pennsylvanian was aloof, stubborn, and contentious. Adhering to "an elevated conception" of politics where men were "called into service" to seek the "common good," he denounced the "mere politicians" and the "sly, whispering, slandering system" which he thought characterized Jackson's White House. His repugnance to the type of men he found in Washington strengthened his resolve to obey his own conscience and resist Jackson's will. Nor was there much hope that the honor of a presidential appointment would inspire a willingness to compromise. "As to gratitude for kindness," commented a leading Pennsylvania politico, "the President may as well seek it in a lizard. He is utterly unaccessible to the feeling."[20]

Jackson's appointment of Duane had been too hastily undertaken. Wrongly assuming that the Pennsylvanian's opposition to Biddle's Bank and loyalty to the Democratic party would make him eager to follow through on removal, Jackson neglected to consult any of his closest advisers prior to the selection. Only after he had fixed his mind on Duane did he ask for an opinion, and then he turned to McLane. Whether McLane knew of Duane's opposition to state banking is a moot question. Whatever the truth, he raised no objections to the appointment and without further ado, Jackson invited Duane into the cabinet. It was a serious blunder.[21]

In March 1833, with nullification safely resolved, Jackson revived the Bank issue on a note of greater urgency. Not only did resentment over the Bank's previous transgressions still fester, but the circumstances surrounding the conclusion of the nullification crisis provided new grounds for concern. The opposition, which had recently appeared so weak and divided that key Democrats considered the possibility of its complete collapse, now appeared revitalized by the alliance between Clay and Calhoun. Their collaboration presaged a stronger opposition party which would find a common denominator in supporting recharter.

No sooner had Clay offered his compromise tariff proposal than Blair denounced the "new coalition" with Calhoun based upon "preserving the protective policy, and accumulating surpluses in the Treasury to sustain the Bank and to be voted out in largesses by Congress." Kendall was even more vivid about the danger. "A new combination is now formed of which the Bank is the nucleus and the citadel," he contended. The reinvigorated opposition would demand internal improvements and high land prices, while "the Bank is to support its supporters, and send its life blood through the arteries of the whole combination. From an overflowing Treasury as well as a corrupt Bank, the presses and instruments of this new scheme are to be fed and rewarded."[22]

To Kendall, the peril was not immediate but lay in the future; the coalition anticipated an "easy victory" over a president who, without Jackson's popularity, attempted to maintain his principles. The destruction of the Bank, he therefore argued, must take place while Jackson's "deep rooted popularity" could offset the Bank's power.

Moreover, this was essential to the perpetuation of the Democratic party. The president's friends were presently in a state of "doubt, hesitation and discouragement," Kendall claimed. They needed "some decisive act to reunite and inspirit them." In short, a dramatic and bold stroke against the Bank would restore energy, coherence, and discipline to the party.[23]

Jackson shared this concern and had undoubtedly discussed the situation at length with Kendall, for he virtually echoed his adviser's argument about the significance of the Clay-Calhoun alliance. Warning a friend that the opposition sought a rechartered Bank as the hub of a system of high land prices, protective tariffs, and internal improvements, Jackson announced his determination to meet the "crisis." He therefore propounded to his cabinet and a select group of advisers a series of questions concerning the government's relationship to the Bank. At the same time he revealed his own stance that no new national bank should be considered until "a full and fair experiment" had been undertaken with state banks. He left open the timing of the move, however, recommending only that the new system "go into operation at such a time as shall upon a careful consideration of the subject be thought most advisable."[24]

If Jackson and Kendall thought removal might infuse new life into the party, the responses to Jackson's propositions demonstrated its potential for discord. The strongest objections came from McLane, who filled ninety pages with disputations about the dangers of disturbing the currency. Arguing that the Bank was safe, McLane suggested that it retain the revenue until the expiration of its charter necessitated a change. He also declared that he would consider a new national bank "with the proper safeguards" financially sounder than a system of state institutions.[25]

Less assertive than McLane, but hardly more reassuring to the president, were some of the other responses. Navy Secretary Woodbury's moderate hard-money views and his assistance at the time of the Bank veto promised some support. But Woodbury was temperamentally cautious, a disposition that was reinforced by strong political and personal ties to conservatives, whose backing he hoped would eventually elevate him to the presidency. He now claimed to be unconvinced by arguments of the Bank's insolvency and advised against undertaking removal until the summer of 1834, when the anticipated demise of the Bank would make a gradual transfer of the government's revenue less controversial. Similar advice came from Tennessee's Senator Hugh Lawson White, who asserted that "public opinion" would not uphold interference with the Bank at this early date. Postmaster General Barry, though more receptive to Jackson's arguments about removal, simply stated that he would leave the issue where he thought it rightfully belonged, to the president and his Treasury secretary.[26]

Jackson, however, received encouragement from other aides. Reuben M. Whitney, a former Philadelphia merchant and director of the Bank, recommended that the president take immediate action. Whitney had arrived in Washington in the spring of 1832 to testify before Congress about the Bank's transgressions and had stayed on to advise Jackson about its activities. He had turned against the Bank partly because he believed Biddle corrupt, but also because he had once been refused a loan when his business was on the brink of collapse. His experience and access to inside information about the institution made him a valuable counterweight to Biddle, who shrouded the Bank's operations in secrecy from the government's directors.[27]

Notwithstanding the opposition's allegations that Whitney was a leading member of the Kitchen Cabinet, Jackson never considered him a confidant. Whitney's obvious desire for a government post marked him as a political opportunist, and his lack of enthusiasm for a hard-money currency, which he regarded as an "absurdity," placed him outside Jackson's inner circle and would eventually cause him to bolt the party.[28] Still, in the spring and summer of 1833, Whitney's familiarity with the detested Bank gave him entrée among Jackson's advisers, and his opinion was for immediate removal.

Whitney's conclusion was seconded by Taney, whose animosity to the Bank's power increasingly drew him into Jackson's confidence. Taney had first argued for removal the previous November, and he now stated that nothing had changed his mind about the Bank's irresponsible management or the dangers inherent in a "monied institution . . . which feels that money gives it power, and that power will bring it money." He also expressed confidence that "judiciously selected" state banks would provide the necessary services for the government as well as furnish a currency "as wholesome and stable as that of the U. States Bank." The "purity of our institutions," he concluded, called for prompt and decisive action.[29]

Kendall was equally ardent in his response to the president. He had been spending hours systematizing his thinking on the issue, outlining a financial system to replace the Bank, and conferring with cabinet members whose opinions he knew the president would request, particularly McLane. Now summarizing his ideas for Jackson, Kendall argued that "that great enemy of republicanism," the Bank, must not be spared. He warned that there was a scheme afoot to renew the corrupt system of internal improvements, the Bank, public lands, and surplus revenue, and that its advocates looked to the period after Jackson's presidency for gaining control of the government. He implored Jackson to "strike from the hands of corruption its means to do mischief," by removing the public deposits, crippling the Bank, and depriving "the conspirators of the aid which they expect from its money and power."[30]

Kendall argued against establishing any other national bank in place of Biddle's, for such an institution "impairs the morals of our people, corrupts our Statesmen and is dangerous to liberty." Instead, he suggested reliance on a few state banks which could perform the Treasury's services, and discounted the possibility that removal would disrupt the country's financial system. By obtaining federal revenue, he claimed, the state banks would be able to resist any policy adopted by the Bank and would become "powerful friends" of the administration in its fight against Biddle.

Once again, Kendall noted the importance of removal for the Democratic party. "The public mind is now at a stand," he declared. Nullification had created doubts about "the future course of the administration and the arrangement of parties," and people were uncertain where to find their political principles and friends. He urged Jackson to chart the party's future and predicted that a decisive thrust against the Bank would inspire the "true men of the country" to rally with new enthusiasm around the administration.

Kendall's advice reflected his unbending conviction of the Bank's corruption and of the need to restore sound and moral principles to government. That it was largely in accord with Jackson's sentiments was evident in May 1833, when the president asked Kendall to prepare the outline of a state banking system that would go into operation before Congress assembled in December. Jackson also indicated his disagreement with McLane's reasoning by sending the secretary's treatise to Blair for critical analysis; the editor responded with a compilation of the Bank's misdeeds designed to highlight its arbitrary and irresponsible ways.[31]

By the time Jackson began his triumphal postnullification tour of eastern cities on 6 June 1833, he had resolved on removing the deposits, but had not made a firm commitment about the timing or details of the change. The disagreement evident among his advisers about the justice and expediency of the policy cautioned him against precipitate action. Moreover, he had encountered an unexpected complication shortly before departing the capital when, on 1 June, Duane assumed office. The secretary, upon learning from Kendall and Whitney that Jackson had decided to withdraw the deposits, marched into the president's office and declared that he would never issue an order to place the government's revenue in state banks. Jackson responded that the Bank had to be put down before it could secure recharter, but he did not pursue matters further, instead promising to send Duane more information while he was on tour.[32]

When the president's caravan reached New York, Jackson found Van Buren receptive to Kendall's plan for early action, though with what degree of enthusiasm it is impossible to say; and he fixed his mind on having the new policy in effect before Congress convened. As Kendall had advised, a bold stroke would force the stragglers into line, and Jackson likened this stratagem to "that of Cortez, who burnt his ships on the shore when he marched on Mexico. Our doubtful friends should have no ship to fly to, no hope but in the success of the Administration."[33] When the tour reached Boston in late June, therefore, Jackson informed Duane that he had "come to the conclusion" that removal should be initiated "at furthest, by the 1st or 15th of September next, so that we may have it in our power to present the new system to Congress, in complete and successful operation, at the commencement of the session."[34]

Jackson also detailed a plan for organizing the state banks that was substantially like Kendall's, with a small number of primary and secondary banks which would be responsible for the federal funds. The banks would provide the same financial services as the Bank of the United States, and would be required to make frequent reports about their operations to the Treasury secretary. He then recommended Kendall as the "proper person" to carry out the negotiations with the state banks.[35]

A few days later, Jackson became ill and cut short the rest of his New England tour. Back in Washington to recuperate, he found Duane adamant in opposing Kendall's plan. The secretary agreed that Biddle's bank was "unconstitutional and of evil tendency," but he declared the state banks equally unconstitutional as well as irresponsible and inefficient. In his opinion, the time was right to develop a permanent solution to the nation's financial needs, and he suggested that Congress "appoint a commission, to consider the whole question of our currency, banking, &c."[36]

Duane's objections may have been financially sound, but they were politically naive and impractical, and his suggestion of an independent commission totally ignored the Bank's continuing quest for a new charter. Even though Jackson and his Kitchen Cabinet exaggerated the Bank's power to influence politics, they were undoubtedly correct in assuming that the prompt withdrawal of the deposits would severely diminish the prospects for recharter. Duane seemed oblivious to the evident truth that economic decisions cannot be divorced from politics, and as a result, he became an unwitting ally of an institution that he condemned.[37]

For two weeks during the middle of July, Jackson and Duane debated the legality and expediency of removing the deposits, and finally Duane agreed to a mission by Kendall inquiring whether the state banks would accept the government's plan. Jackson and Kendall then privately conferred on the latter's instructions, wording them in such a way that the envoy was permitted to assure bankers that the deposits were going to be removed whether or not any particular bank agreed to accept them. The phrasing was critical because both men realized that bankers would be reluctant to challenge Biddle unless they believed the decision to remove was irrevocable.[38]

When Kendall left Washington at the end of July, his purpose was to provide Jackson with positive evidence that the state banks were willing to become the government's bankers. And it would be difficult to imagine a more zealous agent, for Kendall believed that the Bank must be crushed or the republic would soon be saddled again with the monster. The whole of his anti-Bank career seemed to climax on this errand, and he was determined to succeed. "If we do not now overcome this Bank influence and carry the point of removal we may give up all for lost," he wrote Blair from one of his stops. "I can retire into the shell of the 4th Auditor's Office; but you—what will you do? The enemies of the Bank will be insulted and trodden upon, and it will require much courage to hold up our heads. On the contrary, if the point be carried, we shall have a firm, zealous party and shall have put down the Bank forever."[39]

Kendall skillfully went about his business. Knowing the state banks' fear of Biddle, he played upon their desire for the government's money. And emphasizing that the deposits were, in fact, being withdrawn from the Bank, he provided an "excuse to their master if he should call them to account. They may say to him, 'really, my liege, we could see no objection to undertaking this business after your death, or if *sufficient reasons* should exist for taking it from you' etc." The tactic was evidently successful, for Kendall was generally received warmly by state bankers wherever he went.[40]

Although the primary purpose of Kendall's mission was to solicit state bank cooperation, he and Jackson hoped that a favorable response would also overcome the cabinet's doubts and objections. Unity in the cabinet would help assure the policy's acceptance in Congress and the country. But as the summer progressed, opposition to removal intensified. Duane, McLane, and Woodbury remained adverse in varying degrees, and on the presidential tour of the Northeast, Cass also revealed his disagreement. Towards the end of July, Lewis reported "a good deal of unpleasant feeling in the cabinet," and Woodbury later recalled that the majority was so strongly hostile to immediate removal that even the zealous Taney wavered momentarily.[41] Lewis, who thought removal would disrupt the economy and shatter the party, urged Blair to moderate his demands for early action, and he collaborated with Ritchie to formulate arguments against the policy. He admitted, however, that their arguments were "thrown away upon . . . [Blair] and some other Anti-Bank men here."[42]

The magnitude of this resistance seems to have surprised and unsettled Jackson. Hoping to moderate its severity, he considered the possibility of having the new banking system ready to operate when Congress convened but delaying the actual withdrawal until 1

January, when Congress was in session. By not presenting the legislature with a fait accompli, this alternative appeared more respectful of its power over the purse. As July drew to a close, Jackson asked Van Buren for his opinion and then fled the capital's summer heat for the Rip Raps, a vacation spot in Virginia, to ponder his decision while awaiting Van Buren's reply. Significantly, he asked Blair, an avid proponent of immediate removal, to accompany him.[43]

At the Rip Raps, Jackson received letters from Kendall, Taney, and Whitney urging immediate action against the Bank, and Blair was always at his side advancing the case for a coup de grace. With this encouragement, Jackson again resolved to complete the removal process before Congress assembled. He would not hazard his policy by any delays just to satisfy his cabinet's scruples. He and Blair therefore worked on a formal message justifying his decision to be presented to the cabinet; by 12 August the rough draft was finished and Jackson sent it to Van Buren for inspection. "Every investigation develops some more corruption of this mamoth [sic] of power, and brings to view the necessity of separating it from the Government as early as possible," he declared in a covering letter.[44]

Evidence of discord, however, continued to confront the president. Kendall reported rumors in New York and Philadelphia to the effect that Duane and McLane were conspiring to prevent removal. Jackson relayed this "truly mortifying" information to Van Buren, warning that such stories would injure McLane and undermine the vice-president's popularity, "it being well understood the confidence and friendship that exists between you & him."[45]

Even more distressing were reports about Van Buren's own activity. Whitney reported to Blair that he had seen McLane and Georgia's Senator John Forsyth hurrying to New York. Forsyth, he had learned, was alarmed at the prospect of removing the deposits and was now going to see Van Buren. He surmised that McLane's purpose was the same. Just two days after Whitney wrote his letter, Kendall informed Jackson that he had been surprised to find McLane and Van Buren having breakfast together at a hotel in New York. The two men had then suggested to Kendall that the state bank system be organized immediately but that removal be delayed until 1 January, leaving Congress time to legislate on the whole banking question before the president acted on his own.[46]

Kendall first suspected that McLane had devised the proposal in hopes that Congress would prevent removal. But the two men argued that their object was to unite the cabinet behind the president's policy and to prevent the administration from acting in defiance of the legislature. His fears only partially allayed, Kendall confided to Jackson that he would support this proposal *"provided"* that McLane and Duane gave firm assurances they would use their influence to sustain removal should Congress fail to adopt a satisfactory alternative to the present deposit system. If they should renege on their promise and use their influence to defeat removal, Kendall warned, there was "a probability that they and the Bank would carry two-thirds against it and we should be in a worse condition than ever." The only *"certain"* course, he concluded, was to remove the deposits before Congress met, but if the whole cabinet agreed to the plan, he would acquiesce.[47]

McLane's idea, which was later referred to as his "middle course," was similar to the one that Jackson had just rejected, largely at the urging of Blair. McLane's scheme, however, was slightly more elaborate since it entailed his and Duane's commitment to support removal after 1 January. It also had conservative overtones. What he and Duane considered appropriate congressional action on the government's fiscal system might differ considerably from what Jackson would accept. If Congress should pass another national bank bill, the secretaries might consider their part of the bargain fulfilled.

In any case, McLane's proposal was a dangerous gambit for the administration. It gave Congress time to cause mischief or even enact legislation preventing removal. It is therefore likely that Kendall was initially correct in suspecting that McLane offered the scheme in hopes of sabotaging Jackson's plan. McLane had in fact first proposed to Van Buren that Jackson do nothing more than direct Congress's attention to the financial problems caused by the Bank veto and initiate removal only if Congress failed to legislate a solution. Moreover, Duane later denied that he had ever consented to McLane's idea, claiming that he would never agree to any plan involving the use of state banks.[48]

On the other hand, Van Buren's participation probably had nothing to do with blocking the president's will. Indeed, he had emphatically rejected McLane's first proposal as "useless and discreditable." But the vice-president found the middle course attractive because it offered the prospect of uniting the party behind Jackson's policy. As Forsyth's trip to New York indicated, many of Van Buren's southern allies feared Jackson would act on his own before Congress assembled. McLane's proposal might pacify them and, at the same time, allow McLane to remain in the party. Van Buren, therefore, retreated from his previous support of early removal.[49]

When news of the Van Buren–McLane conference reached the Rip Raps, Jackson was determined to seize the initiative, and it was undoubtedly with his approbation that Blair dispatched a letter to Van Buren denouncing the middle course. "What has the president to expect from procrastination," he asked the vice-president. "Nothing but division among his friends in Congress, and impregnable phalanx drawn together under Messrs. Clay, Webster, & Calhoun to sustain . . . [the Bank] in its present position."[50]

Blair mockingly expressed wonder that such a Bank partisan as McLane was prepared to become the Bank's enemy on 1 January. "The fact is," the editor declared, "disguise it as you may, Mr. McLane cannot be true to his own principles and to those of the President. He knows that the Bank's power is the last hope of Federalism and he is fighting for it." The only solution to the Bank question, Blair continued, was to rally the party behind a measure designed to cut "the connection between the Bank & the Govt." It was a severe tongue-lashing, the kind Blair usually reserved for Clay.[51]

Meanwhile, Van Buren himself remained silent about removal. Jackson had asked for his opinion in late July, just before leaving for the Rip Raps, and Van Buren had waited until 19 August before requesting more time to speak with his friends on the subject. He also indicated that he might not agree with the president about removal but declared he would nonetheless stand with Jackson "agt. the world, whether it respects men or things."[52]

Finally on 4 September, Van Buren responded to Jackson's July request, and though he must have known from Blair's letter that the president desired immediate removal, he refused to commit himself. Stating that both he and Silas Wright preferred to delay removal until 1 January because it would show greater respect for Congress, he also declared his willingness to support any course the president chose. It was a yea-nay letter, hedging on the issue of timing, yet solicitously worded so as to retain Jackson's regard.[53]

The president responded with an argument for immediate removal. "To prolong the deposits until after the meeting of Congress," he warned Van Buren, "would be to do the very act [the Bank] wishes." He said he counted on Van Buren's support and requested the vice-president's presence in Washington by early October. "It is possible that your friends hesitate, and are overawed by the power of the Bank," Jackson chided. "It cannot overawe me."[54]

Still Van Buren hesitated. Although acknowledging that the president's rebuke had "very much weakened" his preference for delay, he would not endorse action before Congress met. He also resisted the suggestion that he be in Washington when the deposits were withdrawn, declaring that his appearance would encourage insinuations that the policy had been dictated by "a monied junto in N. York." It would be better to deprive the opposition of such diversions, he argued, and let them confront instead the president's "well deserved popularity."[55]

Van Buren, of course, had a point. Those who pressed hardest for removal—Kendall, Blair, and Taney—all relied upon Jackson's popularity to sustain the policy. But it is equally clear that the vice-president preferred to remain away from the battleground. He had agreed to support any decision made by Jackson and would come to Washington if the president insisted, but he wanted if possible to avoid personal association with a potentially divisive measure.

Ignoring Van Buren's misgivings, Jackson called a cabinet meeting on 10 September to declare that Kendall's trip had been completely successful in demonstrating the readiness and ability of the state banks to handle the public money. There could now be "no excuse for further delay," he maintained. He asked the cabinet to read Kendall's report and said he hoped they would agree to immediate action.[56]

For a week, Jackson tried to sway McLane and Duane to his point of view, but when the cabinet met again on 17 September, he found them still opposed. Cass also resisted, while Woodbury entered into a lengthy discussion of the question, sometimes supporting, sometimes opposing, but finally backing the president. Only Taney fully endorsed the step.[57]

On the following day, the cabinet gathered to hear Jackson's statement defending removal. The document had been drafted at the Rip Raps with Blair and then been revised by Taney and Kendall.[58] In reciting once again the litany of sins that Jackson considered evidence of the Bank's "faithlessness and corruption"—its self-serving loan policy, the circulation of Bank propaganda, autocratic management, and disregard of the public interest and its own charter in managing the 3 percent certificates—the paper portrayed the Bank as a perpetual threat to liberty. It therefore concluded that removal was necessary to "preserve the morals of the people, the freedom of the press, and the purity of the elective franchise . . ." At the same time, it claimed that the state banks would provide equivalent services and security to the public without the dangerous concentration of power inherent in a national bank.[59]

In order to institute the new system, Jackson had to dismiss Duane, who refused to issue an order changing the government's depository. The president certainly had legitimate grounds for dissatisfaction, for Duane had engaged in a policy of delay and obstruction to prevent removal. If in some respects, he was more faithful to Jacksonian antibank thinking than Jackson himself, he nevertheless failed to appreciate that removal was initially more concerned with destroying the Bank than with reforming the nation's currency.[60] Confronted with the possibility of a stronger political opposition which would seek a new Bank charter after Jackson left office, and presented with what they considered continuing evidence of the Bank's corruption, removal's most strenuous backers viewed the "monster's" demise as essential to the preservation of republican institutions. Duane's resistance, therefore, directly challenged Jackson's policy as well as his authority, and the president, who now regarded Duane as "either the weakest mortal, or the most strange composition I have ever met with," relieved the secretary of his duties and on 23 September, replaced him with Taney.[61]

The Treasury order to withdraw the deposits represented a signal victory for Kendall and Blair. Along with Taney, they had called for early and decisive action, and had convinced Jackson to remain steadfast in his preference for immediate removal. Their influence on Jackson's policy, however, was not a matter of manipulation but of shared ideas. All believed that a quick thrust would not only permanently ruin the Bank's prospects for recharter, but would reanimate the Democratic party.

Once announced, Jackson and his advisers attempted to give removal "the character of a *party measure*." The *Globe* warned that restoration of the deposits would defy Jackson's wishes, and promised that "the sincere opponents of the Bank, and the sincere friends of the President, however much they may have differed upon the expediency of removing the deposits, *will present an unbroken front on the question of restoration*." In order to attract the support of as many Democrats as possible, the paper generally did not focus on the president's reasons for removal, but rather on the consequences of returning the deposits. Warning that a reversal of Jackson's order would lead to recharter, the *Globe* declared that the fundamental question was "Shall the United States Bank be restored?"[62]

To some extent, this strategy succeeded in producing greater unity in the executive office. Woodbury rallied loyally to Jackson's side and later became an efficient administrator of the state banking system as Taney's successor in the Treasury Department. Van Buren also fell into line. Perceiving that the party would suffer a stinging defeat if Jackson's decision were reversed, the vice-president prodded reluctant Democrats to defend removal and held weekly dinners for party leaders in Congress to coordinate their efforts. "The fate of this administration if not the character of that which is to come after it depends upon the result of the great question which now agitates the country," he concluded.[63]

Cass and McLane, however, refused to sanction the policy, and, recognizing that it would be made a party question, informed Jackson that although they preferred to remain in the cabinet, the awkwardness of their situation might require them to resign. Rather than provoke a cabinet shakeup, Jackson agreed to avow publicly in his official message on removal his full responsibility for the decision, and he placed in the *Globe* a notice confirming that removal was "not to be considered as a cabinet measure."[64]

This settlement did not please the president's zealous anti-Bank advisers, who thought Cass and McLane should be compelled to adhere to the party's program or be discharged. Taney claimed that the compromise had saved Cass and McLane, allowing them to do further mischief. "But for it they would have gone out and have been ruined," he explained to Blair.[65] Blair and Kendall also urged greater disciplinary control over the secretaries. As the removal controversy intensified in Congress, they complained to Jackson that the public's impression of a divided cabinet was divesting the policy of its partisan quality. Blair recommended that Jackson adopt "a bold & decisive course" by printing an editorial drafted by Kendall arguing that no "real friend" of the president could favor returning the government's money. "We shall have an unmasking on this question," the essay threateningly concluded, "and it will afford a sure test to discriminate friends from foes." Meanwhile, rumors circulated in Washington of an impending cabinet change, which one prominent politician attributed to a design to force McLane's resignation. "The K[itchen] C[abinet] hate him mortally," he asserted, no doubt accurately.[66]

But Jackson refused to permit publication of Kendall's editorial. According to Woodbury, the article was set aside partly at the urging of Van Buren, who sought to avert both a final break with McLane and any implication in the proposed statement of his own approbation of Jackson's act. The vice-president wanted to let public opinion settle before explicitly revealing his own thinking about removal. Although Woodbury's suspiciousness of Van Buren cautions against accepting his allegation at face value, it is generally consistent with the vice-president's attempts throughout Jackson's presidency to moderate public controversy. In any case, it is evident that Jackson agreed to print nothing more about cabinet-level opposition to removal, and he thereby permitted his secretaries to disagree, in silence. As he informed McLane, all he wanted of them was "to attend to the duties of their respective departments."[67]

Knowing that removal would stir up a storm of protest, especially with the opposition in control of the Senate, Jackson and his aides applied most of their energies to gaining an endorsement from the House. Since the Speaker appointed all committees and helped control the flow of business, Jackson viewed the position with special concern. The previous Speaker, Andrew Stevenson of Virginia, had been offered an appointment as minister to Great Britain, and a number of prominent Democrats, including Polk and James M. Wayne of Georgia, aspired to his office. But faced with an anticipated crisis, Jackson and his advisers decided to delay Stevenson's nomination and return him to the House as Speaker. Stevenson, however, was uncertain that under the circumstances he would have enough support, and Jackson, determined to leave nothing to chance, ordered "that noses ought to be counted." Stevenson was found to have sufficient strength and was reelected.[68]

In selecting the House committees, Stevenson appointed the hardworking and loyal Polk as chairman of the crucial Ways and Means Committee, which would report on removal, and Polk rapidly assumed the position of administration floor leader. Jackson, however, carefully monitored the efforts of his followers, and William B. Lewis's appearances on the House floor were so conspicuous that an opposition member offered a motion to bar him from the House. It lost in a close vote, 92 yeas to 107 nays.[69] In the end, with the support of key party leaders and extensive White House efforts, Jackson finally triumphed. On 4 April 1834, after intense and prolonged debate, the House adopted four resolutions presented by Polk sustaining the president's Bank veto as well as his removal of the deposits.[70]

"The People have triumphed!" the *Globe* announced jubilantly after the House vote. "The sound thereof . . . will reanimate the democracy of the Union and strengthen the enemies of corrupt monopolies so that they will not faint or falter, till the Constitution be rescued, and the cause of equal privileges be vindicated."[71] Yet it was evident that removal had weakened the Democratic party, fully justifying Van Buren's early fears. In Pennsylvania, the policy added another strain to the state organization, and though many Democratic leaders like Governor George Wolf eventually soured on Biddle and his Bank and reluctantly supported removal, a significant loss of party support occurred. Only eleven of Pennsylvania's twenty-eight congressmen held firm on the House resolution opposing restoration of the deposits. Elsewhere, in the Ohio Valley as well as in Connecticut, the Democrats also suffered significant electoral losses in the aftermath of removal, though the return of prosperity following Biddle's monetary contraction brought a resurgence of Democratic strength by the spring of 1835.[72]

The House vote also demonstrated the impact of removal on the South. The first Polk resolution, which declared that the Bank ought not to be rechartered, passed easily by 134 votes to 82, with members from the slaveholding states approving by 61 to 27. However, on the second resolution, which declared that the deposits ought not to be restored, the administration's majority shrank to 118 votes to 103, with the majority of members from the slaveholding states voting against removal. The administration's loss of support was most evident in the Virginia delegation, where seven members who voted against the Bank also voted to restore the deposits, leaving a delegation which had voted against the Bank by 13 to 5 with an overwhelming majority of 12 to 6 against removal.[73]

While a large number of southern Jacksonians, including prominent leaders like North Carolina's Jesse Speight and Virginia's John Y. Mason, voted consistently for Jackson's policy, the House vote indicated serious reservations in the South about the president's action. Ritchie's *Enquirer*, for example, protested his dismissal of Duane as an abuse of executive powers, and only after continual prodding by Blair and Jackson did he endorse removal. Even more serious, removal provided an excuse for Democrats who for one reason or another were disgruntled with Jackson to move into the opposition. Most of these were southern states' rights radicals, who used the issue of "executive usurpation" as a pretext for joining the newly emerging Whig party. Virginia, the hub of Van Buren's southern following, became a Whig state until late 1835, and removal also strengthened the Whig party in North Carolina and Georgia. Calhoun rejoiced at this situation, declaring that the deposit question was "a load too heavy" for the Democrats, and though the South Carolinian exaggerated its effects, even Kendall admitted that "a few men" had bolted.[74]

But removal also benefited the Democracy. Most significantly, it provided a clear rallying point by bringing the party back to its anti-Bank, antimonopoly, and limited government standard. During the nullification winter of 1832–33, party lines had been blurred when Jackson and Webster marched hand in hand against the nullifiers. But as Kendall had forecast in the spring of 1833, removal once more identified the party with opposition to the Bank. Party lines were again distinct and men like Webster went into opposition.

The withdrawal of the deposits also dealt the Bank a decisive blow, effectively ending its hopes for recharter. For someone like Louis McLane, who hoped to steer the party to a moderate pro-Bank position, the decision conclusively demonstrated the impracticality of such notions. Stripped of power, McLane soon left the cabinet and by 1840 was supporting the Whig presidential candidate.[75]

While removal concluded Jackson's war against the Bank, it also marked the beginning of his assault on the paper-money system. Admittedly, it appears inconsistent that a president who professed hard-money principles should buttress the power of state banks by providing them with government revenue; and indeed, some historians have questioned the sincerity of Jackson's principles and claimed that his destruction of Biddle's bank worked in the interests of state bankers, men-on-the-make, and the general expansion of American laissez faire capitalism.[76] Nevertheless, as formulated by Jackson and his advisers, removal was intended not only to eliminate the threat of a concentrated monied power, but also to promote a stable specie currency and to check banking excesses.

According to the plan initially devised by Kendall and Jackson, the government was to use only a "few" safe banks, and there was to be a superintendent with an office in the Bank of the Metropolis in Washington who would oversee the smooth and safe functioning of the deposit system. Jackson hoped Kendall would assume this position, but when Kendall preferred to stay in the government, the president dropped the idea of making the Washington bank a central coordinating office. Nevertheless, until the close of his presidency, the number of deposit banks remained small and their performance creditable.[77] To Jackson, the state banks provided the government with all necessary services without the dangers inherent in connecting the country's political institutions with a monopolistic monied power. "From their number and dispersed situation," he claimed of the state banks, "they can not combine for the purposes of political influence, and whatever may be the dispositions of some of them their power of mischief must necessarily be confined to a narrow space and felt only in their immediate neighborhoods." The deposit system, then, was fully in keeping with Jackson's belief in the principles of limited government and decentralized power.[78]

Jackson also made clear that he expected the substitution of state banks for the national bank to be followed by a reform of the nation's currency. In March 1834, the *Globe* summarized in official fashion Jackson's monetary thinking and made distinct what the Bank veto had left vague—that Jackson considered the only constitutional currency to be "a metallic one," and that "among the great . . . evils" of the Bank had been its tendency to subvert this principle. While the president was sensible of the embarrassments that an immediate return to specie would entail, the notice continued, he was turning his attention "to such expedients as would mitigate the evils growing out of the present system." The following day, Blair attacked the Bank as "the head and master of the whole paper system," and labeled gold and silver coin as "JACKSON MONEY." [79]

As his second term progressed, Jackson's hard-money bias came increasingly to the fore as he attempted to restrain the undue influence of local banks on the nation's money supply. Although he devoted some attention to the economic effect of the paper system in stimulating a boom-bust cycle, the president especially emphasized its social and political consequences for a republican society. He charged that paper money inspired speculation which sapped "public virtue," undermined "the purity of our virtuous Government as left us by our fathers," and robbed "honest labour of its earnings to make knaves rich, powerful & dangerous." Like the Bank, the paper system sacrificed the interests of the great body of the people—"the planter, the farmer, the mechanic, and the laborer"—who recognized that their success depended "upon their own industry and economy." Paper-money banking was, therefore, indistinguishable from the spirit of monopoly and special privilege which was "at war with the genius of all our institutions." [80]

In decrying the insidious influence of paper money, Jackson harked back to Jeffersonian doctrine, but as in his Bank veto message, he accentuated its egalitarian implications. He warned that the "resort to implied powers and the use of corporations clothed with privileges" would be the means by which the few would first attempt to gain "control over the labor and earnings" of the people. Ultimately, however, there would be an alliance with government itself, resulting in a concentration of power, tyranny, and despotism. In sum, the pathology of the paper-money system terminated in the loss of liberty. Jackson conceded the impracticability of returning the country to what he considered the exemplary days of the Founding Fathers, but he urged the necessity of preventing new abuses from undermining republican society. [81]

In order to avert the evils of paper money, Jackson recommended the suppression of small bank notes, an increase in the specie reserves of pet banks, the revaluation of gold to encourage its circulation, and, by his Specie Circular, the substitution of specie for worthless paper in the purchase of public lands. As he explained to Congress in December 1835, "proper regulations" can "secure a practical return . . . of the currency to the constitutional medium." He also called for greater efforts in the states to regulate the currency and check the abuses of "monopoly and exclusive privileges."[82] As recent scholarship has demonstrated, the Jackson administration strived to maintain the safety of the government's revenue, to control the note issues of state banks, and to introduce greater amounts of specie into the money supply. While Democrats were not full-fledged economic regulators, neither were they dogmatic adherents to laissez faire economics.[83]

As in other cases, Jackson availed himself of the assistance of a number of people in pursuing his hard-money program. Taney's loyalty and zeal earned him the president's confidence and personal friendship, and even after the Senate rejected his appointment as Treasury secretary, he continued to advise Jackson on monetary and banking matters.[84] Similarly, Missouri's Senator Thomas Hart Benton came into increasing prominence during Jackson's second term. Although he had had little to do with the president's decision to remove the deposits, Benton was soon working closely with the White House to advance the hard-money cause. He collaborated on Treasury Department regulations to suppress small notes, sponsored a bill to revaluate gold, helped Jackson draft his Specie Circular, and like his counterpart in the House, James K. Polk, became the administration's unofficial floor leader on currency matters. Benton's enthusiasm for specie gained him the sobriquet "Old Bullion," as well as the president's warm praise. In Jackson's estimation, Benton, along with Taney and Polk, deserved "not only golden medals, but the gratitude of their country" for assailing "the destructive and corrupting paper system."[85]

Others, like Woodbury and Whitney, developed rules and procedures for regulating state banks and implementing Jackson's hardmoney notions, but contributed little to such major policy decisions as the Specie Circular.[86] As for Van Buren, it is probable that he simply acquiesced in Jackson's course. While sympathetic to policies designed to end speculation, he did not share the president's hardmoney radicalism and feared, with good reason, the political consequences of such rapid movement towards a specie currency.[87]

It seems evident, then, that with the significant exception of Taney, Jackson's efforts at monetary reform were most conspicuously seconded by a group of border-state western advisers, notably Kendall, Blair, Benton, and Polk. They represented that segment of western society which still exhibited a Jeffersonian hostility to irresponsible banking and which, during the panic of 1837, would generally adopt more stringent antibank measures than their eastern colleagues. The advantages of hard money were by no means limited to the West, but to Jackson it seemed to have a special appropriateness for that section. As the *Globe* announced in defending the Specie Circular, "for farmers, mechanics, laborers of all classes, especially *back-woods people*, who have but little money . . . [Jackson] thinks gold and silver the best. They never have more than they can carry about. It is convenient as change, safe to keep, and less of it will supply their wants."[88]

Jackson's program to substitute a metallic currency for paper money had only limited success. Not only did the Whig majority in the Senate prevent for two years the passage of an administration-sponsored bill regulating the deposit banks, but the unveiling of Jackson's hard-money ideas provoked opposition from an element of the Democratic party more favorably disposed to the credit system and the note issues of state banks. While a full-scale schism was avoided until Van Buren's presidency, the resistance of Conservative Democrats like William C. Rives and Nathaniel Tallmadge to the antibanking and hard-money wing of the Democracy hampered administration efforts to pass regulatory measures. It is also evident that the president's reliance on state governments to restrain their banks naively exaggerated the popularity of a specie currency. Although Jacksonians made serious efforts to control bank issues, their accomplishments were inconsiderable. Jackson was, therefore, compelled to rely on executive action to reduce the flow of paper, an expedient which had only a limited effect.[89]

In retrospect, it appears that the President's banking program contained mutually incompatible objectives. By decentralizing economic power, he counteracted the dangers posed by a concentrated monied institution like the Bank, but at the cost of reducing prospects for currency reform. Limitations on banking would have to be enacted by each state as well as by the national government. Furthermore, Jackson's determination to sever economic power from political authority, which he saw joined in the charter of the national bank, clashed with congressional or presidential efforts to reform banking abuses. Ironically, in order to restrain paper issues, Jackson had to resort to powers he avowedly disdained.[90]

Even with these handicaps, the deposit banks served the government well until 1836 when Congress, responding to inflationary pressures in the economy, the appearance of a rapidly increasing federal surplus, and the imminence of a presidential election, passed the Deposit Act. This measure, while it contained some of the bank reforms that Jackson had urged, allocated the government's surplus funds to the states and limited the amount of revenue any one bank could hold. Its effect was to expand the number of deposit banks, making their management even more difficult, and to encourage inflation and speculation. Despite its implications for Jackson's hard-money program, the Deposit Act passed Congress by overwhelming majorities. Only four other senators, for example, joined Benton and New York's Silas Wright in opposition.[91]

Jackson initially intended to veto the bill, for however much he endorsed its regulatory provisions, he found distribution objectionable. The *Globe* prepared the public for a veto by declaring that the administration regarded distribution with an "absolute revolt of feeling," and Jackson privately requested Taney to draft a veto message. Taney responded with a paper denouncing the act as an unconstitutional extension of federal power and warning that it created a precedent for government loans to private corporations, investments in the stock of companies undertaking local improvements, and additional imposts to protect manufacturers.[92]

Jackson, however, withheld his veto and reluctantly signed the bill. Many years later, Benton explained the president's change of mind by claiming that "some of Mr. Van Buren's friends" strongly urged approval. To be sure, Van Buren himself opposed distribution, and his associate, Silas Wright, conspicuously fought the measure on the Senate floor. But it seems likely that Van Buren sympathizers reminded Jackson that a veto would damage Van Buren's presidential campaign. Certainly, the vice-president neither encouraged opposition to the bill nor recommended a veto. Moreover, as Benton also acknowledged, a presidential rejection might have proved ineffectual. In an election year with Democrats collaborating with Whigs to distribute money to the states, Congress probably would have overridden Jackson's veto.[93]

Whatever his reasons, Jackson informed House Democrats after the bill passed the Senate on 17 June that he would approve it if certain changes were made. The Senate version provided that the federal surplus be loaned to the states and that retrieval be dependent on state consent rather than Treasury Department needs. Jackson wanted the funds to be designated in the states as a deposit rather than a loan, and to be subject to recall by the secretary of the treasury. These alterations were merely cosmetic, since the states treated the deposits as a permanent distribution, but they assuaged Jackson's scruples and avoided a confrontation with his own party. "I never have witnessed such rejoicing, as I have this day among our friends, as soon as I gave assurances to most of them, that you would approve of the deposit principle, with the States; but that you would veto a bonus or loaning," Richard M. Johnson reported to the president. An amendment embracing Jackson's wishes won acceptance "like wild fire," and the bill passed the House by a vote of 155 to 38. The Senate then concurred in the House's action.[94]

Although the Deposit Act was now law, Jackson announced through the *Globe* that he still considered it "impolitic and unsafe to mix up the affairs of the United States with those of the several States," and that he would not countenance the idea of distributing federal funds rather than depositing them with the states. In the coming months, the *Globe* continued to inveigh against the measure, decrying its tendency to increase the tariff, to inspire extravagant improvements projects, and to blur the lines separating federal and state governments. "We apprehend that the people of this country are not yet prepared to support a band of excise men, custom-house officers, tax gatherers, and land officers, for the purpose of collecting money one day from them to be returned shortly after—not to them, but to some wily politicians . . . to be employed by them in promoting their own schemes of individual ambition and personal aggrandizement," Blair asserted.[95]

The Deposit Act represented a deviation from Jackson's hard-money principles, but neither he nor such key advisers as Kendall, Blair, Taney, Benton, or Polk were responsible. They did not propose or endorse it. Indeed, the *Globe* immediately urged its repeal and claimed that the question of distribution would "hereafter discrimi-

nate parties, as the tariff, the bank, the system of internal improvements, have heretofore done." Yet while the administration thus
vented its anger, the exigencies of politics dictated that it yield to the
public will. Jackson himself conceded that he was compelled to moderate his criticism of "the Deposit bill, alias distribution bill" because
he "did not wish to do any thing that might embarrass others coming
after me." [96]

There were, however, limits to Jackson's flexibility. In the winter of
1837, Congress passed a bill repealing the Specie Circular, and
Jackson, after lobbying futilely to prevent passage, employed a pocket
veto. "I would yield much to my friends and particularly now as I am
going out of office and I may say out of life," he explained to Blair. "But
I have the great republican principles to sustain, the constitution to
preserve, protect and defend, and the most vital principle in it is the
currency, and I have to maintain a consistency of character in all my
acts to make my administration beneficial to republicanism." [97]

As his presidency drew to a close, Jackson realized that his deposit
system had failed to promote a specie currency. He always regarded
the use of state banks as an "experiment," and while he considered
them safer than Biddle's institution, he also warned his countrymen
that "in the present state of the currency these banks may and do
operate injuriously upon the habits of business, the pecuniary concerns, and the moral tone of society." [98] In the fall of 1836, disil-
lusioned with the conduct of the state banks, Jackson asked Kendall to
devise a bank, located in the District of Columbia, which would be
based "upon real Banking principles." He wanted this bank to serve as
a "model for the states," issuing no bills under twenty dollars and
publicizing all its loans. Jackson never submitted such a project to
Congress, probably because he did not want to commit Van Buren,
now president-elect, to any particular solution to the country's financial problems. But he demonstrated his awareness that the experiment
with state banks should be concluded and new measures adopted to
deal with the government's fiscal and monetary responsibilities. [99]

8

A New Leader

During the last two years of Jackson's presidency, the question of his successor was conclusively resolved in favor of Van Buren. Yet because of the prominence of western influence in the White House, the selection of Van Buren as the Democracy's new leader implied a shift in the party's control and required an accommodation between the Van Burenites and Jackson's western advisers. The transfer of command was successfully accomplished, but the selection of Kentucky's Richard M. Johnson as Van Buren's running mate illuminated once again the clash of interests which had characterized the White House throughout Jackson's presidency, and demonstrated the ability of Jackson's western advisers to shape the party's structure even as Van Buren assumed the leadership of the Democratic party.

When Congress adjourned in the spring of 1834, Van Buren was generally acknowledged to be the most likely Democratic nominee for the presidency. In view of the "Magician's" guarded and equivocal response to most of Jackson's policies, this high standing requires an explanation.

In part, Van Buren's ability to recover can be attributed to his tact and personal charm. One reads Van Buren's letters to Jackson with a painful awareness of his calculated and ingratiating style, which skillfully combined professions of loyalty and lavish praise with mild criticism. His objections to Jackson's course never reached the point of outright opposition and were always couched in the language of suggestion. Van Buren recognized Jackson's control of his administration, and he never defied or challenged the president's authority.[1]

More importantly, Van Buren could generally promise to sustain Jackson's final decision "with immovable constancy," for whatever their disagreement over strategy and tactics the two men shared similar political principles. Considering themselves states' rights disciples of Jefferson, they opposed the Bank and federal aid for local internal improvements and favored increasing the specie basis of the nation's currency. Thus, although Van Buren's cautious temperament and solicitousness of his southern allies' feelings frequently nettled Jackson, the breach was quickly repaired by the vice-president's affirmation of basic agreement.[2]

Significantly, there was also no one else of Van Buren's stature who came this close to sharing Jackson's ideas. Men like Kendall and Blair were more in tune with the president's personal style—his energetic thrusts against the opposition—but they lacked Van Buren's political prominence. Kendall, for example, came to Washington in 1828 without experience in national politics, and however much Jackson soon sought his counsel, both he and the president acknowledged the difficulties of placing the Kentuckian in the cabinet. "I am too new a man to be sustained in such a station by public opinion," Kendall confided to Blair in January 1830. "General Jackson knows this as well as I do." Even in 1835, when Jackson appointed Kendall as postmaster general, many Democrats, especially from the South, opposed the choice of "such a low fellow as Amos." Indeed, though he quickly changed his mind, Kendall initially rejected the offer because he "had not occupied any of those prominent positions which the practice of the government had made prerequisites for cabinet appointments." Like most key presidential advisers, Kendall's and Blair's status derived from signs of Jackson's favor rather than an independent political base.[3]

Van Buren, however, had occupied "prominent positions," including the State Department and the vice-presidency; he was a seasoned political leader. No one else was as prominent or as loyal. The nation's other outstanding political figures were either firmly allied with the opposition or were conspicuous dissenters from Jackson's policies. Webster, Calhoun, and Clay were Whigs, while Cass, McLane, and John McLean could not endorse Jackson's program with the same conviction as Van Buren. The New Yorker, therefore, provided the best prospect for perpetuating the principles established during Jackson's presidency, and by the summer of 1834, the president was declaring that all Democrats must stand against the Bank and for Van Buren.[4]

In order to assure his position as the heir apparent, Van Buren needed only to confirm his ability to win votes, and the New York elections of 1834 provided an appropriate opportunity. Many Democrats doubted Van Buren's popular appeal; if he were unable to rally his own state behind the president's removal policy, party leaders might be compelled to search for a more attractive candidate. Calhoun probably exaggerated when he declared that a Whig victory in New York would force Van Buren to retire, but even the vice-president's warmest supporters revealed their anxiety when they noted the importance of the New York elections. Alfred Balch, a Tennessee Van Burenite, maintained that a victory would make Van Buren "the Lord of the Ascendant," obliging doubters to "jump down on *his* side," and Jackson himself reminded Van Buren that a triumph would put "to rest *all opposition* and maneuvering." The vice-president understood the situation, calling New York the "battle ground" between the parties, and promised extensive efforts to retain control of the state.[5]

The New York elections of October 1834 resulted in a tremendous Democratic victory. After defending Jackson's Bank and removal policy, the party's ticket for governor and lieutenant-governor triumphed handily, while most Democratic candidates for the legislature and Congress outpolled their opponents by substantial majorities. The Democratic surge secured Van Buren's position as the party's front-runner. "The New York elections are gratifying even beyond what I had ventured to hope for," Taney reported to Jackson. "They are indeed decisive and final, & we shall now have peace for many years."[6]

Although by 1834 almost all party leaders recognized Van Buren's claim, they did so with varying degrees of enthusiasm. Jackson and Taney were strongly behind the New Yorker, and William B. Lewis used his special position as the president's friend to urge Democrats to support Jackson's choice. But others were less ardent in their support. Woodbury thought Van Buren too "aristocratic in habits & in social intercourse" to be a popular president, and Barry was even cooler, preferring fellow westerner Richard M. Johnson for the presidency.[7]

Blair and Kendall backed Van Buren, but not with the enthusiasm or devotion that derives from personal attachment to a candidate. The Kentuckians continued to fix their loyalty on Jackson, and their support of Van Buren was based primarily upon their recognition that the vice-president was the best available successor. In November 1832, for example, Kendall informed Van Buren that "the democratic party of the West . . . now look to you as the . . . man who is destined to receive the mantle of our departing Chief and perpetuate his principles in the administration of the government." But Kendall also made clear that his own commitment was contingent upon Van Buren's support of Jackson's policies and his ability to lead the party. "The events of a few years may make it necessary to . . . [the party's] preponderance that its favor and support shall be bestowed upon another," he asserted.[8]

By 1834, Kendall was firmly behind Van Buren, but it was evident that their association lacked the familiarity of his relationship with Jackson. When Van Buren was elected president, Washington politicos even speculated that Kendall would be dropped from the new cabinet. Although these rumors proved unfounded and Kendall continued to serve Van Buren as postmaster general, his influence never matched that of Van Buren's New York friends Benjamin Butler and Silas Wright.[9]

By 1834, Blair also privately supported Van Buren, but he refused to endorse him in the *Globe* or to give the presidential issue much attention. The party's determination to hold a national convention in May 1835 probably accounted for a large part of Blair's reticence; it would have been unseemly for the administration's newspaper to close off debate on the presidential nomination by proclaiming the virtues of Van Buren. But it is also likely that Blair preferred to use his editorial space defending Jackson's policies against opposition attacks. The *Globe*, grumbled one prominent Connecticut politician, was "a mere executive organ & not the organ of the party."[10]

While Kendall's independence of the Van Burenites was relatively inconspicuous, Blair's position as administration editor made him more visible, and it is apparent that the vice-president's friends continued to doubt his trustworthiness. Blair's public neutrality by no means indicated hostility to Van Buren, but the New Yorker's followers revealed their dissatisfaction with his direction of the *Globe* when in 1834 Washington witnessed two attempts to establish a pro–Van Buren newspaper.

The prospectus for the *National Standard* first appeared in the *Globe* on 14 February 1834. It promised to support the administration and promote Van Buren for the presidency. Significantly, the Albany *Argus*, Van Buren's New York newspaper, approved the establishment of this "co-laborer with the Globe," and the announcement of the new paper also coincided with the publication of rumors that Van Buren was having difficulty managing "the kitchen." Blair, however, quickly scotched the potential competitor. Noting that its editor was a South Carolinian who had formerly worked with Duff Green, Blair implied that it was sponsored by nullifiers interested in dividing the Democracy. It is impossible to determine whether Blair was correct, for the *National Standard* never appeared. But the *Argus's* response indicated that the Van Buren forces wanted a paper in Washington explicitly devoted to their leader.[11]

Shortly after this abortive effort, a pro–Van Buren newspaper actually was established in Washington. In early April 1834, a Pennsylvania Democrat printed the first copy of the *North American*, a decidedly Democratic sheet that staunchly supported Jackson's policies. Its editor, however, contended that the *Globe* was too closely identified with the president and that the party demanded a "firm, devoted Jackson, Van Buren Democratic paper in Washington." The *North American* applauded the call for a second Democratic national convention, but unlike the *Globe*, it formally endorsed Van Buren for the nomination.[12]

While one suspects that the *National Standard* had originated in opposition attempts to divide and embarrass the Democratic party, there seems little reason to question the *North American's* legitimacy. Instead of ridicule, it was greeted by Blair with profound silence. Ignored by the Albany *Argus* as well, the *North American* appeared sporadically until it ceased publication in early 1835. Nevertheless, while it lived, the paper's very existence was interpreted by some journals as an indication of Van Burenite dissatisfaction with the *Globe*, and even after its demise, Blair was warned by a Virginia friend that disgruntled party leaders in Virginia and Pennsylvania were contemplating the establishment of another journal in Washington.[13]

Although tension between the Van Burenites and Blair should not be exaggerated, the impending transfer of power to Van Buren plainly revealed lines of stress among Jackson's advisers. Knowing that his energetic editorial policy had occasionally discomforted the cautious Van Buren, Blair recognized the possibility that their lack of personal intimacy might lead Van Buren to seek a new editor once he became president. In April 1834, when the *North American* was first issued, Blair's brother-in-law warned him that "Van will not want you!" and in early 1835 his father declared he was gratified to learn that Blair intended to settle in Illinois. To be sure, these letters could indicate nothing more than temporary despondency or pique. But one must note that after his election, Van Buren seriously entertained suggestions from prominent Democrats that he replace Blair, and the editor himself offered to resign so that the New Yorker could choose as his replacement one "who must to some extent have confidential relations with the Administration." In the end, however, Van Buren asked Blair to remain.[14]

By the fall of 1834, virtually every party leader accepted the primacy of Van Buren's claim to the Democratic nomination, but no similar consensus had emerged on the vice-presidential nomination. Two candidates, the Kentuckian Richard M. Johnson and the Virginian William C. Rives, vied for the second spot on the ticket in a contest that involved more than personal rivalry. Around them coalesced the clashing interests of the western and Van Burenite wings of the party.

Johnson's appeal was that of complementing Van Buren with a celebrated westerner who would ensure his section's attachment to the Democratic party. To those who believed that the South had no other choice but to support the party's ticket and that attention should be directed to the West, Johnson was a logical choice. His considerable popularity in that section as well as his extensive support among eastern workingmen had made him the Kitchen Cabinet's choice for the vice-presidency in 1832 until the Senate rejected Van Buren's nomination as minister to Britain.

As the Democratic convention of May 1835 approached, Johnson's qualities once again attracted favorable notice from party leaders concerned about the West. The Whig strategy was to throw the election of 1836 into the House of Representatives by offering a number of regional candidates to challenge Van Buren. In the West, William Henry Harrison was creating difficulties for Democrats, and there was the even more worrisome possibility that Clay might make a last minute bid for the presidency. In the border-state West, as well as the South, the candidacy of Tennessee's Hugh Lawson White was also playing havoc with the Democracy's hopes of victory. Jackson's own state was preparing to ignore his wishes and abandon the party's choice in order to support White.[15]

As in the past, Blair and Kendall were foremost among Johnson's boosters. As Blair explained to Virginia Democrats, it was important to rally "to Mr. Van Buren & his administration (if he should be elected) the sturdy Democracy of the West, which must have some bond of union with him in the person of some popular citizen to become thoroughly identified with him." Although the evidence is not conclusive, it appears that Jackson, suspecting that Clay would announce his candidacy, also supported Johnson. One of the president's close political and personal friends reported after a visit to Washington in early 1835 that Johnson was a sure bet for the nomination, and the delegates who assembled at the Democratic convention a few months later also assumed that Johnson was the president's choice.[16]

But Johnson's candidacy was opposed by those Democrats who worried more about the South than the West. He had had a mulatto mistress and had made no effort to conceal his relationship or his two daughters by her. The Tennessee Van Burenite Alfred Balch warned Jackson that the Kentuckian was socially unacceptable to the South, and Jackson's close friend John Catron asserted that Johnson's social life made him "not only positively unpopular . . . but affirmatively odious. . . . In every slaveholding country this must be so, and ought to be so."[17]

Even were the Kentuckian morally sounder, southern Democrats still would prefer having one of their own as vice-president to signal the party's adherence to states' rights principles and to recognize the South's loyalty to the Democratic cause. Jackson had done much for the South by limiting internal improvements expenditures, revising the tariff, and reaffirming the benefits of Jeffersonian doctrine. But he had also ruffled southern sensibilities. Southern Democrats, particularly Virginians, had taken exception to his nullification proclamation and Force Bill message, his peremptory discharge of Duane, and his withdrawal of the government's deposits from the Bank. They therefore rallied to Rives's standard to enhance the party's appeal in their section. As Ritchie observed, if Rives were the vice-presidential candidate "Virginia, & the South, will be safe—with Col. Johnson, less than safe."[18]

Southern insistence on Rives increased after December 1834, when Judge Hugh Lawson White's presidential campaign gathered momentum. Support for White appeared among disparate groups. Some southern radicals, led by Duff Green, disregarded White's opposition to nullification in order to capitalize on an opportunity to defeat Van Buren and weaken the Democratic party's grip on the South.[19] But also among White's sponsors were a number of disgruntled Tennessee Democrats like John Bell, politicians with close ties to the state's business and banking communities, who had always opposed Jackson's anti-Bank program but had never been strong enough to challenge Old Hickory's popularity at home. They would soon form the backbone of Tennessee's Whig party. White himself opposed the Bank, but once under Bell's influence, he agreed that he would not veto another Bank bill if it were passed by Congress.[20] William B. Lewis was associated with this faction and his refusal to denounce White antagonized Jackson and the "*Simon Pures* of the party." His personal relations with the president, which had somehow survived their basic political disagreements, distinctly cooled.[21]

White's foremost appeal, however, was to southern anti–Van Buren and antinorthern sentiment. Indeed, from the outset of Jackson's presidency, White's own animus against Van Buren and Van Buren promoters like Eaton and Lewis had distanced him from Jackson, and he had even declined to serve as Eaton's replacement after the cabinet reorganization of 1831. White's constancy in supporting Jackson's program, including a senatorial effort defending removal, and his reputation for political integrity enabled him to exploit southern anxieties, regardless of party, about Van Buren's northern background and association with machine-style politics. By the spring of 1835, White had effectively raised doubts about Van Buren's fidelity to the South and slavery, and had thereby interjected a distinctly sectional tone to the presidential canvas. Ritchie complained that White supporters were capitalizing on Van Buren's apparent stand in favor of slavery restriction during the Missouri debates as well as "his general views of *slavery*." Rives reported that the Tennessean had "produced a good deal of disarray & confusion," while the *Globe* denounced efforts "to build up a Southern party on sectional considerations *solely* . . . upon the question of slavery, and its concomitant interests." To many southern Jacksonians, the future looked gloomy if White remained in the contest.[22]

Realizing that they would have to defend Van Buren to the South under the sensitive conditions created by White's candidacy, the Rives men urged the necessity of placing the Virginian on the ticket.

Rives himself put the issue squarely before Van Buren, warning that nothing must be done to alienate Virginia from the Republican fold. He pointed out that the idea of a southern confederacy had taken a firm hold in the South and that "the only means of defeating it, is to keep Virginia as the *fulcrum* of the South in harmonious relations with the administration of the General government."[23]

The second Democratic national convention convened in Baltimore on 20 May 1835. Ironically, Jackson's own state failed to send an official delegation, so great had been the inroads made by White among Tennessee Democrats. Even staunch Van Buren men deemed it prudent to stay away, and Tennessee's votes were cast by an ordinary citizen who happened to be in Baltimore when the convention assembled.[24]

Like Jackson's selection three years before, Van Buren's nomination was uncontested, but the significance of the convention's designation was much greater. Lacking Jackson's personal magnetism, Van Buren relied to a greater extent than his predecessor on the bonds of party loyalty and the benefits of political organization to achieve victory. Confronted by White's strenuous efforts to win over Jackson supporters, the convention enabled Van Buren to establish himself as the exclusive bearer of the party's name and principles.

Party leaders were fully cognizant of the convention's value. Jackson recommended that it be held early so that people's attention could be directed towards one candidate, thereby minimizing the possibilities of division. "Creating divisions among the people *as to men* is one of the artifices, essential to the success of the *few* over the *many*," he declared in defense of the convention. "It is therefore of the utmost importance, that the majority should adopt some means to prevent such divisions." A leading Virginia Van Burenite agreed. "Our best safeguard (so far as the presidential contest is involved)," he advised Van Buren shortly before the convention assembled, "appears to be in a well organized and discreetly conducted national convention. . . . Its united and imposing voice more than any other means will be influential in putting down the rash and disjointed attempts of petty factions." Thus when Blair officially announced the call for the 1835 convention, he asserted that only "by union, harmony, [and] concert of action" could Jeffersonian principles triumph over latter-day Federalism. [25]

Nevertheless, the major issue before the delegates was the vice-presidential contest between Johnson and Rives. With Blair in attendance, urging the Kentuckian's claims and coaxing Rives's supporters with the possibility of electing a Virginian as the next Speaker of the House of Representatives, it was evident that Johnson would receive the nomination. As one of Rives's friends noted, "the fiat had gone forth" that the westerner should be selected.[26]

The New York delegation held the key to the outcome. To the surprise of at least one prominent politician, Van Buren's own state lined up firmly behind Johnson. Rives men had hoped that Van Buren would stand by his Virginia allies, and Ritchie had been so confident that Rives's nomination "was fixed" that he concerned himself little with the problem. Indeed, Van Buren probably did prefer the Virginian, and he had assured Rives that he agreed "precisely" on the need to secure southern support of the party. But Johnson had the endorsement of Jackson and the Kitchen Cabinet, and the New Yorker would not defy their wishes. Thus when the delegates assembled, the New York members were decidedly for Johnson.[27]

Even before the voting began, Rives's friends realized they had lost, and their bitter disappointment was exhibited in the announcement by one delegate that Virginia would disavow any candidate "who does not carry out or maintain the political principles Virginia ever held dear." That this declaration was more than a rhetorical flourish became clear after the votes were counted and Johnson had won the necessary two-thirds majority. The Virginia delegation refused to make the nomination unanimous and advised the convention that they would not recommend Johnson to their constituents. The Old Dominion representatives were piqued at what they considered the party's deplorable strategy of looking to "the corrupt west," and assuming "that the gallantry of the south could be relied upon to sustain itself & the cause." Virginia would remain obdurate to the very end, giving its vice-presidential electoral votes to Judge William Smith of Alabama.[28]

Johnson's nomination was a symbolic victory for the Kitchen Cabinet. Few party leaders seriously considered the Kentuckian presidential timber and his selection had little bearing on the question of the succession after Van Buren. But the placement of a westerner on the ticket showed the special influence of the West during

Jackson's administration, for even as power was flowing into Van Buren's hands, the national convention had focused its attention on the West, believing the South would be sufficiently satisfied with the ticket not to bolt. It is impossible to think that if Van Buren had had a free hand, he would have selected Johnson for his running mate. Van Buren's political base was the New York–Virginia alliance, and Johnson was anathema to the Richmond Junto.

The period between the Democratic convention and the inauguration of Van Buren was a time of accommodation and adjustment between the Van Burenites and the Kitchen Cabinet. Once the convention adjourned, Blair gave his full endorsement to Van Buren's election. Whatever their previous disagreements, Van Buren was the party's choice and the candidate most likely to carry on Jackson's policies. Blair therefore urged his friends to "bring the democratic countrymen to the polls" and used his influence to mend factional rifts within state organizations, sometimes irritating hard-money radicals who worried that the editor was abandoning their cause.[29]

Blair also tactfully acknowledged Van Buren's new status by placing the *Globe* at the candidate's disposal, allowing Van Buren to insert propaganda which then circulated to Van Buren committees throughout the country. The *Globe* proved especially effective in evoking party loyalty by affirming Van Buren's position as the only legitimate Republican candidate. In response to White's criticism of party organization and dictation, Blair denounced such antiparty notions as inimical to majority rule and the maintenance of republican government. "The spirit which would extinguish popular power in the government, by defeating the only mode of giving prevalence to the will of the majority, is precisely the same which is always at work to give all authority to the designing few," he contended. "If bankism, nullification, . . . anti-Jacksonian, and every thing that is anti-republican, rallies under the White flag, and Van Burenism be the opposite," he asked, "who should hesitate to give a preference to Van Buren?" The Republican party, he promised, would "adhere to principle, regardless of names." And he attempted to assuage the South's disappointment with Johnson's nomination by arguing, with some exaggeration, that the Kentuckian had fully supported the president's measures and had helped make Virginia's principles popular throughout the West. It was therefore to Virginia's "interest . . . to support the Western candidate and to encourage . . . the inclination, which the growing West has shown in support of the principles she has so potently inculcated."[30]

Friction with the Van Burenites did not entirely cease, however, and some Democrats grumbled that Blair still devoted too much attention to the West. "Blair can fight the Bank very well, and make war upon Clay, and write about Kentucky," Gideon Welles complained shortly after Van Buren's victory, "but that is about all. The *Globe* had more columns devoted to Kentucky politics during the year preceding Mr. Van Buren's election, than to all the Union besides (except Tennessee). . . ." The charge had some validity, since Blair's loyalty to Jackson made him especially eager to avert a Whig victory in Tennessee. When he learned that North Carolina's state elections in the summer of 1836 had ended in an opposition victory, Blair informed Jackson of his disappointment, declaring that he was "vexed most at the bad effect it will have in Tennessee, for which I would swap the whole south, beyond Virginia."[31] Nevertheless, Van Buren was sufficiently satisfied with the *Globe*'s performance, and when Blair offered his resignation to allow Van Buren the selection of another official spokesman, it was rejected. Blair then bought a permanent residence in Washington and prepared to use his pen to support Jackson's successor.[32]

Van Buren also contributed to party harmony by prodding disaffected Virginia Democrats to back the party's ticket and by publicly avowing his agreement with Jackson's banking, tariff, and internal improvements policies.[33] At the same time, he continued to defer to the president during the last months of his administration and remained in the background when Jackson issued his Specie Circular to halt inflation and the overissue of worthless bank paper. Van Buren's opinion of this measure is uncertain, but it is difficult to believe he was enthusiastic about an act which was opposed by a majority of the Congress and of the cabinet, and which therefore threatened to divide the party in the midst of a presidential election. Although he probably agreed with it in principle, he must have regretted its timing. Whatever the truth, Van Buren said nothing, and there was no repetition of the tension between president and vice-president that had occurred during the removal controversy.[34]

With Van Buren presaging a continuation of Jackson's policies, and with the president and Kitchen Cabinet behind him, the Democratic ticket triumphed. The victory was not a resounding one. Van Buren won 170 electoral votes to his opponents' 73, compared to Jackson's 1832 margin of 219 to 49, and his margin in popular votes dropped almost 6 percentage points compared to Jackson's 1832 total. He won a bare majority of 50.9 percent of the popular votes, as Ohio, Indiana, Georgia, and Tennessee moved into the Whig column. Even where Van Buren prevailed, he did so by smaller margins than Jackson's, indicating a closer party balance across the country.[35]

Regional and local realignments during this election produced the heaviest Democratic losses in the slaveholding states. According to Joel Silbey's calculations, the Democrats suffered an 18 percent loss of support in that section. Thus while Jackson had garnered 70 percent of North Carolina's vote and had been unopposed in Alabama in 1832, Van Buren attracted, respectively, only 53 percent and 56 percent of the turnout. The Democrats remained the majority party in most southern states, but they now faced a powerful Whig minority. Four years earlier, the South had given Jackson his greatest margin of victory, but in 1836 the strongest Democratic vote came from the Middle Atlantic states.[36] The impact of Jackson's policies, Van Buren's northern birth, and White's attractiveness had taken its toll. One of Van Buren's first acts as president, therefore, was to appoint another southerner to the cabinet, hoping to assuage the feelings of his Virginia allies and to strengthen the Democratic party in that section.[37]

If Van Buren's margin of victory was smaller than Jackson's in 1828 or 1832, he nevertheless had the advantage of being placed in power by a party whose principles were better defined. For eight years Jackson had hammered out a program derived from Jeffersonian limited government and antimonopoly tenets, and as a consequence, many original Jackson men of 1828 were now to be found in the opposition ranks. Although the cautious Van Buren was, on the whole, less responsible for this program than Jackson, Kendall and Blair, he was generally in agreement with their actions. Now, as he prepared to assume the presidency, Van Buren found the party increasingly divided between the supporters and opponents of Jackson's hard-money program. It would be his responsibility to determine whether to back off or to continue efforts to reform the nation's money supply. When, after appropriate hesitation, he decided to align himself with the hard-money cause, and indeed to extend its objectives to encompass the divorce of government from banking, he won the enthusiastic endorsement of Andrew Jackson.[38]

Conclusion

On New Year's Day 1840, John Quincy Adams recorded in his diary what he took to be the lesson of American politics since the establishment of the Constitution. The key to political success, he observed, was the alliance forged by Thomas Jefferson combining "the Southern interest in domestic Slavery with the Northern riotous Democracy." Dedicated to states' rights principles, this combination had given Virginia control of national politics for twenty-four years before the Jacksonians revitalized the alliance and once again placed the federal government at the service of southern interests.[1]

Adams's assessment was not a sudden revelation, but the product of long, and often painful, reflection on the course of national development. Almost ten years earlier he had made a similar claim watching disconsolately as Andrew Jackson rejected his idea that government should promote by positive deeds the physical and moral improvement of the country. In the aftermath of the Maysville Road veto, the former president had concluded that Jackson had "thrown his whole weight into the slave-holding scale," and he had forecast the demise of the cause of internal improvements and domestic industry.[2]

To some extent, Adams was correct. Not only was Jackson more disposed than his predecessor to apply Jeffersonian states' rights principles to government, but through his selection of Martin Van Buren as his successor and political confidant, he placed the preeminent spokesman for the New York–Virginia alliance among his inner circle of advisers. Moreover, Jackson was solicitous to appoint southerners to prominent positions and to alleviate the inequities produced by large-scale government programs.[3] Van Buren took it upon himself to publicize the benefits that Jackson provided. "My object is to place before the nation, and particularly your southern *friends*, what has been effected through your instrumentality upon this great subject," Van Buren advised the president in submitting a statement on internal improvements for Jackson's sixth annual message.[4] The South, then, constituted an important bloc of Jackson's support, and he rarely made a significant decision without consulting Van Buren.

Nevertheless, a study of White House politics during Jackson's presidency reveals that the primary inspiration for the Democratic party's program came not from Van Buren and his New York–Virginia axis, but from Jackson and the border-state West. Jackson himself remained at the center of the decision-making process, seeking aid from a large number of advisers, both official and informal, but concentrating responsibility in his own hands. Throughout these years, however, he gave special consideration to the counsel of the two former Kentucky relief men, Amos Kendall and Francis Blair, whose political views and temperaments closely matched his own. The Kentuckians shared his suspicion of paper-money banking and his hostility to the Bank of the United States. They also distrusted what they conceived to be an established economic and political "aristocracy," whose power they sought to counter through an aggressive political style combining dramatic popular appeals with efficient political organization. Westerners themselves, they often took the South's support for granted while focusing attention on welding the West to the Democratic party. They were devoted first and foremost to Jackson, a matter of considerable importance to a president who abided by traditional notions of loyalty and trust, and who felt most comfortable associating with other westerners.

The coolness with which Van Buren and his southern allies greeted certain major policy and organizational decisions attested to the primacy of the Jackson-Kendall-Blair axis. The Bank War, and especially the removal of the government's deposits, nullification, Blair's management of the *Globe*, and the selection of the party's vice-presidential candidates were among the actions that provoked criticism from Van Burenites. One prominent southern Democrat, citing the lack of southerners in Jackson's cabinet, even asked if there were "a fixed policy in the administration to keep all southern men out of the Cabinet?" Although this situation was brought about more by accident than by insufficient concern for the South, at the end of Jackson's presidency, Van Buren noted that there was only one cabinet member from that section, and he "felt it to be . . . [his] duty to go south" for his first appointment.[5] One must avoid exaggerating such contention, for it took place within a broad area of agreement, and especially in Van Buren's case, reflected considerations of timing and temperament more than differences of principle. Nevertheless, these considerations make it impossible to maintain that Jackson's presidency was, fundamentally, an assertion of southern power in national politics.

Equally significant, Jackson's program belied the parochialism and narrow sectional purposes that Adams attributed to it. Instead, it bore the unmistakable imprint of Jackson's commitment to revitalize and perpetuate republican ideals. Republican ideology, as it had been interpreted and expounded by the Jeffersonians in the 1790s, continued to vibrate in Jackson's thoughts. It was not the only philosophical influence on him or his advisers, but a concern for liberty and virtue animated his campaign against corrupt institutions and political practices. Identifying privileged monopolies, paper-money banking, speculation, excessive government expenditures, burdensome taxation, and consolidated power as diseases that sapped the vitality of the people and endangered their republican institutions, Jackson embarked on a program to sustain "the great republican principles." Historians may long debate whether Jackson's political program evidenced a genuine ideology, but there is no reason to doubt that he possessed a set of ideas based upon republican theory and the Jeffersonian tradition that provided him with a means of understanding and relating to his society.[6]

To be sure, Jeffersonian principles had always been especially identified with the South, and Jackson's thinking did owe much to southern politicians and ideologues like Jefferson, Macon, Randolph, and Taylor. But Jeffersonian doctrine was increasingly employed in that section as part of a struggle to protect southern interests from northern encroachments. Jackson, however, in emphasizing Jeffersonianism's egalitarian implications, struck a responsive chord throughout the country. By circumscribing government's power and severing its connection with special privilege, he sought to preserve—for adult white males—equality of opportunity, individual enterprise, and public virtue as the foundation of a republican society. While his actions sometimes had reactionary consequences, as in the case of Indian removal, for the most part his program was in harmony with the democratic mood of his era.[7]

Jackson, of course, no more monopolized republican ideology than the Jeffersonians did in contending against Federalism. Republicanism was a common language, spoken in a variety of dialects, in antebellum America. In the South, nullifiers urged state interposition as an antidote to a diseased political system, while other southerners followed Jefferson's own lead in defending their way of life against northern commercial, speculative, and centralizing values. Whigs also appealed to this ideology, not least in their choice of a party label that harked back to the Revolution's victory over tyrannical executive authority. The assumptions of republicanism, therefore, provided the cognitive framework for much of the political debate in the Jacksonian period.[8]

The persistence of republican ideology into the nineteenth century helps explain the unusual sensitivity of Jacksonian politicians towards the themes of corruption, tyranny, special privilege, monopoly, and a monied aristocracy. Republican doctrine assumed a perpetual conflict between virtue and corruption, and between liberty and power; and it demanded continual vigilance on behalf of freedom. Inherent in this construct, therefore, were elements of anxiety and, sometimes, even paranoia. Without denying that the material development which was rapidly transforming nineteenth-century America posed real dangers to the ideal of a republican society, the rhetoric of Jacksonian politics still seems disproportionate to the threat. But republican ideology, while directing attention to areas of vulnerability in free societies, also predisposed politicians to exaggerate the motives and actions of their opponents.[9]

Why the West was so conspicuous a source of Jacksonianism must remain a matter of conjecture. Little is known about the experiences and outlook of westerners in the early nineteenth century. Certainly, historians have too often been swayed by a concept of the West as monotonously speculative, inflationary, and striving. The West was no more monolithic than any other section, and westerners like John Eaton, William B. Lewis, and Andrew Jackson Donelson, to mention only Jackson men, often disapproved of the president's course. They provided personal friendship, discretion in the performance of political chores, and, in Donelson's case, the security of a confidential private secretary—important functions of presidential aides. But there is no evidence that they contributed significantly to policy making.

Kendall and Blair, however, represented a different West, one which kept alive the Jeffersonian antipathy to paper-money banking and expansive governmental powers. As Bray Hammond has shown, this was a major current of western thought, and it is not anomalous that men like Jackson, Kendall, and Blair emerged from the West to challenge the national bank. While it would therefore be simplistic to replace recent interpretations of Jacksonianism with a narrowly sectional and environmental one, it is evident that Jackson's political program and style owed much to the experiences and attitudes of one segment of western society.[10]

The West's experience in the panic of 1819 provided an appropriate background for Jackson's presidency. The panic generated grass-roots political activity, inspired attacks against special privilege, re-awakened a Jeffersonian animus against lawyers and bankers, and renewed latent misgivings about a national government both remote and unresponsive. The depression of the early 1820s was especially severe in the West and South, and in Kentucky it was followed by further contention in the Old Court–New Court battles. Controversies over currency, banking, the role of government in aiding the farming and mechanic population, and the relationship between elected representatives and appointed judges furnished Blair's and Kendall's formal political training. Although they differed with Jackson over specific relief issues during the 1820s, they were later able to put the results of their education to use in Jackson's administration because their values and philosophies were fundamentally similar.

Of more general significance may be the idea that social and economic change was more visible in the West than in other areas of the country. The western environment was relatively plastic, absorbing the rapid changes that accompanied the transition from an isolated and self-sufficient society to one that was increasingly market oriented, complex, and modern. Western institutions, such as banks, were primitive and unsophisticated compared to the older Northeast and Southeast regions, and as Kendall found when he moved to Lexington, western society, however pretentious, lacked the rigidity of that of Massachusetts.[11] Westerners could see land opened for settlement and cultivation, new towns founded, and a social structure develop. At the same time, for many people the West carried the idealistic burden of America's hopes for perpetuating a free, prosperous, and virtuous republican nation. The immediacy and high visibility of social change, in light of western hopes and ideals, may have increased the awareness of, and resentment against, "speculative" and "idle" gains made by the few. Similarly, the section's more fluid social divisions, its flexible political structure, and its incentives for political participation encouraged politicians to look to the people for support by adopting a more popular and participatory style of politics.[12]

The special contribution of the West to the early Democratic party, as well as the continued relevancy of republican ideology after the War of 1812, may well contain a warning to historians now detailing the impact of slavery on antebellum politics. However menacing the slavery issue began to appear in the mid-1830s, it had very little effect on the perceptions of men like Jackson, Kendall, and Blair. Reflecting their Jeffersonian heritage, they considered slavery not as a permanent fixture, but as a blight that, somehow, Time and Providence would eradicate. "On principle, slavery has no advocates North or South of the Potomac," the *Globe* explained. "The present generation finds the evil entailed on it . . . [and] Providence . . . will, no doubt, in the course of time, relieve the American people of their share of this misfortune." Jackson censured abolitionists and proslavery enthusiasts alike as fanatics who endangered sectional peace, subverted the republic, and jeopardized this preordained progress towards freedom.[13] And throughout his presidency, issues relating to slavery remained a minor, though ominous, undercurrent.[14] Much more prominent was his concern to preserve republican institutions by adjusting and reconciling Jeffersonianism to an increasingly expansive and pluralistic society.

Notes

Introduction

1. Four useful historiographical surveys of Jacksonian scholarship are Charles G. Sellers, Jr., "Andrew Jackson Versus the Historians," *Mississippi Valley Historical Review* 44 (1958):615–34; John William Ward, "The Age of the Common Man," in *The Reconstruction of American History*, ed. John Higham, pp. 82–97; Alfred A. Cave, *Jacksonian Democracy and the Historians*; and Ronald P. Formisano, "Toward a Reorientation of Jacksonian Politics: A Review of the Literature, 1959–1975," *Journal of American History* 63 (1976):42–65.

2. Lee Benson, *The Concept of Jacksonian Democracy*; Ronald P. Formisano, *The Birth of Mass Political Parties*; William G. Shade, *Banks or No Banks*. Critical evaluations of the ethnocultural school of history can be found in James E. Wright, "The Ethnocultural Model of Voting: A Behavioral and Historical Critique," *American Behavioral Scientist* 16 (1973):653–74; Richard L. McCormick, "Ethnocultural Interpretations of Nineteenth-Century American Voting Behavior," *Political Science Quarterly* 89 (1974):351–77; and Richard B. Latner and Peter Levine, "Perspectives on Antebellum Pietistic Politics," *Reviews in American History* 4 (1976):15–24.

3. Throughout this study, I have used the terms "Democratic party," "Republican party," "Democratic Republican party," and "the Democracy" to designate the followers of Jackson. My use of multiple titles risks confusion when the Jacksonians are being compared with the Jeffersonian Republicans, but there seems to be no other recourse because party terminology was inconsistent during the years of Jackson's political career. Thus at their 1832 convention, the Jacksonians officially adopted the name "Republican," but Jackson men also commonly referred to themselves as "Democrats" or "Democratic Republicans." At their 1835 convention, the Jacksonians officially changed their name to "Democratic Republicans," but many still referred to themselves as "Republicans" or "Democrats." I have attempted, of course, to make clear when I am describing the Jacksonians in contrast to the Jeffersonians. See Samuel Rhea Gammon, Jr., *The Presidential Campaign of 1832*, pp. 157–62; Amos Kendall, *Autobiography of Amos Kendall*, pp. 449–53; Washington *Globe*, 27 May 1835.

4. Stephen Hess, *Organizing the Presidency*, pp. vii, 3–4.

5. *Niles' Weekly Register* 45 (30 November 1833):209; Lynn L. Marshall, "The Strange Stillbirth of the Whig Party," *American Historical Review* 72 (1967):445–47.

6. Richard P. Longaker, "Was Jackson's Kitchen Cabinet a Cabinet?" *Mississippi Valley Historical Review* 44 (1957):94–108.

7. A seminal study using the "reputational" approach is Floyd Hunter, *Community Power Structure.* A classic example of the "case study" technique is Robert A. Dahl, *Who Governs?* See also Peter Bachrach and Morton S. Baratz, "Two Faces of Power," *American Political Science Review* 56 (1962):947–52; and Bachrach and Baratz, "Decisions and Nondecisions: An Analytical Framework," *American Political Science Review* 57 (1963):632–42.

8. See, for example, James C. Curtis, *Andrew Jackson and the Search for Vindication,* pp. 12, 169; and Michael Paul Rogin, *Fathers and Children,* pp. 13–15, 285–88.

9. See, for example, Bray Hammond, *Banks and Politics in America from the Revolution to the Civil War,* pp. 359–60; Charles M. Wiltse, *John C. Calhoun,* 2:49; Carl Brent Swisher, *Roger B. Taney,* p. 302.

10. Charles G. Sellers, Jr., *James K. Polk,* 2:14–18 (vol. 1 hereinafter cited as Sellers, *Polk: Jacksonian;* vol. 2 hereinafter cited as Sellers, *Polk: Continentalist).* See also Marvin Meyers, *The Jacksonian Persuasion,* pp. 7–10; Albert Somit, "Andrew Jackson as Political Theorist," *Tennessee Historical Quarterly* 8 (1949):99–126.

11. Clifford Geertz, "Ideology as a Cultural System," in *Ideology and Discontent,* ed. David E. Apter, pp. 57–65; Gene Wise, *American Historical Explanations,* pp. 3–22; Robert E. Shalhope, "Thomas Jefferson's Republicanism and Antebellum Southern Thought," *Journal of Southern History* 42 (1976):529–36.

12. Frederick Jackson Turner, *The United States: 1830–1850,* pp. 30–33, 213. See also John Catron to Jackson, 21 March 1835, Andrew Jackson, *Correspondence of Andrew Jackson,* 5:331–32; James D. Richardson, comp., *A Compilation of the Messages and Papers of the Presidents,* 3:1142.

13. For an analysis of anti-Jackson sentiment in the West, see Everett W. Kindig, "Western Opposition to Jackson's 'Democracy': The Ohio Valley as a Case Study, 1827–1836" (Ph.D. diss., Stanford University, 1974).

14. Martin Van Buren, *The Autobiography of Martin Van Buren,* 2:275.

Chapter 1. The Victorious Coalition

1. Robert V. Remini, *The Election of Andrew Jackson,* pp. 187–91; Samuel Flagg Bemis, *John Quincy Adams and the Union,* pp. 150–51; Mrs. Samuel Harrison Smith, *The First Forty Years of Washington Society,* p. 257.

2. Memorandum by Daniel Webster, [February 1829], *The Letters of Daniel Webster,* p. 142.

3. George Dangerfield, *The Awakening of American Nationalism: 1815–1828,* pp. 1–35; Harry Ammon, *James Monroe,* pp. 369–72, 380–85.

4. Charles S. Sydnor, *The Development of Southern Sectionalism: 1819–1848,* pp. 134–56; James Sterling Young, *The Washington Community:*

1800–1828, pp. 142, 222–26; Ammon, *James Monroe,* pp. 384–85; James S. Chase, *Emergence of the Presidential Nominating Convention: 1789–1832,* pp. 24–26.

5. Richard P. McCormick, *The Second American Party System,* pp. 28–30; Chilton Williamson, *American Suffrage from Property to Democracy: 1760–1860,* pp. 208–9, 223, 264, 277–80. On the decline of deferential politics in the early nineteenth century, see Moisei I. Ostrogorski, *Democracy and the Party System in the United States,* pp. 10–11; Marshall, "Strange Stillbirth of the Whig Party," pp. 453–55; and David Hackett Fischer, *The Revolution of American Conservatism,* pp. xi–xx, 1–28. Perry M. Goldman, "Political Virtue in the Age of Jackson," *Political Science Quarterly* 87 (1972):46–62, discusses the popular politician in Jacksonian America. Ronald P. Formisano, "Deferential-Participant Politics: The Early Republic's Political Culture, 1789–1840," *American Political Science Review* 68 (1974):473–87, perceptively analyzes the gradual shift from "a traditional, notable-oriented and deferential politics . . . to a party, electorate-oriented and egalitarian style of politics." John Niven, *Gideon Welles,* pp. 32–34, draws an apt parallel between evangelical religion and Jacksonian politics.

6. Van Buren, *Autobiography,* 2:10–13; Kendall, *Autobiography,* pp. 1–25, 66–67; William E. Smith, *The Francis Preston Blair Family in Politics,* 1:18–21; Cyrus Bradley, *Biography of Isaac Hill, of New-Hampshire;* Michael Wallace, "Changing Concepts of Party in the United States: New York, 1815–1828," *American Historical Review* 74 (1968):453–92; Formisano, "Toward a Reorientation of Jacksonian Politics," p. 55n; Niven, *Gideon Welles,* pp. 90–91; Whitman H. Ridgway, "Community Leadership: Baltimore During the First and Second Party Systems," *Maryland Historical Magazine* 71 (1976):346–48. A useful essay on American attitudes towards politics and politicians in the antebellum period is Richard Hofstadter, *The Idea of a Party System.*

7. Sidney H. Aronson, *Status and Kinship in the Higher Civil Service,* pp. 60–66, 90–105; McCormick, *Second American Party System,* pp. 351–52; Hofstadter, *Idea of a Party System,* pp. 239–48; Lynn L. Marshall, "The Genesis of Grass-roots Democracy in Kentucky," *Mid-America* 47 (1965): 269–87. Marshall's article makes the significant point that voter participation is not the only index of democracy. It is also necessary to know how the voter and the politician perceived politics.

8. There is no comprehensive study of the political and social consequences of the panic of 1819, but some of its effects can be traced in Murray N. Rothbard, *The Panic of 1819;* Samuel Rezneck, "The Depression of 1819–22, A Social History," *American Historical Review* 39 (1933):28–47; William Graham Sumner, *Andrew Jackson,* chap. 10; Dangerfield, *Awakening of American Nationalism,* chap. 6; Frederick Jackson Turner, *Rise of the New West: 1819–1829,* chap. 9; Richard P. McCormick, "New Perspectives on Jacksonian Politics," *American Historical Review* 65 (1960):292–94.

9. Charles G. Sellers, Jr., "Banking and Politics in Jackson's Tennessee,

1817–1827," *Mississippi Valley Historical Review* 41 (1954–55):67–71; Rothbard, *Panic of 1819*, pp. 47–51.

10. John Quincy Adams, *Memoirs of John Quincy Adams*, 5:128. See also *Argus of Western America*, 5 July 1821.

11. My description of Tennessee politics in the 1820s relies strongly on Charles G. Sellers, Jr., "Jackson Men with Feet of Clay," *American Historical Review* 62 (1957):537–51; Sellers, "Banking and Politics in Jackson's Tennessee," pp. 61–84; and Sellers, *Polk: Jacksonian*, pp. 66–134.

12. For Jackson's popular appeal, see John William Ward, *Andrew Jackson: Symbol for an Age*. Curtis, *Andrew Jackson*, pp. 1–92, places Jackson's presidential career in the context of national development. A provocative analysis of charisma can be found in Max Weber, "The Sociology of Charismatic Authority," in *From Max Weber*, pp. 245–48; Albert Somit, "The Political and Administrative Ideas of Andrew Jackson" (Ph.D. diss., University of Chicago, 1947), p. 42.

13. Donald J. Ratcliffe, "The Role of Voters and Issues in Party Formation: Ohio, 1824," *Journal of American History* 59 (1973):847–70; Marshall, "Grass-roots Democracy in Kentucky," pp. 284–87; Robert P. Hay, "The Case for Andrew Jackson in 1824: Eaton's *Wyoming Letters*," *Tennessee Historical Quarterly* 29 (1970–71):139–51; Kim T. Phillips, "The Pennsylvania Origins of the Jackson Movement," *Political Science Quarterly* 91 (1976):490–93, 503, 508. See also Robert E. Shalhope, "Jacksonian Politics in Missouri: A Comment on the McCormick Thesis," *Civil War History* 15 (1969):210–25.

14. For election statistics and analysis, see Edward Stanwood, *A History of Presidential Elections*, pp. 96–101; Sydnor, *Development of Southern Sectionalism*, p. 171; R. Carlyle Buley, *The Old Northwest*, 2:26–28; Dangerfield, *Awakening of American Nationalism*, p. 222.

15. William W. Freehling, *Prelude to Civil War*, pp. 118–19; Remini, *Election of Jackson*, p. 25; Calhoun to Littleton W. Tazewell, 15 August 1827, John C. Calhoun Papers, Library of Congress.

16. Calhoun's changing positions can be studied in Freehling, *Prelude to Civil War*, pp. 89–133; and Wiltse, *John C. Calhoun*, 1:passim.

17. For a study of the Old Republicans, see Norman K. Risjord, *The Old Republicans*. Also useful are Manning J. Dauer and Hans Hammond, "John Taylor: Democrat or Aristocrat?" *Journal of Politics* 6 (1944):381–403; and Eugene Tenbroeck Mudge, *The Social Philosophy of John Taylor of Caroline*. The flavor of Old Republican thought is captured best in their own writings. See especially John Taylor, *An Inquiry into the Principles and Policy of the Government of the United States*.

18. Turner, *Rise of the New West*, pp. 277–80; Sydnor, *Development of Southern Sectionalism*, pp. 134–56, 177–202; Richard H. Brown, "The Missouri Crisis, Slavery, and the Politics of Jacksonianism," *South Atlantic Quarterly* 65 (1966):55–72.

19. Troup's statement is quoted in Turner, *Rise of the New West*, p. 278;

Randolph's is from *Annals of Congress*, 18 Cong., 1 Sess., p. 1308; Brown, "Missouri Crisis," p. 58; Risjord, *Old Republicans*, pp. 221–27; Shalhope, "Thomas Jefferson's Republicanism," pp. 538–56.

20. The reasons for South Carolina's being more extreme than other southern states form the theme of Freehling's *Prelude to Civil War*; Calhoun to Jackson, 10 July 1828, Jackson, *Correspondence*, 3:415.

21. Gammon, *Campaign of 1832*, pp. 72–73; Arthur B. Darling, *Political Changes in Massachusetts: 1824–1848*, p. 62; Levi Woodbury to Elizabeth Woodbury, 11 December 1829, Levi Woodbury Papers, Library of Congress.

22. Gammon, *Campaign of 1832*, p. 73; Freehling, *Prelude to Civil War*, p. 131.

23. Since Van Buren was primarily responsible for building the faction that supported William Harris Crawford in 1824, and since he became the acknowledged leader of that faction after 1824, I have used the terms "Van Burenites" and "Crawfordites" interchangeably in this essay.

24. Excellent discussions of Van Buren's activities in the 1820s are found in Brown, "Missouri Crisis," pp. 55–72; Remini, *Election of Jackson*; and Remini, *Martin Van Buren and the Making of the Democratic Party*. See also Van Buren to Thomas Ritchie, 13 January 1827, Martin Van Buren Papers, Library of Congress.

25. Van Buren, *Autobiography*, 2:8, 28; Remini, *Van Buren and the Democratic Party*, pp. 2–15; James C. Curtis, *The Fox at Bay*, pp. 6–27; Edward M. Shepard, *Martin Van Buren*, pp. 16–18; Max M. Mintz, "The Political Ideas of Martin Van Buren," *New York History* 30 (1949):422–48. Even Bray Hammond, a severe critic of Van Buren, admits that the New Yorker was a sincere follower of Jeffersonian principles. See Hammond, *Banks and Politics*, pp. 351–55.

26. Van Buren, *Autobiography*, 2:159, 183, 193; Gammon, *Campaign of 1832*, p. 26; Brown, "Missouri Crisis," pp. 64–70. See also Joseph Hobson Harrison, Jr., "Martin Van Buren and His Southern Supporters," *Journal of Southern History* 22 (1956):438–58; and Harrison, "Oligarchs and Democrats: The Richmond Junto," *Virginia Magazine of History and Biography* 78 (1970):184–98.

27. Van Buren, *Autobiography*, 2:196.

28. Remini, *Election of Jackson*, pp. 47–50, 54–55; Van Buren, *Autobiography*, 2:198.

29. Willie Mangum to Charity Mangum, 8 April 1826, Willie Person Mangum, *The Papers of Willie Person Mangum*, 1:268; Remini, *Election of Jackson*, pp. 57–58.

30. Gammon, *Campaign of 1832*, p. 74.

31. Shaw Livermore, Jr., *The Twilight of Federalism*, pp. 223, 240–41; Swisher, *Roger B. Taney*, pp. 119–31.

32. For events in Kentucky during the 1820s, see Arndt M. Stickles, *The Critical Court Struggle in Kentucky: 1819–1829*; Sumner, *Andrew Jackson*,

chap. 6; and two excellent unpublished works: Lynn L. Marshall, "The Early Career of Amos Kendall: The Making of a Jacksonian" (Ph.D. diss., University of California, Berkeley, 1962); and Dale Maurice Royalty, "Banking, Politics, and the Commonwealth: Kentucky, 1800–1825" (Ph.D. diss., University of Kentucky, 1972).

33. Marshall, "Early Career of Amos Kendall," pp. 3–47; Kendall, *Autobiography*, pp. 1–15, 59–61, 68–120, 125; Kendall to John Kendall, 22 April 1849, Amos Kendall Papers, Massachusetts Historical Society.

34. Kendall, *Autobiography*, pp. 119–20, 126; Marshall, "Early Career of Amos Kendall," pp. 76–82.

35. Kendall, *Autobiography*, pp. 156–81; Marshall, "Early Career of Amos Kendall," pp. 117–18.

36. Marshall, "Early Career of Amos Kendall," pp. 220–22, 250–56, 301; Royalty, "Banking, Politics, and the Commonwealth," pp. 260–61; McCormick, *Second American Party System*, pp. 209–22. See also Powrie Vaux Doctor, "Amos Kendall: Propagandist of Jacksonian Democracy, 1828–1836" (Ph.D. diss., Georgetown University, 1939).

37. Georgetown *Patriot*, 11 May 1816. Kendall was part owner and editor of this paper shortly before taking control of the *Argus of Western America*.

38. *Argus of Western America*, 4 September 1818, 1 January, 2 April, 14 May, 23 July 1819, 15 February, 5 July 1821, 25 July 1822, 6 April 1825; Royalty, "Banking, Politics, and the Commonwealth," p. 277.

39. Smith, *Blair Family in Politics*, 1:12–18, 20.

40. Smith, *Blair Family in Politics*, 1:19–28; Marshall, "Early Career of Amos Kendall," p. 201.

41. *Argus of Western America*, 1 January, 10 September 1819, 10 February 1820 (quotation), 1 March 1821, 28 March, 2 May (quotation) 1822; Marshall, "Early Career of Amos Kendall," pp. 240–44, 260–61.

42. *Argus of Western America*, 21 May, 11 June (quotation) 1819, 15 February 1821, 28 March, 4 April (quotation) 1822, 23 December 1829 (quotation).

43. *Argus of Western America*, 8 June, 28 June, 5 July (quotation) 1821, 1 October 1823, 6 April 1825.

44. Hammond, *Banks and Politics*, pp. 332–34; and Lynn L. Marshall, "The Authorship of Jackson's Bank Veto Message," *Mississippi Valley Historical Review* 50 (1963):476, both distort and exaggerate Kendall's entrepreneurial motivation. Not until 1845, after suffering considerable financial losses and with his political influence diminished, did Kendall form a lucrative business association with Samuel F. B. Morse. Kendall, *Autobiography*, pp. 507, 525–28; Kendall to Jane Kendall, 14 April 1845, Amos Kendall Papers, Library of Congress. For the persistence of antibank thinking in the West, see Bray Hammond, "Banking in the Early West: Monopoly, Prohibition, and Laissez Faire," *Journal of Economic History* 8 (1948):1–25; Hammond, *Banks and Politics*, pp. 605–30; James Roger Sharp, *The Jacksonians versus the Banks*, pp. 322–23.

45. *Argus of Western America*, 7 January, 11 August, 3 September 1824, 6

April 1825, 2 August 1826 (quotation); Royalty, "Banking, Politics, and the Commonwealth," pp. 318–23.

46. Marshall, "Early Career of Amos Kendall," pp. 354, 383–85.

47. *Argus of Western America,* 22 February 1822.

48. Blair to Clay, 3 October 1827, Washington *Globe,* 16 March 1841; *Argus of Western America,* 1 November 1826. See also *Argus of Western America,* 27 January 1830.

49. Marshall, "Grass-roots Democracy in Kentucky," pp. 269–87; Kindig, "Western Opposition to Jackson's 'Democracy,'" pp. 159–60.

50. Ben: Perley Poore, *Perley's Reminiscences of Sixty Years in the National Metropolis,* 1:104.

51. Despite their overemphasis on ethnic and religious variables in explaining voter behavior, the "new" political historians have made a valuable contribution in directing attention to the nonmaterial or "symbolic" dimension of political issues. See Shade, *Banks or No Banks,* pp. 16–19; and Formisano, *Birth of Mass Political Parties,* pp. 10–14.

52. George Dangerfield, *The Era of Good Feelings,* p. 7; Florence Weston, *The Presidential Election of 1828,* pp. 155–80; Sydnor, *Development of Southern Sectionalism,* p. 191; Jackson to Andrew Jackson Donelson, 20 May 1822, Jackson, *Correspondence,* 3:162; John Spencer Bassett, *The Life of Andrew Jackson,* pp. 396–97; Van Buren to Jackson, 14 September 1827, Van Buren Papers.

53. N.s. to Jackson, n.d., placed at end of 1827 letters, Andrew Jackson Papers, Library of Congress; Van Buren to Jackson, 14 September 1827, Van Buren Papers; Robert Hayne to Jackson, 3 September 1828, Jackson, *Correspondence,* 3:433–35; Central Jackson Committee of Kentucky to Jackson, 5 December 1828, Jackson Papers.

54. Ward, *Andrew Jackson,* pp. 48–50; Thomas Perkins Abernethy, *From Frontier to Plantation in Tennessee,* p. 248.

55. In applying the words "persuasion," "ideology," and "philosophy" to Jackson's thinking, I am following the example of a number of historians who, by eschewing an excessive rigidity of definition, have provided imaginative insights into historical phenomena. All three words signify a coherent set of ideas, values, or beliefs. See Meyers, *Jacksonian Persuasion,* p. 6; Richard Buel, Jr., *Securing the Revolution,* pp. xi–xii; Eric Foner, *Free Soil, Free Labor, Free Men,* pp. 4–5; Wise, *American Historical Explanations,* pp. 8, 13.

56. Robert E. Shalhope, "Toward a Republican Synthesis: The Emergence of an Understanding of Republicanism in American Historiography," *William and Mary Quarterly* 29 (1972):49–80. Especially pertinent is Gordon Wood's outstanding study *The Creation of the American Republic;* Buel, *Securing the Revolution;* Library of Congress Symposia on the American Revolution, *The Development of a Revolutionary Mentality;* J. G. A. Pocock, "Machiavelli, Harrington and English Political Ideologies in the Eighteenth Century," in *Politics, Language and Time: Essays on Political Thought and History,* pp. 104–47; Isaac Kramnick, *Bolingbroke and His Circle,* pp. 70–83; Joyce

Appleby, "The Social Origins of American Revolutionary Ideology," *Journal of American History* 64 (1978):938–40; and John R. Howe, *From the Revolution through the Age of Jackson.*

57. J. G. A. Pocock, *The Machiavellian Moment*, pp. 526–45; Lance Banning, "Republican Ideology and the Triumph of the Constitution, 1789 to 1793," *William and Mary Quarterly* 31 (1974):179–88; Buel, *Securing the Revolution*, pp. 294–95; Howe, *From the Revolution through the Age of Jackson*, pp. 89–93; Rodger D. Parker, "The Bolingbrokean Origins of Jeffersonian Republicanism," pp. 14–20. Professor Parker kindly allowed me to read his unpublished essay. Cf. Shalhope, "Thomas Jefferson's Republicanism," pp. 529–56.

58. For Jackson's recollection of the sacrifices made during the Revolution to achieve "a republican government," see Jackson to Willie Blount, 4 January 1813, Jackson, *Correspondence*, 1:255. Rogin, *Fathers and Children*, p. 14, considers the "revolutionary fathers" one of two cultural symbols that dominated Jackson's life. The other was Indians.

59. Jackson to L. H. Coleman, 26 April 1824, Jackson, *Correspondence*, 3:249–50; Jackson to James W. Lanier, 15? May 1824, *Correspondence*, 3:253; Jackson to John Coffee, 7 May 1824, *Correspondence*, 3:252; Jackson to Monroe, 12 November 1816, *Correspondence*, 2:264–65; Abernethy, *From Frontier to Plantation*, pp. 244–49.

60. Jackson to Andrew Jackson Donelson, 21 March, 6 August 1822, 26 February 1824, Jackson, *Correspondence*, 3:156–67, 174, 230.

61. Jackson to John Overton, 22 January 1798, Jackson, *Correspondence*, 1:43; Jackson to William Dickson, 1 September 1801, *Correspondence*, 1:58–59; S. Williams to Jackson, 25 April 1808, *Correspondence*, 1:189; Robert V. Remini, *Andrew Jackson*, pp. 37, 43–44. Mary T. Orr claims that John Overton, one of Jackson's earliest friends in Tennessee, stimulated his interest in Jeffersonianism. Overton was a distant relative of Jefferson and had been a neighbor before he moved to Tennessee. See Orr, "John Overton and Traveler's Rest," *Tennessee Historical Quarterly* 15 (1956):217.

62. Jackson to Monroe, 26 July 1822, Jackson, *Correspondence*, 3:171; Jackson to Captain John Donelson, 3 September 1821, *Correspondence*, 3:117; Jackson to Andrew Jackson Donelson, 8 February 1823, *Correspondence*, 3:186–87; Jackson to Calhoun, August 1823, *Correspondence*, 3:202. While Jackson's association with the antirelief Blount-Overton faction helps explain his opposition to Felix Grundy's state bank scheme, his hard-money views were more influential. See Sellers, "Banking and Politics in Jackson's Tennessee," pp. 76–78.

63. Jackson to L. H. Coleman, 26 April 1824, Jackson, *Correspondence*, 3:250; Jackson to William S. Fulton, 4 July 1824, *Correspondence*, 3:259–60.

64. Jackson to Calhoun, 26 July 1826, Jackson, *Correspondence*, 3:307; Jackson to John Coffee, 12 May 1828, *Correspondence*, 3:402; Jackson to James Hamilton, Jr., 29 June 1828, *Correspondence*, 3:412.

65. Jackson to John Branch, 3 March 1826, Branch Family Papers, Southern

Historical Collection, University of North Carolina; Boyd McNairy to Clay, 24 March 1828, Henry Clay Papers, Library of Congress.

66. Jackson to L. H. Coleman, 26 April 1824, Jackson, *Correspondence*, 3:249–51; Robert Hayne to Jackson, 3 September 1828, *Correspondence*, 3:433–35.

67. Jackson to John Branch, 3 March 1826, Branch Family Papers; Kendall to Blair, 7 March 1829, Blair-Lee Papers, Princeton University Library.

68. For Adams's statement that "liberty is power," see Richardson, *Messages and Papers*, 2:882.

69. Roy F. Nichols, *The Invention of the American Political Parties*, pp. 371–72. My discussion of the Jackson organization of 1828 is largely a summary of the findings in Remini, *Election of Jackson*. See also Ronald P. Formisano, "Political Character, Antipartyism and the Second Party System," *American Quarterly* 21 (1969):683–709, for a discussion of the Jacksonians' greater acceptance of political parties.

70. Remini, *Election of Jackson*, pp. 34–50; Fletcher M. Green, "Duff Green, Militant Journalist of the Old School," *American Historical Review* 52 (1946–47):247–51, 263–64; Young, *Washington Community*, pp. 173–74; Leonard D. White, *The Jacksonians*, pp. 284–86; Frederic Hudson, *Journalism in the United States: 1690–1872*, pp. 231–40.

71. Remini, *Election of Jackson*, pp. 70–71, 86–94.

72. Remini, *Election of Jackson*, pp. 63–65; James Parton, *Life of Andrew Jackson*, 3:142.

73. Remini, *Election of Jackson*, pp. 101–2; McCormick, *Second American Party System*, pp. 346–49; James S. Chase, "Jacksonian Democracy and the Rise of the Nominating Convention," *Mid-America* 45 (1963):231–34; Young, *Washington Community*, p. 35.

74. Jackson to Andrew Jackson Donelson, 11 April 1824, Jackson, *Correspondence*, 3:246; Jackson to Samuel Swartwout, 22 February 1825, *Correspondence*, 3:279.

75. Jackson to William B. Lewis, 8 March 1828, original in J. Pierpont Morgan Library, reproduction read in Jackson-Lewis Papers, New York Public Library; Jackson to Lewis, 13 August 1828, Jackson-Lewis Papers. The New York Public Library's collection of Jackson-Lewis correspondence provides abundant testimony of the commanding position taken by Jackson in his campaign.

76. Van Buren, *Autobiography*, 2:515; Wiltse, *John C. Calhoun*, 2:76–79.

Chapter 2. Cabinet Formation and Jackson's Advisory System

1. Van Buren, *Autobiography*, 2:244.

2. Young, *Washington Community*, pp. 230–39; Leonard D. White, *The Jeffersonians*, pp. 77–86.

3. Leonard D. White, *The Federalists*, pp. 88–96; White, *Jeffersonians*, pp. 29–44; Young, *Washington Community*, pp. 187–96; Dumas Malone, *Jeffer-*

son the President: First Term, p. 28; memorandum in Jackson's handwriting, 9 December 1828, Jackson, *Correspondence*, 3:451.

4. Jackson's recommendation of a constitutional amendment limiting the president to one term was in keeping with Jeffersonian principles, but he never made this proposal a priority. See Richardson, *Messages and Papers*, 3:1011.

5. Kendall to Blair, 14 February 1829, Blair-Lee Papers; Jackson to Richard K. Call, 15 November 1821, Jackson, *Correspondence*, 3:130; Curtis, *Andrew Jackson*, p. 79; Albert Somit, "Andrew Jackson as Administrator," *Public Administration Review* 8 (1948):188–89, 194. As a senator, Jackson also indicated the influence of his early life on his attitude towards advisers. "The best lesson learnt me in my youth, was to pursue principle and never depart from my own judgt when matured. treat all with complacency, but make confidents [*sic*] of but few. I have profitted much by an adherence to this rule, but still I have been deceived as you know in men." Jackson to John Coffee, 27 December 1824, Jackson, *Correspondence*, 3:270.

6. Van Buren, *Autobiography*, 2:253, 255; Jackson to John Coffee, 12 May, 11 December 1828, Jackson, *Correspondence*, 3:402, 458. Richardson, *Messages and Papers*, 3:1309; Parton, *Life of Jackson*, 3:77; Young, *Washington Community*, pp. 240–41; Arthur M. Schlesinger, Jr., *The Age of Jackson*, p. 66; White, *Jacksonians*, pp. 20–28, 87, 93, 504; Somit, "Political and Administrative Ideas," pp. 161–62.

7. *Niles' Register* 40 (30 April 1831):145; Henry S. Foote, *Casket of Reminiscences*, p. 102; White, *Federalists*, pp. 36–37, 510; White, *Jeffersonians*, pp. 30–31; Malone, *Jefferson the President: First Term*, p. 28; Richardson, *Messages and Papers*, 3:1312; Somit, "Andrew Jackson as Political Theorist," p. 103.

8. Kendall to Blair, 7 March 1829, Blair-Lee Papers; "Statement of Andrew Jackson Donelson," 10 November 1830, Jackson, *Correspondence*, 4:200–205; James Buchanan to Benjamin Porter, 22 January 1829, James Buchanan Miscellaneous Papers, New-York Historical Society.

9. Daniel Webster to Ezekiel Webster, 23 February 1829, Webster, *Letters*, p. 142; Memorandum by Webster, [February 1829], *Letters*, p. 142. The importance of molding institutions while still in their formative stage is discussed in another context in Arthur E. Bestor, Jr., "Patent-Office Models of the Good Society: Some Relationships between Social Reform and Westward Expansion," *American Historical Review* 58 (1952):505–26. Also suggestive is John R. Howe, Jr., "Republican Thought and the Political Violence of the 1790's," *American Quarterly* 19 (1967):147–65.

10. Johnathan Degraff to Azariah Flagg, 21 December 1828, Azariah Flagg Papers, New York Public Library; Green to John Pope, 11 December 1828, Duff Green Papers, Library of Congress; Balch to Van Buren, 27 November 1828, Van Buren Papers; *United States' Telegraph*, 20 January 1829; Green to Mordecai M. Noah, 21 April 1829, Green Papers, Library of Congress.

11. Kendall to Blair, 14 February 1829, Blair-Lee Papers.

12. Bassett, *Life of Jackson*, p. 410; Sellers, *Polk: Jacksonian*, p. 137; Kendall to John Pope, 11 January 1829, Blair-Lee Papers; Kendall to his wife, 23 January 1829, Kendall, *Autobiography*, p. 281; Hess, *Organizing the Presidency*, p. 161.

13. Sellers, *Polk: Jacksonian*, pp. 67–69, 171–76, 196–98; Poore, *Perley's Reminiscences*, 1:88; Louis R. Harlan, "Public Career of William Berkeley Lewis," *Tennessee Historical Quarterly* 7 (1948):18–27; Abernethy, *From Frontier to Plantation*, p. 241; Gabriel L. Lowe, Jr., "John H. Eaton, Jackson's Campaign Manager," *Tennessee Historical Quarterly* 11 (1952):99–147.

14. Kendall to Blair, 22 November 1829, Blair-Lee Papers. See also Jackson to Andrew Jackson Donelson, 26 February 1824, Jackson, *Correspondence*, 3:231.

15. Harlan, "Career of Lewis," pp. 3–38, 118–52; Sellers, *Polk: Jacksonian*, pp. 67–69, 171–76, 196–98; Lewis to Jackson, 8 February 1813, Jackson, *Correspondence*, 1:276; Abernethy, *From Frontier to Plantation*, p. 241.

16. Lowe, "John H. Eaton," p. 126; Jackson to Polk, 13 December 1844, Jackson, *Correspondence*, 6:339.

17. Sellers, *Polk: Jacksonian*, p. 197; Claude G. Bowers, *The Party Battles of the Jackson Period*, pp. 427–28; Hugh Lawson White, *A Memoir of Hugh Lawson White*, pp. 243–44; Jackson to White, 31 December 1828, White, *Memoir*, p. 246; Jackson to Andrew Jackson Donelson, 27 July 1831, Andrew Jackson Donelson Papers, Library of Congress.

18. James A. Hamilton, *Reminiscences of James A. Hamilton*, pp. 86–87; Adams, *Memoirs*, 8:136.

19. Hamilton, *Reminiscences*, p. 88.

20. Harlan, "Career of Lewis," p. 33; Lewis to Allan Hall, 12 July 1837, Lewis to Elijah Hayward, 28 March 1827, Jackson-Lewis Papers; Sellers, *Polk: Jacksonian*, p. 137; James A. Hamilton to Van Buren, 21 February 1829, Van Buren Papers.

21. Hamilton, *Reminiscences*, pp. 90–91; James A. Hamilton to Van Buren, 19 February 1829, Van Buren Papers.

22. Kendall to Blair, 7 March 1829, Blair-Lee Papers; Parton, *Life of Jackson*, 3:176; Hamilton, *Reminiscences*, p. 89; William T. Barry to daughter, 16 May 1829, "Letters of William T. Barry," *William and Mary College Quarterly Historical Magazine* 13(1904-5):239; Sellers, *Polk: Jacksonian*, p. 142; Jackson to Samuel Swartwout, 27 September 1829, Jackson, *Correspondence*, 4:78.

23. Kendall to Blair, 7 March 1829, Blair-Lee Papers; James Hamilton, Jr., to Van Buren, 19 February 1829, Van Buren Papers; Hamilton, *Reminiscences*, p. 89.

24. James Hamilton, Jr., to Van Buren, 19 February 1829, Van Buren Papers; Philip S. Klein, *Pennsylvania Politics: 1817–1832*, p. 255; Kendall to Blair, 7 March 1829, Blair-Lee Papers.

25. Klein, *Pennsylvania Politics*, pp. 121–22, 214–18; 253–54.

26. W. A. Ingham, *Samuel D. Ingham*, pp. 6–8, 15; Klein, *Pennsylvania*

Politics, pp. 127, 241, 246; *Register of Debates in Congress*, 19 Cong., 2 Sess., p. 1099; Phillips, "Pennsylvania Origins of the Jackson Movement," p. 505.

27. Andrew Jackson to Andrew Jackson Donelson, 27 July 1831, Donelson Papers; "Mr. Calhoun & Seminole Affair," manuscript in Jackson's handwriting, at end of 1832 papers, Jackson Papers; "Major Eaton's Reply," *Niles' Register* 41 (17 September 1831):50.

28. Bassett, *Life of Jackson*, p. 414; William S. Hoffmann, "John Branch and the Origins of the Whig Party in North Carolina," *North Carolina Historical Review* 35 (1958):299–315; Kendall to Blair, 7 March 1829, Blair-Lee Papers; James A. Hamilton to Van Buren, 21 February 1829, Van Buren Papers; Hamilton, *Reminiscences*, p. 102. Branch's son was born on 8 January, the anniversary of Jackson's victory at New Orleans. When informed of this, Jackson noted that the child would clearly be "a true patriot." Jackson to Branch, 3 March 1826, Branch Family Papers.

29. William S. Hoffmann, *Andrew Jackson and North Carolina Politics*, pp. 37–38; James A. Hamilton to Van Buren, 21 February 1829, Van Buren Papers.

30. Royce Coggins McCrary, Jr., "John Macpherson Berrien of Georgia (1781–1856): A Political Biography" (Ph.D. diss., University of Georgia, 1971), pp. v–vi, 90–91, 100–103, 113, 147; Van Buren, *Autobiography*, 2:216.

31. Thomas P. Govan, "John M. Berrien and the Administration of Andrew Jackson," *Journal of Southern History* 5 (1939):449; McCrary, "John Macpherson Berrien," pp. 144–46.

32. James A. Hamilton to Van Buren, 13 February 1829, Van Buren Papers; Kendall to Blair, 7 March 1829, Blair-Lee Papers; Dorothy G. Fowler, *The Cabinet Politician*, p. 2.

33. James A. Hamilton to Van Buren, 19 February 1829, Van Buren Papers.

34. James Hamilton, Jr., to Van Buren, 23 January, 19 February 1829, Van Buren Papers.

35. James Hamilton, Jr., to Van Buren, 19 February 1829, Van Buren Papers.

36. James Hamilton, Jr., to Van Buren, 5 March 1829, Van Buren Papers; J. H. Scinner to James Barbour, 22 February 1829, James Barbour Papers, New York Public Library.

37. *U.S. Telegraph*, 14 April 1831; Green to Kendall, 10 August, 17 September 1828, Green Papers, Library of Congress; Kendall to Blair, 3 February 1829, Blair-Lee Papers.

38. Sellers, *Polk: Jacksonian*, pp. 137–43; Andrew Jackson Donelson to Emily Donelson, 15 January 1831, Donelson Papers; Emily Donelson to Polly Coffee, 27 March 1829, quoted in Pauline Wilcox Burke, *Emily Donelson of Tennessee*, 1:178; Donelson to———, 20 September 1829, Donelson to John Coffee, 27 August 1829, Donelson Papers; Van Buren, *Autobiography*, 2:345; James A. Hamilton to Van Buren, 23 February 1829, Van Buren Papers.

39. Margaret Eaton, *The Autobiography of Peggy Eaton*, pp. 32, 208. See also Queena Pollack, *Peggy Eaton*; C. C. Cambreleng to Van Buren, 1 January 1829, Van Buren Papers; Smith, *First Forty Years*, p. 282.

40. Gideon Welles to John M. Niles, 29 February 1829, Gideon Welles Papers, Library of Congress; Kendall to Blair, 7 March 1829, Blair-Lee Papers.

41. The complicated maneuvers involving the cabinet seats can be reconstructed from the following: Kendall to Blair, 7 March, 10 March, 30 April 1829, Blair-Lee Papers; James A. Hamilton to Van Buren, 23 February 1829, Van Buren Papers; Hoffmann, *Jackson and North Carolina Politics*, pp. 39–40; White, *Jeffersonians*, p. 318; Adams, *Memoirs*, 8:112–13; Branch to Col. Bell, 26 September 1831, Branch Family Papers; Smith, *First Forty Years*, p. 282.

42. Julius Franz Kany, "The Career of William Taylor Barry" (M.A. thesis, Western Kentucky State Teachers College, 1934), pp. 1–2, 28–55; Jackson to Andrew Jackson Donelson, 21 March, 5 July, 11 October 1822, Jackson, *Correspondence*, 3:156, 167, 179.

43. Kany, "Career of William Taylor Barry," pp. 3, 8, 57–61; Kendall to Blair, 14 February, 7 March 1829, Blair-Lee Papers; Frances Clifton, "John Overton as Andrew Jackson's Friend," *Tennessee Historical Quarterly* 11 (1952):40.

44. Kany, "Career of William Taylor Barry," pp. 24–26; Barry to daughter, 16 May 1829, "Letters of William T. Barry," 13:240–41.

45. Jackson to John McLemore, April 1829, Jackson, *Correspondence*, 4:20; Webster to Ezekiel Webster, 26 February 1829, Webster, *Letters*, p. 144; McLane to Van Buren, 19 February 1829, Van Buren Papers; James Campbell to Gulian Verplanck, 7 February [March?] 1829, Gulian Verplanck Papers, New-York Historical Society.

46. Hamilton, *Reminiscences*, p. 243; William B. Lewis to Azariah Flagg, 14 February 1832, Flagg Papers; Cambreleng to Van Buren, 1 March 1829, Van Buren Papers.

47. Barry to daughter, 25 February 1830, "Letters of William T. Barry," *William and Mary College Quarterly Historical Magazine* 14(1905–6):20; Hoffmann, "Branch and the Whig Party," pp. 299–315; Branch to Messrs. Alex. W. Mebane, Geo. B. Outlaw, &c., 20 August 1831, *Niles' Register* 41 (17 September 1831):38; Govan, "Berrien and the Administration of Andrew Jackson," pp. 447–68; Berrien to George Gilmer, 3 February 1855, John McPherson Berrien Papers, Southern Historical Collection, University of North Carolina; McCrary, "John Macpherson Berrien," pp. 126–27.

48. Wiltse, *John C. Calhoun*, 2:19–25; Calhoun to Littleton W. Tazewell, 14 April 1829, Calhoun Papers, Library of Congress; Hamilton, *Reminiscences*, p. 93; Van Buren to C. C. Cambreleng, 17 December 1828, Van Buren Papers; Van Buren, *Autobiography*, 2:231; James A. Hamilton to Van Buren, 13 February, 19 February 1829, Van Buren Papers.

49. Parton, *Life of Jackson*, 3:174; Kendall to Blair, 7 March 1829, Blair-Lee Papers; Cambreleng to Van Buren, 1 March 1829, Van Buren Papers; Kany, "Career of William Taylor Barry," p. 11; Livermore, *Twilight of Federalism*, p. 245.

50. Washington *Globe*, 8 August 1831; Kendall to Blair, 28 January 1830, Blair-Lee Papers; White, *Jacksonians*, p. 94; Aronson, *Status and Kinship*, p.

158; George M. Dallas to George Wolf, 27 March 1835, George M. Wolf Papers, Historical Society of Pennsylvania.

51. Van Buren, *Autobiography*, 2:250–51; *Niles' Register* 36 (11 July 1829):317, 41 (3 December 1831):264; Hamilton, *Reminiscences*, p. 191.

52. *U.S. Telegraph*, 28 November 1831; Edward Livingston to James Barbour [1831], James Barbour Papers; Jackson to Kendall, n.d., Kendall Papers, Massachusetts Historical Society; Mahlon Dickerson, "Diary, 1832–1845," Mahlon Dickerson Papers, New Jersey Historical Society; John Sergeant to Nicholas Biddle, 27 February 1834, Nicholas Biddle, *The Correspondence of Nicholas Biddle Dealing with National Affairs: 1807–1844*, p. 223; Levi Woodbury, 10 January 1834, "Sundry Exercises or Moral Self-examinations, Resolutions, and Intimate Memoranda, January 19, 1823–March 9, 1834," Box 29, Woodbury Papers; James C. Curtis, "Andrew Jackson and His Cabinet: Some New Evidence," *Tennessee Historical Quarterly* 27 (1968):158–59.

53. Hess, *Organizing the Presidency*, p. 43; Richard F. Fenno, Jr., *The President's Cabinet*, pp. 5, 160–86; Young, *Washington Community*, pp. 230–37; James A. Hamilton to William C. Rives, 8 September 1831, William C. Rives Papers, Library of Congress; Dickerson, Diary, 1 December 1834, 18 June, 29 November 1836, 30 January 1837, Dickerson Papers; Thomas Hart Benton, *Thirty Years' View*, 1:678; McLane to Jackson, 27 December [1831?], placed at end of 1832 letters, Jackson Papers; Edward Livingston to James Barbour [1831], James Barbour Papers; Curtis, "Andrew Jackson and His Cabinet," p. 163.

54. Blair to Mrs. Gratz, 29 August 1831, Thomas Clay, ed., "Two Years with Old Hickory," *Atlantic Monthly* 60 (August 1887):197–98; Blair to [Abraham Lincoln], n.d., Blair-Lee Papers; Kendall, *Autobiography*, p. 635; Washington *Globe*, 12 March, 9 September 1831; Benton, *Thirty Years' View*, 1:678. James C. Curtis argues that Jackson occasionally polled his cabinet, but his evidence is not conclusive. See Curtis, "Andrew Jackson and His Cabinet," p. 161.

55. Jackson to Van Buren, 6 December 1831, Jackson, *Correspondence*, 4:379; Roger B. Taney, "Roger B. Taney's 'Bank War Manuscript,'" *Maryland Historical Magazine* 53 (1958):128–29.

56. Jackson to William B. Lewis, 19 October 1839, Jackson-Lewis Papers; Van Buren, *Autobiography*, 2:704.

57. Kendall to Blair, 3 February, 7 March 1829, 28 January 1830, Blair-Lee Papers; Kendall to Joseph Desha, 9 April 1831, "Correspondence between Governor Joseph Desha and Amos Kendall: 1831–1835," ed. James A. Padgett, *Register of the Kentucky State Historical Society* 38 (1940):8; Hamilton, *Reminiscences*, p. 130; Kendall, *Autobiography*, p. 285.

58. Kendall to Blair, 7 March 1829, Blair-Lee Papers; Blair to Jackson, 26 August 1834, Jackson to Blair, 6 September 1834, Blair Family Papers, Library of Congress; Van Buren, *Autobiography*, 2:321; Richard Parker to Van Buren, 25 December 1835, Van Buren Papers; Willie P. Mangum to James Iredell, 11 February 1832, James Iredell Papers, Duke University Library.

59. Kendall to Blair, 10 March 1829, Blair-Lee Papers.

60. Kendall to Blair, 9 January, 3 February 1829, Blair-Lee Papers; Jackson to William B. Lewis, 19 October 1839, Jackson-Lewis Papers.

61. Kendall to Blair, 7 March 1829, Blair-Lee Papers. See also, Jackson to John Coffee, 10 April 1830, Jackson, *Correspondence*, 4:134; James Hamilton, Jr., to Van Buren, 19 February 1829, Van Buren Papers; Washington *Globe*, 29 July 1834.

62. Georgetown *Patriot*, 20 April, 16 November 1816; *Argus of Western America*, 18 June 1819, 30 May 1822, 18 February 1824.

63. *Argus of Western America*, 29 November 1826, 24 January, 31 January (quotation), 25 April (quotation), 7 November (quotation), 26 December 1827, 28 February 1828.

64. Kendall to Blair, 21 June 1829 (quotation), 21 April, 25 April, 24 May 1830, Blair-Lee Papers; Kendall to Gideon Welles, 13 September 1830, Welles Papers; Jackson to John Coffee, 30 May 1829, Jackson, *Correspondence*, 4:39; Jackson to Jno. C. McLemore, 28 September 1829, Andrew Jackson Miscellaneous Papers, New-York Historical Society; Jackson to William B. Lewis, 10 August 1830, Jackson-Lewis Papers; Adams, *Memoirs*, 8:141, 144.

65. *Argus of Western America*, 2 January 1828; Kendall to John Pope, 11 January 1829, Blair-Lee Papers.

66. Richard B. Morris, ed., *Encyclopedia of American History*, p. 163; James Truslow Adams, ed., *Dictionary of American History*, 3:213; White, *Jacksonians*, pp. 94–95; Parton, *Life of Jackson*, 3:183; Longaker, "Jackson's Kitchen Cabinet," p. 108; Louis W. Koenig, *The Invisible Presidency*, pp. 40–45; Marshall, "Strange Stillbirth of the Whig Party," pp. 450–52.

67. Blair to Mrs. Gratz, 29 August 1831 [1833], Clay, ed., "Two Years with Old Hickory," pp. 197–98; Robert M. Gibbes to Biddle, 11 December 1831, Nicholas Biddle Papers, Library of Congress; Washington *Globe*, 29 March, 8 September 1832, 29 November 1833, 14 July 1834; Green to Richard K. Crallé, 30 April 1832, Green Papers, Library of Congress; *U.S. Telegraph*, 13 March, 27 March, 29 September, 6 October 1832, 2 August 1833; *National Intelligencer*, 16 June 1832, 10 January, 2 October, 6 November 1833; Andrew Stevenson to Blair, 2 April 1833, Henry Toland to Blair, 10 November 1832, Blair-Lee Papers. Poindexter's responsibility for publicizing the phrase "Kitchen Cabinet" is discussed in Richard B. Latner, "The Kitchen Cabinet and Andrew Jackson's Advisory System," *Journal of American History* 65 (1978):374–77. It is likely that Poindexter coined the phrase as well. I wish to thank Professor Edwin A. Miles for directing me to evidence that Poindexter originated the term.

68. Longaker, "Jackson's Kitchen Cabinet," p. 100; Fenno, *The President's Cabinet*, pp. 4–5; Hess, *Organizing the Presidency*, p. 206. See also Matthew A. Crenson, *The Federal Machine*, pp. 57–58.

69. Lester Seligman, "Presidential Leadership: The Inner Circle and Institutionalization," *Journal of Politics* 18 (1956):413; Theodore C. Sorensen, *Decision-Making in the White House*, pp. 70–71; Hess, *Organizing the Presidency*, pp. 174–75; Richard T. Johnson, "Presidential

Style," in *Perspectives on the Presidency*, ed. Aaron Wildavsky, pp. 263–66.

70. Hess, *Organizing the Presidency*, pp. 1–11, 160–62, 174–75. Louis W. Koenig, in analyzing different types of presidential advisers, distinguishes gradations of influence even within the president's inner circle. He labels those with freer access to the president "favored members." Koenig, *Invisible Presidency*, p. 22.

71. For Jackson's expansion of presidential powers, see White, *Jacksonians*, pp. 20–49; Robert V. Remini, *Andrew Jackson and the Bank War*, pp. 176–78; Ralph M. Goldman, *The Democratic Party in American Politics*, p. 45.

72. Hess, *Organizing the Presidency*, pp. 39, 150; *National Intelligencer*, 4 January, 2 October 1833.

73. *U.S. Telegraph*, 2 August 1833.

74. Washington *Globe*, 9 September 1831; Billy Gratz to Blair, 31 May 1831, Blair Family Papers; Amos Kendall, "Anecdotes of General Jackson," *United States Magazine and Democratic Review* 11 (1842):273–74; Koenig, *Invisible Presidency*, pp. 407–9; Crenson, *Federal Machine*, p. 61; Curtis, *Andrew Jackson*, pp. 11–12, 82, 144.

75. Nathaniel Niles to William C. Rives, 23 July 1833, Rives Papers; Blair to Mrs. Gratz, 10 May 1831, Clay, ed., "Two Years with Old Hickory," p. 193.

76. Jackson to Taney, 13 October, 8 November 1834, 14 April 1838, Andrew Jackson, "Letters of Andrew Jackson to Roger Brooke Taney," *Maryland Historical Magazine* 4 (1909):303, 304, 305; Taney, "'Bank War Manuscript,'" p. 117.

77. Jackson to Kendall, n.d. [September–October 1834], Andrew DeCoppett Collection, Princeton University Library; Benton, *Thirty Years' View*, 1:678.

78. Kendall to————, 10 April 1831, Welles Papers; Blair to Mrs. Gratz, 20 April 1831, Clay, ed., "Two Years with Old Hickory," p. 192; Washington *Globe*, 16 November 1835; Kendall to Jackson, 3 December 1831, Blair-Lee Papers.

79. *U.S. Telegraph*, 28 August 1832; Van Buren to Lewis, 17 January 1856, Lewis to Allen A. Hall, 12 July 1837, Jackson-Lewis Papers; Van Buren to Benjamin F. Butler, June 1835, Benjamin F. Butler Papers, Princeton University Library.

80. George M. Dallas to Samuel Ingham, 15 May 1831, George M. Dallas Papers, Historical Society of Pennsylvania; Polk to Donelson, 28 April 1835, Donelson Papers; Lewis to Blair, 23 August 1832, J. S. Barbour to Blair, 9 November 1831, T. Bland to Blair, 2 July 1835, Thomas P. Moore to Blair, 4 September 1833, Blair-Lee Papers; Lewis to Jackson, 20 August 1834, Jackson Papers; Lewis to Blair, 17 May 1831, Blair-Lee Papers; *U.S. Telegraph*, 13 August 1831.

81. *Niles' Register* 36 (6 June 1829):244, 37(10 October 1829):97–98, 42 (16 June 1832):292; Hamilton, *Reminiscences*, pp. 212, 250; Isaac Hill to————, 15 August 1833, New Hampshire Whig Papers, Houghton Library,

Harvard University; Jackson to Van Buren, 5 September 1831, Jackson, *Correspondence*, 4:347; Barry to daughter, 24 May 1831, 10 April 1832, 22 February, 8 March 1834, "Letters of William T. Barry," 14:231, 232, 239–40; William J. Duane, *Narrative and Correspondence Concerning the Removal of the Deposits*, p. 57; Gideon Welles to Hill, 25 March 1829, Isaac Hill Papers, New Hampshire Historical Society (unless otherwise noted, all future Hill Papers references are to this collection); Hill to A. A. Burk, 16 November 1833, New Hampshire Whig Papers; Francis O. Smith to Blair, 11 July 1834, Blair-Lee Papers; Hill to———, 15 August 1833, Isaac Hill Papers, Library of Congress.

82. Woodbury, 10 January 1834, "Sundry Exercises," Woodbury Papers; John M. McFaul and Frank Otto Gatell, "The Outcast Insider: Reuben M. Whitney and the Bank War," *Pennsylvania Magazine of History and Biography* 91 (1967):120–24; Thomas Ellicott to Jackson, 6 April 1833, Jackson, *Correspondence*, 4:49–52; Johnson, "Presidential Style," p. 262.

83. Woodbury, 10 January 1834, "Sundry Exercises," Woodbury Papers.

84. Kendall to Blair, 14 February 1829, Blair-Lee Papers; Crenson, *Federal Machine*, p. 61.

85. Blair to Mrs. Gratz, 29 August 1831, Clay, ed., "Two Years with Old Hickory," p. 198; Kendall to James Gordon Bennett, 31 July 1833, quoted in Hudson, *Journalism in the United States*, p. 446; Jackson to John Randolph, 11 November 1831, Jackson, *Correspondence*, 4:372.

Chapter 3. A More Cohesive Party

1. Poem by Andrew Jackson, n.d., Rives Papers.
2. Kendall to Blair, 25 April 1830, Blair-Lee Papers.
3. Parton, *Life of Jackson*, 3:287–88.
4. Brown, "Missouri Crisis," pp. 68–72; Remini, *Election of Jackson*, pp. 114–15; David Rankin Barbee, "Andrew Jackson and Peggy O'Neale," *Tennessee Historical Quarterly* 15 (1956):37–52.
5. Smith, *First Forty Years*, p. 298; Constance McLaughlin Green, *Washington: Village and Capital*, pp. 122–23.
6. Adams, *Memoirs*, 8:138; Aronson, *Status and Kinship*, pp. 82, 90.
7. Smith, *First Forty Years*, p. 344; William C. Rives to wife, 4 December 1836, Rives Papers.
8. Barry to daughter, 16 May 1829, "Letters of William T. Barry," 13:239; Kendall to Blair, 29 October 1830, Blair-Lee Papers; Kendall, *Autobiography*, pp. 278, 284; Blair's sister to Blair, April———, Blair-Lee Papers; Jackson to Samuel Swartwout, 27 September 1829, Jackson, *Correspondence*, 4:79.
9. Smith, *First Forty Years*, p. 344.
10. Green, *Washington*, pp. 121–22.
11. Smith, *First Forty Years*, p. 288.
12. Jackson to Captain John Donelson, 7 June 1829, Jackson, *Corre-*

spondence, 4:41–42; Jackson to Robert Call, 5 July 1829, *Correspondence*, 4:51–52. On the implications of the Eaton affair for Jackson's elevated concept of the family, see Curtis, *Andrew Jackson*, pp. 94–100; and Rogin, *Fathers and Children*, pp. 268–72.

13. Parton, *Life of Jackson*, 3:195; Barry to daughter, 16 May 1829, "Letters of William T. Barry," 13:239.

14. Van Buren, *Autobiography*, 2:231, 266–67, 342–43, 363, 406; Hamilton, *Reminiscences*, pp. 92–93.

15. Kendall, *Autobiography*, p. 360; Blair to Van Buren, 9 December 1858, Van Buren Papers.

16. Jackson to Robert Call, 5 July 1829, Jackson, *Correspondence*, 4:51–52; Parton, *Life of Jackson*, 3:203–5; Jackson to John McLemore, 24 November 1829, Jackson, *Correspondence*, 4:88–89.

17. Wiltse, *John C. Calhoun*, 2:36; Jackson, "Mr. Calhoun & Seminole Affair," at end of 1832 papers, Jackson Papers.

18. Barry to daughter, 25 February 1830, "Letters of William T. Barry," 14:19–20.

19. Kendall to Blair, 28 January 1830, Blair-Lee Papers.

20. Remini, *Andrew Jackson*, pp. 114–15; Schlesinger, *Age of Jackson*, p. 54.

21. George M. Dallas to George Wolf, 24 April 1834, Wolf Papers.

22. Hayne to Woodbury, 10 July 1828, Woodbury Papers; Green to Calhoun, 1 August 1830, Duff Green Papers, Southern Historical Collection, University of North Carolina; *U.S. Telegraph*, 18 March, 23 August 1831. Two excellent discussions of the Tariff of 1828 are Remini, *Election of Jackson*, pp. 166–80; and Dangerfield, *Awakening of American Nationalism*, pp. 275–83.

23. Albany *Argus*, 2 March 1829.

24. Branch to Messrs. Alex. W. Mebane, Geo. B. Outlaw, &c., 20 August 1831, in *Niles' Register* 41 (17 September 1831):38; James A. Hamilton to Van Buren, 21 February 1829, Van Buren Papers; Branch to——— Bond, 26 July 1839, Branch Papers; Branch to James Iredell, 31 March 1832, Iredell Papers; Kendall to Blair, 29 October 1830, Blair-Lee Papers; Hoffmann, "Branch and the Whig Party," pp. 299–315.

25. Berrien to George Gilmer, 3 February 1855, Berrien Papers; Berrien to Duff Green, 4 August 1837, Green Papers, Southern Historical Collection; McCrary, "John Macpherson Berrien," pp. 90–91, 147–48.

26. *Niles' Register* 35 (31 January 1829):379, 43 (1 September 1832):9; James Hamilton, Jr., to Berrien, 29 July 1831, Berrien Papers; McCrary, "John Macpherson Berrien," pp. 137–43, 196–209.

27. Van Buren, *Autobiography*, 2:346; Donelson to———, 20 September 1829, Donelson to John McLemore, 20 April 1830, 9 January 1831, Donelson to Genl [Coffee], 20 May 1831, Donelson to John Branch, 21 May 1831, Donelson Papers. The marriage of Donelson's brother to one of Branch's daughters helped cement Donelson's attachment to the anti-Eaton forces. See Burke, *Emily Donelson*, 1:245–46.

28. Jackson to Donelson, 30 October 1830, Jackson, *Correspondence*, 4:194; Parton, *Life of Jackson*, 3:337; Donelson to John McLemore, 9 January 1831, Donelson to John Branch, 30 August 1832, Donelson Papers.

29. Remini, *Andrew Jackson*, pp. 79–86; Harlan, "Career of Lewis," p. 33.

30. Jackson to R. G. Dunlap, 29 August 1831, Jackson Papers; Wiltse, *John C. Calhoun*, 2:77–79; Parton, *Life of Jackson*, 3:321–26.

31. Jackson to Calhoun, 13 May 1830, Jackson, *Correspondence*, 4:136; "Correspondence Between Gen. Andrew Jackson and John C. Calhoun," *Niles' Register* 40 (5 March 1831):11.

32. Jackson to John Coffee, 10 April 1830, Jackson, *Correspondence*, 4:134; Van Buren, *Autobiography*, 2:372–73.

33. Jackson to John Overton, 31 December 1829, Jackson, *Correspondence*, 4:109.

34. Webster to Mr. Mann, 19 March 1830, Daniel Webster Papers, Massachusetts Historical Society.

35. Jackson to Van Buren, 1 November 1830, Van Buren Papers; Kendall to Blair, 7 March 1829, Blair-Lee Papers; James Hamilton, Jr., to Van Buren, 19 February 1829, Van Buren Papers; Richardson, *Messages and Papers*, 3:1012–13.

36. Richardson, *Messages and Papers*, 3:1014–15; Jackson to John Overton, 31 December 1829, Jackson, *Correspondence*, 4:109.

37. Richardson, *Messages and Papers*, 3:1077–80; Van Buren to Jackson, 18 November 1832, Van Buren Papers; Kendall to Blair, 25 April, 2 October 1830, Blair-Lee Papers; Van Buren, *Autobiography*, 2:171; Albany *Argus*, 23 December 1830.

38. Calhoun to Christopher Van Deventer, 25 May 1831, John C. Calhoun Papers, South Caroliniana Library, University of South Carolina.

39. Freehling, *Prelude to Civil War*, pp. 157–59; Calhoun to Samuel Ingham, 30 October 1830, 4 May 1831, Calhoun to Alexander Hamilton, March 1831, Calhoun Papers, South Caroliniana Library; Adams, *Memoirs*, 8:166.

40. Jackson to John Overton, 31 December 1829, Jackson, *Correspondence*, 4:109; *Niles' Register* 37 (6 February 1830):393; M. Rives to William C. Rives, 24 January 1830, Rives Papers; Freehling, *Prelude to Civil War*, pp. 192–93.

41. Calhoun to Ingham, 30 October 1830, Calhoun Papers, South Caroliniana Library.

42. Hill to Gideon Welles, 20 April 1830, Welles Papers; Jonathan Harvey to William Prescott, 27 April 1830, Jonathan Harvey Papers, New Hampshire Historical Society; Jackson to John Overton, 31 December 1829, Jackson, *Correspondence*, 4:108–9.

43. Parton, *Life of Jackson*, 3:284; Freehling, *Prelude to Civil War*, p. 192; Kendall to Blair, 25 April 1830, Blair-Lee Papers.

44. Kendall to Blair, 1 March, 2 October 1830, Blair-Lee Papers; Green to Calhoun, 19 November 1830, Green Papers, Southern Historical Collection.

45. Calhoun to Ingham, 30 October 1830, Calhoun to Christopher Van

Deventer, 12 May 1830, Calhoun to James H. Hammond, 15 January 1831, Calhoun Papers, South Caroliniana Library.

46. Jackson to John Overton, 31 December 1829, Jackson, *Correspondence*, 4:108–9.

47. Van Buren, *Autobiography*, 2:231–32, 343; Hamilton, *Reminiscences*, p. 94.

48. Sorensen, *Decision-Making in the White House*, p. 74; Van Buren, *Autobiography*, 2:231, 266–67; Van Buren to C. C. Cambreleng, 23 April 1829, Van Buren Papers.

49. Jackson to John Overton, 31 December 1829, Jackson, *Correspondence*, 4:108; Smith, *First Forty Years*, p. 310.

50. Green to Edward Bellview, 8 October 1830, Green Papers, Southern Historical Collection.

51. Van Buren, *Autobiography*, 2:171–72; Jackson to John Coffee, 10 April 1830, Jackson, *Correspondence*, 4:134; Jackson to John Overton, 31 December 1829, *Correspondence*, 4:108; Kendall to Blair, 25 April 1830, Kendall to Jackson, 3 December 1831, Blair-Lee Papers.

52. Kendall to Blair, 22 November 1829, 28 January 1830, Blair-Lee Papers. See drafts of Jackson's first and second annual messages for evidence of Kendall's contribution, in Presidential Messages, Jackson Papers.

53. Kendall to Blair, 9 January 1829, Blair-Lee Papers; Silas Wright to Van Buren, 9 December 1828, Van Buren Papers; Green to Worden Pope, 15 August 1829, Green Papers, Library of Congress; *U.S. Telegraph*, 14 April 1831.

54. Green to [Calhoun], 16 June 1829, Green Papers, Library of Congress; Kendall to Blair, 14 March, 12 April, 21 June 1829, Blair-Lee Papers; Green to John Pope, 11 April 1829, Green to William T. Barry, 11 July 1829, Green Papers, Library of Congress; Green to Dr. Lane, 21 October 1830, Green Papers, Southern Historical Collection; *U.S. Telegraph*, 14 January 1830.

55. Hill to [Welles], 20 April, 7 May 1830, Welles Papers; Kendall to Blair, 25 April, 30 April, 2 October 1830, Blair-Lee Papers; *U.S. Telegraph*, 8 June 1830.

56. Green to James Hamilton, Jr., 29 September, 15 August 1830, Green to Calhoun, 1 August 1830, Green Papers, Southern Historical Collection; *U.S. Telegraph*, 20 April 1830; Kendall to Blair, 25 April, 2 October 1830, Blair-Lee Papers.

57. Calhoun to Alexander Hamilton, March 1830, Calhoun Papers, Library of Congress; James A. Hamilton to Jackson, 29 July 1830, Jackson Papers; Jackson to Lewis, 26 June 1830, Jackson, *Correspondence*, 4:156.

58. Kendall to Blair, 28 January, 3 February, 11 February 1830, Blair-Lee Papers; Green to Calhoun, 1 August 1830, Green to Edward Bellview, 8 October 1830, Green Papers, Southern Historical Collection; Parton, *Life of Jackson*, 3:335; Kendall to Blair, 22 August 1830, Blair-Lee Papers.

59. Kendall to Blair, 9 January 1829, 4 September 1830, Blair-Lee Papers.

60. Kendall to Jackson, 3 December 1831, Kendall to Blair, 9 January, 19 July, 22 August, 2 October 1830, Blair-Lee Papers.

61. Kendall to Blair, 2 October 1830, Blair-Lee Papers.

62. Blair to Green, 13 October 1830, Blair-Lee Papers; Kendall to Green, 7 November 1830, Washington *Globe*, 30 March 1831; Kendall to Blair, 2 October, 4 October 1830, Blair-Lee Papers; Kendall to Virgil Maxcy, 12 November 1830, Amos Kendall Miscellaneous Papers, New York Public Library; Green to James Hamilton, Jr., 29 September 1830, Green to Calhoun, 19 November 1830, Green Papers, Southern Historical Collection; Kendall to Isaac Hill, 26 November 1830, Kendall Miscellaneous Papers, New-York Historical Society.

63. Van Buren, *Autobiography*, 2:377; William S. Archer to Van Buren, 12 March 1831, Van Buren Papers; Blair to Mrs. Gratz, 23 February 1831, Clay, ed., "Two Years with Old Hickory," p. 191; Van Buren to Blair, 21 May 1856, Blair Family Papers; Blair to Van Buren, 17 May 1856, Van Buren Papers.

64. Parton, *Life of Jackson*, 3:337.

65. *Argus of Western America*, 23 December, 24 December, 30 December 1829, 21 March, 28 July 1830; Blair to Green, 13 October 1830, Blair-Lee Papers; Smith, *Blair Family in Politics*, 1:21–47.

66. *U.S. Telegraph*, 25 September 1830.

67. Washington *Globe*, 20 July 1833; Andrew Jackson Donelson to Blair, 1 January 1832, Edwin Crosswell to Blair, 10 September 1835, William B. Lewis to Blair, 17 May 1831, Blair-Lee Papers; Kendall to Isaac Hill, 15 July 1831, Hill Papers; William Potter to Blair, 18 June 1831, Blair-Lee Papers.

68. Duff Green to Richard K. Crallé, 16 December 1832, Green Papers, Library of Congress; John Reynolds to Blair, 20 August 1835, Amos Lane to Blair, 2 September 1831, Blair-Lee Papers; Jackson to Kendall, 23 July 1832, Jackson Papers; Blair to Jackson, 24 March 1845, Blair Family Papers; Young, *Washington Community*, pp. 208–9.

69. Blair to Jno. Maquire, 11 August 1869, Blair Family Papers; Parton, *Life of Jackson*, 3:337–38; Billy Gratz to Blair, 31 May 1831, Van Buren to Blair, 21 May 1856, Blair Family Papers; Blair to Mrs. Gratz, 5 February 1831, Clay, ed., "Two Years with Old Hickory," pp. 190–91; Bassett, *Life of Jackson*, p. 705; Smith, *Blair Family in Politics*, 1:68–70.

70. Green to Ninean Edwards, 18 August 1829, Green to Worden Pope, 15 August 1829, Green to James Hamilton, Jr., 29 September 1830, Green Papers, Library of Congress; Calhoun to Samuel Ingham, 4 May 1831, Calhoun Papers, South Caroliniana Library; Green to Calhoun, 7 September 1829, Green Papers, Library of Congress; Parton, *Life of Jackson*, 3:297; Hamilton, *Reminiscences*, p. 243; William B. Lewis to Azariah Flagg, 14 February 1832, Flagg Papers; J. S. Barbour to James Barbour, 1 March 1830, James Barbour Papers.

71. Barry to daughter, 25 February 1830, "Letters of William T. Barry," 14:20; Kendall to Blair, 18 March 1830, Blair-Lee Papers.

72. J. S. Barbour to James Barbour, 1 March 1830, James Barbour Papers; Kendall to Blair, 25 April 1830, Blair-Lee Papers; Daniel Webster to Jeremiah Mason, 27 February 1830, Daniel Webster Papers, Massachusetts Historical Society; Parton, *Life of Jackson*, 3:296, 299.

73. Wiltse, *John C. Calhoun*, 2:84; *U.S. Telegraph*, 16 March 1830; Green to Ritchie, 30 March 1830, Green Papers, Library of Congress; Kendall to Blair, 18 March 1830, Blair-Lee Papers.

74. Lewis to Col. L. C. Stanbaugh, 11 March 1830, Parton, *Life of Jackson*, 3:300; *Niles' Register* 38 (24 April 1830):169–70.

75. Kendall to Blair, 18 March 1830, Blair-Lee Papers; C. C. Cambreleng to Azariah Flagg, 5 April 1830, Flagg Papers; Gammon, *Campaign of 1832*, pp. 87–88; Jackson to John Coffee, 10 April 1830, Jackson, *Correspondence*, 4:134.

76. Adams, *Memoirs*, 8:209; Van Buren to William C. Rives, 6 April 1830, Rives Papers; Morton to Calhoun, 18 April 1830, Marcus Morton Papers, Massachusetts Historical Society.

77. Kendall to Gideon Welles, 21 February 1831, Welles Papers; Washington *Globe*, 19 January, 9 March 1831.

78. Charles McDonald to Calhoun, 30 May 1831, Calhoun Papers, South Caroliniana Library; George M. Dallas to Samuel Ingham, 29 May 1831, Dallas Papers; Morton to Calhoun, 7 March 1831, Morton Papers.

79. Washington *Globe*, 13 July, 9 September 1831; Samuel McKean to Ingham, 30 May 1831, Simon Gratz Collection, Case 1, Box 39, Historical Society of Pennsylvania.

80. Calhoun to Samuel Ingham, 4 May 1831, Calhoun Papers, South Caroliniana Library; William S. Archer to Van Buren, 12 March 1831, Van Buren Papers.

81. Richmond *Enquirer*, 1 November 1831; Green to George McDuffie, 14 July 1830, Green to B. W. Leigh, 9 October 1832, Green Papers, Southern Historical Collection.

82. Jackson to John Overton, 31 December 1829, Jackson, *Correspondence*, 4:108–9; Branch to Edmund Freeman, 22 August 1831, Washington *Globe*, 31 August 1831.

83. Van Buren, *Autobiography*, 2:577, 704–5; *Niles' Register* 30 (7 May 1831):169; Jackson to Hugh Lawson White, 29 April 1831, Jackson Papers.

84. Isaac Hill to Kendall, 26 April 1831, New Hampshire Whig Papers; Andrew C. McLaughlin, *Lewis Cass*; Swisher, *Roger B. Taney*; Samuel Tyler, *Memoir of Roger Brooke Taney*; Levi Woodbury, "Levi Woodbury's 'Intimate Memoranda' of the Jackson Administration," ed. Ari Hoogenboom and Herbert Ershkowitz, *Pennsylvania Magazine of History and Biography* 92 (1968):507–8.

85. Calhoun to James H. Hammond, 16 May 1831, Calhoun Papers, South Caroliniana Library; White, *Memoirs*, pp. 266–67.

86. *U.S. Telegraph*, 13 August, 8 October, 13 October 1831; Green to John

Floyd, 4 April 1831, Green Papers, Southern Historical Collection; Kendall to Blair, 22 November 1829, Blair-Lee Papers; Lewis to Jackson, 1 July 1831, Jackson, *Correspondence*, 4:309; Kendall to Gideon Welles, 1 April 1831, Welles Papers; Blair to Mrs. Gratz, 2 March 1831, Clay, ed., "Two Years with Old Hickory," p. 102; Kendall to Joseph Desha, 30 June 1831, "Correspondence between Governor Joseph Desha and Amos Kendall," pp. 20–21.

87. Gammon, *Campaign of 1832*, p. 90; Marquis James, *The Life of Andrew Jackson*, p. 279; Bassett, *Life of Jackson*, pp. 540, 705.

88. Blair to Jno. Maquire, 11 August 1869, Blair Family Papers.

89. Van Buren, *Autobiography*, 2:446; Hamilton, *Reminiscences*, p. 219; James A. Hamilton to Jackson, 15 August 1831, Jackson Papers.

Chapter 4. Elaborating a Program

1. Meyers, *Jacksonian Persuasion*, pp. 8–10.

2. Benton, *Thirty Years' View*, 1:738; Foote, *Casket of Reminiscences*, p. 102; Thomas Ritchie to Isabella Harrison, 20 August 1830, Thomas Ritchie Papers, Library of Congress. For a different interpretation, see Curtis, *Andrew Jackson*, pp. 82–83, 111–12.

3. Kendall, *Autobiography*, p. 453.

4. Adams, *Memoirs*, 8:180; *U.S. Telegraph*, 6 November 1829.

5. Bemis, *Adams and the Union*, p. 85; Richardson, *Messages and Papers*, 2:938; Lynn Hudson Parsons, "'A Perpetual Harrow Upon My Feelings': John Quincy Adams and the American Indian," *New England Quarterly* 46 (1973):353–55.

6. Wilson Lumpkin, *The Removal of the Cherokee Indians from Georgia*, 1:42; Ronald N. Satz, *American Indian Policy in the Jacksonian Era*, pp. 1–6; Mary Elizabeth Young, *Redskins, Ruffleshirts, and Rednecks*, pp. 13–18.

7. *Niles' Register* 36 (30 May 1829):231, 36 (13 June 1829):258–59.

8. Richardson, *Messages and Papers*, 3:1019–22. For Kendall's and Donelson's assistance, see Presidential Messages, First Annual Message, Jackson Papers.

9. Richardson, *Messages and Papers*, 3:982; *Niles' Register* 35 (13 December 1828):250, 37 (19 December 1829):257; Bernard W. Sheehan, *Seeds of Extinction*, pp. 243–50; Satz, *American Indian Policy*, p. 406. See also *Niles' Register* 36 (13 June 1829):250, 36 (8 August 1829):388.

10. F. P. Prucha, "Andrew Jackson's Indian Policy: A Reassessment," *Journal of American History* 56 (1969):527–39; Satz, *American Indian Policy*, pp. 9–10. See also Rogin, *Fathers and Children*, especially pp. 206–48.

11. Curtis, *Andrew Jackson*, p. 70; Jackson to James Monroe, 4 March 1817, Jackson, *Correspondence*, 2:279–81; Jackson to Secretary of War,

[1831?], *Correspondence*, 4:220; Jackson to Calhoun, 2 September 1820, 18 January 1821, *Correspondence*, 3:32, 38.

12. Jackson to Monroe, 4 March 1817, Jackson, *Correspondence*, 2:280–81; Jackson to Calhoun, August 1823, *Correspondence*, 3:202; Jackson to Coffee, 25 September 1826, *Correspondence*, 3:314–15. Jackson's belief that civilized society was progressive and superior to primitive society in social, technical, and moral matters was generally shared by his contemporaries. The idea derived in large part from the popularization of the writings of the Scottish common sense school. See Roy Harvey Pearce, *The Savages of America*, pp. 82–91. See also, Richardson, *Messages and Papers*, 3:1084.

13. Jackson to Col. James Gadsden, 12 October 1829, Jackson to Major David Haley, 13 October 1829, Jackson Papers; Richardson, *Messages and Papers*, 3:1020; Jackson to Col. Robert Butler, 21 June 1817, Jackson, *Correspondence*, 2:299; Jackson to William B. Lewis, 31 August 1830, *Correspondence*, 4:178–79; Jackson to Calhoun, 19 June 1820, *Correspondence*, 3:27; Young, *Redskins, Ruffleshirts, and Rednecks*, pp. 9–11; William G. McLaughlin and Walter H. Conser, Jr., "The Cherokees in Transition: A Statistical Analysis of the Federal Cherokee Census of 1835," *Journal of American History* 64(1977):678–80.

14. Jackson to Secretary of War, [1831?], Jackson, *Correspondence*, 4:220; Jackson to John Coffee, 7 April 1832, *Correspondence*, 4:430.

15. Jackson to John Pitchlynn, 5 August 1830, Jackson, *Correspondence*, 4:169; "Indian case," scrap in Jackson's handwriting at end of 1829 letters, Jackson Papers; Jackson to Edward G. W. Butler, 25 July 1825, Jackson, *Correspondence*, 3:289; Richardson, *Messages and Papers*, 3:1099–1104; John Eaton to John Donelly, 4 August 1830, Jackson Papers; Curtis, *Andrew Jackson*, p. 72.

16. Van Buren, *Autobiography*, 2:295; Jackson to John Pitchlynn, 5 August 1830, Jackson, *Correspondence*, 4:169; Jackson to Blair, 4 June 1838, *Correspondence*, 5:553.

17. *Niles' Register* 39 (18 September 1830):68, 37 (12 September 1829):41; Eaton to Jackson, 8 February 1827, Jackson Papers; Hamilton, *Reminiscences*, p. 134; Presidential Messages, Special Message to the Senate, 22 February 1831, Jackson Papers.

18. Hamilton, *Reminiscences*, p. 134; Kendall, *Autobiography*, p. 686; *Argus of Western America*, 5 March 1823.

19. Hamilton, *Reminiscences*, p. 134; Van Buren, *Autobiography*, 2:289, 293–95; Van Buren to James R. Beys, 24 October 1848, Van Buren to John Forsyth, 18 December 1832, Van Buren Papers; *U.S. Telegraph*, 4 January 1833; *Niles' Register* 44 (27 July 1833):259–60; Edwin A. Miles, "After John Marshall's Decision: *Worcester v. Georgia* and the Nullification Crisis," *Journal of Southern History* 39 (1973):519–44. Although historians generally believe that the issue of Indian affairs provided an inducement for Berrien's appointment to the cabinet, Jackson's willingness to send the Georgian

abroad in April 1829 argues against exaggerating the importance of this consideration. See Jackson to Berrien, 6 April 1829, Berrien Papers.

20. *U.S. Telegraph*, 8 August, 8 September 1829; Richmond *Enquirer*, 8 September 1829; Albany *Argus*, 12 December 1829.

21. Joseph Howard Parks, *John Bell of Tennessee*, p. 37; L. Paul Gresham, "The Public Career of Hugh Lawson White," *Tennessee Historical Quarterly* 3 (1944):303.

22. *Register of Debates*, 21 Cong., 1 Sess., pp. 319–20, 380–82, 997, 1026, 1111.

23. *Register of Debates*, 21 Cong., 1 Sess., pp. 328, 336, 1021.

24. On Jackson's concern about the organization of the House committee, see scrap of paper in his handwriting at end of the 1829 papers, Jackson Papers; *Register of Debates*, 21 Cong., 1 Sess., p. 1124; Michael Hoffman to Van Buren, 9 December 1832, Van Buren Papers.

25. Daniel Webster to Joseph Story, 10 April [1830], Webster Papers; *Register of Debates*, 21 Cong., 1 Sess., p. 1141; *U.S. Telegraph*, 28 May 1830.

26. Webster to James Barbour, 24 May 1830, James Barbour Papers; *Niles' Register* 38 (5 June 1830):269; "Washington Correspondence," Richmond *Enquirer*, 1 June 1830.

27. *Niles' Register* 38 (5 June 1830):269; *U.S. Telegraph*, 5 May 1830; Curtis, *Andrew Jackson*, p. 107. For purposes of tabulation, I have listed Virginia, North Carolina, South Carolina, and Georgia as the Southeast; Louisiana, Mississippi, and Alabama as the Southwest; Kentucky, Tennessee, and Missouri as the border-West; Ohio, Indiana, and Illinois as the Old Northwest; Maine, Massachusetts, Rhode Island, Connecticut, New Hampshire, and Vermont as New England; and New York, New Jersey, Pennsylvania, Delaware, and Maryland as the Middle Atlantic region. My conclusions agree with those arrived at independently by Parsons, "John Quincy Adams and the American Indian," pp. 361–62; and John Andrew, "The Nature of Jacksonian Politics: A Reconsideration," pp. 15–18. Professor Andrew kindly permitted me to read his unpublished manuscript.

28. *Niles' Register* 38 (5 June 1830):269; Webster to Clay, 29 May 1830, Henry Clay, *The Private Correspondence of Henry Clay*, pp. 274–75; Andrew, "Nature of Jacksonian Politics," p. 10. Everett W. Kindig notes considerable opposition to Jackson's removal plan in the older states of the Ohio Valley, particularly Kentucky and Ohio. In the newer states, such as Illinois, Indiana, and Missouri, removal was more popular, though opposition was still evident. He concludes that removal "was not a measure of great popularity in the Valley, as so often depicted in the histories of the period." See Kindig, "Western Opposition to Jackson's 'Democracy,'" pp. 234–61 (quotation on p. 261).

29. Jackson to Andrew Jackson Donelson, 24 March 1831, Donelson Papers; C. B. Gardiner, "Notes Sent to Jackson by C. B. Gardiner," 22 March 1831, Jackson, *Correspondence*, 4:249; Van Buren, *Autobiography*, 2:293.

30. Adams, *Memoirs*, 8:229; *Niles' Register* 41 (24 December 1831):311.

31. Richardson, *Messages and Papers*, 3:1390–91.

32. *Argus of Western America*, 24 February 1830; Washington *Globe*, 26 February 1831. See also *Argus of Western America*, 31 March, 28 July 1830.

33. Washington *Globe*, 5 January, 2 February, 26 February 1831.

34. Washington *Globe*, 22 January 1831.

35. Washington *Globe*, 2 January, 5 February, 16 February 1831, 24 October, 3 November, 15 November 1832.

36. Ronald N. Satz, "Indian Policy in the Jacksonian Era: The Old Northwest as a Test Case," *Michigan History* 60 (1976):75–82; Richardson, *Messages and Papers*, 4:1513. The process of Indian removal is ably traced in Satz, *American Indian Policy*; Young, *Redskins, Ruffleshirts, and Rednecks*; and Grant Foreman, *Indian Removal: The Emigration of the Five Civilized Tribes of Indians*.

37. *Niles' Register* 42 (31 March 1832):78; Richmond *Enquirer*, 26 February 1830, 8 March 1832.

38. Washington *Globe*, 26 February 1831, 19 May 1836; "Speech of Benjamin F. Butler," Albany *Argus*, 29 October 1832; Parsons, "John Quincy Adams and the American Indian," pp. 361–62. My analysis of the Senate vote on removal confirms Parsons. See also Andrew, "Nature of Jacksonian Politics," pp. 13–18.

39. Kendall to Blair, 7 March 1829, Blair-Lee Papers; James Hamilton, Jr., to Van Buren, 19 February 1829, Van Buren Papers; "Address from the Central Hickory Club (of Washington) to the Republican Citizens of the United States," Washington *Globe*, 13 October 1832.

40. For a different view, see Rogin, *Fathers and Children*, pp. 4, 166–67, 182–83.

41. Kendall to Blair, 7 March 1829, Blair-Lee Papers; Richardson, *Messages and Papers*, 3:1015.

42. Jackson to Monroe, 26 July 1822, Jackson, *Correspondence*, 3:171; Jackson, "Notes for the Maysville Road Veto," [19–26? May 1830], *Correspondence*, 4:138; Richardson, *Messages and Papers*, 3:1000, 1014, 1052; Jackson to L. H. Coleman, 26 April 1824, *Correspondence*, 3:249.

43. Jackson to John Overton, 31 December 1829, Jackson, *Correspondence*, 4:109; Richardson, *Messages and Papers*, 3:1076.

44. George R. Taylor, *The Transportation Revolution: 1815–1860*, pp. 21–22; Albany *Argus*, 22 May 1830; Richardson, *Messages and Papers*, 3:1015.

45. Van Buren, *Autobiography*, 2:312; Remini, *Van Buren and the Democratic Party*, pp. 30–31, 102–3; Brown, "Missouri Crisis," pp. 63–64, 70.

46. Van Buren, *Autobiography*, 2:312; "Notes Sent to Jackson by C. B. Gardiner," 22 March 1831, Jackson, *Correspondence*, 4:249.

47. Van Buren, *Autobiography*, 2:324; James, *Life of Jackson*, p. 526; Washington *Globe*, 7 June 1833; Harlan, "Career of Lewis," p. 31.

48. Georgetown *Patriot*, 2 April, 16 November 1816; *Argus of Western*

America, 24 January, 31 January, 26 December (quotation) 1827, 11 February 1829; Kendall to Blair, 7 March, 2 October 1830, Blair-Lee Papers.

49. Hoffmann, *Jackson and North Carolina Politics*, p. 54; McCrary, "John Macpherson Berrien," pp. 141–42.

50. Jackson to Van Buren, 15 May 1830, Van Buren, *Autobiography*, 2:322.

51. *Register of Debates*, 21 Cong., 1 Sess., p. 820; Glyndon G. Van Deusen, *The Jacksonian Era: 1828–1848*, p. 52. According to Everett W. Kindig, the Maysville Road was also potentially part of a suggested southwestern national road, beginning at Zanesville, Ohio, on the Cumberland Road, passing through Maysville and Lexington, Kentucky, and terminating in New Orleans. See Kindig, "Western Opposition to Jackson's 'Democracy,'" p. 362.

52. *Register of Debates*, 21 Cong., 1 Sess., pp. 827, 838, 840; William Nisbet Chambers, *Old Bullion Benton*, p. 166; William B. Hatcher, *Edward Livingston*, pp. 340–41.

53. *Register of Debates*, 21 Cong., 1 Sess., pp. 832, 840–41; Sellers, *Polk: Jacksonian*, pp. 96–98, 119–20, 150–55.

54. Van Buren, *Autobiography*, 2:320–21.

55. Polk had a minor role in drafting the constitutional arguments in the Maysville Road veto. See Presidential Messages, Maysville Road Veto, Jackson Papers; Van Buren, *Autobiography*, 2:323; Daniel Webster to James Barbour, 24 May 1830, James Barbour Papers.

56. "Notes—The Maysville road bill," at end of 1830 papers, Jackson Papers; Ritchie to [Van Buren], n.d., located in 1830 section, Van Buren Papers; Richardson, *Messages and Papers*, 3:1049–50. Madison believed the veto had inaccurately summarized his views on the constitutionality of internal improvements expenditures. See Van Buren, *Autobiography*, 2:330–35 for his objections.

57. Richardson, *Messages and Papers*, 3:1052–53.

58. Ritchie to Archibald Ritchie, 8 June 1830, "Unpublished Letters of Thomas Ritchie," *The John P. Branch Historical Papers of Randolph-Macon College* 3 (1911):208–9; *Register of Debates*, 21 Cong., 1 Sess., p. 1144; "Mr. Eaton's Reply," Washington *Globe*, 15 September 1831; Washington *Globe*, 23 February 1831.

59. Van Buren, *Autobiography*, 2:327.

60. *Register of Debates*, 21 Cong., 1 Sess., pp. 1140, 382; *Niles' Register* 38 (8 May 1830):207–8. The two other congressmen were James Shields of Ohio and George Leiper of Pennsylvania.

61. Jackson to Van Buren, 4 May 1830, Van Buren, *Autobiography*, 2:321; *U.S. Telegraph*, 2 June 1830; Andrew Jackson to a committee of friends in Frederick, Maryland, *Niles' Register* 38 (3 July 1830):338.

62. Turner, *United States: 1830–1850*, pp. 390–91; Kindig, "Western Opposition to Jackson's 'Democracy,'" pp. 83–86, 389, 398.

63. Kindig, "Western Opposition to Jackson's 'Democracy,'" pp. 396–97;

Buley, *The Old Northwest*, 2:169–70; Homer J. Webster, *A History of the Democratic Party Organization in the Northwest: 1824–1840*, p. 38; Gammon, *Election of 1832*, p. 138; "Notes Sent to Jackson by C. B. Gardiner," 22 March 1831, Jackson, *Correspondence*, 4:249; *U.S. Telegraph*, 12 February 1831; *Register of Debates*, 21 Cong., 1 Sess., p. 1140.

64. Hill to Azariah Flagg, 19 July 1830, Flagg Papers; Van Buren to Jackson, 25 July 1830, Jackson, *Correspondence*, 4:166. See also Louis McLane to Van Buren, 20 July 1830, Van Buren Papers.

65. Kindig, "Western Opposition to Jackson's 'Democracy,'" pp. 399–400.

66. Kendall to Blair, 28 September 1830, Jesse Bledsoe to Barry, 25 November 1830, Charles S. Bibb to Blair, 28 December 1830, Blair-Lee Papers; Felix Grundy to Jackson, 31 July 1830, Jackson Papers.

67. Jackson to William B. Lewis, 28 June 1830, Jackson, *Correspondence*, 4:157; Washington *Globe*, 14 December 1830, 8 June 1831; *U.S. Telegraph*, 12 February 1831.

68. See especially Jackson's sixth annual message of December 1834, Richardson, *Messages and Papers*, 3:1337–42. For Jackson's shift on distribution, see Richardson, *Messages and Papers*, 3:1464–65; Jackson to Van Buren, 24 July, 30 July 1833, Van Buren Papers; Duff Green to Richard K. Crallé, 5 December 1831, Green Papers, Library of Congress; Washington *Globe*, 7 May 1831, 27 July, 7 December 1832.

69. Thomas Ritchie to Van Buren, 10 July 1832, Van Buren Papers; Van Buren, *Autobiography*, 2:171–72; Leland Winfield Meyer, *The Life and Times of Colonel Richard M. Johnson of Kentucky*, pp. 274–76. According to Everett W. Kindig, Jackson's river and harbor improvements vetoes were more politically damaging than his road vetoes. "Ideology," Kindig concludes, "had triumphed over the exigencies of politics." Kindig, "Western Opposition to Jackson's 'Democracy,'" pp. 408, 414 (quotation). For another view, see Carlton Jackson, "The Internal Improvement Vetoes of Andrew Jackson," *Tennessee Historical Quarterly* 25 (1966):261–79.

70. "Address from the Central Hickory Club (of Washington) to the Republican Citizens of the United States," Washington *Globe*, 13 October 1832. There is no question that Kendall penned the address: cf. Kendall, *Autobiography*, pp. 429–32. Washington *Globe*, 14 July 1831. See also Washington *Globe*, 19 July 1831.

71. Taylor, *Transportation Revolution*, pp. 372–78; Robert A. Lively, "The American System: A Review Article," *Business History Review* 29 (1955):85–88.

72. Jackson to Van Buren, 5 September, 17 December 1831, Van Buren to Jackson, 13 January 1832, Van Buren Papers. Van Buren called the Bank "the vital question of his [Jackson's] administration." See Van Buren, *Autobiography*, 2:705.

73. Hammond, *Banks and Politics*, pp. 605–30. In the 1790s Jackson suffered a painful economic loss in a land speculation, the Allison affair. It was years before he extricated himself from its embarrassments, and he

avoided further speculative ventures. Sellers, "Banking and Politics in Jackson's Tennessee," p. 76. For conjectures about the psychological consequences of the Allison affair, see Curtis, *Andrew Jackson*, pp. 33–35; and Rogin, *Fathers and Children*, pp. 95–101.

74. Jackson to John Donelson, 3 September 1821, Jackson, *Correspondence*, 3:117; Jackson to Andrew Jackson Donelson, 8 February 1823, *Correspondence*, 3:186–87; Sellers, "Banking and Politics in Jackson's Tennessee," pp. 61–84; Jackson to Thomas Hart Benton, [June 1832?], *Correspondence*, 4:446.

75. Hamilton, *Reminiscences*, p. 236; Washington *Globe*, 29 July 1834; Lewis to Jackson, 2 November 1839, Jackson-Lewis Papers; Sellers, *Polk: Jacksonian*, p. 179; Ralph C. H. Catterall, *The Second Bank of the United States*, p. 184n.

76. Ingham to Jackson, 26 November 1829, Jackson Papers; Nicholas Biddle to S. Frothingham, 30 June 1830, J. Kelsey Burr Collection, Box 3, Library of Congress; Berrien to Jackson, 27 November 1829, Jackson Papers; McCrary, "John Macpherson Berrien," p. 170; James A. Hamilton to Jackson, 8 December 1833, Jackson Papers; Washington *Globe*, 12 March 1831, 8 September 1832.

77. Jean Alexander Wilburn, *Biddle's Bank*, pp. 44–45, 64–65; John M. McFaul, *The Politics of Jacksonian Finance*, pp. 26–28; Frank Otto Gatell, "Sober Second Thoughts on Van Buren, the Albany Regency, and the Wall Street Conspiracy," *Journal of American History* 53 (1966):19–41; Van Buren, *Autobiography*, 2:221; Remini, *Van Buren and the Democratic Party*, pp. 97–98.

78. Charles H. Ambler, *Thomas Ritchie*, p. 177; Stevenson to Blair, n.d., Blair-Lee Papers; Martin Van Buren, *Inquiry into the Origin and Course of Political Parties in the United States*, p. 322; McFaul, *Jacksonian Finance*, pp. 20–22, 27; Sydnor, *Development of Southern Sectionalism*, pp. 136–38. Cf. Wilburn, *Biddle's Bank*, pp. 61–62.

79. R. L. Colt to Biddle, 14 December 1829, 14 May 1830, Samuel S. Smith to Biddle, 26 December 1829, 14 May 1830, Biddle Papers. Duff Green was also unsure about Van Buren's position on the Bank, claiming that the "shuffling and cutting" by the New York Van Buren papers made it difficult for him to establish a firm Bank policy in the *U.S. Telegraph*. See Green to John S. Lytle, 16 July 1831, Green Papers, Southern Historical Collection. On the other hand, Van Buren's anti-Bank ideas were suspected in R. L. Colt to Biddle, 16 January 1830, Biddle to Albert Gallatin, 30 November 1830, and Biddle to J. Hunter, 4 May 1831, Biddle Papers.

80. Washington *Globe*, 12 March 1831; Hamilton, *Reminiscences*, pp. 149–50. See also paper in Kendall's handwriting listed under "Dec 1830" discussing Bank interference in Kentucky elections, with an endorsement by Jackson, Jackson Papers.

81. Kendall to Blair, 22 November 1829, 22 August 1830, Blair-Lee Papers.

82. Hamilton, *Reminiscences*, p. 150; Presidential Messages, First Annual

Message, Jackson Papers; Catterall, *Second Bank*, p. 180; Jackson to William B. Lewis, 27 June 1830, Jackson-Lewis Papers; Kendall to Blair, 1 March, 22 August 1830, Blair-Lee Papers.

83. Washington *Globe*, 19 January 1831; Isaac Hill to Gideon Welles, 14 December 1831, Welles Papers; Kendall to Hill, 15 July 1831, Hill Papers; Kendall to Blair, 1 March 1830, Lewis to Blair, 17 May, 10 May 1831, Blair-Lee Papers; Blair to Mrs. Gratz, 2 March, 10 May 1831, Clay, ed., "Two Years with Old Hickory," pp. 192–93; Blair to Jno. Maquire, 11 August 1869, Blair Family Papers.

84. Felix Grundy to Jackson, 22 May 1829, Jackson Papers; Richardson, *Messages and Papers*, 3:1025; Kendall to Blair, 9 January 1829, Blair-Lee Papers; Jackson to Moses Dawson, 17 July 1830, Jackson, *Correspondence*, 4:161–62; Catterall, *Second Bank*, pp. 187–92; Hugh Russell Fraser, *Democracy in the Making*, p. 31.

85. Scrap in Blair's handwriting, at end of 1830 letters, Jackson Papers. The resemblance between this note and the final wording of Jackson's second annual message makes it apparent that the note was prepared for that message.

86. Richardson, *Messages and Papers*, 3:1091–92; Jackson to Van Buren, 1 November 1830, Van Buren Papers; Van Buren, *Origin and Course of Political Parties*, pp. 314–15; Hamilton, *Reminiscences*, p. 191; Biddle to Joseph Hemphill, 14 December 1830, Biddle Papers; Gatell, "Sober Second Thoughts," p. 39.

87. Biddle to George Hoffman, 15 December 1829, John Norvall to Biddle, 7 December 1830, Biddle Papers.

88. McLane to Van Buren, 20 July 1830, Van Buren Papers; Biddle to J. Hunter, 4 May 1831, Biddle Papers; John A. Munroe, *Louis McLane*, pp. 151–52.

89. Biddle to J. Hunter, 4 May 1831, Biddle Papers; Van Buren to Jackson, 19 August 1833, Jackson Papers; Charles Jared Ingersoll to Biddle, 21 February 1832, Biddle, *Correspondence*, p. 183; Hatcher, *Livingston*, pp. 364–65.

90. Thomas Cadwalader to Biddle, 26 December 1831, Biddle, *Correspondence*, pp. 160–61; Randolph Bunner to Gulian Verplanck, 31 May 1832, Verplanck Papers; Woodbury to William Plummer, Jr., 6 January 1832, William Plummer, Jr., Miscellaneous Papers, New-York Historical Society; Plummer to Woodbury, 20 January, 1 March 1832, Woodbury Papers; Donelson to John McLemore, 9 January 1831, Donelson Papers; James, *Life of Jackson*, p. 285; Vincent J. Capowski, "The Making of a Jacksonian Democrat: Levi Woodbury, 1789–1831" (Ph.D. diss., Fordham University, 1966), p. 202.

91. Thomas Cadwalader to Biddle, 21 December 1831, Biddle, *Correspondence*, p. 150; Robert Gibbes to Biddle, 11 December 1831, Biddle, *Correspondence*, p. 139; C. C. Cambreleng to Van Buren, 4 January 1832, Van Buren Papers; Jackson to Van Buren, 5 September 1831, Jackson, *Correspondence*, 4:347; Taney, "'Bank War Manuscript,'" p. 127.

92. Swisher, *Roger B. Taney*, pp. 91–92, 201; Cambreleng to Van Buren, 4 January 1832, Van Buren Papers. For Taney's limited influence during

Jackson's first term, see Taney, "'Bank War Manuscript,'" pp. 109, 117, 216, 224.

93. Jackson to Van Buren, 5 September 1831, 17 December 1831, Jackson, *Correspondence*, 4:347, 385.

94. "Memorandum by Biddle," 19 October 1831, Biddle, *Correspondence*, pp. 128–31.

95. Kendall's unused draft of the Bank section is in Presidential Messages, Third Annual Message, Jackson Papers; McLane to Van Buren, 14 December 1831, Van Buren Papers; Taney, "'Bank War Manuscript,'" pp. 116–28, 215; Swisher, *Roger B. Taney*, pp. 160–61.

96. "Memorandum by Biddle," 19 October 1831, Biddle, *Correspondence*, pp. 128–31; Richardson, *Messages and Papers*, 3:1121; Taney, "'Bank War Manuscript,'" pp. 122–28, 215.

97. Jackson to John Randolph, 22 December 1831, Jackson Papers; Lewis to James A. Hamilton, 1 January 1832, Hamilton, *Reminiscences*, p. 236.

98. McLane to Gulian Verplanck, 24 January 1832, Verplanck Papers; John Randolph to Jackson, 19 December 1831, Jackson Papers; Van Buren to William C. Rives, 25 January 1832, Rives Papers; Van Buren to C. C. Cambreleng, 19 January 1832, Van Buren Papers; Washington *Globe*, 9 December 1831.

99. McLane to Blair, 19 December 1831, Blair-Lee Papers; McLane to Van Buren, 14 December 1831, Hoyt to Van Buren, 7 February 1832, Cambreleng to Van Buren, 4 February 1832, Webb to Van Buren, 5 February 1832, Van Buren Papers.

100. Montgomery Blair, "Sketch of F. P. Blair, Sr.," [13 May 1858?], Blair-Lee Papers. I suggest Noah as a possible replacement for Blair because in early 1833, Blair was apparently pressed by some Van Buren men to form a partnership with Noah. See Benjamin Gratz to Blair, 24 January, 21 February 1833, Blair-Lee Papers. Another possibility is James Gordon Bennett. See Bennett to Van Buren, 1 December 1832, Van Buren Papers.

101. Blair to Edward Livingston, 21 June [1832], Blair to "Gentlemen," n.d., Montgomery Blair, "Sketch," [13 May 1858?], Blair-Lee Papers; Blair to Jackson, 30 April 1845, Jackson to Blair, 17 January 1843, Blair Family Papers.

102. Blair to Livingston, 18 June, 21 June 1832, Livingston to Blair, 20 June 1832, Blair-Lee Papers; Blair to Jackson, with Jackson's endorsement, n.d., Jackson Papers.

103. Biddle to A. Dickins, 20 December 1831, Biddle Papers.

104. McLane to Biddle, 5 January 1832, Biddle, *Correspondence*, pp. 167–68; Lewis to Blair, 12 August 1832, Blair-Lee Papers; Jackson to Van Buren, 14 January 1832, Jackson, *Correspondence*, 4:448; Charles Jared Ingersoll to Biddle, 21 February 1832, Biddle, *Correspondence*, pp. 183–85.

105. Biddle to Thomas Cadwalader, 3 July 1832, Biddle Papers; Taney to Van Buren, 2 June 1835, Van Buren Papers; Taney, "'Bank War Manuscript,'" p. 226.

106. Jackson to Van Buren, 14 June 1832, Van Buren Papers; Marshall,

"Jackson's Bank Veto Message," p. 470; Van Buren, *Origin and Course of Political Parties*, pp. 314–15.

107. Richardson, *Messages and Papers*, 3:1142–43, 1147–51. Compare with Kendall's anti-Bank editorials in the *Argus of Western America*, 21 May, 23 July 1819; Kendall, *Autobiography*, pp. 207–22; Taney, " 'Bank War Manuscript,' " pp. 226–27.

108. Richardson, *Messages and Papers*, 3:1153.

109. Richardson, *Messages and Papers*, 3:1153–54.

110. Richardson, *Messages and Papers*, 3:1141.

111. Richardson, *Messages and Papers*, 3:1141–42, 1149.

112. Washington *Globe*, 20 July, 28 July, 20 August, 30 August, 8 September, 28 September 1832; Schlesinger, *Age of Jackson*, pp. 91–92; *National Intelligencer*, 19 December 1832. It was generally known that Kendall had prepared the Bank message. See *U.S. Telegraph*, 15 September 1832.

113. Stanwood, *Presidential Elections*, pp. 100–101; Remini, *Jackson and the Bank War*, p. 106; Robert V. Remini, "Election of 1832," in *History of American Presidential Elections: 1789–1968*, ed. Arthur M. Schlesinger, Jr., 1:515–16; McCormick, "New Perspectives," p. 292; Kindig, "Western Opposition to Jackson's 'Democracy,' " pp. v–vi, 20.

114. McCormick, "New Perspectives," pp. 292, 300; Philip A. Grant, Jr., "The Bank Controversy and Connecticut Politics, 1834," *Connecticut Historical Society Bulletin* 33 (1968):90.

115. Barry to daughter, 4 July 1832, "Letters of William T. Barry," 14:233; *U.S. Telegraph*, 15 September 1832.

116. Dallas to Henry D. Gilpin, 10 July, 13 July 1832, Dallas Papers; Isaac Hill to Gideon Welles, 14 December 1832, Welles Papers.

117. Washington *Globe*, 13 October 1832.

118. Useful discussions of the concept of modernization and its relationship to nineteenth-century America are found in Richard D. Brown, *Modernization*, especially pp. 122–58; Brown, "Modernization and the Modern Personality in Early America, 1600–1865: A Sketch of a Synthesis," *Journal of Interdisciplinary History* 2 (1971–72):201–28; Eric Foner, "The Causes of the American Civil War: Recent Interpretations and New Directions," *Civil War History* 20 (1974):197–214.

119. Washington *Globe*, 13 October 1832, 19 July 1831; Kendall, *Autobiography*, p. 432. For the Whig party's emphasis on social and class homogeneity, see Glyndon G. Van Deusen, "Some Aspects of Whig Thought and Theory in the Jacksonian Period," *American Historical Review* 63 (1958):307–9; Formisano, "Political Character, Antipartyism and the Second Party System," pp. 707–9; Sydney Nathans, *Daniel Webster and Jacksonian Democracy*, pp. 6–7; Elliott R. Barkan, "The Emergence of a Whig Persuasion: Conservatism, Democratism, and the New York State Whigs," *New York History* 52 (1971):367–95.

120. Donald B. Cole, *Jacksonian Democracy in New Hampshire: 1800–1851*, pp. 136–59; John Vollmer Mering, *The Whig Party in Missouri*, pp.

54–70; Benson, *Concept of Jacksonian Democracy*, pp. 171–73; Formisano, *Birth of Mass Political Parties*, pp. 179–82. The relationship between class and partisan affiliation in the Jacksonian period is controversial. For a recent summary of the historical literature, see Edward Pessen, *Jacksonian America: Society, Personality, and Politics*, pp. 248–74.

121. Hammond, *Banks and Politics*, pp. 338–39.

122. Washington *Globe*, 13 October 1832.

123. Jackson to Taney, 13 October 1836, Jackson, *Correspondence*, 5:430; Richardson, *Messages and Papers*, 4:1523, 1526–27. Ethnocultural historians have stressed the influence of Protestant morality on the Whig Party. See Formisano, *Birth of Mass Political Parties*, pp. 102–36; Benson, *Concept of Jacksonian Democracy*, pp. 198–207; Shade, *Banks or No Banks*, p. 144. Two works that consider the moral basis of Jackson's appeal, however, provide useful antidotes: see Meyers, *Jacksonian Persuasion*, passim; and McFaul, *Jacksonian Finance*, pp. 210–16.

Chapter 5. Van Buren for Vice-President

1. Green to John Floyd, 2 April 1831, Green Papers, Southern Historical Collection; William B. Lewis to Blair, 17 May 1831, Blair-Lee Papers; Kendall to Lewis, 17 May 1831, "Origin of the Democratic National Convention," *American Historical Magazine* 7 (1902):268.

2. Jackson to Van Buren, 8 August, 5 September 1831, Jackson, *Correspondence*, 4:329, 348; Jackson to Van Buren, 18 September, 17 December 1831, Van Buren Papers.

3. Van Buren, *Autobiography*, 2:445–46; James A. Hamilton to Jackson, 15 August 1831, Jackson Papers; Ritchie to Van Buren, 20–21 April, 30 April 1831, Van Buren Papers; Van Buren to William C. Rives, 1 November 1831, Rives Papers. Van Buren's Regency organ, the Albany *Argus*, also denied Van Buren's vice-presidential intentions. See Albany *Argus*, 2 June, 23 July 1831.

4. Kendall to Lewis, 17 May 1831, "Origin of the Democratic National Convention," pp. 267–70.

5. Lewis to Kendall, 25 May 1831, "Origin of the Democratic National Convention," pp. 270–72; Washington *Globe*, 6 July, 19 July 1831, 1 June 1832; Kendall to Blair, 28 January 1830, Blair-Lee Papers.

6. Chase, *Emergence of the Presidential Nominating Convention*, pp. ix–x; Chase, "Jacksonian Democracy and the Rise of the Nominating Convention," p. 229. In the South, however, the state convention was slow to gain acceptance before the 1840s. See McCormick, *Second American Party System*, pp. 346–48.

7. Van Buren to Thomas Ritchie, 13 January 1827, Van Buren Papers.

8. Kendall to Blair, 9 January 1829, 28 January, 18 March 1830, Blair to Kendall, 11 February 1830, Blair-Lee Papers; Washington *Globe*, 6 July, 19 July 1831.

9. Jackson to Joseph Conn Guild, 24 April 1835, Jackson, *Correspondence*, 5:338–39. See also Washington *Globe*, 7 August 1835.

10. Hofstadter, *Idea of a Party System*, pp. 12–13, 22–23, 27, 50–53, 122–28, 151, 188, 204–5, 223–26.

11. Jackson to Joseph Conn Guild, 24 April 1835, Jackson, *Correspondence*, 5:341; Jackson to Blair, 19 April 1841, *Correspondence*, 6:105. See also Jackson to Rev. Hardy M. Cryer, 7 April 1833, Jackson, *Correspondence*, 5:53; Jackson to Henry Horn, 25 January 1835, *Correspondence*, 5:321; Jackson to Van Buren, 24 November 1840, *Correspondence*, 6:83.

12. Jackson to Blair, 18 March 1845, Jackson, *Correspondence*, 6:385; Jackson to Alfred Balch, 16 February 1835, *Correspondence*, 5:328; Jackson to William B. Lewis, 18 August 1832, *Correspondence*, 4:467.

13. See above pp. 156–58.

14. Jackson to Tilghman A. Howard, 20 August 1833, Jackson, *Correspondence*, 5:166; Jackson to William B. Lewis, 18 August 1832, *Correspondence*, 4:467. Cf. Curtis, *Andrew Jackson*, pp. 155–57, 169.

15. Washington *Globe*, 24 May 1832; Chase, *Emergence of the Presidential Nominating Convention*, pp. 279–81.

16. Ritchie to William C. Rives, 26 August 1833, Rives Papers; Chambers, *Old Bullion Benton*, p. 189; "Address to the Democratic Republicans of the United States," Washington *Globe*, 6 August 1835; Chase, *Emergence of the Presidential Nominating Convention*, pp. 291–92.

17. Gammon, *Election of 1832*, pp. 97–98.

18. *U.S. Telegraph*, 7 January, 27 January 1832; Washington *Globe*, 27 October, 2 December 1831.

19. Meyer, *Richard M. Johnson*, pp. 207–89; Isaac Hill to Gideon Welles, 12 December 1831, Welles Papers; Richard M. Johnson to Blair, n.d. [1834?], Blair-Lee Papers.

20. Johnson to Blair, 4 October, 10 October 1831, Blair-Lee Papers; Kendall to William B. Lewis, 17 May 1831, "Origin of the Democratic National Convention," p. 269; James Watson Webb to Van Buren, 31 December 1831, Van Buren Papers; Green to John Floyd, 5 December 1831, Green Papers, Library of Congress.

21. Blair to Van Buren, 28 January 1832, Van Buren Papers; Kendall to Blair, 10 March, 30 April 1829, Blair-Lee Papers.

22. Webb to Van Buren, 31 December 1831, Van Buren Papers; Noah to Woodbury, 21 December 1831, Woodbury Papers; Cambreleng to Van Buren, 4 January 1832, Van Buren Papers; Benton, *Thirty Years' View*, 1:218.

23. Van Buren, *Autobiography*, 2:454.

24. Jackson to John Coffee, 27 January, 9 March 1832, Jackson, *Correspondence*, 4:402, 417; Jackson to James A. Hamilton, 27 January 1832, *Correspondence*, 4:402–3; Andrew Stevenson to Thomas Ritchie, 4 February 1832, Van Buren Papers; Felix Grundy to Jackson, 4 February 1832, William Carroll to Jackson, 14 February 1832, Jackson Papers; Lewis to James A. Hamilton,

1832, Hamilton, *Reminiscences*, p. 243; Lewis to Azariah Flagg, 14 February 1832, Flagg Papers.

25. Kendall to [John M. Niles], 26 January 1832, Welles Papers; Blair to Van Buren, 28 January 1832, Van Buren Papers; Washington *Globe*, 30 January 1832.

26. Van Buren to William C. Rives, 13 March 1832, Rives Papers; Van Buren to Jackson, 20 February 1832, Van Buren Papers; Van Buren to William Marcy, 14 March 1832, Van Buren, *Autobiography*, 2:509.

27. Duff Green to Richard K. Crallé, 3 January 1832, Green Papers, Library of Congress; Green to William Ingalls, 22 March 1832, Green Papers, Southern Historical Collection.

28. Charles Manfred Thompson, "Attitude of Western Whigs Towards the Convention System," *Proceedings of the Mississippi Valley Historical Association* 5 (1911–12):176–77; Gammon, *Election of 1832*, p. 98; Klein, *Pennsylvania Politics*, p. 315; Levi Reynolds, Jr., to William B. Lewis, 5 August 1832, Blair-Lee Papers.

29. Drayton to Joel Poinsett, 2 May 1832, Joel Poinsett Papers, Historical Society of Pennsylvania; Iredell to John Branch, 7 March 1832, Branch Papers; Gammon, *Election of 1832*, p. 98; Andrew Stevenson to Thomas Ritchie, 4 February 1832, Van Buren Papers; Charles H. Ambler, *Sectionalism in Virginia from 1776–1861*, pp. 146–49; John Floyd to Calhoun, 2 January 1832, John Floyd Papers, Library of Congress.

30. John Branch to James Iredell, 31 March 1832, Iredell Papers; Blair to Van Buren, 28 January 1832, Van Buren Papers; Adams, *Memoirs*, 8:482; Hoffmann, *Jackson and North Carolina Politics*, p. 49; McCormick, *Second American Party System*, p. 192.

31. Albany *Argus*, 29 June 1832; Andrew Stevenson to Thomas Ritchie, 4 February 1832, Van Buren Papers; *Niles' Register* 42 (10 March 1832):21; John Floyd to Calhoun, 2 January 1832, Floyd Papers; Hoffmann, *Jackson and North Carolina Politics*, p. 54.

32. Benton, *Thirty Years' View*, 1:219; C. C. Cambreleng to Van Buren, 4 January, 4 February 1832, Van Buren Papers; William B. Lewis to James A. Hamilton, 1832, Hamilton, *Reminiscences*, p. 243; James Watson Webb to Van Buren, 31 December 1831, Van Buren Papers; Duff Green to Richard K. Crallé, 30 April 1832, Green Papers, Library of Congress.

33. Charles Dayan to Azariah Flagg, 12 February 1832, Flagg Papers; Jesse Hoyt to Van Buren, 7 February 1832, C. C. Cambreleng to Van Buren, 4 February 1832, Van Buren Papers.

34. James Watson Webb to Van Buren, 31 December 1831, Van Buren Papers. For Blair's more favorable public attitude towards Van Buren as the convention approached, see Washington *Globe*, 8 May 1832.

35. Chase, *Emergence of the Presidential Nominating Convention*, p. 263.

36. *Niles' Register* 42 (26 May 1832):234.

37. *Niles' Register* 42 (26 May 1832):235.

38. James S. Chase argues cogently that national nominating conventions depend on the existence of national parties, and that they represent the apogee of the process of party construction. Chase, *Emergence of the Presidential Nominating Convention*, pp. x, 229. Although his theory exaggerates the development of the National Republican and Antimasonic parties in 1832, it seems evident that conventions both stimulated and responded to the evolving party system.

39. Washington *Globe*, 24 May 1832; *U.S. Telegraph*, 1 September 1832.

40. Rudolph Bunner to Gulian Verplanck, 23 October 1833, Verplanck Papers; McCormick, *Second American Party System*, pp. 347–49.

41. Chase, *Emergence of the Presidential Nominating Convention*, pp. 276–95.

42. Judge Richard Parker to Van Buren, 5 September 1832, Van Buren Papers; Washington *Globe*, 30 July, 11 August 1832; *Niles' Register* 42 (7 July 1832):339, 42 (23 June 1832):303–4; Gammon, *Election of 1832*, p. 145.

43. William B. Lewis to Blair, 26 August 1832, Blair-Lee Papers; J. S. Barbour to James Barbour, 26 March 1832, James Barbour Papers; James Iredell to John Branch, 7 March 1832, Branch Papers.

44. P. P. Barbour to Thomas Gilmer, 24 October 1832, Washington *Globe*, 29 October 1832; *Niles' Register* 43 (1 December 1832):214–15.

45. Kendall to———, 23 April 1832, *Niles' Register* 42 (4 August 1832):406; Amos Kendall to [John M. Niles], 26 January 1832, Welles Papers.

46. Duff Green to Dr. Hagan, 23 October 1832, Green to Calhoun, 23 October 1832, Green Papers, Southern Historical Collection; Adams, *Memoirs*, 9:430.

47. "Address," Washington *Globe*, 13 October 1832.

48. *U.S. Telegraph*, 8 November 1832; William J. Rensom to Blair, 12 August 1831, William B. Lewis to Blair, 23 August 1832, Levi Reynolds, Jr., to William B. Lewis, 5 August 1832, Blair-Lee Papers; Jackson to Lewis, 18 August 1832, Jackson-Lewis Papers; Jackson to Van Buren, 18 November 1832, Van Buren Papers.

Chapter 6. Nullification

1. A somewhat different version of this chapter has been published as "The Nullification Crisis and Republican Subversion," *Journal of Southern History* 43 (1977):19–38.

2. Freehling, *Prelude to Civil War*, pp. 192–95; *Niles' Register* 37 (6 February 1830):393; Charleston *Mercury*, 13 January, 1 May, 3 May, 30 May 1830.

3. Calhoun to Samuel Ingham, 16 June 1831, Calhoun Papers, South Caroliniana Library; Calhoun to Ingham, 31 July 1831, DeCoppet Collection; Calhoun to James Edward Calhoun, 25 December 1831, Calhoun Papers, South Caroliniana Library.

4. Jackson to Van Buren, 23 December, 25 December 1832, Jackson, *Corre-*

spondence, 4:504, 506; Robert Hayne to Jackson, 4 February 1831, with Jackson's endorsement, Jackson Papers.

5. James Hamilton, Jr., to Van Buren, 5 March 1829, Van Buren Papers; Kendall to Blair, 7 March 1829, Blair-Lee Papers; J. H. Scinner to James Barbour, 22 February 1829, James Barbour Papers; Jackson to James Hamilton, Jr., 29 March 1828, Jackson, *Correspondence*, 3:411–12.

6. Richardson, *Messages and Papers*, 3:1223. One must exercise caution in attributing to the West such qualities as nationalism. Still, the West was particularly dependent on the national government in matters relating to Indians, internal improvements, and land settlement. See Turner, *Rise of the New West*, pp. 110, 185–91. For the depth of union sentiment in Jackson's home state, see Paul H. Bergeron, "Tennessee's Response to the Nullification Crisis," *Journal of Southern History* 39 (1973):23–44.

7. Kendall to Gideon Welles, 21 February 1831, Welles Papers; Blair to Mrs. Gratz, 16 July 1831, Clay, ed., "Two Years with Old Hickory," p. 196; Washington *Globe*, 2 March 1831; *Argus of Western America*, 24 December 1828.

8. Jackson to John Coffee, 17 July 1832, Jackson, *Correspondence*, 4:462–63; Jackson to Joel Poinsett, 9 December 1832, *Correspondence*, 4:498; Jackson to John Coffee, 9 April 1833, *Correspondence*, 5:56.

9. Jackson to William B. Lewis, 25 August 1830, Jackson, *Correspondence*, 4:177; Jackson to John Coffee, 13 May 1831, *Correspondence*, 4:282; Jackson to Van Buren, 17 December 1831, *Correspondence*, 4:384.

10. Washington *Globe*, 1 February, 9 November 1832. See also Washington *Globe*, 4 September, 9 November, 10 November, 14 November, 17 December 1832.

11. *U.S. Telegraph*, 18 December, 21 November 1832. See also *U.S. Telegraph*, 30 November 1832.

12. Jackson to John Coffee, 10 April, 18 December 1830, 13 May 1831, Jackson, *Correspondence*, 4:134, 216, 281; Richardson, *Messages and Papers*, 4:1523. For a discussion of conspiratorial thinking in the early republic, see J. Wendell Knox, *Conspiracy in American Politics: 1789–1815*. It is ironic that Calhoun's enemies accused him of inordinate political ambition. As William W. Freehling has shown, Calhoun greatly feared power-grasping politicians, office seekers, and political spoils. He viewed nullification as a means of reducing revenue and patronage and thereby diminishing the power of spoilsmen. William W. Freehling, "Spoilsmen and Interests in the Thought and Career of John C. Calhoun," *Journal of American History* 52 (1965): 25–42.

13. Richardson, *Messages and Papers*, 4:1526–27; Jackson to Taney, 15 October 1836, Jackson, *Correspondence*, 5:430. See Meyers, *Jacksonian Persuasion*, chap. 2.

14. Joel Poinsett, the South Carolina Unionist upon whom Jackson relied for information about nullifier activity, reported Calhoun's moderating

influence and cautioned Jackson against "making this man of too much importance." Poinsett to Jackson, 20 January 1833, Jackson, *Correspondence*, 5:9. Calhoun's moderate position among the nullifiers is stressed by Freehling, *Prelude to Civil War*, pp. 134–76.

15. Charleston *Mercury*, 8 March, 3 May, 24 May, 28 July 1832; Frederic Bancroft, *Calhoun and the South Carolina Nullification Movement*, pp. 19–22, 114–16, 184–85; Chauncey S. Boucher, *The Nullification Controversy in South Carolina*, p. 107; David F. Houston, *A Critical Study of Nullification in South Carolina*, pp. 47–52; Freehling, *Prelude to Civil War*, pp. xi–xii, 255–59; Calhoun to Virgil Maxcy, 11 September 1830, Galloway-Maxcy-Markoe Papers, Library of Congress.

16. Freehling, *Prelude to Civil War*, pp. xi–xii, 255–59, and passim. Paul H. Bergeron has recently subjected Freehling's thesis to incisive questioning, and though he offers no alternative explanation for South Carolina's extremism, his work provides a useful corrective to Freehling's argument. See Bergeron, "The Nullification Crisis Revisited," *Tennessee Historical Quarterly* 35 (1976):263–75.

17. Washington *Globe*, 4 August 1832. See also Washington *Globe*, 27 June, 3 July, 30 August, 9 November, 26 November, 29 December 1832.

18. Jackson to Van Buren, 14 November 1831, Jackson Papers; Jackson to James A. Hamilton, 12 November 1831, Hamilton, *Reminiscences*, p. 231.

19. Richardson, *Messages and Papers*, 3:1087–88; Jackson to Van Buren, 14 November 1831, Jackson Papers; F. W. Taussig, *The Tariff History of the United States*, pp. 102–3.

20. Richardson, *Messages and Papers*, 3:1119.

21. Presidential Messages, Second Annual Message, Jackson Papers; Washington *Globe*, 27 July 1832; Richardson, *Messages and Papers*, 3:1161–62; Blair to Van Buren, 28 January 1832, Van Buren Papers. See also Washington *Globe*, 29 April, 14 July 1832.

22. Van Buren, *Autobiography*, 2:569; C. C. Cambreleng to Van Buren, 18 December 1832, Van Buren Papers; Silas Wright to Azariah Flagg, 20 January 1833, Flagg Papers.

23. McLane to Jackson, 5 May 1832, Jackson Papers; Cambreleng to Van Buren, 18 December 1832, Van Buren Papers; Washington *Globe*, 14 July 1832.

24. Parton, *Life of Jackson*, 3:451–52; Richmond *Enquirer*, 3 July 1832; Washington *Globe*, 14 July, 23 July, 24 July 1832.

25. Van Buren to James A. Hamilton, 15 July 1832, Hamilton, *Reminiscences*, p. 246; Jackson to John Coffee, 17 July 1832, Jackson, *Correspondence*, 4:462–63; Washington *Globe*, 13 October 1832.

26. John C. Calhoun to Richard K. Crallé, May 1832, Calhoun Papers, South Caroliniana Library. Like Calhoun, the nullifiers also employed the vocabulary of republican ideology in presenting their case. They charged that consolidationist principles, as manifested in the American System, oppressed the South, violated the Constitution, and endangered liberty, and they urged

interposition as an antidote for a diseased political system. Their interpretation of republican ideology differed, of course, from that of Jackson. See Latner, "Nullification Crisis and Republican Subversion," pp. 29–30.

27. Charleston *Mercury*, 20 August 1832; General Court of Massachusetts, *State Papers on Nullification* . . . , p. 31; Freehling, *Prelude to Civil War*, pp. 248–54, 262–64.

28. Jackson to Van Buren, 14 November 1831, Jackson, *Correspondence*, 4:374; Jackson to John Coffee, 23 October 1831, *Correspondence*, 4:362; Washington *Globe*, 21 January 1833. See also Washington *Globe*, 3 July, 14 July, 30 November, 4 December 1832.

29. Jackson to John Coffee, 17 July 1832, Jackson, *Correspondence*, 4:462; Hamilton, *Reminiscences*, p. 231; Jackson to Poinsett, 7 November 1832, Jackson, *Correspondence*, 4:486; Jackson to Van Buren, 23 October 1832, Van Buren Papers; Jackson to Van Buren, 18 November 1832, Jackson, *Correspondence*, 4:489; Jackson to Cass, 29 October 1832, *Correspondence*, 4:483.

30. Kendall to Van Buren, 10 November 1832, Van Buren Papers; Jackson to John Coffee, 14 December 1832, Jackson, *Correspondence*, 4:500; Jackson to Poinsett, 2 December, 9 December 1832, *Correspondence*, 4:493–94, 497–98; Jackson to Van Buren, 25 December 1832, *Correspondence*, 4:505–6; Hamilton, *Reminiscences*, p. 248.

31. Kendall to Littleton Dennis Teackle, 1 December 1832, Kendall Miscellaneous Papers, New-York Historical Society; Washington *Globe*, 30 August, 5 November 1832.

32. Jackson to Anthony Butler, 4 December 1832, Jackson, *Correspondence*, 4:496; Jackson to Van Buren, 13 January 1833, *Correspondence*, 5:3; Silas Wright to Van Buren, 13 January 1833, Van Buren Papers; Richardson, *Messages and Papers*, 3:1160–62; Munroe, *Louis McLane*, p. 369.

33. Kendall's draft of a proclamation is found in Presidential Messages, Nullification Proclamation, Jackson Papers.

34. Livingston to Poinsett, 11 December 1832, Poinsett Papers; Jackson to Livingston, 4 December 1832, Jackson, *Correspondence*, 4:495; Smith, *Blair Family in Politics*, 1:117.

35. Richardson, *Messages and Papers*, 3:1206, 1211–12.

36. Richardson, *Messages and Papers*, 3:1216–19.

37. Jackson to Joel Poinsett, 9 December 1832, Jackson, *Correspondence*, 4:498.

38. Jackson to Poinsett, 24 January 1833, Jackson, *Correspondence*, 5:11–12; Jackson to Van Buren, 13 January 1833, Van Buren Papers; Kendall, *Autobiography*, p. 631.

39. McLane to Gulian Verplanck, 16 January [1833], Verplanck Papers; Woodbury, 10 January 1834, "Sundry Exercises," Woodbury Papers; Munroe, *Louis McLane*, p. 369.

40. Freehling, *Prelude to Civil War*, pp. 284–86.

41. Richardson, *Messages and Papers*, 3:1192–94; Washington *Globe*, 29 January 1833.

42. Bergeron, "Tennessee and Nullification," pp. 33–35.

43. Ritchie to Van Buren, 25 June 1832, Van Buren Papers; Richmond *Enquirer*, 24 April 1830. See also Richmond *Enquirer*, 30 March, 17 April, 21 August, 30 November 1832, 22 January, 26 January, 12 February 1833.

44. Van Buren, *Autobiography*, 2:547; Richmond *Enquirer*, 13 December 1832; *Niles' Register* 43 (19 January 1833):345.

45. Richmond *Enquirer*, 8 January, 15 March 1833. See also Richmond *Enquirer*, 22 January, 26 January, 19 February 1833; Calhoun to Armistead Burt, 15 January 1833, John C. Calhoun Papers, Duke University Library. Not all southern Democrats agreed with Ritchie. Andrew Stevenson argued against his position on secession. See Jackson to Van Buren, 25 January 1833, Jackson, *Correspondence*, 5:13; Albany *Argus*, 15 February 1833.

46. Woodbury, 10 January 1834, "Sundry Exercises," Woodbury Papers; Tyler, *Memoir of Roger Brooke Taney*, pp. 188–89.

47. Cambreleng to Van Buren, 25 December 1832, Van Buren Papers; Wright to Azariah Flagg, 29 January 1833, Flagg Papers; John Eaton to Van Buren, 2 January 1833, Van Buren Papers.

48. Albany *Argus*, 25 February, 14 May, 10 August 1832; Van Buren, *Autobiography*, 2:171–72; Jackson to Van Buren, 1 November 1830, Thomas Ritchie to Van Buren, 25 June 1832, Van Buren Papers; Louis McLane to Jackson, 5 May 1832, Jackson Papers. On the Albany *Argus*'s solicitude for New York State's wool growers, see Albany *Argus*, 14 May, 28 May 1832.

49. On Thomas Ritchie's unhappiness with Van Buren's tariff position, see Richmond *Enquirer*, 28 February, 27 April, 1 June, 19 October 1832.

50. Van Buren to Jackson, 22 December 1832, 20 February 1833, Van Buren Papers; Van Buren to Jackson, 21 September, 11 October 1831, Jackson, *Correspondence*, 4:352, 358.

51. Van Buren, *Autobiography*, 2:547; Van Buren to Jackson, 22 December 1832, Van Buren Papers; Van Buren to Jackson, 27 December 1832, Jackson, *Correspondence*, 4:507; Albany *Argus*, 22 December 1832. See also Curtis, *Fox at Bay*, pp. 40–45.

52. Van Buren to Jackson, 27 December 1832, Jackson, *Correspondence*, 4:506–7.

53. Van Buren to Jackson, 9 January, 20 February 1833, Van Buren to Silas Wright, 4 February 1833, Van Buren Papers; James A. Hamilton to Jackson, 22 January 1833, Jackson Papers; Van Buren, *Autobiography*, 2:558–59. Silas Wright, however, urged passage of the Force Bill. See Wright to John M. Niles, 3 February 1833, Welles Papers.

54. Van Buren, *Autobiography*, 2:706–7; Jackson to Van Buren, 13 January 1833, Van Buren Papers; Jackson to Joel Poinsett, 16 January 1833, Jackson, *Correspondence*, 5:5. Van Buren later claimed that the proclamation's errors were due to Jackson's carelessness. See Van Buren, *Autobiography*, 2:546. The evidence cited makes Van Buren's contention unlikely; Jackson took pride in the document.

55. Jackson to Van Buren, 13 January 1833, Van Buren Papers; Washington *Globe*, 8 January, 6 September 1833; Silas Wright to Van Buren, 13 January 1833, Van Buren Papers. See also Washington *Globe*, 19 December 1832, 2 January, 9 January, 21 January, 2 February, 8 March 1833.

56. Richardson, *Messages and Papers*, 3:1203–19, esp. p. 1211; Washington *Globe*, 19 December 1832, 2 January, 8 January 1833; Richmond *Enquirer*, 12 February, 14 February, 24 September 1833; Van Buren, *Autobiography*, 2:549–53; Nathaniel Macon to John Randolph, 28 October 1831, extract, Jackson Papers; Freehling, *Prelude to Civil War*, pp. 207–8.

57. Kendall to Van Buren, 2 November 1832, Van Buren Papers.

58. Van Buren's reaction is implied in Kendall's response to his letter. See Kendall to Van Buren, 10 November 1832, Van Buren Papers.

59. Kendall to Van Buren, 10 November 1832, Van Buren Papers.

60. Washington *Globe*, 9 November, 14 November, 26 November, 29 November 1832.

61. Silas Wright to John M. Niles, 13 February 1833, Welles Papers; Washington *Globe*, 6 December, 27 December 1832, 18 February, 23 March 1833; Jackson to Joel Poinsett, 17 February 1833, Jackson, *Correspondence*, 5:18; John Eaton to Van Buren, 2 January 1833, Van Buren Papers. See also Washington *Globe*, 27 May, 24 June, 28 November 1833.

62. For a discussion of the Jackson-Webster movement, see Norman D. Brown, "Webster-Jackson Movement for a Constitution and Union Party in 1833," *Mid-America* 46 (1964):147–71; Brown, *Daniel Webster and the Politics of Availability*, pp. 15–52; Nathans, *Daniel Webster*, pp. 48–73. On Livingston and Cass, see George Ticknor Curtis, *Life of Daniel Webster*, 1:464; Daniel Webster, *The Private Correspondence of Daniel Webster*, 1:536–37; Van Buren, *Autobiography*, 2:704–7.

63. Albany *Argus*, 9 July 1833; Washington *Globe*, 10 May, 17 May 1833; Van Buren, *Autobiography*, 2:678–79.

64. Kendall to Van Buren, 2 November 1832, Van Buren Papers; Washington *Globe*, 25 June 1833; Hamilton, *Reminiscences*, p. 259.

65. Washington *Globe*, 28 November, 19 December 1833, 23 January, 13 February, 22 February, 25 February, 26 February 1834; William T. Barry to Van Buren, 7 July 1833, Van Buren Papers; *U.S. Telegraph*, 15 July 1833, quoted in Brown, *Daniel Webster*, p. 44.

66. Benjamin Gratz to Blair, 21 February 1833, Blair-Lee Papers; Washington *Globe*, 16 January 1833.

67. Silas Wright to Azariah Flagg, 25 February 1833, Flagg Papers; Jackson to Van Buren, 13 January 1833, Van Buren Papers.

68. Jackson to Joel Poinsett, 24 January, 6 March 1833, Jackson, *Correspondence*, 5:11–12, 29; Jackson to Van Buren, 25 January 1833, Van Buren Papers. See also Nathans, *Daniel Webster*, pp. 60–61.

69. Washington *Globe*, 21 January 1833; *Register of Debates*, 22 Cong., 2 Sess., pp. 688, 1903; Brown, *Daniel Webster*, p. 22.

70. Jackson to Joel Poinsett, 6 March 1833, Jackson, *Correspondence*, 5:29; Silas Wright to John M. Niles, 13 February 1833, Van Buren Papers; Wright to Azariah Flagg, 25 February 1833, Flagg Papers.

71. George M. Dallas to Henry Gilpin, 1 December 1832, Dallas Papers.

72. Van Buren, *Autobiography*, 2:452–53; *Register of Debates*, 22 Cong., 2 Sess., p. 688.

73. Brown, *Daniel Webster*, p. 29; Kendall to Jackson, 20 March 1833, Jackson Papers.

74. Arthur C. Cole, *The Whig Party in the South*, pp. 21–22; Hoffmann, *Jackson and North Carolina Politics*, pp. 63–68; Freehling, *Prelude to Civil War*, p. 287; Richmond *Enquirer*, 1 November 1831, 8 December 1832.

75. Jackson to Hugh Lawson White, 24 March 1833, Jackson, *Correspondence*, 5:46; Kendall to Blair, 20 March 1833, Jackson Papers; Washington *Globe*, 7 December 1832.

76. Jackson to John Coffee, 9 April 1833, Jackson, *Correspondence*, 5:56; Jackson to Andrew J. Crawford, 1 May 1833, Jackson Papers [misfiled under 1 May 1832].

77. Washington *Globe*, 11 June 1833. The parallels between the *Globe*'s argument and Professor William W. Freehling's thesis are apparent. Both emphasize the leadership of rice planters among the nullifiers while discounting economic hardship as a cause of their anger. Freehling, however, sees the planters' fears about the stability of slavery as central to their participation in the nullification movement, while the *Globe* concludes that political ambition lay behind South Carolina radicalism. Freehling, *Prelude to Civil War*, pp. xii, 255–59. See also Washington *Globe*, 26 November 1832.

78. Charleston *Mercury*, 19 March, 19 April, 22 April, 26 April 1833; *U.S. Telegraph*, 23 April 1833.

79. Jackson to Andrew J. Crawford, 1 May 1833, Jackson Papers; Washington *Globe*, 5 April, 12 April, 20 April 1833.

80. In his study of nullification, William W. Freehling claims that throughout the nullification episode, South Carolina's radicals engaged in a "frenzied response" to the abolitionists' "innocuous" attacks. Freehling, *Prelude to Civil War*, p. 49. He has since, however, changed his opinion and now holds that the nullifiers' fears were rational. For his reasons, see Freehling, "Paranoia and American History," *New York Review of Books* 18 (23 September 1971):36–39.

81. Jackson to John Coffee, 9 April 1833, Jackson, *Correspondence*, 5:56; Washington *Globe*, 20 April 1833. The relationship between politics and slavery during Jackson's presidency awaits scholarly treatment. Suggestive discussions are Gerald S. Henig, "The Jacksonian Attitude Toward Abolitionism in the 1830's," *Tennessee Historical Quarterly* 28 (1969):42–56; George M. Fredrickson, *The Black Image in the White Mind*, pp. 58–70; and John M. McFaul, "Expediency vs. Morality: Jacksonian Politics and Slavery," *Journal of American History* 62 (1975):24–39.

Chapter 7. Destroying the Bank

1. Jackson to Van Buren, 16 August 1833, Van Buren Papers.

2. For an excellent review of the literature on the consequences of Jackson's banking program, see Harry N. Scheiber, "The Pet Banks in Jacksonian Politics and Finance, 1833–1841," *Journal of Economic History* 23 (1963):196–214. Also see McFaul, *Jacksonian Finance*; and Peter Temin, *The Jacksonian Economy*. Remini, *Jackson and the Bank War*, pp. 177–78, emphasizes the effects of removal on the presidency.

3. Richardson, *Messages and Papers*, 3:1226; Duff Green to Dr. James Hagan, 24 October 1832, Green Papers, Southern Historical Collection; Catterall, *Second Bank*, p. 90.

4. Jackson to William B. Lewis, 18 August 1832, Jackson-Lewis Papers; Jackson to James K. Polk, 16 December 1832, Jackson, *Correspondence*, 4:501; Sister M. Grace Madeleine, *Monetary and Banking Theories of Jacksonian Democracy*, p. 54.

5. Taney, "'Bank War Manuscript,'" pp. 234–36.

6. Richardson, *Messages and Papers*, 3:1163.

7. Washington *Globe*, 17 September, 17 December 1832, 5 January, 7 January, 22 January 1833.

8. Kendall, *Autobiography*, p. 376; Parton, *Life of Jackson*, 3:503–4; Reuben M. Whitney to Blair, 17 May 1836, Blair-Lee Papers.

9. Taney, "'Bank War Manuscript,'" pp. 236–37.

10. Taney, "'Bank War Manuscript,'" pp. 234–35.

11. Kendall, *Autobiography*, p. 376; Parton, *Life of Jackson*, 3:503–4; Van Buren to Blair, 15 October 1845, Blair Family Papers; Curtis, *Fox at Bay*, p. 45.

12. Van Buren, *Autobiography*, 2:575–77; Nathaniel Niles to William C. Rives, 23 July 1833, Rives Papers; Woodbury, 10 January 1834, "Sundry Exercises," Woodbury Papers.

13. McFaul, *Jacksonian Finance*, pp. 27, 39–40.

14. Freehling, "Spoilsmen and Interests," pp. 25–42; John Floyd, *Diary of John Floyd*, pp. 229–33; Ritchie to Andrew Stevenson, n.d., Andrew Stevenson Papers, Library of Congress. Internal evidence reveals that the letter was composed in the spring or early summer of 1834 but speaks of earlier events.

15. Silas Wright to Azariah Flagg, 8 August 1833, Flagg Papers; Van Buren to Jackson, 8 August, 14 September 1833, Jackson Papers.

16. Parton, *Life of Jackson*, 3:505.

17. Jackson to Van Buren, 17 December 1831, Van Buren Papers; Jackson to James A. Hamilton, 28 March 1832, James A. Hamilton Miscellaneous Papers, New-York Historical Society; Blair to Van Buren, 10 October 1845, Van Buren Papers; Van Buren, *Autobiography*, 2:593.

18. Jackson to Van Buren, 18 November 1832, Van Buren Papers; Jackson to Van Buren, 25 November 1832, Van Buren, *Autobiography*, 2:595–96; Louis

McLane to Van Buren, 26 November 1832, *Autobiography*, 2:596–98; Klein, *Pennsylvania Politics*, p. 350.

19. William Duane to———, 3 November 1837, Duane, *Narrative*, pp. 170–73, 176; Jackson to Duane, 17 July 1833, Jackson Papers.

20. Duane to———, 23 August 1833, Duane to J. S. Littell, 20 February 1834, Duane, *Narrative*, pp. 130–31, 146–47; George M. Dallas to Samuel Ingham, 8 July 1829, Dallas Papers.

21. McLane to Van Buren, 26 November 1832, Van Buren, *Autobiography*, 2:596–98; Roger Taney to Van Buren, 8 March 1860, Van Buren Papers; Van Buren to Blair, 15 October 1845, Blair Family Papers; Blair to Van Buren, 10 October 1845, Van Buren Papers; Duane, *Narrative*, pp. 1–2.

22. Washington *Globe*, 18 February 1833; Kendall to Louis McLane, 16 March 1833, Kendall to Jackson, 20 March 1833, Jackson Papers.

23. Kendall to McLane, 16 March 1833, Jackson Papers.

24. Jackson to Hugh Lawson White, 24 March 1833, Jackson Papers; Jackson, "Directions as to BUS, submitted to Cabinet," 19 March 1833, Jackson Papers; Jackson to Roger Taney, 12 March 1833, Roger B. Taney Papers, Maryland Historical Society.

25. McLane to Jackson, 20 May 1833, Jackson Papers.

26. Woodbury to Jackson, 2 April 1833, Jackson Papers; Capowski, "The Making of a Jacksonian Democrat," pp. 194–95, 202; Philip D. Wheaton, "Levi Woodbury: Jacksonian Financier" (Ph.D. diss., University of Maryland, 1955), pp. 43–44, 126; Niven, *Gideon Welles*, pp. 116–18; White to Jackson, 11 April 1833, Barry to Jackson, April 1833, Jackson Papers.

27. Whitney to Jackson, 18 March 1833, Jackson Papers; Whitney to Blair, 16 August 1833, Blair-Lee Papers; McFaul and Gatell, "The Outcast Insider," pp. 118–20.

28. Whitney to Jackson, 6 October 1834, Jackson Papers; Blair to Jackson, 21 July 1837, 5 January 1839, Blair Family Papers; McFaul, *Jacksonian Finance*, p. 69.

29. Taney to Jackson, n.d., Jackson Papers. Taney's letter has a penciled date, not in his handwriting, of "April 3, 1833."

30. Kendall to Jackson, 20 March 1833, Kendall to McLane, 16 March 1833, Jackson Papers. Kendall enclosed his letter to McLane in his statement to Jackson. See also Thomas Ellicott to Kendall, 13 April 1833, Roger B. Taney Papers, Library of Congress.

31. Kendall to Van Buren, 9 June 1833, Jackson to Van Buren, 24 July 1833, Van Buren Papers; Francis Blair, "Notes on Treasury Opinion," [May 1833], Jackson, *Correspondence*, 5:102–4; Robert Gibbes to Nicholas Biddle, 13 April 1833, Biddle, *Correspondence*, pp. 205–6.

32. Duane, *Narrative*, pp. 5–9.

33. Van Buren to Blair, 15 October 1845, Blair Family Papers; Blair to Van Buren, 17 August 1833, Van Buren Papers. Woodbury recalled that Van Buren's enthusiasm for removal during the spring of 1833 "got Pre[si]d[en]t so

excited he would listen to no longer delay." Woodbury, 10 January 1834, "Sundry Exercises," Woodbury Papers.

34. Jackson to Duane, 26 June 1833, Jackson Papers.

35. Jackson to Duane, 26 June 1833, Jackson Papers.

36. Duane to Col. Duane, 2 July 1833, Duane, *Narrative*, pp. 10–11.

37. Biddle to Thomas Cooper, 31 July 1833, Biddle, *Correspondence*, pp. 213–14; Catterall, *Second Bank*, p. 285.

38. Duane to Jackson, 10 July 1833, Jackson Papers; Duane, *Narrative*, pp. 84–92.

39. Kendall to Blair, 11 August 1833, Blair-Lee Papers.

40. Kendall to Blair, 3 August 1833, Blair-Lee Papers.

41. Kendall to Jackson, 11 August 1833, Jackson Papers; Kendall, *Autobiography*, p. 378; Lewis to Blair, 24 July 1833, Blair-Lee Papers; Duane, *Narrative*, p. 100; Woodbury, 10 January 1834, "Sundry Exercises," Woodbury Papers; McLaughlin, *Lewis Cass*, pp. 154–55.

42. Lewis to Blair, 24 July 1833, Blair-Lee Papers; Lewis to Jackson, 3 April 1833, Jackson Papers; Lewis to Ritchie, 28 August 1833, Jackson-Lewis Papers.

43. Jackson to Van Buren, 24 July 1833, Van Buren Papers; Parton, *Life of Jackson*, 3:504–5; Lewis to Ritchie, 28 August 1833, Jackson-Lewis Papers; Lewis to Jackson, 3 April 1833, Jackson Papers.

44. Blair to Van Buren, 13 November 1859, Van Buren, *Autobiography*, 2:607–8; Jackson to Van Buren, 12 August 1833, Van Buren Papers; Taney to Jackson, 3 August 1833, Jackson Papers; Whitney to Blair, 16 August 1833, Blair-Lee Papers; Blair to Van Buren, 17 August 1833, Van Buren Papers.

45. Kendall to Jackson, 11 August 1833, Jackson Papers; Jackson to Van Buren, 16 August 1833, Van Buren Papers.

46. Whitney to Blair, 12 August 1833, Blair-Lee Papers; Kendall to Jackson, 14 August 1833, Van Buren to Jackson, 4 September 1833, Jackson Papers; Kendall, *Autobiography*, pp. 382–83.

47. Kendall to Jackson, 14 August 1833, Jackson Papers.

48. Duane, *Narrative*, p. 93; Washington *Globe*, 14 March 1834. Cf. Munroe, *Louis McLane*, pp. 399–400.

49. Van Buren to Jackson, 4 September 1833, Jackson Papers.

50. Blair to Van Buren, 17 August 1833, Van Buren Papers.

51. Blair to Van Buren, 17 August 1833, Van Buren Papers.

52. Van Buren to Jackson, 19 August 1833, Jackson Papers.

53. Van Buren to Jackson, 4 September 1833, Jackson Papers.

54. Jackson to Van Buren, 8 September 1833, Van Buren Papers.

55. Van Buren to Jackson, 11 September, 14 September 1833, Jackson Papers.

56. Duane, *Narrative*, pp. 97–98.

57. Duane, *Narrative*, pp. 99–100.

58. Blair to Van Buren, 13 November 1859, Van Buren, *Autobiogra-*

phy, 2:608; Presidential Messages, Removal of Deposits, Jackson Papers.

59. Richardson, *Messages and Papers,* 3:1237–38.

60. Duane, *Narrative,* p. 96.

61. Jackson to Van Buren, 22 September, 23 September 1833, Van Buren Papers. John M. McFaul traces the development of currency reform after removal; see McFaul, *Jacksonian Finance,* pp. 11–12, 206–9. Richardson, *Messages and Papers,* 4:1470.

62. Blair to Jackson, 7 January 1834, Jackson Papers; Washington *Globe,* 28 November 1833, 28 March 1834. See also Washington *Globe,* 30 September, 11 October 1833, 1 January, 26 February, 28 November 1834.

63. Van Buren to John Van Buren, 2 February 1834, Van Buren Papers; Van Buren, *Autobiography,* 2:729–31; Van Buren to Woodbury, 29 January 1834, Woodbury Papers; McFaul, *Jacksonian Finance,* pp. 143–77.

64. Jackson to Van Buren, 24 September, 25 September 1833, Van Buren, *Autobiography,* 2:603–4; Blair to Van Buren, 13 November 1859, Van Buren, *Autobiography,* 2:608; Paper in Francis Blair's handwriting entitled "McLane & Cass, The Settlement," Box 33, Blair-Lee Papers; Washington *Globe,* 26 September 1833.

65. Blair to Van Buren, 13 November 1859, Van Buren, *Autobiography,* 2:608.

66. Blair to Jackson, 7 January 1834, Jackson Papers; Kendall, "Kendall about a divided Cabinet," Blair-Lee Papers; Richard H. Wilde to Gulian Verplanck, 22 February 1834, Verplanck Papers. Taney may have suggested the idea of the editorial. See Woodbury, 11 January 1834, "Sundry Exercises," Woodbury Papers.

67. Woodbury, 10 January, 11 January 1834, "Sundry Exercises," Woodbury Papers; Jackson to Van Buren, 24 September 1833, Van Buren, *Autobiography,* 2:604.

68. James K. Polk to William B. Lewis, 13 August 1833, Jackson-Lewis Papers; Stevenson to Blair, n.d. but internal evidence indicates March–April 1833, Blair-Lee Papers; Richard H. Wilde to Gulian Verplanck, 21 November 1833, Verplanck Papers; Jackson to Blair, 30 November 1833, Jackson Papers.

69. Adams, *Memoirs,* 9:64, 56; *Register of Debates,* 23 Cong., 1 Sess., p. 2222; Sellers, *Polk: Jacksonian,* pp. 213–14.

70. *Register of Debates,* 23 Cong., 1 Sess., pp. 3473–76.

71. Washington *Globe,* 7 April 1834.

72. George M. Dallas to George Wolf, 2 March 1834, Wolf Papers; *Register of Debates,* 23 Cong., 1 Sess., pp. 3474–75; Charles McCool Snyder, *The Jacksonian Heritage,* pp. 37–43; Kindig, "Western Opposition to Jackson's 'Democracy,' " pp. 482–83; Grant, "The Bank Controversy and Connecticut Politics, 1834," p. 96; Philip A. Grant, Jr., "Jacksonian Democracy Triumphs in Connecticut," *The Connecticut Historical Society Bulletin* 33 (1968):118–20.

73. *Register of Debates,* 23 Cong., 1 Sess., pp. 3474–75. My calculations are in basic agreement with those arrived at by John M. McFaul. See McFaul, *Jacksonian Finance,* pp. 111–13.

74. Washington *Globe*, 9 October 1833; Jackson to Blair, 14 December 1844, in Hudson, *Journalism in the United States*, p. 269; Adams, *Memoirs*, 9:57, 82; Calhoun to Lewis Coryell, 24 June 1834, Lewis Coryell Papers, Historical Society of Pennsylvania; Kendall to William D. Lewis, 30 June 1834, Lewis-Nielson Papers, Historical Society of Pennsylvania; McFaul, *Jacksonian Finance*, pp. 111–13; Cole, *Whig Party in the South*, pp. 27–30; McCormick, *Second American Party System*, pp. 220–24.

75. McLane to Gulian Verplanck, 4 January 1838, Verplanck Papers.

76. Hammond, *Banks and Politics*, pp. 326–29.

77. Kendall to Van Buren, 9 June 1833, Van Buren Papers; Kendall to Jackson, 20 March 1833, Jackson Papers; Kendall, *Autobiography*, pp. 387–89; Scheiber, "Pet Banks in Jacksonian Politics and Finance," pp. 197–202; McFaul, *Jacksonian Finance*, pp. 149–50. Peter Temin attributes the economic instability of the mid-1830s and early 1840s to international monetary and commodity movements, not to Andrew Jackson's banking program. Temin, *Jacksonian Economy*, pp. 22–27, 172–77.

78. Jackson to Duane, 26 June 1833, Jackson Papers; Richardson, *Messages and Papers*, 4:1522.

79. Washington *Globe*, 28 March, 29 March 1834.

80. Richardson, *Messages and Papers*, 3:1383–84, 4:1520–21, 1524–25; Jackson to Taney, 13 October 1836, Jackson, *Correspondence*, 5:430.

81. Richardson, *Messages and Papers*, 3:1383–84, 4:1525.

82. Richardson, *Messages and Papers*, 3:1385, 4:1525; Jackson to Woodbury, 3 July 1834, Woodbury Papers; Jackson to Kendall, n.d. [1836], Jackson Papers.

83. McFaul, *Jacksonian Finance*, pp. 4–5.

84. Taney to Jackson, 27 June 1836, Jackson Papers; Jackson to Taney, 13 October 1836, Jackson, *Correspondence*, 5:429–30.

85. Benton, *Thirty Years' View*, 1:373–74, 379, 676–78; Benton to Taney, n.d. [1834], Taney Papers, Maryland Historical Society; Benton to Jackson, 11 June 1834, Donelson Papers; Benton to Woodbury, 28 December 1835, Woodbury Papers; Jackson to William Findlay, 20 August 1834, Jackson, *Correspondence*, 5:285–86; Chambers, *Old Bullion Benton*, pp. 195–221; Sellers, *Polk: Jacksonian*, pp. 226–33.

86. James K. Polk to Woodbury, 27 February 1834 [1835?], Woodbury to Benton, 29 December 1835, Woodbury Papers; McFaul, *Jacksonian Finance*, pp. 170, 173; Wheaton, "Levi Woodbury," pp. 110, 252–53.

87. Curtis, *Fox at Bay*, pp. 65–70; Benton, *Thirty Years' View*, 1:658, 2:10–11.

88. Washington *Globe*, 18 July 1836. On western hard-money radicalism after the panic of 1837, see Sharp, *Jacksonians versus the Banks*, pp. 212–13.

89. Sellers, *Polk: Jacksonian*, pp. 225–32; Benton, *Thirty Years' View*, 1:700–705; McFaul, *Jacksonian Finance*, pp. 116–35, 172–73, 178–79; John M. Niles to Gideon Welles, 9 January 1837, Welles Papers; Calhoun to James H. Hammond, 18 February 1837, James Henry Hammond Papers, Library of

Congress; William B. Lewis to Andrew Stevenson, 13 March 1837, Stevenson Papers. For a discussion of the Conservative Democrats, see Howard Braverman, "The Economic and Political Background of the Conservative Revolt in Virginia," *Virginia Magazine of History and Biography* 60 (1952):266–87.

90. Richardson, *Messages and Papers*, 3:1385–86; Sellers, *Polk: Jacksonian*, pp. 225, 232.

91. Remini, *Jackson and the Bank War*, pp. 169–72; Benton, *Thirty Years' View*, 1:649–57; *Register of Debates*, 24 Cong., 1 Sess., pp. 1845–46.

92. Washington *Globe*, 16 June, 24 June 1836; Taney to Jackson, 20 June 1836, Jackson Papers; Taney, "Proposed Veto of the Surplus Revenue Bill of 1836," 20 June 1836, Jackson, *Correspondence*, 5:404–9. Jackson also seems to have prepared a veto message. Filed at the end of his 1833 correspondence in the Jackson Papers is a draft in Jackson's hand of a veto, which internal evidence indicates was intended for the Deposit Act. In it, Jackson complained that the measure was unconstitutional as well as impolitic and would "compel Congress to increase the Tariff, which lead [*sic*] to the recharter of the U. States Bank, and restore the system of internal improvement, consolidate the Government, corrupt the morals of the people & destroy our liberties."

93. Benton, *Thirty Years' View*, 1:657–58; McFaul, *Jacksonian Finance*, p. 137; Curtis, *Fox at Bay*, pp. 65–70; Washington *Globe*, 20 August 1836.

94. *Register of Debates*, 24 Cong., 1 Sess., pp. 4350–52, 4359, 1859; Johnson to Jackson, 21 June 1836, Jackson Papers; William C. Rives to wife, 23 June 1836, Rives Papers; Washington *Globe*, 24 June 1836; Swisher, *Roger B. Taney*, pp. 328–30. While the amended bill was before the Senate, Calhoun asserted that "the principle of the bill had not been changed. . . . No Secretary of the Treasury will ever call for this money." His statement went unchallenged by the Jacksonians. See *Register of Debates*, 24 Cong., 1 Sess., p. 1859.

95. Washington *Globe*, 24 June, 8 July, 21 July, 23 July, 8 September 1836.

96. Washington *Globe*, 29 March 1836; Blair to Jackson, 30 July 1836, Jackson Papers; McFaul, *Jacksonian Finance*, pp. 116–19; Jackson to Taney, 6 December 1836, Taney Papers, Maryland Historical Society.

97. Jackson to Blair, [January 1837?], 20 February 1839, Blair Family Papers; Richardson, *Messages and Papers*, 4:1501–7.

98. Jackson to James A. Hamilton, 2 February 1834, Hamilton, *Reminiscences*, pp. 269–70; Benton, *Thirty Years' View*, 1:158; Richardson, *Messages and Papers*, 4:1522.

99. Jackson to Kendall, 24 November 1836, Jackson Papers.

Chapter 8. A New Leader

1. Van Buren to Jackson, 27 December 1832, Van Buren Papers; Curtis, *Fox at Bay*, p. 50.

2. Van Buren to Jackson, 11 September 1833, Jackson Papers.

3. Van Buren to Blair, 16 May 1856, Blair Family Papers; Kendall to Blair, 28 January 1830, Blair-Lee Papers; Romulous M. Saunders to William C.

Rives, 23 March 1835, Rives Papers; Kendall, *Autobiography*, p. 335. According to Louis W. Koenig, the presidential adviser's status "is the subtle, changeable, but unmistakable florescence of the President's mind." It is invested neither with title nor permanence. See Koenig, *Invisible Presidency*, p. 45.

4. Jackson to John Overton, 31 December 1829, Jackson, *Correspondence*, 4:108–9; Jackson to Van Buren, 8 August 1834, Van Buren Papers.

5. Calhoun to Duff Green, 10 November 1834, Calhoun Papers, South Caroliniana Library; Balch to Jackson, 30 October 1834, Jackson Papers; Jackson to Van Buren, 14 September 1834, Van Buren to Jackson, 25 July 1834, Van Buren Papers.

6. DeAlva Stanwood Alexander, *A Political History of the State of New York*, 1:404–5; Taney to Jackson, 2 November 1834, Jackson Papers.

7. Lewis to James A. Hamilton, 22 June 1833, 30 March 1834, Hamilton, *Reminiscences*, pp. 259, 282; Woodbury, 10 January 1834, "Sundry Exercises," Woodbury Papers; Barry to daughter, 22 February 1834, "Letters of William T. Barry," 14:238.

8. Kendall to Van Buren, 2 November, 10 November 1832, Van Buren Papers.

9. Barry to daughter, 22 February 1834, "Letters of William T. Barry," 14:238; Harriet Martineau, *Retrospect of Western Travel*, 1:157; Curtis, *Fox at Bay*, p. 61.

10. Smith, *Blair Family in Politics*, 1:121; John M. Niles to Gideon Welles, 15 May 1836, Welles Papers.

11. Washington *Globe*, 14 February, 11 March, 21 March 1834; *U.S. Telegraph*, 7 February, 20 March 1834; Albany *Argus*, 13 March 1834. When the *Argus* learned that Blair had not approved the new paper, it withdrew its support. Albany *Argus*, 14 March 1834.

12. *North American*, 12 April 1834. A complete file of the paper, the only one extant, is in the Library of Congress.

13. *Niles' Register* 46 (3 May 1834):147; *Pennsylvania Inquirer*, 9 October 1834; H. Haines to Blair, 16 November 1835, Blair-Lee Papers.

14. Benjamin Gratz to Blair, 3 April 1834, James Blair to Blair, 18 January 1835, Blair-Lee Papers; Blair to Van Buren, 17 May 1856, 8 October 1836, Van Buren Papers; Niven, *Gideon Welles*, pp. 175–76.

15. Meyer, *Richard M. Johnson*, pp. 406–10; Jackson to Henry Horn, 25 January 1835, Jackson, *Correspondence*, 5:321; Sellers, *Polk: Jacksonian*, pp. 251–52, 269–73. Joel H. Silbey, "Election of 1836," in *History of American Presidential Elections*, ed. Schlesinger, 1:577–640, provides both data and a perceptive analysis of this election.

16. Nathaniel Niles to William C. Rives, 23 July 1833, 25 May 1835, Rives Papers; Blair to Jackson, 19 May 1835, Jackson Papers; John Catron to Jackson, 21 March 1835, Jackson, *Correspondence*, 5:331.

17. Balch to Jackson, 4 April 1835, Jackson Papers; Catron to Jackson, 21 March 1835, Jackson, *Correspondence*, 5:331.

18. John Randolph to Jackson, 8 November 1831, Jackson Papers; Andrew Stevenson to Van Buren, 19 April 1829, Van Buren Papers; Ritchie to William C. Rives, 19 May 1835, Rives Papers; Ambler, *Thomas Ritchie*, pp. 169–70, 223–24.

19. Green to Hugh Lawson White, 11 April 1835, Green Papers, Southern Historical Collection; Green to Calhoun, 2 March 1835, John C. Calhoun Papers, Clemson University (copy in Calhoun Papers, South Caroliniana Library); Calhoun to Benjamin W. Leigh, 22 May 1835, Benjamin Watkins Leigh Papers, University of Virginia Library (copy in Calhoun Papers, South Caroliniana Library); Calhoun to William Gordon, 22 May 1835, Calhoun Papers, Duke University Library; John Tyler to James Iredell, 10 January 1835, Iredell Papers; George McDuffie to Richard H. Wilde, 10 May 1835, George McDuffie Papers, South Caroliniana Library.

20. Powell Moore, "The Revolt Against Jackson in Tennessee, 1835–1836," *Journal of Southern History* 2 (1936):335–39; Thomas P. Abernethy, "The Origin of the Whig Party in Tennessee," *Mississippi Valley Historical Review* 12 (1926):504–22; Parks, *John Bell*, pp. 84–99; Sellers, *Polk: Jacksonian*, pp. 251–66.

21. Lewis to Jackson, 30 August 1839, Jackson-Lewis Papers.

22. White, *Memoirs*, pp. 144–45, 254–64; Ritchie to William C. Rives, 21 March 1835, Rives Papers; Rives to Woodbury, 8 April 1835, Woodbury Papers; Washington *Globe*, 2 May 1835; Peter V. Daniel to Van Buren, 9 March 1835, Van Buren Papers. See also Hoffmann, *Jackson and North Carolina Politics*, pp. 102–14; Sellers, *Polk: Jacksonian*, pp. 250–66, 273–80. For Van Buren's cautious and unsubstantial support of slavery restriction in Missouri, see Dangerfield, *Awakening of American Nationalism*, pp. 120–21; Van Buren, *Autobiography*, 2:99–100; Shepard, *Van Buren*, pp. 62–63.

23. Rives to Van Buren, 10 April 1835, Rives Papers.

24. Sellers, *Polk: Jacksonian*, pp. 270–73. The proceedings of the Democratic convention can be found in the Washington *Globe*, 27 May 1835. A summary of its activity appears in Richard C. Bain and Judith H. Parris, *Convention Decisions and Voting Records*, pp. 20–23.

25. Jackson to Van Buren, 5 October 1834, Van Buren Papers; Jackson to Tilghman A. Howard, 20 August 1833, Jackson Papers; Peter V. Daniel to Van Buren, 9 March 1835, Van Buren Papers; Washington *Globe*, 30 January 1835; Woodbury, 10 January 1834, "Sundry Exercises," Woodbury Papers.

26. Blair to Jackson, 19 May 1835, Jackson Papers; Blair to H. Haines, 24 August 1835, Blair-Lee Papers; Nathaniel Niles to Rives, 27 May 1835, Rives Papers.

27. George M. Dallas to George Wolf, 21 May 1835, Dallas Papers; Van Buren to Mrs. Rives, 21 April 1835, Ritchie to William C. Rives, 19 May 1835, Rives Papers; Blair to Jackson, 19 May 1835, Jackson Papers.

28. Washington *Globe*, 27 May 1835; Rives to Van Buren, 2 June 1835, Nathaniel Niles to Rives, 30 May 1835, Rives Papers.

29. Blair to Van Buren, 28 August 1836, Van Buren Papers; Niven, *Gideon Welles*, pp. 147–49.

30. Van Buren to Blair, 25 August 1836, Blair Family Papers; Blair to Van Buren, 28 August 1836, Van Buren Papers; Washington *Globe*, 9 October, 19 March, 8 June 1835; Smith, *Blair Family in Politics*, 1:122.

31. Welles to Silas Wright, 11 January 1837, John M. Niles to Welles, 15 May 1836, Welles Papers; Washington *Globe*, 13 March 1837; Blair to Jackson, 21 August 1836, Jackson Papers.

32. Blair to Van Buren, 17 May 1856, 8 October 1836, Van Buren Papers.

33. Van Buren to Rives, 26 May 1835, Rives Papers; Van Buren to Sherrod Williams, 9 June 1836, Washington *Globe*, 20 August 1836; Curtis, *Fox at Bay*, pp. 48–51.

34. Benton, *Thirty Years' View*, 1:676–78; William B. Lewis to Rives, 10 July 1836, Rives Papers; Jackson to Kendall, 5 July 1836, Jackson Papers; Kendall to Woodbury, 11 July 1836, Woodbury Papers; Washington *Globe*, 18 July 1836.

35. My discussion of the 1836 election relies heavily on the data and analyses presented by Richard McCormick, "New Perspectives," especially p. 300; and Joel Silbey, "Election of 1836," pp. 595–98, 640.

36. Silbey, "Election of 1836," p. 597.

37. Van Buren to George M. Dallas, 16 February 1837, Van Buren Papers.

38. Andrew Jackson Donelson to———, 9 August 1835, Donelson Papers; Curtis, *Fox at Bay*, pp. 67–71, 90.

Conclusion

1. John Quincy Adams, *The Diary of John Quincy Adams: 1794–1845*, p. 503.

2. Adams, *Memoirs*, 8:232.

3. Brown, "Missouri Crisis," pp. 70–72; Van Buren to Benjamin F. Butler, 8 November 1833, Butler Papers.

4. Van Buren to Jackson, 5 November 1834, Jackson, *Correspondence*, 5:306; Richardson, *Messages and Papers*, 3:1337–42.

5. John Forsyth to Van Buren, 29 June 1833, Van Buren to George M. Dallas, 16 February 1837, Van Buren Papers. Van Buren appointed Joel Poinsett as secretary of war. Among the southerners who declined an appointment to Jackson's cabinet were William Drayton of South Carolina and Peter V. Daniel of Virginia. See Jackson to Van Buren, 11 July 1831, Van Buren Papers; Andrew Stevenson to Roger Taney, 5 November 1833, Taney Papers, Maryland Historical Society.

6. Richardson, *Messages and Papers*, 4:1511–27; Jackson to Taney, 13 October 1836, Jackson, *Correspondence*, 5:430; Jackson to Blair, January 1837, *Correspondence*, 5:444; Meyers, *Jacksonian Persuasion*, pp. 7–17. For an especially lucid and able discussion of the relationship between percep-

tion, ideology, and objective reality, see Shalhope, "Thomas Jefferson's Republicanism," pp. 529–56.

7. Sellers, *Polk: Continentalist*, pp. 14–18. For a discussion of the egalitarian and conservative edges of states' rights principles, see Robert J. Harris, "Chief Justice Taney: Prophet of Reform and Reaction," *Vanderbilt Law Review* 10 (1957):227–57.

8. Charleston *Mercury*, 28 August 1832, 22 February, 28 February, 3 April 1833; Calhoun to Samuel Ingham, 22 December 1831, Calhoun Papers, South Caroliniana Library; Shalhope, "Thomas Jefferson's Republicanism," pp. 547–56. See the excellent collection of documents on the Whig party in Daniel Walker Howe, ed., *The American Whigs*, especially pp. 79–88.

9. Bernard Bailyn, *The Ideological Origins of the American Revolution*, pp. 144–59; Wood, *Creation of the American Republic*, pp. 36–43, 413–25. For a discussion of the prevalence of conspiratorial thinking in the early republic, see Knox, *Conspiracy in American Politics: 1789–1815*.

10. Hammond, "Banking in the Early West," pp. 1–25.

11. Sharp, *Jacksonians versus the Banks*, p. 323; Marshall, "Early Career of Amos Kendall," pp. 76–79.

12. Stanley Elkins and Eric McKitrick, "A Meaning for Turner's Frontier: Part I: Democracy in the Old Northwest," *Political Science Quarterly* 69 (1954):321–53; Marshall, "Grass-roots Democracy in Kentucky," pp. 269–87; Bestor, "Patent-Office Models of the Good Society," pp. 505–26; Richard Wade, *The Urban Frontier*; Merle E. Curti, *The Making of an American Community*.

13. Washington *Globe*, 24 April 1833; Jackson to Kendall, 9 August 1835, Jackson, *Correspondence*, 5:360–61; Jackson to Andrew J. Crawford, 1 May 1833, Jackson to Taney, 13 October 1836, Jackson Papers. See also Washington *Globe*, 19 September 1831, 29 December 1832, 1 February, 5 April 1833, 29 August 1834, 18 September 1835, 11 February, 14 February 1837.

14. McFaul, "Expediency vs. Morality," pp. 25–26.

Bibliography

I. Primary Sources

A. Manuscript Collections

BALTIMORE. Maryland Historical Society.
  Roger B. Taney Papers.
BOSTON. Massachusetts Historical Society.
  Amos Kendall Papers.
  Marcus Morton Papers.
  Daniel Webster Papers.
CAMBRIDGE. Houghton Library, Harvard University.
  New Hampshire Whig Papers.
CHAPEL HILL. Southern Historical Collection, University of North Carolina.
  John McPherson Berrien Papers.
  Branch Family Papers.
  Duff Green Papers.
COLUMBIA. South Caroliniana Library, University of South Carolina.
  John C. Calhoun Papers.
  George McDuffie Papers.
CONCORD. New Hampshire Historical Society.
  Jonathan Harvey Papers.
  Isaac Hill Papers.
DISTRICT OF COLUMBIA. Library of Congress.
  Nicholas Biddle Papers.
  Blair Family Papers.
  J. Kelsey Burr Collection.
  John C. Calhoun Papers.
  Henry Clay Papers.
  Andrew Jackson Donelson Papers.
  John Floyd Papers.
  Galloway-Maxcy-Markoe Papers.
  Duff Green Papers.
  James Henry Hammond Papers.
  Isaac Hill Papers.
  Andrew Jackson Papers.
  Amos Kendall Papers.
  Thomas Ritchie Papers.
  William C. Rives Papers.

Andrew Stevenson Papers.
Roger B. Taney Papers.
Martin Van Buren Papers.
Gideon Welles Papers.
Levi Woodbury Papers.
DURHAM. Duke University Library.
John C. Calhoun Papers.
James Iredell Papers.
NEWARK. New Jersey Historical Society.
Mahlon Dickerson Papers.
NEW YORK. New-York Historical Society.
James Buchanan Miscellaneous Papers.
James A. Hamilton Miscellaneous Papers.
Andrew Jackson Miscellaneous Papers.
Amos Kendall Miscellaneous Papers.
William Plummer, Jr., Miscellaneous Papers.
Gulian Verplanck Papers.
New York Public Library.
James Barbour Papers.
Azariah Flagg Papers.
Jackson-Lewis Papers.
Amos Kendall Miscellaneous Papers.
PHILADELPHIA. Historical Society of Pennsylvania.
Lewis Coryell Papers.
George M. Dallas Papers.
Simon Gratz Collection.
Lewis-Neilson Papers.
Joel Poinsett Papers.
George M. Wolf Papers.
PRINCETON. Princeton University Library.
Blair-Lee Papers.
Benjamin F. Butler Papers.
Andrew DeCoppett Collection.

B. Printed Correspondence, Personal Memoirs, and Travel Accounts

Adams, John Quincy. *The Diary of John Quincy Adams: 1794–1845.* Edited
    by Allan Nevins. New York: Longmans, Green, and Co., 1951.
———. *Memoirs of John Quincy Adams, Comprising Portions of His Diary
    from 1795–1848.* Edited by Charles Francis Adams. 12 vols. Philadelphia:
    J. B. Lippincott Co., 1874–77.
Barry, William T. "Letters of William T. Barry." *William and Mary College
    Quarterly Historical Magazine* 13(1904–5):236–44, 14(1905–6):19–23,
    230–41.
Benton, Thomas Hart. *Thirty Years' View.* 2 vols. New York: D. Appleton and
    Co., 1854.

Biddle, Nicholas. *The Correspondence of Nicholas Biddle Dealing with National Affairs: 1807–1844*. Edited by Reginald C. McGrane. New York: Houghton Mifflin Co., 1919.

Clay, Henry. *The Private Correspondence of Henry Clay*. Edited by Calvin Colton. New York: A. S. Barnes & Co., 1855.

"Correspondence between Governor Joseph Desha and Amos Kendall: 1831–1835." Edited by James A. Padgett. *Register of the Kentucky State Historical Society* 38 (1940):5–24.

Duane, William J. *Narrative and Correspondence Concerning the Removal of the Deposits*. Philadelphia: n.p., 1838.

Eaton, Margaret. *The Autobiography of Peggy Eaton*. Edited by Charles F. Deems. New York: Charles Scribner's Sons, 1932.

Floyd, John. *Diary of John Floyd*. Edited by Charles H. Ambler. *The John P. Branch Historical Papers of Randolph-Macon College* 5 (1918):119–233.

Foote, Henry S. *Casket of Reminiscences*. Washington, D.C.: Chronicle Publishing Co., 1874.

Hamilton, James A. *Reminiscences of James A. Hamilton*. New York: Charles Scribner's Sons, 1869.

Jackson, Andrew. *Correspondence of Andrew Jackson*. Edited by John Spencer Bassett and J. Franklin Jameson. 7 vols. Washington, D.C.: Carnegie Institution of Washington, 1926–35.

————. "Letters of Andrew Jackson to Roger Brooke Taney." *Maryland Historical Magazine* 4 (1909):297–313.

Kendall, Amos. "Anecdotes of General Jackson." *United States Magazine and Democratic Review* 11 (1842):270–74.

————. *Autobiography of Amos Kendall*. Edited by William Stickney. Boston: Lee & Shepard, 1872.

Lumpkin, Wilson. *The Removal of the Cherokee Indians from Georgia*. 2 vols. New York: Dodd, Mead & Co., 1907.

Mangum, Willie Person. *The Papers of Willie Person Mangum*. Edited by Henry T. Shanks. 5 vols. Raleigh, N.C.: State Department of Archives and History, 1950–56.

Martineau, Harriet. *Retrospect of Western Travel*. 2 vols. New York: Harper and Brothers, 1838.

"Origin of the Democratic National Convention." *American Historical Magazine* 7 (1902):267–73.

Poore, Ben: Perley. *Perley's Reminiscences of Sixty Years in the National Metropolis*. 2 vols. Philadelphia: Hubbard Brothers, 1886.

Ritchie, Thomas. "Unpublished Letters of Thomas Ritchie." Edited by Charles H. Ambler. *The John P. Branch Historical Papers of Randolph-Macon College* 3 (1911):199–252.

Smith, Mrs. Samuel Harrison. *The First Forty Years of Washington Society*. Edited by Gaillard Hunt. New York: Charles Scribner's Sons, 1906.

Taney, Roger B. "Roger B. Taney's 'Bank War Manuscript.'" Edited by Carl Brent Swisher. *Maryland Historical Magazine* 53 (1958):103–31, 215–37.

"Two Years with Old Hickory." Edited by Thomas M. Clay. *Atlantic Monthly* 60 (1887):187–99.

Van Buren, Martin. *The Autobiography of Martin Van Buren*. Edited by John C. Fitzpatrick. American Historical Association, Annual Report, 1918, vol. 2. Washington, D.C.: Government Printing Office, 1920.

Webster, Daniel. *The Letters of Daniel Webster*. Edited by C. H. Van Tyne. New York: McClure, Phillips & Co., 1902.

————. *The Private Correspondence of Daniel Webster*. Edited by Fletcher Webster. 2 vols. Boston: Little, Brown and Co., 1857.

White, Hugh Lawson. *A Memoir of Hugh Lawson White*. Edited by Nancy N. Scott. Philadelphia: J. B. Lippincott Co., 1856.

Woodbury, Levi. "Levi Woodbury's 'Intimate Memoranda' of the Jackson Administration." Edited by Ari Hoogenboom and Herbert Ershkowitz. *Pennsylvania Magazine of History and Biography* 92 (1968):507–15.

C. Federal Documents

Annals of Congress.

Register of Debates in Congress.

Richardson, James D., comp. *A Compilation of the Messages and Papers of the Presidents*. 22 vols. New York: Bureau of National Literature, 1897–1922.

D. Newspapers and Periodicals

Albany *Argus*. Albany, New York.

Argus of Western America. Frankfort, Kentucky.

Charleston *Mercury*. Charleston, South Carolina.

Georgetown *Patriot*. Georgetown, Kentucky.

National Intelligencer. Washington, D.C.

Niles' Weekly Register. Baltimore, Maryland.

North American. Washington, D.C.

Pennsylvania Inquirer. Philadelphia, Pennsylvania.

Richmond *Enquirer*. Richmond, Virginia.

United States' Telegraph. Washington, D.C.

Washington *Globe*. Washington, D.C.

II. Secondary Works

A. Books

Abernethy, Thomas P. *From Frontier to Plantation in Tennessee: A Study in Frontier Democracy*. Chapel Hill: University of North Carolina Press, 1932.

Adams, James Truslow, ed. *Dictionary of American History*. 5 vols. New York: Charles Scribner's Sons, 1940.

Alexander, DeAlva Stanwood. *A Political History of the State of New York.* 3 vols. New York: Henry Holt and Co., 1906.

Ambler, Charles H. *Sectionalism in Virginia from 1776–1861.* Chicago: University of Chicago Press, 1910.

———. *Thomas Ritchie: A Study in Virginia Politics.* Richmond: Bell Book & Stationery Co., 1913.

Ammon, Harry. *James Monroe: The Quest for National Identity.* New York: McGraw-Hill, 1971.

Apter, David E., ed., *Ideology and Discontent.* New York: Free Press, 1964.

Aronson, Sidney H. *Status and Kinship in the Higher Civil Service: Standards of Selection in the Administrations of John Adams, Thomas Jefferson, and Andrew Jackson.* Cambridge, Mass.: Harvard University Press, 1964.

Bailyn, Bernard. *The Ideological Origins of the American Revolution.* Cambridge, Mass.: Harvard University Press, Belknap Press, 1967.

Bain, Richard C., and Parris, Judith H. *Convention Decisions and Voting Records.* 2d ed. Washington, D.C.: Brookings Institution, 1973.

Bancroft, Frederic. *Calhoun and the South Carolina Nullification Movement.* Baltimore: Johns Hopkins University Press, 1928.

Bassett, John Spencer. *The Life of Andrew Jackson.* New ed., 2 vols. in 1. New York: Macmillan Co., 1928.

Bemis, Samuel Flagg. *John Quincy Adams and the Union.* New York: Alfred A. Knopf, 1956.

Benson, Lee. *The Concept of Jacksonian Democracy: New York as a Test Case.* Princeton: Princeton University Press, 1961.

Boucher, Chauncey S. *The Nullification Controversy in South Carolina.* Chicago: University of Chicago Press, 1916.

Bowers, Claude G. *The Party Battles of the Jackson Period.* Boston: Houghton Mifflin Co., 1922.

Bradley, Cyrus. *Biography of Isaac Hill, of New-Hampshire.* Concord: J. F. Brown, 1835.

Brown, Norman D. *Daniel Webster and the Politics of Availability.* Athens: University of Georgia Press, 1969.

Brown, Richard D. *Modernization: The Transformation of American Life, 1600–1865.* New York: Hill and Wang, 1976.

Buel, Richard, Jr. *Securing the Revolution: Ideology in American Politics, 1789–1815.* Ithaca: Cornell University Press, 1972.

Buley, R. Carlyle. *The Old Northwest: Pioneer Period, 1815–1840.* 2 vols. Indianapolis: Indiana Historical Society, 1950.

Burke, Pauline Wilcox. *Emily Donelson of Tennessee.* 2 vols. Richmond: Garrett and Massie, 1941.

Catterall, Ralph C. H. *The Second Bank of the United States.* Chicago: University of Chicago Press, 1903.

Cave, Alfred A. *Jacksonian Democracy and the Historians.* Gainesville: University of Florida Press, 1964.

Chambers, William Nisbet. *Old Bullion Benton: Senator from the New West.* Boston: Little, Brown and Co., 1956.

Chase, James S. *Emergence of the Presidential Nominating Convention: 1789–1832.* Urbana: University of Illinois Press, 1973.

Cole, Arthur C. *The Whig Party in the South.* Washington, D.C.: American Historical Association, 1913.

Cole, Donald B. *Jacksonian Democracy in New Hampshire: 1800–1851.* Cambridge, Mass.: Harvard University Press, 1970.

Crenson, Matthew A. *The Federal Machine: Beginnings of Bureaucracy in Jacksonian America.* Baltimore: Johns Hopkins University Press, 1975.

Curti, Merle E. *The Making of an American Community: A Case Study of Democracy in a Frontier County.* Stanford: Stanford University Press, 1959.

Curtis, George Ticknor. *Life of Daniel Webster.* 2 vols. New York: D. Appleton and Co., 1870.

Curtis, James C. *Andrew Jackson and the Search for Vindication.* Boston: Little, Brown and Co., 1976.

———. *The Fox at Bay: Martin Van Buren and the Presidency, 1837–1841.* Lexington: University Press of Kentucky, 1970.

Dahl, Robert A. *Who Governs?* New Haven: Yale University Press, 1961.

Dangerfield, George. *The Awakening of American Nationalism: 1815–1828.* New York: Harper and Row, 1965.

———. *The Era of Good Feelings.* New York: Harcourt, Brace and Co., 1952.

Darling, Arthur B. *Political Changes in Massachusetts: 1824–1848.* New Haven: Yale University Press, 1925.

Fenno, Richard F., Jr. *The President's Cabinet: An Analysis in the Period from Wilson to Eisenhower.* Cambridge, Mass.: Harvard University Press, 1959.

Fischer, David Hackett. *The Revolution in American Conservatism: The Federalist Party in the Era of Jeffersonian Democracy.* New York: Harper and Row, 1965.

Fish, Carl R. *The Civil Service and the Patronage.* New York: Longmans, Green, and Co., 1905.

Foner, Eric. *Free Soil, Free Labor, Free Men: The Ideology of the Republican Party before the Civil War.* New York: Oxford University Press, 1970.

Foreman, Grant. *Indian Removal: The Emigration of the Five Civilized Tribes of Indians.* Norman: University of Oklahoma Press, 1932.

Formisano, Ronald P. *The Birth of Mass Political Parties: Michigan, 1827–1861.* Princeton: Princeton University Press, 1971.

Fowler, Dorothy G. *The Cabinet Politician: The Postmasters General, 1829–1909.* New York: Columbia University Press, 1943.

Fraser, Hugh Russell. *Democracy in the Making: The Jackson-Tyler Era.* Indianapolis: Bobbs-Merrill Co., 1938.

Fredrickson, George M. *The Black Image in the White Mind: The Debate on Afro-American Character and Destiny, 1817–1914.* New York: Harper and Row, 1971.

Freehling, William W. *Prelude to Civil War: The Nullification Controversy in South Carolina, 1816–1836*. New York: Harper and Row, 1966.

Gammon, Samuel Rhea, Jr. *The Presidential Campaign of 1832*. Baltimore: Johns Hopkins University Press, 1922.

General Court of Massachusetts. *State Papers on Nullification . . . .* Boston: Dutton and Wentworth, 1834.

Goldman, Ralph M. *The Democratic Party in American Politics*. New York: Macmillan Co., 1966.

Green, Constance McLaughlin. *Washington: Village and Capital, 1800–1878*. Princeton: Princeton University Press, 1962.

Hammond, Bray. *Banks and Politics in America: From the Revolution to the Civil War*. Princeton: Princeton University Press, 1957.

Hatcher, William B. *Edward Livingston: Jeffersonian Republican and Jacksonian Democrat*. University, La.: Louisiana State University Press, 1940.

Hess, Stephen. *Organizing the Presidency*. Washington, D.C.: Brookings Institution, 1976.

Higham, John, ed. *The Reconstruction of American History*. New York: Harper and Row, 1962.

Hoffmann, William S. *Andrew Jackson and North Carolina Politics*. Chapel Hill: University of North Carolina Press, 1958.

Hofstadter, Richard. *The Idea of a Party System: The Rise of Legitimate Opposition in the United States, 1780–1840*. Berkeley: University of California Press, 1969.

Houston, David F. *A Critical Study of Nullification in South Carolina*. New York: Longmans, Green, and Co., 1896.

Howe, Daniel Walker, ed. *The American Whigs: An Anthology*. New York: John Wiley and Sons, 1973.

Howe, John R. *From the Revolution through the Age of Jackson: Innocence and Empire in the Young Republic*. Englewood Cliffs, N.J.: Prentice-Hall, 1973.

Hudson, Frederic. *Journalism in the United States: 1690–1872*. New York: Harper and Brothers, 1873.

Hunter, Floyd. *Community Power Structure*. Chapel Hill: University of North Carolina Press, 1953.

Ingham, W. A. *Samuel D. Ingham*. Philadelphia: printed for the author, 1910.

James, Marquis. *The Life of Andrew Jackson*. 2 vols. in 1. Indianapolis: Bobbs-Merrill Co., 1938.

Klein, Philip S. *Pennsylvania Politics: 1817–1832, A Game without Rules*. Philadelphia: Historical Society of Pennsylvania, 1940.

Knox, J. Wendell. *Conspiracy in American Politics: 1789–1815*. New York: Arno Press, 1972.

Koenig, Louis W. *The Invisible Presidency*. New York: Rinehart and Co., 1960.

Kramnick, Isaac. *Bolingbroke and His Circle: The Politics of Nostalgia in the Age of Walpole*. Cambridge, Mass.: Harvard University Press, 1968.

Library of Congress Symposia on the American Revolution. *The Development of a Revolutionary Mentality*. Washington, D.C.: Library of Congress, 1972.

Livermore, Shaw, Jr. *The Twilight of Federalism: The Disintegration of the Federalist Party, 1815–1830*. Princeton: Princeton University Press, 1962.

McCormick, Richard P. *The Second American Party System: Party Formation in the Jacksonian Era*. Chapel Hill: University of North Carolina Press, 1966.

McFaul, John M. *The Politics of Jacksonian Finance*. Ithaca: Cornell University Press, 1972.

McLaughlin, A. C. *Lewis Cass*. Boston: Houghton Mifflin Co., 1899.

Madeleine, Sister M. Grace. *Monetary and Banking Theories of Jacksonian Democracy*. Philadelphia: University of Pennsylvania Press, 1943.

Malone, Dumas. *Jefferson the President: First Term, 1801–1805*. Boston: Little, Brown and Co., 1970.

Mering, John Vollmer. *The Whig Party in Missouri*. Columbia, Mo.: University of Missouri Press, 1967.

Meyer, Leland W. *The Life and Times of Colonel Richard M. Johnson of Kentucky*. New York: Columbia University Press, 1932.

Meyers, Marvin. *The Jacksonian Persuasion*. Stanford: Stanford University Press, 1957.

Morris, Richard B., ed. *Encyclopedia of American History*. New York: Harper and Row, 1953.

Mudge, Eugene Tenbroeck. *The Social Philosophy of John Taylor of Caroline*. New York: Columbia University Press, 1939.

Munroe, John A. *Louis McLane: Federalist and Jacksonian*. New Brunswick: Rutgers University Press, 1973.

Nathans, Sydney. *Daniel Webster and Jacksonian Democracy*. Baltimore: Johns Hopkins University Press, 1973.

Nichols, Roy F. *The Invention of the American Political Parties: A Study of Political Improvisation*. New York: Macmillan Co., 1967.

Niven, John. *Gideon Welles: Lincoln's Secretary of the Navy*. New York: Oxford University Press, 1973.

Ostrogorski, Moisei I. *Democracy and the Party System in the United States: A Study in Extra-Constitutional Government*. New York: Macmillan Co., 1910.

Parks, Joseph Howard. *John Bell of Tennessee*. Baton Rouge: Louisiana State University Press, 1950.

Parton, James. *Life of Andrew Jackson*. 3 vols. New York: Mason Brothers, 1860.

Pearce, Roy Harvey. *The Savages of America: A Study of the Indian and the Idea of Civilization*. Baltimore: Johns Hopkins University Press, 1953.

Pessen, Edward. *Jacksonian America: Society, Personality, and Politics*. Homewood, Ill.: Dorsey Press, 1969.

Pocock, J. G. A. *The Machiavellian Moment: Florentine Political Thought and the Atlantic Republican Tradition*. Princeton: Princeton University Press, 1975.

———. *Politics, Language and Time: Essays on Political Thought and History*. New York: Atheneum, 1971.

Pollack, Queena. *Peggy Eaton: Democracy's Mistress*. New York: Minton, Balch and Co., 1932.

Remini, Robert V. *Andrew Jackson*. New York: Twayne Publishers, 1966.

———. *Andrew Jackson and the Bank War: A Study in the Growth of Presidential Power*. New York: W. W. Norton and Co., 1967.

———. *The Election of Andrew Jackson*. Philadelphia: J. B. Lippincott Co., 1963.

———. *Martin Van Buren and the Making of the Democratic Party*. New York: Columbia University Press, 1959.

Risjord, Norman K. *The Old Republicans: Southern Conservatism in the Age of Jefferson*. New York: Columbia University Press, 1965.

Rogin, Michael Paul. *Fathers and Children: Andrew Jackson and the Subjugation of the American Indian*. New York: Alfred A. Knopf, 1975.

Rothbard, Murray N. *The Panic of 1819: Reactions and Politics*. New York: Columbia University Press, 1962.

Satz, Ronald N. *American Indian Policy in the Jacksonian Era*. Lincoln: University of Nebraska Press, 1975.

Schlesinger, Arthur M., Jr. *The Age of Jackson*. Boston: Little, Brown and Co., 1945.

———, ed. *History of American Presidential Elections: 1789–1968*. 4 vols. New York: Chelsea House, 1971.

Sellers, Charles G., Jr. *James K. Polk*. 2 vols. Princeton: Princeton University Press, 1957–66.

Shade, William G. *Banks or No Banks: The Money Question in Western Politics, 1832–1865*. Detroit: Wayne State University Press, 1972.

Sharp, James Roger. *The Jacksonians versus the Banks: Politics in the States After the Panic of 1837*. New York: Columbia University Press, 1970.

Sheehan, Bernard W. *Seeds of Extinction: Jeffersonian Philanthropy and the American Indian*. Chapel Hill: University of North Carolina Press, 1973.

Shepard, Edward M. *Martin Van Buren*. Boston: Houghton Mifflin Co., 1889.

Smith, William E. *The Francis Preston Blair Family in Politics*. 2 vols. New York: Macmillan Co., 1933.

Snyder, Charles McCool. *The Jacksonian Heritage: Pennsylvania Politics*. Harrisburg: Pennsylvania Historical and Museum Commission, 1958.

Sorensen, Theodore C. *Decision-Making in the White House: The Olive Branch or the Arrows*. New York: Columbia University Press, 1963.

Stanwood, Edward. *A History of Presidential Elections*. 4th ed., rev. Boston: Houghton Mifflin Co., 1896.

Stickles, Arndt M. *The Critical Court Struggle in Kentucky: 1819–1829*. Bloomington: Graduate Council, Indiana University, 1929.

Sumner, William Graham. *Andrew Jackson*. Boston: Houghton Mifflin Co., 1899.

Swisher, Carl Brent. *Roger B. Taney*. New York: Macmillan Co., 1935.

Sydnor, Charles S. *The Development of Southern Sectionalism: 1819–1848*. Baton Rouge: Louisiana State University Press, 1948.

Taussig, F. W. *The Tariff History of the United States*. 7th ed., rev. New York: G. P. Putnam's Sons, 1923.

Taylor, George R. *The Transportation Revolution: 1815–1860*. New York: Rinehart and Co., 1951.

Taylor, John. *An Inquiry into the Principles and Policy of the Government of the United States*. Fredericksburg, Va.: Green and Cady, 1814.

Temin, Peter. *The Jacksonian Economy*. New York: W. W. Norton and Co., 1969.

Turner, Frederick Jackson. *Rise of the New West: 1819–1829*. New York: Harper and Brothers, 1907.

———. *The United States: 1830–1850*. New York: Henry Holt and Co., 1935.

Tyler, Samuel. *Memoir of Roger Brooke Taney, LL.D*. Baltimore: John Murphy and Co., 1872.

Van Buren, Martin. *Inquiry into the Origin and Course of Political Parties in the United States*. New York: Hurd and Houghton, 1867.

Van Deusen, Glyndon G. *The Jacksonian Era: 1828–1848*. New York: Harper and Row, 1959.

Wade, Richard. *The Urban Frontier: The Rise of Western Cities, 1790–1830*. Cambridge, Mass.: Harvard University Press, 1959.

Ward, John William. *Andrew Jackson: Symbol for an Age*. New York: Oxford University Press, 1955.

Weber, Max. *From Max Weber: Essays in Sociology*. Edited by H. H. Gerth and C. Wright Mills. New York: Oxford University Press, 1946.

Webster, Homer, J. *A History of the Democratic Party Organization in the Northwest: 1824–1840*. Columbus, Ohio: F. J. Heer, 1915.

Weston, Florence. *The Presidential Election of 1828*. Washington, D.C.: Ruddick Press, 1938.

White, Leonard D. *The Federalists: A Study in Administrative History, 1789–1801*. New York: Macmillan Co., 1948.

———. *The Jacksonians: A Study in Administrative History, 1829–1861*. New York: Macmillan Co., 1954.

———. *The Jeffersonians: A Study in Administrative History, 1801–1829*. New York: Macmillan Co., 1951.

Wilburn, Jean Alexander. *Biddle's Bank: The Crucial Years*. New York: Columbia University Press, 1967.

Wildavsky, Aaron, ed. *Perspectives on the Presidency*. Boston: Little, Brown and Co., 1975.

Williamson, Chilton. *American Suffrage from Property to Democracy: 1760–1860*. Princeton: Princeton University Press, 1961.

Wiltse, Charles M. *John C. Calhoun*. 3 vols. Indianapolis: Bobbs-Merrill Co., 1944–51.

Wise, Gene. *American Historical Explanations: A Strategy for Grounded Inquiry*. Homewood, Ill.: Dorsey Press, 1973.

Wood, Gordon. *The Creation of the American Republic*. Chapel Hill: University of North Carolina Press, 1969.

Young, James Sterling. *The Washington Community: 1800–1828*. New York: Columbia University Press, 1966.

Young, Mary Elizabeth. *Redskins, Ruffleshirts, and Rednecks: Indian Allotments in Alabama and Mississippi, 1830–1860*. Norman: University of Oklahoma Press, 1961.

B. Articles

Abernethy, Thomas P. "The Origin of the Whig Party in Tennessee." *Mississippi Valley Historical Review* 12 (1926):504–22.

Appleby, Joyce. "The Social Origins of American Revolutionary Ideology." *Journal of American History* 64 (1978):935–58.

Bachrach, Peter, and Baratz, Morton S. "Decisions and Nondecisions: An Analytical Framework." *American Political Science Review* 57 (1963): 632–42.

———. "Two Faces of Power." *American Political Science Review* 56 (1962):947–52.

Banning, Lance. "Republican Ideology and the Triumph of the Constitution, 1789 to 1793." *William and Mary Quarterly* 31 (1974):167–88.

Barbee, David Rankin. "Andrew Jackson and Peggy O'Neale." *Tennessee Historical Quarterly* 15 (1956):37–52.

Barkan, Elliott R. "The Emergence of a Whig Persuasion: Conservatism, Democratism, and the New York State Whigs." *New York History* 52 (1971):367–95.

Bergeron, Paul H. "The Nullification Crisis Revisted." *Tennessee Historical Quarterly* 35 (1976):263–75.

———. "Tennessee's Response to the Nullification Crisis." *Journal of Southern History* 39 (1973):23–44.

Bestor, Arthur E. "Patent-Office Models of the Good Society: Some Relationships between Social Reform and Westward Expansion." *American Historical Review* 58 (1953):505–26.

Braverman, Howard. "The Economic and Political Background of the Conservative Revolt in Virginia." *Virginia Magazine of History and Biography* 60 (1952):266–87.

Brown, Norman D. "Webster-Jackson Movement for a Constitution and Union Party in 1833." *Mid-America* 46 (1964):147–71.

Brown, Richard D. "Modernization and the Modern Personality in Early America: 1600–1865." *Journal of Interdisciplinary History* 2 (1971–72):201–28.

Brown, Richard H. "The Missouri Crisis, Slavery, and the Politics of Jacksonianism." *South Atlantic Quarterly* 65 (1966):55–72.

Chase, James S. "Jacksonian Democracy and the Rise of the Nominating Convention." *Mid-America* 45 (1963):229–49.

Clifton, Frances. "John Overton as Andrew Jackson's Friend." *Tennessee Historical Quarterly* 11 (1952):23–40.

Curtis, James C. "Andrew Jackson and His Cabinet: Some New Evidence." *Tennessee Historical Quarterly* 27 (1968):157–64.

Dauer, Manning J., and Hammond, Hans. "John Taylor: Democrat or Aristocrat?" *Journal of Politics* 6 (1944):381–403.

Elkins, Stanley, and McKitrick, Eric. "A Meaning for Turner's Frontier: Part I: Democracy in the Old Northwest." *Political Science Quarterly* 69 (1954):321–53.

Foner, Eric. "The Causes of the American Civil War: Recent Interpretations and New Directions." *Civil War History* 20 (1974):197–214.

Formisano, Ronald P. "Deferential-Participant Politics: The Early Republic's Political Culture, 1789–1840." *American Political Science Review* 68 (1974):473–87.

———. "Political Character, Antipartyism and the Second Party System." *American Quarterly* 21 (1969):683–709.

———. "Toward a Reorientation of Jacksonian Politics: A Review of the Literature, 1959–1975." *Journal of American History* 63 (1976):42–65.

Freehling, William W. "Paranoia and American History." *New York Review of Books* 18 (1971):36–39.

———. "Spoilsmen and Interests in the Thought and Career of John C. Calhoun." *Journal of American History* 52 (1965):25–42.

Gatell, Frank Otto. "Sober Second Thoughts on Van Buren, the Albany Regency, and the Wall Street Conspiracy." *Journal of American History* 53 (1966):19–41.

Goldman, Perry M. "Political Virtue in the Age of Jackson." *Political Science Quarterly* 87 (1972):46–62.

Govan, Thomas P. "John M. Berrien and the Administration of Andrew Jackson." *Journal of Southern History* 5 (1939):447–68.

Grant, Philip A., Jr. "The Bank Controversy and Connecticut Politics, 1834." *Connecticut Historical Society Bulletin* 33 (1968):90–96.

———. "Jacksonian Democracy Triumphs in Connecticut." *Connecticut Historical Society Bulletin* 33 (1968):117–24.

Green, Fletcher M. "Duff Green, Militant Journalist of the Old School." *American Historical Review* 52 (1946–47):247–64.

Gresham, L. Paul. "The Public Career of Hugh Lawson White." *Tennessee Historical Quarterly* 3 (1944):291–318.

Hammond, Bray. "Banking in the Early West: Monopoly, Prohibition, and Laissez Faire." *Journal of Economic History* 8 (1948):1–25.

Harlan, Louis R. "Public Career of William Berkeley Lewis." *Tennessee Historical Quarterly* 7 (1948):3–38, 118–52.

Harris, Robert J. "Chief Justice Taney: Prophet of Reform and Reaction." *Vanderbilt Law Review* 10 (1957):227–57.

Harrison, Joseph Hobson, Jr. "Martin Van Buren and His Southern Supporters." *Journal of Southern History* 22 (1956):438–58.

———. "Oligarchs and Democrats: The Richmond Junto." *Virginia Magazine of History and Biography* 78 (1970):184–98.

Hay, Robert P. "The Case for Andrew Jackson in 1824: Eaton's *Wyoming Letters*." *Tennessee Historical Quarterly* 29 (1970–71):139–51.

Henig, Gerald S. "The Jacksonian Attitude Toward Abolitionism in the 1830's." *Tennessee Historical Quarterly* 28 (1969):42–56.

Hoffmann, William S. "John Branch and the Origins of the Whig Party in North Carolina." *North Carolina Historical Review* 35 (1958):299–315.

Howe, John R., Jr. "Republican Thought and the Political Violence of the 1790's." *American Quarterly* 19 (1967):147–65.

Jackson, Carlton. "The Internal Improvement Vetoes of Andrew Jackson." *Tennessee Historical Quarterly* 25 (1966):261–79.

Latner, Richard B. "The Kitchen Cabinet and Andrew Jackson's Advisory System," *Journal of American History* 65(1978):367–88.

———. "The Nullification Crisis and Republican Subversion." *Journal of Southern History* 43 (1977):19–38.

Latner, Richard B. and Levine, Peter. "Perspectives on Antebellum Pietistic Politics." *Reviews in American History* 4 (1976):15–24.

Lively, Robert A. "The American System: A Review Article." *Business History Review* 29 (1955):81–96.

Longaker, Richard P. "Was Jackson's Kitchen Cabinet a Cabinet?" *Mississippi Valley Historical Review* 44 (1957):94–108.

Lowe, Gabriel L., Jr. "John H. Eaton, Jackson's Campaign Manager." *Tennessee Historical Quarterly* 11 (1952):99–147.

McCormick, Richard L. "Ethno-Cultural Interpretations of Nineteenth-Century American Voting Behavior." *Political Science Quarterly* 89 (1974):351–77.

McCormick, Richard P. "New Perspectives on Jacksonian Politics." *American Historical Review* 65 (1960):288–301.

McFaul, John M. "Expediency vs. Morality: Jacksonian Politics and Slavery." *Journal of American History* 62 (1975):24–39.

McFaul, John M., and Gatell, Frank Otto. "The Outcast Insider: Reuben M. Whitney and the Bank War." *Pennsylvania Magazine of History and Biography* 91 (1967):115–44.

McLaughlin, William G., and Conser, Walter H., Jr. "The Cherokees in Transition: A Statistical Analysis of the Federal Cherokee Census of 1835." *Journal of American History* 64 (1977):678–703.

Marshall, Lynn L. "The Authorship of Jackson's Bank Veto Message." *Mississippi Valley Historical Review* 50 (1963):466–77.

———. "The Genesis of Grass-roots Democracy in Kentucky." *Mid-America* 47 (1965):269–87.

————. "The Strange Stillbirth of the Whig Party." *American Historical Review* 72 (1967):445–68.

Miles, Edwin A. "After John Marshall's Decision: *Worcester* v. *Georgia* and the Nullification Crisis." *Journal of Southern History* 39 (1973):519–44.

Mintz, Max M. "The Political Ideas of Martin Van Buren." *New York History* 30 (1949):422–48.

Moore, Powell. "The Revolt Against Jackson in Tennessee, 1835–1836." *Journal of Southern History* 2 (1936):335–59.

Orr, Mary T. "John Overton and Traveler's Rest." *Tennessee Historical Quarterly,* 15 (1956):216–23.

Parsons, Lynn Hudson. "'A Perpetual Harrow Upon My Feelings': John Quincy Adams and the American Indian." *New England Quarterly* 46 (1973):339–79.

Phillips, Kim T. "The Pennsylvania Origins of the Jackson Movement." *Political Science Quarterly* 91 (1976):489–508.

Prucha, F. P. "Andrew Jackson's Indian Policy: A Reassessment." *Journal of American History* 56 (1969):527–39.

Ratcliffe, Donald J. "The Role of Voters and Issues in Party Formation: Ohio, 1824." *Journal of American History,* 59 (1973):847–70.

Remini, Robert V. "The Albany Regency." *New York History* 39 (1958): 341–55.

Rezneck, Samuel. "The Depression of 1819–1822, A Social History." *American Historical Review* 39 (1933–34):28–47.

Ridgway, Whitman H. "Community Leadership: Baltimore During the First and Second Party Systems." *Maryland Historical Magazine* 71 (1976): 334–48.

Satz, Ronald N. "Indian Policy in the Jacksonian Era: The Old Northwest as a Test Case." *Michigan History* 60 (1976):71–93.

Scheiber, Harry N. "The Pet Banks in Jacksonian Politics and Finance, 1833–1841." *Journal of Economic History* 23 (1963):196–214.

Seligman, Lester G. "Presidential Leadership: The Inner Circle and Institutionalization." *Journal of Politics* 18 (1956):410–26.

Sellers, Charles G., Jr. "Andrew Jackson versus the Historians." *Mississippi Valley Historical Review* 44 (1958):615–34.

————. "Banking and Politics in Jackson's Tennessee, 1817–1827." *Mississippi Valley Historical Review* 41 (1954):61–84.

————. "Jackson Men with Feet of Clay." *American Historical Review* 62 (1957):537–51.

Shalhope, Robert E. "Jacksonian Politics in Missouri: A Comment on the McCormick Thesis." *Civil War History* 15 (1969):210–25.

————. "Thomas Jefferson's Republicanism and Antebellum Southern Thought." *Journal of Southern History* 42 (1976):529–56.

————. "Toward a Republican Synthesis: The Emergence of an Understanding of Republicanism in American Historiography." *William and Mary Quarterly* 29 (1972):49–80.

Somit, Albert. "Andrew Jackson as Administrator." *Public Administration Review* 8 (1948):188–96.

———. "Andrew Jackson as Political Theorist." *Tennessee Historical Quarterly* 8 (1949):99–126.

Thompson, Charles Manfred. "Attitude of Western Whigs Towards the Convention System." *Proceedings of the Mississippi Valley Historical Association* 5 (1911–12):167–89.

Van Deusen, Glyndon G. "Some Aspects of Whig Thought and Theory in the Jacksonian Period." *American Historical Review* 63 (1958):305–22.

Wallace, Michael. "Changing Concepts of Party in the United States: New York, 1815–1828." *American Historical Review* 74 (1966):453–92.

Wright, James E. "The Ethnocultural Model of Voting: A Behavioral and Historical Critique." *American Behavioral Scientist* 16 (1973):653–74.

C. Theses, Dissertations, and Unpublished Papers

Andrew, John. "The Nature of Jacksonian Politics: A Reconsideration." Paper loaned to author.

Capowski, Vincent J. "The Making of a Jacksonian Democrat: Levi Woodbury, 1789–1831." Ph.D. dissertation, Fordham University, 1966.

Doctor, Powrie Vaux. "Amos Kendall: Propagandist of Jacksonian Democracy, 1828–1836." Ph.D. dissertation, Georgetown University, 1939.

Kany, Julius Franz. "The Career of William Taylor Barry." M.A. thesis, Western Kentucky State Teachers College, 1934.

Kindig, Everett W. "Western Opposition to Jackson's 'Democracy': The Ohio Valley as a Case Study, 1827–1836." Ph.D. dissertation, Stanford University, 1974.

McCrary, Royce Coggins. "John Macpherson Berrien of Georgia (1781–1856):A Political Biography." Ph.D. dissertation, University of Georgia, 1971.

Marshall, Lynn L. "The Early Career of Amos Kendall: The Making of a Jacksonian." Ph.D. dissertation, University of California, Berkeley, 1962.

Parker, Rodger D. "The Bolingbrokean Origins of Jeffersonian Republicanism." Paper loaned to author.

Royalty, Dale Maurice. "Banking, Politics, and the Commonwealth: Kentucky, 1800–1825." Ph.D. dissertation, University of Kentucky, 1972.

Somit, Albert. "The Political and Administrative Ideas of Andrew Jackson." Ph.D. dissertation, University of Chicago, 1947.

Wheaton, Philip D. "Levi Woodbury: Jacksonian Financier." Ph.D. dissertation, University of Maryland, 1955.

Index

and election of 1836, 190–91, 198–202, 205. *See also* Election of 1832

Deposit Act. *See under* Banking and fiscal policies

Deposit bank system. *See* Banking and fiscal policies, deposit bank system

Dickerson, Mahlon, 125

Distribution of surplus revenue, 68–70, 77; and Jackson, 26, 50, 68–69, 106, 140, 144

Donelson, Andrew Jackson, 44, 55, 56, 65–66; and Jackson, 5, 66, 210; and Eaton affair, 42, 61, 63, 65–66, 230–31 (n. 27); and Indian policy, 88, 91; and Bank of the United States, 113, 117

Donelson, Emily, 42

Drayton, William, 134, 263 (n. 5)

Duane, William, 169–70; appointed secretary of Treasury, 169–70; on removal of deposits, 174–75, 176, 177, 178, 180; dismissed as secretary of Treasury, 181, 185, 199

Eaton, John H., 11, 28, 35, 39, 62, 65–66, 74, 100; and Jackson, 10–11, 34–35, 54, 55, 84, 210; career of, 35; and Lewis, 35–36; and Calhoun, 36, 45, 62–63; and Van Buren, 36, 45, 46, 61–62, 157; and White, 36, 200; and the cabinet, 37, 39, 41–42, 43, 45, 48, 81; and Kendall, 41–42; and the Eaton affair, 59, 60–66, 67; and tariff and banking policies, 63–65, 108; and Indian policy, 88, 91, 98

Eaton, Margaret (Timberlake), 42–43, 59, 60–63

Eaton affair, 42–43, 58, 59–66, 67, 72, 73, 78, 82, 101, 143, 230–31 (n. 27)

Eaton-Lewis clique, 42

Eisenhower, Dwight David, 52

Election of 1824, 10–12

Election of 1828, 7, 22–23, 27–29, 35, 67

Election of 1832, 95, 98, 114, 115, 120–23, 138–39

Election of 1834, 194–95

Election of 1836, 200–201, 203–5

Electoral reform: in 1820s, 8–10

Ellicott, Thomas, 56

Era of Good Feelings, 8, 127

Erie Canal, 15, 100

Everett, Alexander, 119

Executive office politics, 2, 84. *See also* Presidential advisers, White House politics

"Family party," 38

Federalist party, 8, 17, 33, 35, 40, 46, 88, 127–28; opposition to Federalist principles of, 12–14, 25, 38, 105, 152, 153, 179, 201, 210

Florida and Seminole controversy, 67

Floyd, John, 14, 124

Force Bill, 152, 153–54, 156, 159–60, 252 (n. 53); and Jackson, 150–51, 159; and the South, 167, 199. *See also* nullification

Foreign policy, 73

Forsyth, John, 67, 125, 177, 179

Fort Hill Address, 141

Founding Fathers, 127

Freehling, William W., 69, 144

French spoliation claims, 73

Georgetown *Patriot*, 218 (n. 37)

Georgia, 40, 81, 82, 185, 205; and Indian policy, 40, 87–88, 91–92, 95–96, 97. *See also* Indian policy

Globe. See Washington *Globe*

Gooch, E. W., 75–76

Green, Duff, 29, 60, 73–74, 77, 78, 85, 131, 158, 162, 197, 199; career of, 27–28, 84; and Calhoun, 34, 73–74, 124, 125; and Van Buren, 34, 130, 134, 136; and Eaton, 41–42; and Kendall, 41–42, 49, 139; and Kitchen Cabinet, 52, 53–54, 56; and tariff, 64, 75; and Jackson, 71, 74, 75, 76, 79, 80, 82; and Bank of the United States, 75, 120; and nullification, 75, 142–43; and Blair, 76–77, 110, 142–43; and Indian policy, 87, 92; and Maysville Road veto, 105, 106

Grundy, Felix, 10, 105, 220 (n. 62)

Hamilton, James, Jr., 14, 40–41, 45, 46, 65, 142, 149

Hamilton, James A., 56, 67, 109–10; and Van Buren, 36, 131; and Jackson's first cabinet, 37, 43, 46, 47

Hammond, Bray, 211